Everyday Life
in the
Muslim
Middle
East

Indiana Series in Middle East Studies

Mark Tessler

GENERAL EDITOR

Everyday Life
in the
Muslim
Middle
East

Second Edition

EDITED BY

Donna Lee Bowen and
Evelyn A. Early

Indiana University Press
Bloomington and Indianapolis

This book is a publication of

Indiana University Press
601 North Morton Street
Bloomington, IN 47404-3797 USA

http://iupress.indiana.edu

Telephone orders 800-842-6796
Fax orders 812-855-7931
Orders by e-mail iuporder@indiana.edu

© 2002 by Indiana University Press

First edition © 1993 by Indiana University Press

Paperback cover and design by Linda Dalal Sawaya © 1993

All rights reserved

The paper used in this publication meets the minimum requirements of
American National Standard for Information Sciences—Permanence of Paper for
Printed Library Materials, ANSI Z39.48-1984.

Manufactured in the United States of America

Library of Congress Cataloging-in-Publication Data

Everyday life in the Muslim Middle East / edited by Donna Lee Bowen and
Evelyn A. Early.—2nd ed.
p. cm. — (Indiana series in Middle East studies)
Includes bibliographical references and index.
ISBN 0-253-34010-1 — ISBN 0-253-21490-4 (pbk.)
1. Middle East—Social life and customs. 2. Africa, North—Social life and
customs. I. Bowen, Donna Lee, date II. Early, Evelyn A. III. Series.
DS57 .E94 2002
956—dc21
2001002722

4 5   07 06 05

For our parents
and for
Amelia Aleene Elisabeth

CONTENTS

Part II Gender Relations

Part III Home, Community, and Work

We designed this second edition of *Everyday Life in the Muslim Middle East* to incorporate recent important trends, such as the information technology revolution and reformist Islam. Our original inspiration for this anthology stemmed from our need as professors for sources on the Middle East which described and analyzed real life, such as literature in translation and ethnographic work by social scientists. Both literature and local discourse provide a rich context for understanding Middle Eastern Muslim culture. After ten more years of experience in the Middle East, we continue to be impressed by the importance of religion and politics in the everyday lives of Middle Easterners. Like everyone else's in the world, their beliefs and their life situations form a seamless whole. The incorporation of new technology and the new directions taken by religious movements have important ramifications in Middle Eastern lives. The continued misunderstanding of Middle Eastern Muslims by Western society and its press was our major impetus in deciding to publish a second edition. We believe the best way to combat stereotypes is to meet others on a person-to-person basis, and in order to do so, it is critical to understand how they live.

The second edition retains twelve of our most popular pieces from the first edition, according to polls of students and readers. These twelve include three which are literary excerpts and another five which are local stories and poetry from places like Yemen, Egypt, and Afghanistan. Some of the twenty-three new pieces are recent field studies of problems such as marriage and the forging of social ties in new settings, such as Muscat, Istanbul, and Tehran. Some examine new forms of Muslim thought, such as Dale Eickelman's article on Islamic reform, and new forms of Muslim learning in fora such as the Internet and home study groups in such venues as Syria, Sudan, and Jordan. Others are accounts of local cultural expressions of history and identity in the face of global culture. These include film in Morocco and television in Egypt and Syria. Three pieces by Erika Friedl, Ziba Mir-Hosseini, and Anne Betteridge look at post-Revolution Iranian society, law, and ritual.

While aware of the crushing load that various terrorist acts have laid on the outsider's image of Muslim society, we do not dwell on terrorism in this collection, because Muslim society is no more inherently violent than any other twentieth-century society. However, it is important to understand the impact of conflict, violence, and torture on everyday life. One article deals with the Lebanese civil war's intrusion into everyday life, another with the Intifada's impact on personal and family dynamics, and a third with the personal price paid for government brutality. Another theme which reverberates in the Middle East today is globalization. It supplies a subtext to many of the new articles, such as those on satellite television, the Internet, abortion mores, and even the shaping of standards of beauty.

In our second edition, we focus more on such compelling issues as Islamic knowledge, family values, social change, and global concerns than on gender and on representing each area of the Middle East. Each article stands on its contribution to understanding culture and society via topics ranging from Islamists in Jordan and schoolteachers in Sudan to finding a job in Egypt and negotiating family ties in Oman. The book represents fifteen countries in thirty-two articles. Certain countries, such as Morocco and Egypt, tend to be well represented because of their openness to researchers. Three articles are general and speak of numerous countries.

In our original preface, we thanked many people who helped with the evolution of our project. In addition to thanking all our contributors for their cheerful help and writing, we would like to thank Dale Eickelman for his continual academic and moral support for our project; Janet Rabinowitch and Dee Mortensen of Indiana University Press, who spurred us to edit this second edition; and Allison O. Whitley for her uncomplaining editorial assistance.

NOTE ON TRANSLITERATION

The problems of transliterating terms for this book vividly demonstrate the diversity found in the Middle East. While there are standard transliteration systems for literary Arabic and Persian (e.g., those used by the *International Journal of Middle Eastern Studies*), rendering colloquial dialects from a variety of areas is more problematic. Arabic colloquial dialects have no agreed-upon system of transliteration; pronunciation differs sufficiently to preclude any one standard transliteration for the various colloquial languages. No one system exists which resolves the transliteration conflicts between literary Arabic and colloquial dialects.

It was difficult for us to standardize the transliteration of Arabic and Persian words used in this book in a manner which would make the word clear to the lay reader and evocative of the written or spoken language for the linguist. We aim to make the terms recognizable to students of Arabic or Persian and understandable to readers new to the area. Our solution has been to systematize more than to standardize. We set comprehensive criteria as best we could, but did not attempt to make all terms conform to a single standard. We simplified the transliteration as much as possible while at the same time preserving the sounds of language in the Middle East.

Various consonants in Arabic and Persian are not used in English. The most difficult to transliterate properly are the ayn and the hamza (at times a vowel, at times a glottal stop). We have transliterated the ayn as ʿ. We have transliterated the hamza as ʾ and use it when it is accepted usage or when the author so indicated, but with the goal of simplification we omitted it in the majority of cases where meaning was not compromised.

Arabic has three long vowels, which for the most part we have not represented unless doing so seemed critical to distinguish meaning. Also, we have not differentiated the emphatic consonants from the non-emphatic.

We transliterated terms from colloquial dialects to best represent the pronunciation of that area. The *galabiyya* of Syria becomes the *jellaba* of Morocco. We transliterated some Arabic terms colloquially, to reflect the pronunciation conventions described in a given article (*hshuma*, Moroccan Arabic). The careful reader will also note Arabic terms which have been absorbed into English or French (Bedouin or *caid*). In each of these cases we have noted the derivation of the term in the glossary. Occasionally, we follow the author's use of words or names transliterated in the French convention, such as the French Bou Chaib as opposed to Bou Shaʿib.

We retain media conventions in the transliteration of personal and place names familiar to readers in a certain form (Hussein, Nasser).

We trust that the specialists who read this book will appreciate the reason for discrepancies in our transliteration system. Likewise, we hope that the reader uninitiated in Middle Eastern languages will catch some of the flavor of literature and speech so vital to knowledge of the area.

Everyday Life
in the
Muslim
Middle
East

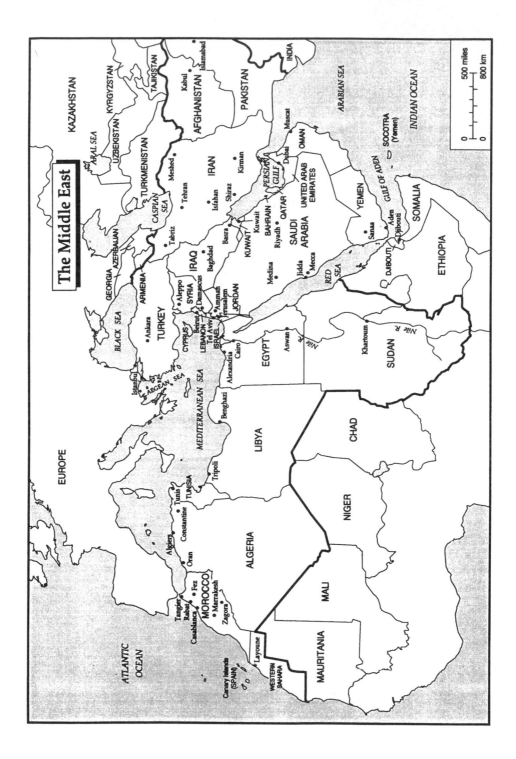

The Middle East

INTRODUCTION

This collection of essays is designed to give Western readers a sense of what it is like to live in the Middle East in the latter part of the twentieth century. The Middle East is perhaps the most difficult region of the world for Westerners to comprehend. We are more familiar with its stereotypes than its specificity. Often the area seems riven by contradictions. Many factors are responsible for this: Westerners tend to be unfamiliar with the region itself, and they know few Middle Easterners personally. Media accounts emphasize the area's convoluted politics and history of conflict. We lack, therefore, the more accurate image which might be garnered from an encounter with the everyday life of ordinary Middle Easterners.

In preparing this book, we have worked from the assumption that one can learn much about another culture by examining everyday, simple acts that are performed by all people, often without their thinking or remarking upon the significance of these acts. The materials presented here emphasize everyday life as Middle Easterners live it. We have chosen to focus on daily life in five areas: life passages or generations; gender relations; home, community, and work; religious expression; and performance and entertainment. To survey the region broadly, examples range from Iran and Afghanistan in the east to Morocco in the west. Essays treat such varied topics as childrearing in a Moroccan town, an Afghani courtship and marriage, Tunisian women university students' concerns about health and sexuality, young men's experience in Gaza, Islam over the Internet, and dramatic Syrian television serials which subvert the official government take on politics.

EVERYDAY LIFE

The everyday life approach utilized here has evolved as social scientists have focused on ordinary people's lives rather than on abstract theories of social action. Fernand Braudel, through his pioneering work in cosmopolitan history, has legitimated the historical study of everyday life. Henri

Lefebvre's *La Vie Quotidienne dans le Monde Moderne*, translated as *Everyday Life in the Modern World*, opened a new chapter in modern social science. Scholars such as Bourdieu, Brugel, Fallers, Geertz, Horton, LeFebvre, and Turner have emphasized how ordinary life is organized and what its cultural principles are. Everyday life studies demonstrate how abstract cultural principles may be utilized in analyses of data drawn from real-life experience. For example, such studies of culture in praxis demonstrate what kinship or religiosity or nationalism means by considering what happens and what is said when someone marries, visits a shrine, seeks medical care, supports a leader, or undertakes a community project.

This everyday approach is extremely helpful in understanding distinctions such as that between "traditional" and "modern" and in analyzing concepts such as patriarchy and honor. What, for instance, do we learn about traditional and modern medicine when a Muslim Middle Eastern woman concerned about infertility consults a doctor in a mother-child health clinic about fertility and also visits a shrine to vow that she will sacrifice a lamb if she becomes pregnant? She relies equally on clinical medicine and a folk interpretation of her religion. Or, in another case, what can we conclude when a devout Muslim merchant strikes a business deal to import revealing sequined Parisian dresses? Does he not see a conflict between his religious belief and the sale of ostentatious products from Western material society?

In the readings that follow, it becomes apparent that Middle Eastern life is based on a foundation of religion and politics. Actions that may seem apolitical to Americans, such as watching satellite television, wearing a scarf tied a certain way, or holding a study group in a scholar's home, have religious and political overtones. Middle Easterners see religious and political implications in their actions. In adhering to tradition or in experimenting with modernity, they are also situating themselves religiously and politically. These decisions illustrate the complex cultural patterns of the Muslim Middle East. Whether their decisions are traditional or modern is hard to say. Most of everyday life is a mix of the old and the new. The cultural system that holds it all together for Muslim Middle Easterners is a rich tapestry woven with strands of Islamic and local custom in a historically determined context. Everyday culture blends classical and local religious traditions to solve problems—finding a job, raising children, mending a quarreling community, combating inflation. It is in this everyday arena that people work out cultural conflicts between tradition and modernity or religiosity and secularism, wrought by the rapid change in the Middle East. They debate whether they or their parents determine their marriage partner, which family networks can help them get a job, and how to celebrate religious holidays.

Only by examining the nuts and bolts of ordinary life do we gain an appreciation of the overlap, the mix, of the old and the new in peoples' lives. Lloyd Fallers, in a study of cultural life in Edremit, Turkey, noted that people live a routine which represents an implicit compromise between Muslim and secular ideologies.

> Ordinary people are not automatons. They are not guided through life by the conventions of "encoded" culture and patterned social relations in an utterly routine way. There are occasions when they reflect, decide, strive and succeed or fail in a highly self-conscious manner. But for most people, most of the time, life is routine. Encoded culture informs their social action quite implicitly—which is why these systems of meaning are often difficult to perceive, because the social action informed by shared meaning flows along almost mechanically. (Fallers 1974, 9–10)

As the people of Edremit juggle different cultural codes, so do all peoples make choices in ordinary life about what cultural codes or guidelines to follow on which occasions: religious? nationalist? traditionalist? secularist? local? patriarchal? Life is lived as a cultural counterpoint between one's heritage and the pragmatic demands of one's life situation.

In the selections in this book, the ordinary and the mundane are seen as a key to understanding Middle Eastern culture. Situated social discourse—how people explain their unique experiences—affords insight into people's view of their culture. This book includes self-conscious studies of the personal discourse of reciting the Qur'an, the social discourse of poetry and folk tales, and the commercial discourse of Ramadan television advertisements. For example, a Yemeni's poetry articulates the political situation. Egyptian Bedouin women's poetry exposes personal emotions. A television quiz show exposes a globalizing trend toward secularizing a religious observance. Some accounts mix the Islamic with the local and the ethnic. Traditional tales and heroes may be celebrated on television programs, at national cultural festivals, or in stories people tell one another.

MIDDLE EASTERN MUSLIM CULTURE

A major part of Middle Eastern experience has been said to be based on Muslim culture. But what is Muslim culture? As many Muslims say, Islam exists for all times and all places. Do the seventh century c.e. Quranic laws and precepts constitute a message limited in time and space, or are they universal in application? And if so, or if not, what does this mean for everyday religious and secular life?

Muslim Middle Easterners from myriad demographic backgrounds do not all describe their experiences, raise children, or practice rituals in the same way. The ideal or typical "Muslim family" may not really exist, given that some Muslims live in extended families in the villages and others in nuclear families in cities. A "Muslim state" or "Muslim society" is difficult to define. Middle Eastern Muslims differ in their geography, ethnicity, religion, class, gender, and local customs. Ethnic differences, as in Iraq, Turkey, and Iran with their Kurdish populations, or in Morocco and Algeria with tribes of Arab and Berber descent, may at times influence politics more than religion does. Upper-class Muslims may feel that they have more in common with members of their class (including Christians) in another country than they do with lower-class fellow nationals. The problems faced by Iranian women who delay marriage resemble those confronted by women throughout the world. The sexual dilemmas of Tunisian university women may remind readers of this book of their own university days, and the decision whether to seek an abortion is difficult to make in all cultures.

Differentiation by religion in the Middle East is tricky. While religious beliefs and sectarian allegiances run deep, there are large areas of commonality as well. Although this book concentrates on Muslims, most of the phenomena observed occur equally among Christians, Jews, and other religious groups long resident in Middle Eastern lands. A common cultural heritage, strong nationalist feelings—whether loyalty to a nation-state or to a sense of, for instance, Arab or Kurdish unity—and a shared political situation can blur religious differences. The sharp political conflict between the Israelis and the Palestinians and other Arabs has developed through factors tied more to politics and land ownership than to religion.

Muslim Middle Easterners draw from varied sources of inspiration and knowledge. Religious sources include passages from the Qurʾan and from prophetic tradition, as well as religious rituals such as the Qurʾan-prescribed pilgrimage to Mecca and visits to local shrines. Another important cultural source for such important Middle Eastern values as honor, bravery, hospitality, and generosity is pre-Islamic Arab poetry. Saudi Arabia is the home not only of the holy cities of Islam but also of the "Arab" (Bedouin) identity celebrated in this poetry. As Michael Sells has explained, "The pre-Islamic ode was infused with the bedouin ethos of honor, courage, generosity and the hero's refusal to let impending death distract him from the pleasure of the moment. . . . Though Islam was to change much of the bedouin ethos, banning the wine drinking and tribal warfare that were so much a part of it, the emphasis on generosity, upon the willingness to spend one's life rather than hoarding it . . . remain[ed]" (Sells, 1988).

Pre-Islamic values of generosity and courage endure in the life of twentieth-century Cairo residents, for whom reciprocity is a prime value for social survival. The pre-Islamic genre of satirical poetry directed at enemy tribes is often transformed into the political humor of cartoons, jokes, and comedies directed against contemporary governments. Pre-Islamic Arab values combine with Islamic values such as piety and reverence and with secular values such as patriarchy to form the rich, complex Middle Eastern Muslim culture we encounter in this collection.

THE HISTORICAL CONTEXT OF MIDDLE EASTERN LIFE

Individual lives tap into a kind of compressed history, a time tunnel which emphasizes certain periods of history and particular events. Most Middle Easterners speak often of two historical periods. The first, which serves to define them and their community, begins with the coming of Islam in the seventh century. Islam is a safe, secure touchstone which ensures that today's Muslim fits within a long, illustrious, and well-defined tradition. The second and less secure period begins with the intrusion of the West. Whether this event is dated from the eleventh century and the Crusades, from the end of the Second World War, or from some date in between, the import of Western incursion remains the same: a challenge to traditional patterns of action and thought, and—most important—a challenge to the supremacy of Islam as the undoubted arbiter of intellectual activity and community guidance.

Although the revelations of Muhammad came in the seventh century, long after the appearance of Judaism and Christianity, they built upon the teachings of the Jewish Torah and the Christian New Testament. Muslims consider that Islam, as God's revelation, has guided humankind since the time of Father Adam. A popular Egyptian television serial, "There Is No God but God," entranced audiences throughout the Middle East a few years ago. Its major premise was that the belief in one god, *the* God, predated Muhammad and was taught through the traditions of the patriarchs as recorded in the Qur'an as well as in the Torah and the Gospels. Television audiences followed complicated subplots of the intrigues of idolatrous Egyptian priests, romances in the royal family, and wars waged against Egypt. But the event which dominated the serial was the conversion of a pharaoh of Egypt to the true faith by believers in the one God of the monotheistic religions of Judaism, Christianity, and Islam.

Islam recognizes its debt to the teachings of the patriarchs of the Torah and the Gospels by calling adherents to Judaism, Christianity, and, later, Zoroastrianism the "People of the Book." This appellation is bestowed in recognition of their scriptures, and gives them special status under Muslim rule. This confidence in an unbroken chain of prophets from Adam to Muhammad and in the oneness of the message of those prophets, together with Islam's emphasis upon the existence of a single deity, established it as a world religion. Within a few decades of its appearance, Islam spread swiftly throughout the Byzantine and Sassanid empires and became a major world force both politically and intellectually.

The sense that the Muslim community (*umma*) has a great destiny was reinforced by a chain of victories which began with the conversion of the city of Mecca and then the rest of Arabia to Islam and continued with the conquest of Syria, Iraq, Egypt, North Africa, Central Asia, parts of Spain, and the Balkans. But within one or two centuries the Islamic empire began to fracture into smaller, geographically distinct entities, some preaching sectarian differences. Rule by caliphs (*khulafa*), understood to be worthy successors of the Prophet Muhammad, was replaced by the rule of princes who were distinguished more by military prowess than by righteousness. Throughout the Middle East and North Africa, and into southern Asia, Muslim scholars and scientists built upon Greek philosophy and science— as well as the scientific traditions of the civilizations of India, Egypt, Mesopotamia, and Iran—to establish a glorious civilization centered on the Qurʾan and Islamic learning.

The second major historical period, the challenge to Islam, began in the eleventh century when the Crusaders mounted a successful campaign against Jerusalem, one of the three holy cities of Islam. Muslims were incredulous that uncultured Frankish barbarians could defeat a Muslim army. In the succeeding centuries, cracks in the facade of the highly polished Muslim civilization widened as European armies laid siege to the capital cities of the Middle East. Napoleon's landing in Egypt in 1798 signaled the era of European occupation and the dawn of imperialism and modernization. For Middle Easterners, the advent of the Europeans was simply the arrival of yet one more outside power ambitious to control the "crossroads of the world" and to exploit the region's natural resources, including local labor. In 1830 the French launched their conquest of Algeria, beginning a century-long wave of conquest and political domination throughout the Middle East.

As the Ottoman Empire declined, special commercial courts guaranteed the rights of resident Europeans to pursue business interests. Europeans both shipped their manufactured goods to the Middle East and extracted the region's resources. The French cultivated grapes in North Africa for their vineyards and, in later years, ran their factories with North African laborers. The British bought cotton from Egypt and Sudan and sold it back as cloth woven in the British mills; French-run tobacco companies grew tobacco in Syria.

Muslim intellectuals realized that military defeats and European occupations stemmed both from the weaknesses of Middle Eastern leaders and from the power of superior European weapons. Ultimately, the most serious threat was that posed by Western rationality and technology to traditional Muslim scholarship and belief systems. Muslim education centered on faithful use of Muslim texts: unquestioned obedience to revelation, steadfast adherence to the *sunna* and *hadith* (words and actions of Muhammad and his community), and study of the vast literature of Islamic jurisprudence and religious principles. Western education focused on empirical knowledge. The collision between reason and faith (in a system modulated over a millennium and a half to emphasize faith over reason) produced an intellectual dilemma. How might a tradition of faith compete in a world based on rationality?

Colonized Middle Easterners—Egyptians, Algerians, Syrians, Moroccans—realized that they must understand, if not use, the sciences and systems of their rulers in order to expel them. Arab nationalism was originally a secular movement formed by both Christian and Muslim Arabs. Struggles for independence were often bitter. Algeria won freedom from France in 1962 after sustained warfare and heavy casualties. Palestine has yet to achieve independence. Most Middle Eastern countries see Israel, itself a nation which fought against the British mandate, as a Western implant which blocks Palestinian independence.

Independence, which came in the 1950s and 1960s, was heady, and newfound nationalism promised to overcome social, ethnic, and religious divisions. But as years have passed and governments have not fulfilled hopes for socioeconomic equity, divisions have come to dominate the political arena. Instability in the form of war, political assassinations, and coups d'état exists in almost every country. Middle Easterners are weary of disrupted lives, violent deaths, broken families, shattered economies, and ravaged croplands. For many, life is on hold.

Today, as well as facing problems of political disunity, Middle Eastern countries lack the economic and technological infrastructure to deal with overpopulation, the fast growth of urban areas, and the resultant struggle over scarce resources. Economically, the presence or absence of oil reserves splits Middle Eastern countries into haves and have-nots. The Middle East is struggling to gain an industrial and technological base.

European influence, occupation, and colonization are constant referents for Middle Easterners today. Many Arabs call the colonial period the "time of imperialism." They are ambivalent, often opposing the West at the same time that they hope to emulate Western successes and to avoid Western failures. Western success is measured in terms of prosperity, technological advancement, national strength, democratization, and popular participation, and, in sum, the ability to go one's own way with one's beliefs intact without being influenced by outside forces. Western failure is gauged in terms of materialism, family breakdown, drugs, consumerism, and loss of religion—to name a few. Middle Easterners are puzzled by a Western society which does not care for its elder population. It seems to them that the moral core of Western society has broken down.

Probably the two political issues which most strongly reinforce this view are Palestine and Iraq. The Muslim Middle East supports the self-determination of the Palestinians and their desire to have Jerusalem as their capital so that all Muslims may have access to holy sites. And whether or not a given nation joined the Western coalition against Saddam Hussein in the 1991 Gulf War, Middle Easterners are united in concern for the Iraqi civilians hard hit by Western sanctions. As they feared for the welfare of Bosnians in the former Yugoslavia, they now emphasize that Iraqis are their brothers and sisters and cannot fathom the seeming Western indifference to their plight. They see this as a question of right, human dignity, and social justice.

The most hotly debated topics in the Middle East today are globalization and human rights. One common view is that the West dictates the terms of both: globalization is understood as Western domination, a new type of colonization, as the Western market, flush with capital and technology, seems primed to dominate the less-competitive Middle East. Human rights is a hot-button topic, not because Middle Easterners do not oppose torture or imprisonment without due process, but because the West defines human rights using Western concepts of individual rights and ignores areas such as community morality and welfare.

The information revolution which accompanies globalization has benefited Middle Easterners. The technology and financing of global forces has brought CNN and the Internet to the Middle East. The advent of satellite television has been instrumental in countering censorship. Once individuals gained access to the Internet, either via a local provider or by dialing to a neighboring country, government control over their access to information crumbled. Irbid, a town in the north of Jordan, probably has the most cybercafes per capita of any city in the world. The openness to the outside which this technology brings ties the Middle East to the rest of the world by making information and technology immediately accessible. Probably the fastest way for students to secure their future is to graduate with expertise in computer systems, for businesses from banks to travel agencies are dependent on computer networks. This technology allows them to bypass government bureaucracy and control. Political liberalization may be forced upon the Middle East from below.

The increasingly free flow of information and increased activity by international human rights watch groups have allowed cases of abuses in the Middle East to be publicized and have spurred the call for reform. The actions of international and national human rights groups have been instrumental in pushing political leaders to back down, free political prisoners, and allow international committees to monitor human rights abuses. There is still much work to do, but leaders have realized that they are on notice, and some have made changes on their own.

Middle Eastern opposition to the West is fueled by memories of colonization coupled with such current realities as economic dependency, political vulnerability, and the series of military losses to Israel. From Morocco to Afghanistan, indigenous political movements, under the rubric of Islamic activism, have attained a high profile in their opposition to Western influence and local political corruption. Islamist movements strive to create a uniquely Muslim society, epistemology, and technology—often through political action. Muslims often express a need to reconcile the spiritual and religious side of life with the political and the commercial.

The application of Islam to an individual's life has taken many forms during past decades. In the late 1970s Iranians used Islam as a rallying point to eject their shah and set up a government predicated on Islamic principles. In the intervening years Iranians have confronted war and political repression, and discovered that their Islamic government doesn't solve their everyday problems any better than any other government. In reality, increased literacy and educational opportunities may make the largest differences. Lay people are beginning to master religious texts and learn about Islam for themselves in home study groups and through published and recorded religious literature, television, and the Internet. In this Islamic Reformation, middle-class Muslims are carefully analyzing the meaning of religion for social and political action.

Historically, Muslims have always referred to their religion—as others have referred to their own beliefs—as a standard for social and political action. In the late twentieth century, groups of Islamic activists became more prominent in the Western news and in the politics of many Middle Eastern countries. In the U.S., we tend to hear only about these groups' sensational and violent activities, while the charitable deeds and efforts toward education and social organization of many go unmentioned. While Osama Bin Laden and Hamas in Palestine have grabbed headlines, others have sought legitimate power through political organization and orderly recourse to the ballot box, as is the case of the Muslim parties in Turkey and Jordan. Every Middle Eastern country has active Islamist groups. Some focus on religious learning and are not politically motivated; others have reformist political agendas. Islamist parties have altered the political landscape in Turkey and Jordan. In Algeria, the desire of Islamists to have a voice in politics resulted in a military suspension of elections and a civil war. In Egypt, the formerly outlawed Muslim Brotherhood is now represented in parliament. Other groups devote themselves to charitable work. As long as politics in the Middle East remains controlled by a coterie of political elites which are not accountable to the mass of the citizenry, Islam and its values of social justice and economic equity will continue to be a vital rallying point for opposition and will likely be used as a rationale for political action.

THE MIDDLE EAST: SOCIAL, DEMOGRAPHIC, AND GLOBAL ECONOMIC CHANGE

The Middle East is an ecologically diverse area with mountain ranges, pastureland, cultivated areas, deserts and oases, and urban areas. Fifty years ago, the majority of the area's inhabitants were agriculturalists. Today the Middle East is becoming highly urbanized, and in some Middle Eastern countries the urban percentage of the population is higher than it is in Europe. While Egypt is 44 percent urban, Saudi Arabia is now 83 percent urban (World Population Data Sheet, 2000).

Urban migrants are as much pushed by land fragmentation as pulled by industrial opportunities, which are often limited. A major factor has been job availability in the labor-hungry Gulf. Countering this trend, the 1991 Gulf War resulted in the exodus of thousands of highly skilled Palestinians and millions of other migrant workers from host countries. Upheavals always spell difficult changes for workers, and this situation may take years to settle again, further straining already stretched economies in the meantime.

Urban areas are growing at a rate roughly double that of the population as a whole, and in most countries the urban population is jammed into one or two major cities. Adding to the demographic load, the population of the Middle East is young, with about 38 percent under the age of fifteen. Although the rate of population growth is still high, family planning programs have succeeded in decreasing the birth rate, and better health care continues to raise life expectancy.

In ancient times, the Middle East was a crossroads of commerce. Today, nation-states of the area trade primarily in agricultural products, oil, and labor. Agricultural producers include Morocco, Syria, Egypt, Iraq, Turkey, and Iran. Oil exporters include Saudi Arabia, Iran, Iraq, Libya, Algeria, Kuwait, the United Arab Emirates, and the small states of the Persian Gulf. Yemen, Egypt, Algeria, Tunisia, and Morocco send workers to Europe as well as to the oil-rich states of the Gulf, Libya, and Saudi Arabia. The disparity in earning power between countries with oil and those without is dramatic. In the United Arab Emirates per capita income in 1998 was $17,870; in Egypt it was $1,290.

The need for economic growth may be the greatest challenge the Middle East faces today. Traditional economies have given way to wage labor in a global economy. The vast majority of urban unemployed are unskilled laborers who may find occasional work in the large informal sector of urban margins. But overeducated college graduates often wait years for placement in overstaffed public-sector bureaucracies while blue-collar skilled-labor jobs go begging. Egyptian office workers moonlight by driving taxis or working in coffee shops. Egyptian professors offer multiple tutorials in an evening to beat inflation and augment their meager salary.

Many skilled workers have left their native countries for more lucrative employment in the Gulf, Libya, or Europe. North African migrants returning home from France, urban-educated children returning to the village, young professionals imbued with the ideas of Western universities—all experience strain readjusting to the communities in which they grew up.

Those left behind face major adjustments as well. Women left at home take on new responsibilities in running their farms and workshops; children miss their absent fathers. The alternative to exporting labor is to compete internationally for industries and high-tech companies that can provide jobs for citizens. One result of globalization is that this is possible; another is that every other country in the world is competing for the same opportunities. In order to be competitive these countries must provide, in addition to factors such as the rule of law and a stable civic society, a labor pool which is educated and trained to be competitive in a global marketplace. Getting a child a good education is one of the problems which galvanizes Middle Easterners.

Middle Easterners thus face multiple and complex concerns. Change, on both individual and societal levels, seems to be the order of the day. Given the challenges of the late twentieth century, how do Middle Easterners keep going? What values—family, religion, honor, generosity—serve as guideposts for their lives? What strengths do Middle Easterners draw from the patterns of their everyday lives? In the face of all this upheaval, we must not lose sight of the fact that most Middle Easterners worry primarily about their families and their communities. As long as these are threatened, the area will not be peaceful. Thus it is with the family, with the generations and life passages, that this book begins.

REFERENCES

Braudel, Fernand. 1981. *Civilization and Capitalism: 15th–18th Century.* 2 vols. Trans. Sian Reynolds. New York: Harper and Row, 1981.
Fallers, Lloyd. 1974. *The Social Anthropology of the Nation State.* Chicago: Aldine Publishing.
LeFebvre, Henri. 1971. *Everyday Life in the Modern World.* Trans. Sacha Rabinovich. New York: Harper and Row.
Population Reference Bureau. 2000. World Population Data Sheet. Washington, D.C.: Population Reference Bureau.
Sells, Michael. 1988. "The Heritage of the Desert." Unpublished manuscript.
World Bank. 1990. *Development Report, 1990.* Washington, D.C.: World Bank.

PART ONE

Generations and Life Passages

Family life, the arena for passage from birth through circumcision, adolescence, marriage, and death, varies less by country than it does by locale. Bedouins and villagers usually live a more traditional life in extended families with all the family's sons and their wives under one roof. More attuned to the rhythm of the seasons and less rushed by the daily press of commuting and the eight-hour shift, rural peoples focus on family ties as a basis for all activities—at home and work, in socializing and entertainment. Urbanites often live in discrete nuclear families. Newly arrived migrants to large cities, separated from grandmother, mother, father, and siblings, search out neighbors as substitutes to help them adjust to their new surroundings. The diversions offered by city living are often a poor substitute for the support system of an extended family. National and international labor migration has disrupted households while simultaneously placing peasants and day laborers in an international market with its remittances and consumerism.

BIRTH AND CHILDHOOD

Children are valuable, and their birth is celebrated. At a seven-day naming ceremony in traditional quarters of Cairo, the newborn is shaken in a sieve while the midwife admonishes the child to obey his or her parents. As a proud American father totes cigars, so the traditional Egyptian mother distributes packets of dried nuts, symbolic of fertility, to her well-wishers.

Children ensure continuation of the family and community; they are, as one *hadith* (religious tradition) states, "the delight of life." Families dote on children, and a toddler amid a group of adolescents or adults is overwhelmed with affection. Susan Davis, in her article on childrearing, describes patterns particular to Morocco and describes how childrearing has changed there over the past three decades.

Muslims are expected to marry and to produce progeny who will increase the Muslim community and bless their own family. This is not a religious commandment but a social norm. An unmarried person is a social, not an economic, misfit and is shielded by family members from want or deprivation. The family into which one is born, the natal family, is the most important social group in one's life. It provides protection, food, shelter, income, reputation, and honor. The family is the reference for assistance as one grows up; finds a spouse, job, and home; raises one's own family; and adjusts to changing social circumstances. The family mediates between the individual and the outside world, and Middle Easterners naturally assume that relatives will be favored. One's family name is a ready-made identification which immediately acquaints others with one's reputation and one's access to assistance.

One's position within a family—whether one is married, single, divorced, or widowed, a parent or childless—also defines one's social status in the community. A man is autonomous upon reaching adulthood, usually eighteen, but he is expected to support his natal family as well as his wife and children. Women's legal and social adulthood is different; traditionally women gain status when they give birth to a male child, and they pour immense energy into his upbringing. When the first son is born, his parents are renamed "mother of Muhammad" and "father of Muhammad." The mother-son tie, which some say is the most powerful relation a woman or man will ever have, is typically a close and loving emotional relationship of strong dependency. While daughters marry and leave the family, sons support their parents in old age.

The tie between brother and sister runs a close second to the mother-son relation. Ideally, brothers will defend a sister in need throughout their lives, just as sisters will care for brothers as a kind of second mother. Although a woman may marry out of her natal family, she always carries its name, continues to be close to her brothers—sometimes closer than to her husband—and remains a potential source of dishonor to them.

Circumcision, which occurs between infancy and age ten, is the main rite of passage between birth and marriage. In countries like Egypt and Morocco, it is celebrated with parties and much congratulation. In traditional quarters of Cairo, there is a striking juxtaposition of a solemn religious event and a carnival. Young boys to be circumcised are dressed in white in the manner of a *hajj* returning from pilgrimage. Mounted on a horse, the boys proceed from the mosque at the time of the sunset prayer. Amongst the throngs of family, friends, and strangers watching and cheering them on are vendors of sweets and multi-colored paper hats. Boys who have not been circumcised receive a paper hat as a consolation prize.

War, in its many forms no stranger to the Middle East, has forced many children to mature rapidly. The impact of war upon children is brought home by Emily Nasrallah's story "Explosion," which illustrates the intrusion of violence into private life.

MARRIAGE

Marriage is a key milestone, and its romantic intrigues and festivities provide great entertainment for all. Young Middle Eastern men and women, contemplating their marriages, whisper about potential spouses and about whether romantic or traditionally arranged marriages are best. They eagerly await wedding parties, where young and old crowd in to listen to music and drink thick, sweet *sharbat*. Even luxurious hotel weddings assume the informality of home as children cavort and women ululate. Despite all this celebration, however, families take marriage seriously. Marriage is an economic contract negotiated by older males of the two families. They determine the bride price (*mahr* or *sadaq*) paid to the woman's father, as well as the clothes, jewelry, and furnishings to be given to the couple by each family. The bride price ideally includes a sum of money to be set aside and paid to the wife in case of divorce.

Once the couple is "engaged" via a legally binding marriage contract, they may visit each other at home and may date. The wedding party and consummation may occur months or even years later. After the party, the couple set up housekeeping together. Courtship, engagement, and marriage customs differ significantly by location, education, and social status. In Afghanistan—as Margaret Mills illustrates in the story "Of the Dust and the Wind"—the bride and groom may not have met before the wedding. In some Berber areas of southern Morocco, the bride lives chastely with the groom's family for months before the wedding in order to become familiar with the routine of the family. In the wealthy strata of Lebanon, Egypt, and Tunisia, wedding guests wearing French designer dresses and holding glasses of Scotch whisky circulate around a hotel ballroom and toast the young couple's health. Some weddings are more traditional, some more modern, in the style of the celebration as well as in how the marriage was contracted. As Jenny White illustrates with her stories of two weddings in contemporary Turkey, friends and relations may marry in diverse ways.

OLD AGE AND DEATH

Within the shelter of the family, old age is a time of reaping what one has sown. Traditionally, younger adults consult their elders about medical treatments, business deals, marriages, and political alliances. Responsibility, but not authority, passes to adult children. A mother is often de facto household head long after her husband is dead and the oldest son has gray hair.

Death is accepted as a natural part of life. Customarily, a funeral procession of wailing women and silent men carries the shrouded body to be buried facing Mecca before the first sunset after the death. It is traditional for the family to receive condolences afterward, either in arabesque tents set up for the occasion or at home. Guests read the *Fatiha* (the first verse of the Qur³an), drink tea or coffee, and listen to Quranic recitation. Women normally receive condolences during the day at home. As Driss Chraibi shows, funerals, by invoking emotions through Quranic readings, tie death to the forces of life.

PASSAGES THROUGH LIFE: DIFFERENT LOCALES

Passages through life are determined by family and by custom. Childhood, marriage, parenting, old age: each is shaped by biology and society. The Middle East embroiders different designs for the rituals marking each stage. Erica Friedl's "Traditional Songs from Boir Ahmad" shows one design in the songs and poetry with which Iranian villagers honor the passages of life. All societies value the family, but not every society values patriarchy and family honor as the Middle East does; even societies with a strong sense of honor may not believe that women's actions can dishonor the family in the way that Middle Easterners traditionally do. Such cultural themes as honor or shame shape the social drama of everyday life.

Until recently, the Middle Eastern family was not beset by Western social problems such as runaway children, the youth drug culture (which, however, has made inroads in the Middle East), or neglected elderly. Indeed, many Middle Easterners still question how Western society can abandon unwanted children or grandparents at the time when they most need family care. Middle Easterners exposed to Western mores while working abroad may, as in Driss Chraibi's "The Son's Return," experience difficulty in shifting gears from one culture to another. Bishara Bahbah describes the conflict between his expectations after completing a Ph.D. in the United States and the reality of work as a journalist in Jerusalem. The impersonal professionalism he had mastered in the U.S. clashed with the personal, kin-based methods of dealing with problems which Palestinian Jerusalem followed.

As we read about different ceremonies, different family expectations for puberty and dating, different definitions of adulthood, we may ask: What is distinctive about growing up in the Middle East? Has the Middle East escaped rebellious youth and the neglect of the elderly? Or are its values already changing? Is Islam critical to the strength of the family, or is something else—such as a strong patriarchy or the centrality of family identity—the linchpin? How do Middle Eastern Muslims accommodate modern ideas about dating and virginity? The details of the individual lives presented in the following selections help address such broad cultural questions.

1. Traditional Songs from Boir Ahmad

Collected and translated by Erika Friedl

The following songs about childbirth, marriage, and death are sung by women of the Boir Ahmad tribe in southwestern Iran during times of life crises. The metaphors range from young women's mascara to daily herding duties. —Eds.

BIRTH

Oh, the red-lipped beauty is in labor pains.
May God make it a boy.

Oh, my dear, oh my sister,
your baby boy is crying.

WEDDING

The songs below comment on the events from courtship to actual wedding and were traditionally sung at the different stages of a wedding. Since the Islamic Revolution in Iran, singing of such songs is forbidden. There is no music at all at weddings in Iran now.

The first seven songs are love songs that could be sung at many occasions, not just at weddings.

Three things I ask of God:
a good horse, a good rifle, and a pair of brown eyes.

Oh my uncles are you heathens?
Speak up for me to get me the red-lipped beauty.

I wish I was your mascara brush
inside your jacket
next to your breasts.

I wish I was your rifle—
on your shoulder by day
and at night under your shawl.

(*a woman is speaking.*)

And if you went up in the sky
to hide behind rainclouds,
my eyes would play in yours.

Tell your mother I am at your service—
The beads around your neck have set me afire.

Last night while you carried your water sack,
    I saw your hips.
If your father asks a thousand Toman for you
    I'll give him more.

Lucky the man who has a strong horse, a good rifle,
a soft-spoken mother-in-law and a pretty bride.

Tomorrow morning we'll fetch the bride
for the lion-groom's pleasure.

How nice it is to mount a brown horse
and ride from morning to night for the bride.

Get up, blossom, put on your shoes, it's time to go.
His horsemen are here, it is time to be bashful.

I tell you, dear, keep your house well.
The bride is crying—I am so young, I won't marry.

(*A young bride and her mother are speaking.*)

Mother of the bride, why are you crying?
On your daughter's cap are a hundred Toman worth of
gold.

(*The gold refers to the gold coins which traditionally were
sewn on a bride's cap.*)

The orange blossom stepped out of her house
when her lion-groom's bridewealth appeared out of the
shade.

My God, how long am I to wait in the crowd outside his
house?

The moon is fading and the morning star is high.

(*A bride is complaining about having to wait in front of her
groom's house—her entourage is singing.*)

The bridal chamber is ready, a rich bridal chamber.
In it the lion-groom is playing with a tiger.

How pleasant is your bride chamber's fragrance.
The lion-groom's hands are in his bride's braids.

You have a rich skirt and a red scarf on your head,
and your husband will take care of all your troubles.

(*Sung for a bride.*)

If you want your husband to like you, swing your hips,
and early in the morning sprinkle rosewater on the bed.

(*Sung for a bride.*)

DEATH

*Songs of mourning are still sung by Iranian women, but only in private, no
longer at funerals.*

Angel of Death, give me time, I haven't yet finished two
tasks:
My oldest I haven't given a wife, my baby I haven't
brought up.

(*For a woman with young children.*)

She was pregnant and asked for a cradle,
but her brother had no plain wood.
For her, he wanted to use the best sandalwood.

(For a pregnant woman, or one who dies in childbirth.)

I went to her house, but she wasn't there.
She left for the high mountain spring to wash her cotton
skirt.

(This and the following eight songs are for women, praising their beauty, wealth, and industry.)

I looked down from the hilltop: she was about to milk her
herd.
The swing rod on her buttering stand was of fragrant
wood, tied with bright cotton.

Don't let her tent come down, it has forty ropes, all in
place.
Tighten them firmly, clouds are in the sky.

The tents were still pitched up in the winter camp, but
she packed for the camp in the mountains.

Don't leave: spin a little more on your spindle, your
dowry isn't yet complete.

(This song is sung mostly for young unmarried women.)

Fold your nice scarf, your pretty shirt, and put them in
the bundle.
It is time to break camp and move up to the mountains.

The beautiful woman's necklace broke.
The beads of coral and gold dropped into her lap.

The woman left for her mother's so fast,
that neither a horseman nor a bird can catch up with her.

The two of us sisters went to pick flowers,
but rain and snow came down hard and we lost sight of
each other.

Child, like a tree with roots in loose gravel,
like a tree, all dried up, you haven't born fruit.

>   (*There are few mourning songs for children. It is said that
>   mourning for children is harmful to the dead child's soul.*)

The master hunter went on a hunt. Night fell, but he
didn't come back.
Either the tiger got his dog, or the night took him by surprise.

>   (*For a hunter, but also for any man.*)

I saw your rifle, its butt full of blood.
Is it yours or that of a wild buck?

>   (*For a hunter who died of bullet wounds, usually in a
>   battle.*)

A partridge with two chicks left them and sat down on a
rock.
It has not come back all summer, and the eagle at the
young.

>   (*For a hunter who leaves young children.*)

The lad with the fine white cap disappeared over the pass.
Don't call him, maybe he'll come back by himself.

>   (*For a young man.*)

This fine young man they put on a stretcher.
His hair has the fragrance of mountain flowers.

>   (*For a young man.*)

The gorge is filled with the thunder of gunshots.
The young man was killed there by a pair of tigers.

(*For a young man killed in a battle.*)

Bang, bang, from the river comes the noise of battle.
The young men spoil for a fight.

(*For a young man killed in a battle.*)

Boir Ahmad boy, let us look at you. A ten-bullet rifle is on
your shoulder,
and a red flower-bullet wound is on your white shirt.

(*For a young fighter.*)

The girl's tears tinkle like bells. I don't know:
does she cry out of her own misery, or for her brother?

(*Sung by a woman for her dead brother.*)

2. Growing up in Morocco

Susan Schaefer Davis

After observing childrearing in a small, north-central Moroccan town in the mid-1970s, Susan Schaefer Davis concluded that children are much more durable than Americans consider them to be. She notes the critical importance of gender and the family patriline in childrearing. Males were preferred, for social and economic reasons more than for religious ones, but that preference, as well as many other things, had changed when she looked at several of these issues again in 2000. —Eds.

INFANCY

Male babies are preferred to female in Morocco. This preference is based on the function of each sex within the family. Since Morocco is a patrilineal society (one in which descent is traced through males), the son will remain a part of the family and eventually be responsible for the support of his mother and father in their old age. The daughter, on the other hand, will marry and reside with her husband; she is considered someone who will be lost to the family at marriage. At least, that's how things were in the 1970s. However, by 2000 families were very glad to have daughters, and women who had none really wanted them. While daughters still move out of the family at marriage, now most sons do too. More importantly, now more women work for a living, and mothers report that daughters are more likely to give money to their natal families than are sons, whose wives want to keep it all within the nuclear family. Another factor contributing to the new view is that sons used to inherit land that they worked to support families, but now many fewer people own land or work in agriculture, so such inheritance is less relevant and less profitable. (Sisters formally in-

Adapted and updated from Susan Schaefer Davis, *Patience and Power: Women's Lives in a Moroccan Village* (Boston: Schenkman Books, 1983).

herit half the land their brothers do, but usually brothers work it and control most of the income from it.) Finally, daughters also remain emotionally closer to their mothers throughout their lives than do sons.

However, having a daughter may be less desirable because the female offspring are considered a threat to the family honor, as was quite clearly revealed in an incident which occurred a few years prior to our residence in a Moroccan village. The daughter of one family had become pregnant by the son of the family next door. While both families seldom mentioned the incident, it was clear from local gossip that the girl was believed to be at fault and that her family had been more dishonored. The boy had left the village to study (his family was embarrassed enough to remove him from the scene), but his family suffered no great stigma. The girl had also left the area and was raising her baby in the city. Meanwhile, her mother and sisters were snubbed by the neighborhood women's groups and seldom participated in their activities, spending most of their time isolated inside their home. By 2000, families still worried about the honor of daughters, but lapses were easier to disguise. A pregnant girl might visit an aunt in another city for a few years, and return "divorced" with a child.

At birth, the preference for males was indicated in the 1970s by the larger celebration held for a boy's naming ceremony. By 2000, ceremonies for both sexes were similar, and smaller than in the past. Boys and girls are treated quite similarly during the period from birth to two years of age. Both are constantly in the company of their mother; babysitters are an unknown institution. An infant may be left in the care of a young girl for a few minutes, but only infrequently.

Since nearly all babies are breastfed (I saw perhaps three baby bottles during my early research in the village), they are never far from their mothers. When the mother is working or walking, she carries the baby in a cloth sling on her back which is then tied in front, one end over the shoulder, the other under the opposite breast. This leaves her hands free, and the baby seems to cause no inconvenience. Children are carried in this way, or ride on the hip of a younger sister when they are old enough, until they can walk well. In the 1990s some women began to use Western-style front carriers for babies, and even strollers in the cities, and I also saw men carrying babies in the street. However, babies are still in nearly constant contact with their mothers and other members of the family.

When they are sitting and visiting, women lay babies across their laps or on a cushion next to them; they are seldom held in the arms except when nursing. It is amazing to see several children sound asleep during an evening women's party with loud music and conversation, but they have learned early to sleep in any environment.

It is interesting that in spite of this constant contact with her child, the mother appears to harbor no resentment toward it. She does not seem to find it a burden or feel that it hinders her from doing other things; whatever she does, the baby comes along, as do everyone's babies. Such toler-

ance may be partially due to the fact that babies do not appear to be a problem or nuisance. They are nursed on demand (even three or four times an
hour) and are never allowed to cry more than a few seconds without being
pacified, usually with the breast. These days, babies are given pacifiers or
bottles containing milk or water, too. In the 1970s, the baby was frequently
wrapped in a cloth, used as a diaper but without pins, that was changed
when soiled. Poorer families still use these makeshift diapers, but if they
can afford them, even small-town families now use specially made or even
disposable diapers from birth. Because of the almost constant bodily contact, mothers also learn to sense when babies are about to urinate or defecate and may then remove them from the sling and hold them out over the
(usually dirt) floor. One mother claimed that her son had been "trained"
at six months: that is, he only urinated and defecated at specific times,
and only when he had been "put aside" to do so. Accidents do occur, but
women never seem irritated or upset about their soiled *jellabas*.

One of the few times when babies do cry is when they are teased, and
this usually does not occur until near the end of infancy; they are not teas-
able until that age. Adults seem to enjoy frustrating a child, perhaps holding a toy just out of reach until it bursts into tears, and then giving it both
the toy and a big, warm hug. They don't seem to want to hurt the child or
see it suffer; rather, it appears that this is one of the few varieties of behavior exhibited by the child and they want to see it perform. The hugs afterward are always very reassuring, and the child is never left to cry uncom-
forted.

When a child is in a group of people with its mother, it becomes the
object of everyone's attention only if there is nothing else to talk about—
that is, the baby will be held and cuddled and briefly admired, but it is not
the focus of the group. Even when alone with its mother, the child is always
attended to when it makes a demand, but otherwise it takes second place
to other activities. One seldom observes women saying "Ma-ma, Ma-ma"
and encouraging the child to repeat the sounds, or helping a child to stand
and take its first steps. The child does these things when it is ready; it is
not pressured or encouraged to be precocious. Conversations about the accomplishments of one's children, so common among women in America,
are not heard in Morocco. To a degree Moroccan women do realize themselves through their children, especially their sons, but they nevertheless
place less emphasis on the process of childrearing than Americans do.

In infancy both sexes are dressed identically, in a little smock in the
summer, with a sweater and long pants added in the winter. One must in-
quire to determine the sex of a child, and a mistake does not upset or offend the mother (which is surprising, in view of the society's great sex-role
differentiation). In fact, what seemed most offensive to mothers was to
be told that their baby was lovely. Initially I thought a woman lacked affection for her child when in response to a compliment she replied, "She's

not pretty at all. Look how wrinkled she is, and just as black as her father!" But when one understands the susceptibility of small babies to illness caused by the evil eye, one learns to either agree with the mother that
the baby is ugly or to preface a compliment with the protective phrase
tbarek Allah (God bless).

EARLY CHILDHOOD

The early childhood period includes the second through fifth years of the
child's life, when it is more mobile than an infant, yet spends most of its
time within the household rather than outdoors playing with peers. During this time the differential treatment of the sexes begins, the child learns
to *hshim* (behave properly), and weaning and toilet training (important in
traditional studies of socialization) occur.

Weaning could be said to occur in either infancy or early childhood,
since it usually happens very close to two years of age. By the time of
weaning most children are also eating bits of food from the table, but this
occurs late in comparison to the American practice. Also, a few children
were observed who refused to ingest anything except their mother's milk;
they spat out any other food offered. Only one such child appeared obviously malnourished; he was very scrawny and unable to walk although he
was over two years old.

Because breastfeeding is believed to prevent pregnancy (a belief which
has some basis in fact), women try to continue it until the child is two.
Weaning occurs if a woman becomes pregnant and her milk supply decreases. It is recognized that weaning is difficult for the child, and it often
occurs on a holiday (*id al-seghir*) on which it is felt to be easier, or with a
new moon. Nevertheless, women say of a newly weaned child, "now he
knows that *ghder* [treachery, betrayal] exists in the world." The feeling
that before this time children are very close to the angels and unaware of
worldly hardships in fact reflects, in metaphor, the real situation.

In the 1970s, the process of weaning was very abrupt; the mother chose
a day, painted her breasts with liver bile or hot pepper to discourage the
child, and from that point did not nurse it again. She bound up her breasts
or wore her dress backward to be sure the child would not "steal" a sip
while sleeping next to her. One might expect that mothers would have re-
lented when they saw how unhappy and upset the child was, but the culture bolstered their resolution through the common belief that their milk
spoils and will poison the child once they stop nursing. One woman described how her baby girl had died at the time of weaning for just this
reason. Although she had not given in and nursed the child, she thought
the baby must have "stolen" some milk during the night. The next day the
baby had diarrhea—from the poison, her mother assumed—and she died

a few days later. I suspect that diarrhea did indeed often occur with weaning, not from poisoned milk but because the infant was then more likely to drink the local water, which contained various germs. Adults are immune to most of them, and also strong enough to endure a round of dysentery, but babies are much more susceptible.

Children would be fussy for the first few days after weaning, and some mothers tried to pacify them with candy or cookies. Others objected, however, saying that the children would then always crave sweets and not eat properly.

Weaning had changed quite a bit by 2000. It now begins much earlier; mothers may stop nursing or begin using supplementary bottles when the baby is three months old. This could be related to working outside the home (although Moroccan law gives mothers nursing breaks), but most women seem to nurse less than in the past. Although I do not have any evidence of an increase of diarrhea (the water is now chlorinated) or other consequences for health, I wonder about this practice. Worldwide, longer nursing is felt to be healthier for babies. In fact, some Moroccan women feel early weaning is better for their own health. It does mean that women can leave babies with others more than in the past, but they so do relatively rarely, and usually with close family members. Babies also begin to eat solid foods much sooner than previously, most beginning with a cereal mixed with milk at about two months and gradually adding other foods. By about a year of age, babies are eating and drinking like other children. The weaning process itself has become less intense. The mother does not put hot pepper or another deterrent on her breasts, but just wears a garment closed in the front so the baby cannot nurse. After about three days, the child is said to forget, and since it has bottle feedings or other food, that is probably the case.

While weaning was quite carefully accomplished, toilet training was and is very relaxed. I noted above that women can often sense when an infant is about to urinate or defecate and they then hold the child away from them, so that a child may be trained quite young. No data were collected regarding specific ages, but it appears that most children are toilet trained by three or four years of age, and some considerably earlier. When infants can sit but not walk, they are often seated on the mother's extended legs so that they can defecate on the floor or ground. This is easily cleaned up and not noted, positively or negatively, by others present. More recently, they are put on a potty seat when the need is noticed in time. When children are able to walk (at about one year), they wear only little smocks and no pants at all in the summer, so that they urinate or defecate wherever they happen to be standing. Again, no fuss is made, though they may be taken outside or to the toilet if they are noticed in time. When they are a little older, they learn to squat while defecating (as do adults), further simplifying the process. Whenever they are seen squatting, they are taken to the proper place, and thus quickly learn the association.

During this period, the differential treatment of the sexes becomes much more apparent. The slight amount of extra attention that infant boys receive increases in early childhood. Fathers now pay more attention—infants are not particularly interesting to them—but mainly to boys; girls are given little. Children of both sexes are hugged and told that they are pretty, but boys more often than girls. Small girls do not cry or demand attention to show they resent being slighted, but just sit quietly and observe.

Another aspect of differential treatment is that little boys are allowed and sometimes even encouraged to hit their older sisters, who are not allowed to retaliate. Little girls seldom strike anyone and are not encouraged to do so. Behavior that we would call "spoiled" (such as tantrums) is both exhibited more often by boys and tolerated more from them. While one seldom meets a spoiled little girl, spoiled youngest boys are the norm.

Moroccan children at this stage are much less sheltered than their American counterparts. They are allowed to roam freely about the house; adults do not take pains to keep them away from the fire in the kitchen or to prevent them from falling down the stairs. It is not that the adults do not care; they are concerned when there is a reasonable danger, but would see most American parents' behavior as overprotective. After a period of residence in Morocco, one comes to the conclusion that children are very durable and that they can assume a great deal of responsibility at an early age.

For example, one little girl was found toddling around on the roof where the rabbits were kept, ingesting their excrement. When the mother was informed, instead of rushing the child to the nearest clinic she merely smiled and remarked, "I guess she thinks those are vitamin pills." Much later, in her twenties, the girl's chubby figure was jokingly attributed to these "vitamins." One local family used to laugh at the way I would nervously watch their five-year-old son whenever he rode his tricycle near a steep flight of cement stairs; he had not fallen down them yet and they felt it unlikely that he would. The same boy failed to come home for dinner about 8 P.M., and his sister said, "He must be at his aunt's house—or somewhere. He'll come home sooner or later." Most American mothers would have considered the possibility of his falling in the river, wandering out into the hills, or meeting some other grim fate. The only time a family appeared worried about a child (for reasons other than illness) was when a local six-year-old was missing overnight, and he was later found staying with relatives in the adjacent town.

While American preschoolers are playing and being sheltered from the hardships of life, Moroccan children are enjoying more independence and learning practical skills. Girls especially begin helping their mothers at this time. While boys sometimes run errands, such help is regarded as cute rather than as a contribution to running the household. Girls, however, begin running errands, washing dishes, sweeping, and caring for younger children at this age. It is not unusual to see a five-year-old carrying a one-year-old on her back.

Children of both sexes begin to hshim at this time. *Hshuma* (shame) and the related concept of ʿqel (discussed below) are both very important in Moroccan childrearing; once children have mastered both, they are grown up. "Hshim" means literally "Show some shame!" or "Behave!" when spoken as a command. To hshim is to behave properly and not to exhibit bad manners or morals. Since the behavior expected of boys and girls varies, so does the meaning of "hshim" as applied to each. For a small boy it means to sit quietly; for a girl it demands bodily modesty in addition to quietness. Three-year-old girls are encouraged to cover their legs with their dresses while seated, and strict parents do not even allow them to wear short, French-style dresses. For a mother to say about her daughter *"Kathshim"* (she's well behaved) implies an element of shyness, since proper behavior for girls includes a demure aspect. Often these girls would stare at the ground and blush while their mothers spoke (appropriate behavior when one is being discussed), leading me to initially understand "kathshim" to mean "she's shy or frightened." It should also be noted that "hshim" applies to observable behavior; it is an external judgment by society of one's actions rather than something felt internally and individually by a person. It can be compared to Western concepts of guilt and shame: guilt is internalized self-punishment, but shame is imposed on one by others. In Morocco shame (hshuma) is the most common means of control of behavior, whereas guilt is of little importance. A child did not feel "bad" about stealing something because one should not steal, but felt "bad" about being caught because this meant public shame. The effectiveness of shame as social control was revealed in a class of preschool children in the village. Because a child would not behave in response to directions or even slaps, the teacher stood him in the corner for a few minutes. That he cried as if his heart were broken is not understandable unless one realizes the impact of being publicly shamed.

Another aspect of child training that begins during early childhood and persists to adulthood may be related to the prevalence of shame over guilt. There is a striking inconsistency in the way in which children are disciplined. The first time a little girl takes a large lump of sugar from the tea tray and begins to suck on it, she may be laughed at or even admired, especially if guests are present. The next time she does it she may be soundly spanked; corporal punishment, while not overly harsh, is frequent. The main variable seems to be the mood of the parent rather than the nature of the act. Thus one would hardly expect the child to develop an internal sense of what is right and wrong, since consequences depend on an exterior factor, the parent. Such methods lead directly to feeling only shame, imposed from outside, when caught. One might also speculate that herein lies the origin of the almost uncanny ability of many Moroccans to "psych out" people; it is a talent they develop early, in self-defense against their parents' moods.

LATE CHILDHOOD

During late childhood further differentiation of the sexes occurs, with boys playing and attending school while girls take on more and more responsibility at home. Probably partially as a consequence of their increased responsibility, girls begin to develop ʿqel, more mature behavior, but boys do not do so until much later. During this stage (and sometimes earlier) boys undergo circumcision, which may have a disturbing psychological effect. Perhaps the most outstanding characteristic of late childhood is the fact that the boys are literally terrors outside the household, and one marvels to think that somehow they will be socialized into very restrained and proper men like their fathers.

Between the ages of six and twelve, girls are of maximum usefulness to the household. Although they further refine their housekeeping skills during adolescence, they are then no longer allowed to go out freely because their families become concerned about their honor. The institution of little-girl maids depends mostly on those in late childhood. Girls in this age category learn to do all the basic household tasks of washing, cleaning, cooking, and childcare, and in addition run errands to buy food or deliver messages. More of these girls have been sent to public school recently, but many are too valuable as assistants for their mothers to spare them. One notes again the pragmatism of this training; it is difficult to imagine an American twelve-year-old so competent to run a household. These girls do play with peers, usually after dinner in the evening when all the work is done.

By the middle 1980s, nearly all girls and boys were sent to primary school. While girls still learned housekeeping skills early, they were less available to work as maids for city families, and indeed there was a shortage of these young maids by the 1990s. Going to school also meant that girls' movements were less restricted as they approached adolescence. Instead of people gossiping about a girl who was "out," they would assume she was going to school in addition to helping her mother.

Boys, on the other hand, seem to spend most of their time playing. Most boys attend the public school for at least three or four years, but it must operate on split shifts because of crowding and thus occupies only a few hours of the day. The rest of the time is spent outside in unsupervised play;

the only household task that might be asked of a boy is shopping or taking a message to his father, and that infrequently. The most reserved or controlled game played by groups of boys is soccer, which is a great favorite. Another common game involves a gang of boys each trying to kick one another in the pants. This seemed more typical of the play of these boys— very active and expressing a lot of aggression.

One wonders where all the aggression comes from, since girls do not seem to exhibit it at all. Is it related to the fact that small boys are spoiled but almost inevitably dethroned by the arrival of a new baby, whereas girls lack this experience? Yet girls receive less attention immediately after infancy than do boys, so that transition could be more difficult for them. Or perhaps it is related to the fact that girls' energy is channeled directly into household activities, while boys' energy lacks a productive or appreciated outlet. While all the above may be contributing factors, I suspect that the circumcision of boys between the ages of four and eight, with no prior warning or explanation, may also play an important role in explaining their aggression. There is no similar event for girls in Morocco.

For boys in the 1970s, however, circumcision (*tahar*) was a major event and grounds for a large celebration, to which friends and relatives were invited. In that regard, circumcision is for boys what a wedding is for girls: the most significant ceremonial event to focus on them. Of course, the groom also celebrates his wedding, but the bride is the center of attention. Boys enjoyed all the attention they received at their circumcision, including wearing fancy clothing, parading through the streets on a white horse, and having musicians play in their honor. They also enjoyed the feast, and at the men's party might be encouraged to smoke, drink wine, and dance with the dancing girls, revealing the initiatory aspect of the circumcision. Since most boys were still very young, their participation in these latter activities was more a charade than a reality.

However, all this celebration usually occurred before the actual circumcision. Mothers explained that it is wiser to wait, for if the child should fall ill as a result of the operation, the mother would have to attend to him and could not see to all her duties as hostess. Boys seemed to be aware of the more glamorous aspects but were not told in advance what the actual operation would involve. By eight years of age or so, children might discuss it among themselves, but younger boys were not prepared by their families.

When one assumes the naiveté of the boy, the actual circumcision must have been quite frightening. After all the music, dancing, and eating were over, several women would file into a house with the boy's mother. He was brought in by an uncle or other male relative (seldom by the father; one wonders if he could not bear it). The operation was usually performed by a barber-surgeon who specialized in it, although it might also be available at health clinics. One village boy of five, waiting near the door as everyone filed in, showed a sense what was impending when he said, "Well, I think

I'll just wait here outside." But it was his circumcision and he had to go in. The male relative held the child steady, the barber-surgeon removed the foreskin, and the women all sang loudly so that the mother would not hear the child cry.

After the operation, the child was placed on his mother's back as if he were an infant, and she bent nearly double as she carried him to the room where he would recuperate for a few days. During this passage both mother and son were covered with a white sheet, presumably as a defense against the evil eye. Friends and relatives then filed in and each gave the child a little money and said something comforting. On one such occasion that I attended, the five-year-old boy cried heartbrokenly, a cry that suggested more than physical pain. He did not even pause when one of his visitors, an old midwife, said, "Don't worry, sonny; it'll grow back as big as this!" and displayed her forearm. One of my bigger regrets was that I did not interview this child in the next few days and ask him just what (he perceived) had happened; he was a very verbal child and would probably have had a lot to say. When I finally did ask him, about six months later, all he said was *"wellit sghrir"* (I became small).

By 2000 the practice of circumcision had changed. Morocco's king had begun sponsoring a circumcision day for the whole nation, when boys could be taken to the hospital and circumcised by a doctor at no charge. Nearly all families seem to use this service, whether wealthy or poor. Circumcision in a hospital probably means there are fewer infections, and perhaps this is why it is now felt proper to circumcise boys at a younger age than in the past, at between three and five years old. Boys that age are unlikely to understand the process, and doing it at a hospital probably adds to their anxiety. Another change is that there is a much smaller celebration for the occasion, perhaps a meal or tea and sweets for the family and a few friends.

While boys seem to become wilder and less controllable during late childhood, girls are the opposite. Girls are allowed to laugh, run, and play in the streets (when they have time), as do their brothers. But as they approach adolescence, girls are encouraged to become quieter and more sedate. One little girl in particular comes to mind; at six she was almost as much a tease as her brother, with a twinkle in her eye and a ready laugh. But by ten she had become more restrained, and by twelve she was a "perfect little lady," seldom running or giggling, and the sparkle had been replaced by soberness and a sense of responsibility.

In fact, the greater responsibility borne by girls is probably one of the main factors in their development of ᶜqel earlier than boys. ᶜQel, or the more common *dir lᶜqel*, means literally "to develop a mind." It refers to development into an intellectually capable, or socially responsible, person. Abdelwahed Radi, a professor at Mohammed V University in Rabat, suggests that ᶜqel involves internalizing the values of one's elders. One sees here an interesting contrast with the American concept of child development. We tend to perceive a child's development as linear through time, beginning in infancy, with each successive stage building on the previous ones. Moroccans do not share the concept of linearity; a child exists for a time, and finally one day it is discovered to have developed ʿqel. Girls act quite sensibly by the end of childhood, and during adolescence most are recognized as having "become responsible." One can leave them in charge of the household and expect everything to be functioning smoothly when one returns. If it is not, they are held responsible and punished.

For boys, however, the picture is different. The last thing one would expect of boys at this age is that they would have ʿqel. Rather, they behave irresponsibly, sometimes even destructively, but are not blamed. People used to warn us never to allow children in our house because "they have not yet 'become responsible' and might steal something." We assumed the warning applied to children under seven, as was in fact correct for girls; the boys they referred to were up to fifteen and evidently not yet held responsible for theft. These differences in the rate of assuming responsibility may be partly due to the fact that the realm of a woman lies inside the household and is fairly easily mastered when young, whereas that of a man involves many and varied interactions with the outside world that cannot be easily learned in the setting of the home, or at play, or in school. However, by 2000 many girls attended school and expected to have a role in the world outside the household, but still developed ʿqel well before boys.

ADOLESCENCE

During their teens girls exhibit relatively little change, except for increased sexual modesty. Boys may begin to develop ʿqel, especially if they must work to support themselves or their families, but they are also expected to sow some wild oats at this time.

Girls' socialization continues to occur within the household, although they may also have friends in the neighborhood. With the onset of puberty girls begin to cover themselves more and are seen less frequently in the street. In the 1970s they quickly learned (if they had not already) that exchanging banter with boys or men was forbidden, and instead they passed by with eyes cast down. Most girls married in late adolescence and were fully prepared to become wives and mothers.

With most girls attending at least primary school and many going further, by 2000 girls were less restricted at puberty than in the past. They may wear more modest clothing, but most are keenly interested in fashion and hairstyles. Since they study in mixed classes with boys, they may talk to boys outside school and such "proper" interactions are accepted. While American-style dating is not accepted in the small town I lived in, boys and girls often find opportunities to get together. The age at marriage has gone up dramatically, so by the early 1980s it was about twenty-four for women in urban Morocco, and five to ten years higher for men. This is probably related to the cost of starting a new household and the limited availability of jobs. For more details, see *Adolescence in a Moroccan Town* by Susan S. Davis and Douglas A. Davis.

Boys are still experimenting during this period, often with smoking, eating ham, drinking, and visiting prostitutes. Obviously most of their socialization now occurs outside the home, with peer groups or with older males with whom they work. The son has a great deal of respect for the authority of his father, and the relations of the two are rather distant by this age. A son will not smoke in front of his father and would be very embarrassed to encounter him in a bar or brothel. Thus the father is not responsible for much of the son's socialization, except as he represents a strong authority figure. The lack of a dependable source of guidance for boys at this age probably contributes to their problems. Many perceive their fathers as old-fashioned and unsuccessful in the modern world.

Mothers may threaten to tell fathers of a son's misbehavior, but in the end the mother more frequently defends him to the father. Mothers hope their sons will love and respect them, and ultimately most do, but not until they are in their twenties. Teenage males often abuse both sisters and mothers, who are hurt but tolerate their behavior. One young man of our acquaintance was very sharp with the female members of his family (he was brusque or silent with his father) and occasionally threw plates of food on the floor when he was especially irritated. Young men in Morocco today do face many problems, the main one being widespread unemployment. Given their lack of power in the society, women are the only available targets for their resentment.

Boys manage to survive adolescence and in the 1970s were usually married in their early twenties. They developed ʿqel around the same time; few families would trust their daughter to an immature husband who had not yet developed ʿqel. By the 1990s, men's age at marriage had increased to the early thirties. In their early twenties, young men were still quite adolescent and not ready to support a family, economically or emotionally. But after marriage, the "socially responsible" couple begin their own cycle of childrearing.

3. Explosion

Emily Nasrallah

Since the end of World War II, practically every country in the Middle East has been involved in war or disturbances of some kind: independence wars, civil wars, revolutions, foreign invasions, armed put-downs of strikes and demonstrations, coups d'état and coup d'état attempts. The Gulf War of 1990–91 and other conflicts, such as the Lebanese civil war, the Palestine-Israel conflict (and the history of wars between Israel and its neighbors), the Iran-Iraq war, and the Soviet presence in Afghanistan, have proved highly disruptive to Middle Eastern citizens. Although parts of life are put on hold, noncombatants work to preserve as much of a normal routine as possible. The experiences linked to war, such as deprivation, bombings, injuries, and death, continue to affect many people years after the event. War dramatizes the unpredictability which life brings. Children are often the innocent victims of war and disproportionately suffer emotional trauma as well as physical injury and death. —Eds.

I do not know who records these words for me. Is it the pen that fled from me in the middle of the road as I ran, dragging my daughter behind me, to reach the nearest shelter? Or is it my body that was lifted from underneath the rubble and the ruins of the inferno to be stuffed into the plastic bag that would become its second skin?

When I speak of the "body," I am talking of what is left of it: the lumps and masses of flesh—skinned, flayed and torn—that bear no resemblance to the tall, svelte figure that had walked into the supermarket earlier, juggling the car keys in one hand and with the other clutching the hand of beautiful, little Neinar.

* * *

This story was previously published in Emily Nasrallah, *A House Not Her Own: Stories from Beirut,* trans. Thuraya Khalil-Khouri (Charlottetown, P.E.I.: Gynergy, 1992). It appears here by permission of the author.

Neinar, the pride and joy of her parents' hearts, the apple of their eye, flower of the four seasons, offering every day a new colour and a fresh fragrance. On that day, a Saturday as I recall, she woke early, came to my bed and shook me awake.

"Get up."

"What is it, my love?" I asked, as I rubbed remnants of sleep from my eyes.

"Get up . . . " she repeated the order. "You promised me that today we'd go to the supermarket that sells the Cabbage Patch doll. I want a Cabbage Patch doll."

I smiled and hugged her, trying to entice her with the warmth of my embrace, but she would not be diverted. She would not climb into bed with me and snuggle in my lap and fill me with the essence of her being. She was adamant in her insistence on going to the supermarket, her single-minded purpose for the day.

I asked her, making light of the matter, "And did you dream of the Cabbage Patch doll in your sleep?"

She did not like my question and did not answer me, but kept pulling at my fingers.

* * *

In truth, I had decided two days before to devote a couple of hours of my Saturday to buying household necessities—things that a home consumes with an insatiable appetite. Neinar's little dream coincided well with my carefully laid out plans for that day. For I am a working mother and must plan every minute of my day to please the Lord and please the Boss and please the Family Head.

* * *

"We have two hours and the supermarket is not too far. I just hope the highway is not as crowded as it normally is," I said to Neinar.

She did not seem to be listening to me. I looked at her in my rear-view mirror. Eyes averted toward the window, she was contemplating the sea absentmindedly, recording all she saw in front of her, giving herself up to a childish wonderment and astonishment. She had forgotten I was there and was deaf to my babbling.

I, on the other hand, was very happy at having reconciled my duties and my daughter's outing. I decided I would take this opportunity to make it up to Neinar for the times I am at work, absent from her. The rest of our day would be filled with as many happy and pleasant moments as possible.

Parking the car not far from the store, I opened the back door to help Neinar climb out. We walked towards the store. Or, rather, I walked; she ran and skipped and bounced about in circles like a bee. Neinar, my little bee with honey eyes and rosy lips and cheeks, and the fragrant flavour of a spring flower.

She went ahead to where the shopping carts were lined up, pulled one out and issued her orders.

"We start from here." Her little finger pointed to the toy section. I tried to convince her that we would return to that magical section after we had finished shopping for the necessities.

She was pleased with the arrangement, but looked up at me with a puzzled frown. "And the toys? Are they not necessary?"

I smiled to hide my unforgivable mistake. "They're the most important," I said. "That is why we're going to leave them until we're finished with all the bothersome things. That way we can devote all our attention to them."

She sensed the sincerity of my tone rather than understood the meaning of my words, and was placated. She walked next to me, occasionally stretching her arm toward the shelves to grab a box here or a bag there, to speed up the shopping process and get down to the *real* reason we had come to the supermarket.

*   *   *

The store was crowded—not unusual for a Saturday. I saw a few friends accompanied, as I was, by children flitting around them awed and happy. They were out of their homes, and an outing these days, no matter how mundane, is more like a journey into the unknown . . . but so are silence and noise, movement and action, alertness and lethargy. All of these words convey danger. For danger is no longer restricted to a time and place. It descends from the unknown, like a winged fate, spreading its feathers over the eves and rooftops of cities and suburbs. And when it folds its wings and flies away, it leaves behind ashes, remnants that barely hint that the place was once inhabited.

This is what happened a few days ago. It is all that remains within this memory as it strolls among the people and with them. Every movement, every turning, each activity brings back the reasons for our anxiety, nay, our terror. Even as we seek solace in forgetfulness, we find ourselves returning to burn in the hell of our memories. Yesterday, *Sad el Bawshrieh,* and before it *Sin el Fil,* and before that *Bir al Abed;* and before it and after it and as a result of it and following it . . . Here and there and everywhere death stalks like a rabid monster, with no end in sight; and no sign as to where, when or how he will pack up and leave us.

*   *   *

"It's a new doll, Mama. In Arabic it's called The Cabbage. It's like a cabbage all wrapped up in cloth. Nana bought one from London, and Joujou's aunt got her one. And you? Will you buy one for me? I love it, Mama. I love it more than anything."

Neinar took the doll without permission. She held it to her and turned round in a little dance, kissing it, hugging it . . . inciting my jealousy.

When I was young we did not have this variety and abundance of toys. The most we had would be a dry stick, a button rejected from the sewing basket, a piece of cloth, a bit of cotton, residues of the sieve, threads. Then the creative process would begin.

A few hours later these sundries would become a rosy-cheeked, red-lipped doll, its hair tied back in a bun or falling coquettishly around its shoulders. Once that creative stage was completed we reached the naming stage. We would choose names that did not exist in the village roster: Marzipan, Furfur, Shenshen, Tuta. Names our imaginations were rife with, meaningless words that only became significant when given to our creations.

Neinar's generation is a lucky one. They receive their dolls wrapped in lace. No effort required; no sewing or pasting; no anxiety that their creation would turn out to be a monstrosity eliciting snickers and mockery from the other children.

In fact, this Cabbage Patch doll, that so awed my daughter and others of her age, could be considered a missing link—something between a human form and a monster. Could this be why they are so attached to it? Or is it merely the result of creative marketing?

Why did I waste my time with such analysis? The important question was: would I pay the exorbitant amount for this awkward, clumsy-looking doll?

Of course, such thoughts I kept to myself. Who dares denigrate this queen of dolls, this Madame Cabbage! Who dares destroy a child's dream? I do not deny that I did try to dissuade Neinar from her choice. I pointed out to her all the other conventional dolls, inspired by the great era of international cinema, wearing the faces of Ava Gardner, Grace Kelly, Greta Garbo, Marilyn Monroe.

But she turned away from them all, "Old fashioned faces . . . not for our age!" she said.

I understand my daughter well. She knows her mind and what she wants. She possesses a keen sense and is able to go to the heart of matters. But I did not, apparently, know her that well. I did not imagine that she would be capable of categorizing in this manner, drawing sharp dividing lines between generations. I should have known that what pleases me shouldn't necessarily please her.

She finally put a stop to my interference and forced me to slip my hand into my purse to count the money I had left. Postponing this was out of the question. I could not bring her home disappointed. Not when she had been such a good girl. She looked at me, her gaze penetrating, touching the most vulnerable part of me, saying wordlessly, "It is now your turn. Will you keep *your* promise to me now?"

I opened my mouth to appease her, my hand still roaming inside my purse, to tell her that the money I have on me is enou . . .

I do not continue.

I open my mouth, and cannot close it again. I feel it tearing, ripping out of its place. I slip my hand in my purse, but my purse flies away from me— as does my shopping cart, stacked with my purchases; the people; the mothers with their carts, surrounded by flocks of angels; the store clerks; the piles of merchandise; the shelves; the cash registers; the surveillance equipment; the entrance door; the exit door. Nothing is left on which to rest the eyes. I feel my daughter is still near me. Neinar. Where has Neinar gone? She was holding the cabbage doll in her arms, clutching it to her chest, resting her cheek on its head. She was with me . . .

With me?

Who is me? Who am I? I am no longer here. I am not there. Faster than the speed of lightning I become disjointed . . . my parts scattered all around the place. But then there is no longer a place . . . no longer a time.

I admit I did not hear the explosion. Maybe I lost my ears before the sound could reach me.

Maybe, I say, because there is no longer any certainty. I am scattered in the corners. My legs remain standing, like the barks of an oak. Then they take off, on their own, aimlessly.

The wings of my memory flutter and I see Neinar's face. No, not her face . . . but an apparition, passing at a distance of years away . . . Then I see it coming toward me and I nearly cry out with joy. But where will my cry come from? I have no throat, no vocal cords . . .

*   *   *

There is my purse.

My memory records it. I see it squeezing through the crowds, looking for a way out. Then it falls. Gone are my possessions—papers, money, identification. They all flee the purse to escape through one of the doors . . . But there are no doors, they too have collapsed . . . they are no longer doors. The ceiling is open to a sky that rains fire and metal.

Yes . . . I remember the smoke in the hall. Thick smoke. Smoke softens the shapes and edges of things, but once it disperses, things return to their original luster. This was a different kind of smoke, I knew that. The smoke was rising from the site of the explosion, expanding, mushrooming, spreading left and right, upward and downward, seeping into the pores. It was not the benign smoke of a country chimney or a campfire. It was a smoke that held within it the explosion of wrath and fury and the power of enmity.

*   *   *

I hope now you will allow me to stop my narrative, after all that I have told you. My lips have parted company with each other, my joints are severed and scattered, part of me is burnt, charred.

And my little flower, my fragrant, sweet rose, Neinar, how is she to leave the store without her doll? And I remember . . . I did not pay for it . . . although there is still enough money left in my purse.

Woman and child in her guest room, Oman. Photo by Birgitte Grue.

Parlor in a home in Istanbul, Turkey. Photo by Jenny B. White.

Mother of the groom dancing after bringing her new daughter-in-law home, Istanbul, Turkey. Photo by Jenny B. White.

Emily Nasrallah, Lebanon.

Men relaxing in the heat of the day at a Harasiis campsite, Oman.
Photo by Dawn Chatty.

Harasiis mother with
her children, Oman.
Photo by Dawn
Chatty.

Women by the fountain in
front of the Shah Cheragh
shrine, Shiraz, Iran. Photo
by Anne Betteridge.

The Seyyed Taj ol-din Gharib
shrine in Shiraz, Iran. Photo by
Anne Betteridge.

A bus stop in Shiraz, Iran. Photo by Anne Betteridge.

A street near Bab al-Zuwaila, Cairo, Egypt. Photo by Donna Lee Bowen.

A young professional commutes to work in Amman, Jordan. Photo by Donna Lee Bowen.

Street market in Tangier, Morocco. Photo by Donna Lee Bowen.

Grandmother and grandchild in Zagora, Morocco. Photo by Donna Lee Bowen.

Girl with her mother and aunt in Zagora, Morocco. Photo by Donna Lee Bowen.

Widowed mother with her three daughters holding the photo of an absent friend, Salé, Morocco. Photo by Donna Lee Bowen.

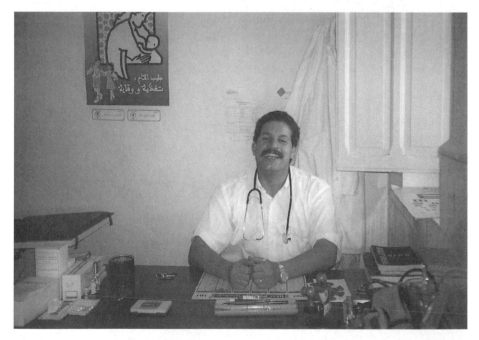

Physician at a public health clinic in al-Jebha, Morocco. Photo by Donna Lee Bowen.

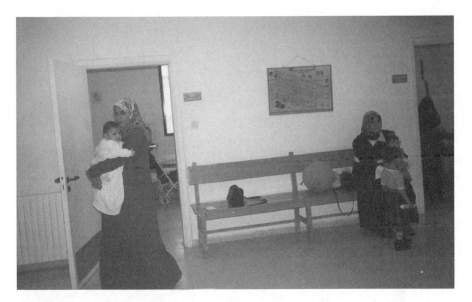

At the Institute for Family Health, Noor al-Hussein Foundation, Sweileh, Jordan. Photo by Gilles François.

Women and children outside traditional homes in Syria. Photo by Gilles François.

Village development committee meeting in Jiblaya, Syria. Photo by Gilles François.

Recipient of a microloan in his market in Al Mukhaibeh, Jordan. Photo by Gilles François.

4. "Of the Dust and the Wind": Arranged Marriage in Afghanistan

Margaret A. Mills

Courtship and weddings, among the most important events in the lives of Middle Easterners, are joyously anticipated as much for the parties and attendant excitement as for the marriage itself. Courtship entails many rituals which must be satisfactorily observed if the wedding is to go forward. Detailed negotiations over the bride's dowry, the furnishing of the house, and attendant matters can consume the attention of the families of the bride and groom for months. —Eds.

This is a story told by Abdul Wahed "Lang" ("the Lame," so called due to a spinal injury at birth which left him partially disabled), a day laborer, about fifty years old, illiterate, never married on account of his poverty, resident at the time of this performance in the household of a nephew in Tau Beriyan village, Herat Province, western Afghanistan, August 31, 1975. I recorded it while conducting research in Afghanistan from 1974 to 1976. Professor Sekandar Amanolahi of Shiraz University, Mr. Muhammad Zaher Sidding, and Mr. Qasim Alami advised me on translation and dialect.

The title, "Xaki o Badi" ("Of the Dust and the Wind"), is a colloquial term for illegitimate birth. In conversation after this tale was told, an elderly male member of the household where I was recording, who had listened to the story, corroborated its relevance to everyday experience with a reminiscence about an actual case of suspected illegitimacy in his village. The tale itself is considered fictional by its teller. For Western readers, it may be somewhat enigmatic in its integration of extremely accurate details of everyday life in Afghanistan and moments of comic absurdity. The storyteller, Wahed, mixes broad foolishness with exuberant enjoyment of the performance opportunities (such as his street vendors' cries, very enthusiastically rendered, which cannot really be done justice in a written translation) and a wry wit concerning life's ironies.

In the story, one central irony concerns the power relationships between men and women, in which men make claims to social initiative and control but really are at the mercy of "women's tricks" (*makre zan*), the latter a common topic in men's humorous storytelling. Among Persian-speaking men with whom I have discussed this story, there is uncertainty about the hero's final attitude toward his wayward wife: whether he remains an innocent dupe, as he has shown himself to be at other moments in the story, or whether his acceptance of five illegitimate children represents a wry resignation toward circumstances which his poverty prevented him from controlling.

Wahed's abrupt switches of narrative voice, from third person to first and back, and finally back to first person again, may also leave an unfamiliar audience wondering how closely to identify with the hero. Wahed turns the entire story of Mir Lal Beg's travels into a personal-experience narrative, perhaps a familiar genre to him from the talk of returning migrant workers. When the hero arrives back in Kabul, he reverts to a third-person object, no longer a reporting subject, during the payoff scene with his father-in-law. Yet he regains his first-person voice as he reluctantly accepts the rationale of his erring wife. First-person narrative, inviting audience identification with the hero, thus correlates with the hero's periods of helplessness: as a poor man abroad, and at home with an unfaithful wife.

The hero's predicament, in which he must defer his marriage for several years in order to raise the required brideprice, was a real one for young men of ordinary means in Afghanistan even in recent years. Employment opportunities as guest workers in Iran or the Gulf States to some extent facilitated the accumulation of capital by working people in recent decades. The effect of the influx of foreign earnings on marriage patterns in Afghanistan since World War II has not, to my knowledge, been studied. In the early 1970s, Afghanistan still had one of the lowest per-capita annual incomes in the world, estimated at $90 (U.S.).

Wahed evokes for us the Afghanistan of his own youth or perhaps that of his father's youth, in references to the old monetary system and the lack of motorized transport, but the circumstances and worries attendant on finding a wife and traveling for work, leaving that wife to the supervision of others, were pertinent ones for young men in Herat in the mid-1970s as well. During the summers of 1975 and 1976 in the Herat area, informants estimated that 50 percent or more of the adult males in some villages were working abroad, in Iran and, to a lesser extent, in the Gulf states, leaving their families in the care of other relatives. The revolutions in Afghanistan and Iran in 1978 and 1979 have of course massively altered the circumstances of migration and work patterns. In the mid-1980s, there were an estimated 1.5 million Afghan refugees in Iran, and another 3 million in Pakistan.

Regional chauvinism and competing cultural claims between major cities such as Kabul, the present capital, and Herat in the west, which historically had much greater cultural and political importance than the modern capital, are also themes which figure in the consciousness and identity of contemporary Afghans. On one level, this is a Herati story making fun of the ostensibly less sophisticated Kabulis.

OF THE DUST AND THE WIND

Once there were two brothers in Kabul, and one had a wife and a house, and one had none. The one said to the other, "Brother, look, even though I don't have any money, I want to look around and find you a fiancee. You go find some work and get some money together, and we'll get you engaged."[1] He said, "Fine." The younger brother was called Lal Mir Khan, and the older was called Sadr Khan.[2] He said, "Brother, do you want So-and-so's daughter, or So-and-so's, or So-and-so's? Tell me who, and I'll go ask for her." He said, "Any girl you choose, and can get for me, would be fine." So he went and came back, and said, "Now Brother, I went and asked for So-and-so's daughter, and they've given their answer. They want thirty thousand rupees from us."[3] He said, "Very good."

"There, now, I've brought your needle and thread."[4] He said, "Now, God willing, you can go off and raise the money, get yourself some kind of work, so you can come back and get married."

"Very good."

The next day, the younger brother went and asked his brother's wife, "Can you give me a few rupees to go visit my fiancee?" She said, "I don't have any cash, but go out to the field and gather yourself a shirttail full of the harvested corn, and take that for your courting." He went out to the pile of harvested ears, and picked a shirttail full of grains off the cobs, but by the time he did that, it was getting dark. When he got to his father-in-law's dooryard, he saw that the gate was shut and locked. He walked all around the compound, and saw that everyone seemed to have gone to bed. He found a place in the wall where sparrows had dug holes for their nests, and tried to use the holes to climb up on top of the compound wall, but a hand-hold gave way and he fell back down, spilled his grain, and bruised himself all over. He gathered up all he could of the grain, then took a better grip, and crept up like a cat to the top of the wall.

He crept over the flat roof, and saw that his father-in-law was asleep to one side, his fiancee to the other, sound asleep. His fiancee had a veil spread over her, and he carefully lifted it off her and spread it out, and put the grain on it.[5] Then he bent his head to give her a kiss, and just as he was about to kiss her, she woke up and socked him in the jaw, so hard it knocked him aside like a cat. He said, "Now, Fuck your father's soul! This is too bad—I came here, and what did you do? By the Qur²an, now I'm going, and I'm not coming back until I get all the money—if I can't bring every bit of the money for your father, I won't come back for you, till I die."[6]

He went back out, over the wall, went back home and the next morning he said to his brother's wife, "Make me up a few pieces of bread—I'm going off to Herat to look for work." She sent him off to the corn pile again to get grain, and to bring her the hand mill for her to make the bread.[7] She made him five or six loaves, and he put them in a knapsack on his back and set off, saying "God keep you! I'm off to Herat to work and make some money, so I can come back and get married."

As he came along the road, he saw a broken piece of melon lying there, and he picked it up and chewed it as he went along. As he walked along, chewing, he met a caravan coming from the direction of Herat, and they greeted him by name and asked him where he was going.[8]

He said, "I'm going to Herat for work—is there work there?" They told him, "Yes, there's plenty of work there, anybody's who's willing to work can make themselves some money." He said (to the caravaneer), "Country-man, the road is long, and it's cold—would you give me your trousers so I won't get cold on the road?" Now those pants were so worn out, that about all that was left of them was the waistband and the cuffs.[9]

When I [the narrator, Wahed, switches to first person here] put them on, I saw that the seat was worn clear through, so I took that piece of dried-out melon skin and stitched it in to cover the hole. Then I set out, walking and walking, and as long as the melon rind was a little bit moist, it was OK and I went along easy. Once it got dry, I went along crackling and crunching.

Finally I got to a big rock, in the middle of nowhere, where I couldn't see either Kabul or Herat, one way or the other. I almost gave up right there. I sat down on that rock, sweating with worry, and ate some of my bread. But finally I got up again, and walking and resting, walking and resting, I came down out of the Hazrajat Mountains. Finally I came down into a town and asked the people, "Is this Herat?" They said, "No brother, they call this Pahlavan Piri." They were making mud bricks to build a qeleh.[10] I said, "Brothers, I'm looking for work, can you give me a share of this job?" They said, "It's late, come back tomorrow and we can give you a qeran[11], and your bread as well." I said, "Fine."

So I worked all the next day, mixing mud for bricks, and they gave me my qeran, and my bread. I put the coin in a little purse, and tied it under my belt. The next day I said, "What about it brothers, do you want me to stay?" "It's early yet—today we'll give you two qeran, and your board." I said "Fine," and I stayed that day.

Once I had three qeran in my pocket, I said, "Forget it. Which way is the city? I'm going to see the city." They said, "If you want to, take that road," and I did and arrived at the Kandahar Gate with all its shops. The shopkeepers all greeted me by name,[12] and I asked them what there was for work. I said, "Can you find me a shop to get started with?" They said, "Did you bring any money, to start a shop?" I said, "Oh, yes—" and got out my three qeran of cash. They said, "Oh—if you took this to the sheepshead-cooker it wouldn't buy you a pound of stew![13] And you want to open a shop—amazing!" There was one Kabuli among the merchants who felt sorry for me, and he said, "If you take this big road, you'll come to Kebabian village. You can buy a donkey-load of carrots there for three qeran. Bring them back and I'll help you find a scale and show you where to sell them. With God's help, maybe it will work out." "Good."

I went off to Kebabian, following the road, and asked around till I found a farmer who would let me help dig and wash the carrots and load them on his donkey, to make up part of the price, and I got a big donkey load for three qeran. When I got back to the city with my load of carrots, my new friend found me a scale and some old stone weights. He showed me a place in the bazaar below the city fort to unload and told me how to call out, "Come on! Sweets of Kebabian! Come on, black carrots! Five sir (half kilogram) for three cents, ten sir for six cents!"[14] I said, "OK." So I unloaded my sacks full of carrots and started in, hawking carrots till the afternoon prayer, and all the carrots were gone, and I saw that I'd doubled my money—six qeran! "Ah! May I be a sacrifice for my countryman's eyes! One qeran profit on every qeran!" So the next morning I went right back to Kebabian, and this time I got a donkeyload of carrots, and another load of turnips. I set up shop in the same spot in the market, and started hollering again, hollered and hollered till afternoon prayer, and I was sweeping up—sold them all. And then I counted and counted—12 qeran! "Ah, I'll be a sacrifice for my countryman's eyes! By God, and I, just for bread—I'm making a qeran for every qeran!"

The next day I went to Kebabian and bought a donkeyload each of carrots and turnips and squash, and I bought a bowl of snuff, too, and I came back and set up my stand, hollering, "Come on, fresh snuff! Come on, black carrots! Come on, turnips! Come on, squash—big squash! Come on, black carrots—sweets of Kebabian! There, now—sweets of Kebabian, five sir three cents, ten sir six cents! Squash, one qeran! There, now, fresh snuff! Fresh snuff! Intoxicating snuff!" So I hollered and hollered, and by the afternoon prayer, I was ready to sweep up, and I saw I had forty qeran! Heaping praise and thanks on my countryman, I went off to Kebabian and got two donkeyloads of each of the vegetables, a bowl of snuff, and a big bowl of yogurt, and hawked all of that. Brother, the people all came crowding around, they bought their own bread from the baker, and I sold them yogurt, half a bowl for the price of a whole bowl.[15] That day I sold clean out, too, and after a while, I was able to get myself a shop, selling yogurt and snuff, brother, and every kind of vegetables, till my shop got to be a thriving business. To make a long story short, I stayed in Herat for seven years.

After seven years, one day a fat envelope arrived from Kabul, brought by some countrymen, and it said, "To Lal Mir Khan! May he be in health! Since he went away to Herat, his household and all his kids are close to starving!" I said, "Hey, now, brother, since when do I have a household full of kids? What's going on? I'd better go to Kabul." I sold my shop and everything I had, and got all the cash together, but it was too much to carry, so I bought gold, and went to get myself a donkey for the trip. I found a good, big, white one with the packsaddle and all the trappings on it for seven hundred rupees. I said, "That's too expensive," but he said, "Baba, that's cheap—look what a good, big donkey it is, with all its gear." So I bought it, anyway—I was rich—and then I wanted a woven-carpet saddle-bag. I saw a guy carrying one around, folded over his shoulder. I asked how much, and he said "five hundred rupees." I bought it from him. Then I saw a nomad with a sword, and I bought that for one thousand rupees.[16]

I brought all that back to the shop—I still had to clean up a few things in the shop, so I took the donkey and tied it in the caravanserai where I had a room, gave the donkey some hay, and went to the shop. The bowl of yogurt was still there, so I decided to test my new sword. I laid the sword's edge on the surface of the yogurt and saw that the yogurt sheared away cleanly below the sword. "Oh, boy, that's a good edge! It cuts yogurt without the slightest trouble!"

Around about dinnertime prayer I went back to my room in the caravanserai, and decided to take the packsaddle off my donkey for the night. When I went to lift the saddle off, it wouldn't come off, and when I yanked it off by force, I saw that the donkey had so many saddle sores, under all the gear, it's like he's been plowed up from his mane to his tail, and the saddle and cinch had stuck to the wounds. But his belly was faultless as a flower. I thought, "If only you had looked at the donkey in the bazaar, taken the gear off to see! Look how you've been tricked—his back is all cut up! Now what? He'll never carry you like this! Well, I'll have to wait around and see if I can heal the sores—I'd better look at the saddlebag, to see if it's full of holes, too!" As soon as I looked it over I saw that it had such holes in it that if you dropped a seven-pound squash into the top it would go right out the bottom. "Oh, curses on his father, what do I do about this saddlebag?" I went off to the bazaar and bought myself about twenty pounds of horsehair thread and a big sack-sewing needle, and came back and sat in a corner of the serai, and there I stayed, putting salves on the donkey's back and feeding it and sewing up all the holes in the sack, for about three weeks, till the thread was all used up and the donkey's back was healed. Then I bought one qeran's worth of tea and one qeran of tea sweets, and filled up the two sides of the saddlebag with that, took up my sword, mounted, and rode off singing "Lady Laili," off toward Kabul.[17]

(In those days, brother, there were no cars—traveling day by day with a donkey it was a month's travel.) We were on the road for a month, till we got to Kabul. I sent word that I'd arrived and my old mother came out, with five kids clinging to her skirts and in her arms, saying, "There now, Lal Mir Khan, your papa, is back! Babies, there now, your papa's back, and welcome! There's your papa, home safely!" She's talking like that, with me coming along the street. Oh, curses on her father, what's this? Whose kids are these? That she's carrying around and they're all clinging to her! Five of them following her, and she's saying, "Here's your papa!" I took the middle one out of my mother's arms, kissed it and gave it back to her, and went on to the house, and there's this huge samovar set up, and my whole family got word, "Lal Mir Khan's back," and came to see me. Each one had to sit and drink tea and eat something, and three days passed that way. I opened the saddle bag, with the tea and sweets, and laid it all out. Then I said to my brother, "This gold—take it to my father-in-law, and ask him to prepare for the wedding."

[Wahed switches back to third person.] He changed the gold back into cash, and went off to his father-in-law's along with his brother. He said to him, "My brother went off to work, and now he's back and he asks permission to claim his wife." He said, "Very good. Did you bring the money?" "Yes." "Give it to me." They poured it all into his lap, to the last qeran. "Now, bring out your daughter, I'm taking her with me." "Fine."

He brought the girl out, and there was that same little boy, at their side, saying, "Ohh, Mama, where are you going? Ohh, Mama, where are you going?" He thought, "Huh? This is a strange business!" As they came out of the house, here she came, with all five of these kids. He said, "Great, fine! Damn your father! Where did all these kids come from?" She said, "Ohh, where do you think they're from? One is from the time you climbed over the wall. When you passed over the roof to get to me, one is from then. One is from when you lifted the veil off me. One is from when you poured the corn into the veil. One is from when you leaned down to kiss me. Are there any extras? Curse your father! What do you mean, where did they all come from? Where else did I get them? Didn't you do these things?" So [switches to first person] I thought it over. "Baba, it's true, you did those things. What a place this Kabul is, that you can get someone pregnant just by setting foot on a roof, or by lifting a veil off someone, or putting grain into the veil, or just leaning down to kiss her! If I had been here in Kabul the whole time, by now I would have five hundred kids!" So I said "OK, now I've taken you from your father, and you bear that in mind—or I swear by the Qur'an, I'll cut you up one side and down the other!" "Fine, that's your choice, it's your authority." So then [switches to third person] he laid that woman down, and that was it, God had given him the five children, and after that they stayed there and I came here.[18]

NOTES

1. Marriage is a family project, usually initiated by the groom's family on his behalf. Either women or men may be the initial negotiators. Final negotiations are conducted between elder male relatives of the prospective bride and groom (fathers or elder brothers by preference). Major items of negotiation are the bride price paid to the girl's father, as compensation for his expense in raising her, the amount of clothing and household goods which the groom and his family will settle on the bride herself, and the amount of divorce compensation to be settled on the bride if the marriage is terminated through no fault of her own. The two former amounts are actual outlays, the latter a form of deterrent, in a setting where no-fault divorce was and is extremely rare and much frowned upon.

It is quite normal still, in all but a minority of urban marriages, for the couple never to have met before their engagement. The groom is expected to visit the bride, with gifts, repeatedly during the period between engagement and marriage, as he attempts to do in this story. Traditionally, a form of bundling was practiced in the Herat area: engaged couples were put to bed together, fully dressed, for courting purposes. The couple was expected to abstain from sexual intercourse until the marriage was finalized.

2. "Khan" is an adult male title. Among nomads, it refers especially to tribal leaders, but settled people use it as a respectful designation for any adult male.

3. Thirty thousand rupees equaled U.S. $600 at the 1975 exchange rate, about six times the annual per capita income at the time. The storyteller mixes terms for two different currency systems—the present one and that prevailing up to approximately the 1920s. His simultaneous intention is to portray a bygone day, when money was worth more and harder to come by than it was in the 1970s, and to portray concerns and realities common to both periods, such as the expense of marriage and the hardship wreaked on prospective grooms by high bride prices.

4. A needle (often actually a decorative stickpin of gold) and thread, together with a silk scarf, are the first, formal gifts from the bride's family to the groom's, which signal agreement to the marriage offer.

5. The *chaderi*, the veil worn by married or engaged women outside their homes in Herat, is a full-length garment with many narrow pleats and an unpleated, knee-length face panel with an eyepiece of embroidery mesh. The cap over the head and the unpleated front panel are often decorated with fine embroidery, and the whole is dyed in one of several vivid colors. The precision of the pleating and the color and the fineness of the embroidery, along with the quality of lace which decorates the traditional white trousers whose hems show below the veil, are all taken by men as hints of physical attractiveness and youth of the woman wearer. A large body of folklore concerns the flirtatious dimensions of veiling. In the story, the girl was using a chaderi as a sheet to cover her in sleep. More typical would have been the use of a so-called *chader shau* ("night veil"), simply a large square of cloth used by village women as a full-length veil (a corner of which is pulled up to cover the face when in view of strangers) and for a variety of purposes, including covering for sleep, around the house.

6. According to tradition, once the engagement agreement is reached, the timing of the wedding is at the discretion of the groom's family, which pays for

the wedding. The bride's family cannot abrogate the agreement, no matter how long the delay, unless formally released from it by the groom's family. This can work a hardship on the bride's family, which must continue to support the woman indefinitely, and in the worst case may find that her marriageability ends before the groom finally releases her. In an actual case of this kind, a woman I knew in Herat City was engaged in childhood, but the groom's family moved away and lost touch with hers. A member of the woman's family told me they had asked a qazi (religious judge) what they should do. He told them to hang the young girl's chaderi veil on the wall, and when it disintegrated and fell off the hook, she would be released to marry someone else. When I knew her, she was about forty and had been married two or three years previously as second wife to a local merchant-land owner. The marriage was childless.

7. This laborious process is narrated in detail. It has been condensed here because of space constraints. Corn, regarded as inferior to wheat, the staple grain, is a poorer food for poor people.

8. The lively greetings and conversation, in Kabul dialect, are repeated verbatim, adding to the verisimilitude of the narrative. Persian-language narrative regularly quotes speech directly rather than indirectly. Wahed explots these opportunities to enhance the sense of realism by using everyday speech and bits of personal detail.

9. These are woolen trousers (*pantlun*) as opposed to traditional, baggy cotton pants (*shalwar*). The humor here again veers toward hyperbole, as it did when the hero was sent out to pick grains of corn off the cobs to take to his fiancee's house, and when. In his poverty, he salvaged a broken bit of melon to chew on as he walked, but here the absurdity becomes more unambiguous. The hero is so naïve that he does not recognize that the caravaneer's traveling pants are worn out.

10. A fortified private residence, built of unbaked mud brick with walls ten or more feet high, the standard architectural form of the countryside, where security from bandits and stock thieves is a concern.

11. The qeran was a currency unit predating today's afghani (known colloquially as a "rupee"); it was integrated into the new system as 1 qeran = 0.5 afs (= approx US $.01 in mid-1970s), but was worth much more in the old system—enough for two or three meals of rice and meat at a bazaar foodstand, for instance. The going price for such a meal in the mid-1970s was about US $.30. A day's pay for an unskilled worker was about 50 afs or US $1.

12. Lael Mir Khan is apparently happy with his earnings, not intending to leave his job permanently, but curious about the city. The merchants he meets are portrayed as having moved there from Kabul. There is an implicit claim for the cultural and commercial superiority of Herat over Kabul, both in this scene, in the hero's inability to distinguish the small town he first approaches from the real city, and in his curiosity. This scene includes a lively exchange of greeting, reported as direct speech, in the original.

13. The heads and feet of goats and sheep are bought from butchers by entrepreneurs who clean and stew them and sell the cooked product for either home or bazaar consumption. Regarded as poor people's food, "heads-and-feet" (*kaleh-pacheh*) are nonetheless humorously enjoyed by many people.

14. These carrots, actually a deep purple color, are very sweet and tender. One sir in Herat is now about 1/4 pound or 100 grams, with ten sir per kilogram. A "cent" (*paisa*) is the smallest currency unit; 100 paisa = 1 afghani (50 paisa = 1 qeran) in the present currency system. The storyteller loudly and enthusiastically repeated the street hawker's cries every time they occurred in the story.

15. The demand for his yogurt was so great that he was able to raise his price over the established rate. Prices of everyday commodities sold in the bazaar are usually very stable and known to regular customers, so that bargaining is minimal. Bread with yogurt and sweetened with tea is a standard noon meal.

16. Perfect verisimilitude in the way things are sold here alternates with comic hyperbole. All these prices are greatly inflated and the hero is being fleeced repeatedly. There is a reference to regional stereotypes in this series of scenes. Heratis have a reputation for being sharp traders, ready to fool the unwary.

17. The tea sweets are *dashlameh,* a boiled candy which is a specialty of Herat, consumed in preference to sugar with tea. "Lady Laili" (literally, *Xanum Laili*) is a traditional song that was very popular several decades ago and is still well remembered.

18. The hero resorts to a vague threat to assert control over his wife, in place of his father-in-law who has failed to control her properly in his absence. The use of the idiom "God gave (a child or children)," is normal in referring to any birth, but here it has an ironic twist. The final statement, "They stayed there and I came here," is a formulaic ending for fictional folktales.

5. Two Weddings

Jenny B. White

Weddings in working-class Istanbul, Turkey, are events that unite families, but they are also individual paths that women tread into the future. Many marriages are arranged, and brides are expected to be modest and obedient, an expectation underlined by the wedding rituals. Often, the couple lives with or near the husband's parents and the bride comes under the authority of her mother-in-law. However, resourceful women can influence whom they marry, under what circumstances, and how they behave after marriage. Marriage is, in many ways, a negotiation of resources. A young woman can make herself attractive to impress mothers looking for brides for their sons. If a woman is industrious, she brings into her marriage a substantial trousseau and the social respect it inspires. By bargaining well during the many rituals surrounding the wedding, the bride and her family can gain financial and material resources for her and her new household. If the bride has a strong personality, she can resist the authority of her mother-in-law. But there are practical limits to a woman's ability to resist society's norms. Flouting them altogether may mean that she loses the resources a traditional wedding would have provided her. —Eds.

I get off the bus at the last stop in the Yenikent[1] neighborhood and walk down the street to Hatije's house. The street is lined with small shops: a pharmacy, a jeweler, a grocery, several stores selling furniture and appliances, stationery shops. Men lean against the wall in front of the shops, chatting and smoking. Women advance purposefully, trailing children or toting plastic bags of purchases. Many of the women wear large, colorful head scarves that drape the forehead, shoulders, and bosom. Others are dressed modestly in long skirts and loose shirts, their hair uncovered. The streets swarm with people. Metin, Hatije's son, comes up beside me by the front door, hand extended. He has been at the coffee house down the street, where his father, Osman, also spends most of his time when he is not at work. Metin is tall and wiry, with a lean, sharp face and a permanently wary expression. He is always edgy, his body moving, eyes shifting, even as he welcomes a guest.

Osman built this house fifteen years ago when he and his wife, Hatije, first moved to Istanbul from their village on the Black Sea coast. Yenikent in those days consisted of wandering dirt roads lined with unevenly staggered, half-built squatter houses. Osman built the house on state land, but managed to get title to the land when politicians up for election distributed deeds to the squatters in his neighborhood. Eventually, Yenikent became part of Istanbul, indistinguishable from any other working-class neighborhood. Osman added a floor to his house whenever he had enough money for material, although once the municipality forced him to raze one floor because he did not have a permit for it. Later he built it again, divided the ground floor into two shops, and rented them out. One shop is a food stand; the other sells used furniture. Most of the houses in Yenikent are designed with this extra source of income in mind. Osman uses the rent from these shops to subsidize his tiny electric shop in the back, which makes only a minimal profit. In the 1980s he used one of the ground-floor spaces as a workshop for a small piece-work business, taking wool and patterns from export merchants and distributing them to neighborhood women, paying them for each sweater they produced. But that business dried up. He explained, "They're using more machines now and set up little factories where they can control the quality better. Our women used to do the work while they were cooking and get egg all over the wool."

I enter the front door and go up the stairs, which have been newly covered with a synthetic green plastic runner. Metin is getting married at the end of the week and moving into the top-floor apartment. The walls have been newly painted. Hatije's mother, visiting from the village, is on her knees at the head of the stairs swiping the new runner with a flimsy plastic cleaning apparatus, a pink box with a rotating brush inside. Hatije greets me but is in a dither, arranging and rearranging doilies and cleaning with a frenetic energy. She is wearing flowered cotton pants under a long blue skirt, a sweater, and a knitted vest, and her head is draped in a red and yellow cotton indoor scarf. Her round face is drawn and pale. The house is full of visiting women, relatives and neighbors, placidly watching and chatting. Only their hands are in constant motion, knitting or crocheting some item they have brought along with them. Occasionally they evaluate each other's work, discussing the stitches, the pattern, what the item is to be used for.

Hatije's daughter, Emine, is in the kitchen washing the dishes used by the previous visitors. Emine is twenty-six years old and lives nearby with her husband, Haluk, and eight-year-old daughter, Serap. She is dressed in jeans and a white V-neck sweater, her shiny black hair gathered in a neat

ponytail. Her enormous, slightly protruding brown eyes add a vulnerability
to her pale full-moon face, like a frightened young doe's. She looks very
tired and whispers to me that she hates coming here because all she ever
ends up doing is working. "I have enough work in my own house."

EMINE:

Ten years before, as a young unmarried girl, Emine had been busy stitch-
ing her trousseau and had worked in her father's piece-work workshop.
She prepared the wool for the women coming in to knit and explained to
them the complicated patterns of the model sweaters. Osman had named
the business after his son and said he hoped Metin would take it over.
Hatije had added, "But we plan to educate him, so maybe he won't be interested." When I asked whether in that case Emine would run the business, they laughed. "If Metin isn't interested, we'll hire a manager. After
all, Emine is going to get married, have children, and leave here." Emine
left school in the fifth grade, her mother told me, because she didn't like
school, but Emine had proudly added that her father needed her to be in
the shop while he looked for buyers.

One night, when Emine was sixteen, we sat together on the floor of the
balcony, where we could not be seen by anyone from the street. She smoked
a cigarette she had stolen from a package in the living room. Everyone else
was asleep. She sat on the rag rug, head back against the wall, looking silently at the night. The gleam of her cigarette rose and fell in the dark like
a beacon. A line of orange car lights snaked along the crest of the hill behind the dark cubes of half-finished houses, their antennae of metal rods
bristling in the shadows. She whispered that she would tell me a secret.
Her friend was engaged but was actually in love with another young man.
She pointed to a lit window a few houses away.

"That's where he lives. They talk by phone, but only as friends." A few
moments later, she added, "He actually loves someone else."

"Who?" I asked.

"Me," she said, laughing.

"And who do you love?"

"I love work."

She told me about the women merchants she had seen when she accompanied her father to downtown Istanbul to deliver sweaters to the merchant
who had ordered them.

"I want to have my own business, bigger than this. And I want to move
to the city."

"Why?"

"Because they're backward here. They won't let you wear pants and you
always have to wear a scarf on your head."

METIN'S WEDDING:

As the day of Metin's wedding approaches, the number of women in Hatije and Osman's house increases. They are in never-ending and constantly changing attendance, arriving and leaving with little fanfare. They fill both the living room and the neighboring guest room, where the women retire if men are present. In this room there are a couch-bed and a smaller couch, as well as a sewing machine, now folded into its wooden case. As in many other Yenikent houses, the internal space is flexible and malleable; walls are moved and rooms change functions. The second-floor balcony has been covered with a roof and the space expanded outward to create a new bedroom for Hatije and Osman. This frees up the third floor for the newlyweds. They will have a living/dining room, a small bedroom, and a fancy new bathroom, with frothy lemon-yellow shower curtains and a matching washing-machine cover. The kitchen is on the second-floor landing and will now serve both apartments. A new balcony has been added onto Hatije and Osman's guest room, so that the women still have a place to sit outside in summer without being seen from the street.

Two of the women accompany me upstairs to view the new bride's trousseau. I have already been to view it in the bride's home, where the towels, scarves, and other items had filled all available space in the living room, draped and stacked, hung on the walls and on a cord stretched across the middle of the room. Yesterday the bride's family brought the trousseau over in boxes and a big cloth-wrapped bundle and arranged it throughout the new apartment. Engagement gifts, like the crystal glasses and china plates, and delicate trousseau items, like the ornate round decorative medallions of silver tin made by the bride, are displayed in the glassed-in vitrine. Arrangements of artificial flowers are on display, some given by the bride's family, others by the groom's. The origin of each object is carefully explained. Ten colorful satin prayer mats, embroidered with loops of flowers, are piled on a chest in the hall, topped by two piles of cotton head scarves, overlapping to display each intricate crocheted edging. On a cabinet is another artfully arranged three-foot high pile of towels edged with crochet work and other embroidered and stitched items. The doors of the hall shoe closet are open to allow views of three new purses and six pairs of fancy new house slippers of embroidered vinyl. In the living room, the display continues—intricate doilies cover every imaginable surface, including the fuse box in the hall. The bride has also made small, artful artificial trees and bowers of wire, beads, and cloth, having learned this skill, along with the silver-colored metalwork, at a course in a girls' art school. Her crafts are distributed around the room and admired by everyone. There are two framed tableau friezes pressed out and etched from the reverse side of the thin silver-colored metal. One is an image of an Ottoman woman under a parasol, smiling through her flimsy veil. The doors to the sideboard are open to display a set of pots and dishes. There is a couch with matching armchairs upholstered in a deep green floral, a square table on a pedestal, a sideboard, and the tall glass-fronted cabinet. The tiny bedroom is dominated by a double bed draped with an embroidered orange satin quilt with matching cushions. One cushion is heart-shaped, with the bride's and groom's initials stitched on it: M, S—Metin and Songül. An embroidered white satin cover contains the bride's and groom's silk nightclothes. An enormous wardrobe takes up one wall. Its mirrored doors slide open, since there is no room for doors that open outward. They are open to display the groom's new shirts and a pile of new sweaters. The drawers of the nightstand and vanity table are also open, staggered so that the contents of each are visible: two dozen head scarves, each with a different embroidered edging; a dozen patterned knit winter bed socks.

I admire everything and return downstairs. I take over the cleaning of the hallway rugs and then am put to work with Emine to wash the dust from the garment and shoe cabinets in the downstairs entry hall and festoon them with doilies crocheted by the bride. The bride has also provided white cloth squares embroidered with pink carnations. The squares are slipped under the dishes in the kitchen cabinet so that triangles of carnations hang down at intervals. I climb on a chair to drape a square on each pot stored atop the cabinets. Curtains of the same pattern have already been hung and a larger cloth of carnations adorns the hood of the stove. The girl's skill is displayed everywhere and marks her territory. This kitchen will be also her kitchen, the hallway her hallway.

We clean and sit and chat, eat sporadically soup, bread and rice, a salad of chopped tomatoes, thinly sliced onions, and fresh crunchy cucumbers from the village in sunflower oil and lemon juice. Emine and I sit on the guest-room bed, pans on newspaper between us, rolling an oiled rice-onion-thyme-mint mixture into grape leaves, also from the village. The assembled women debate the proper way to treat a new bride. One woman is adamant that "you shouldn't spoil them in the beginning. If you're too permissive they become spoiled and refuse to do anything. Look at my brother and his wife. She just does whatever she wants and doesn't treat my parents right at all. She's always gallivanting about. If they had put their foot down right at the beginning this wouldn't have happened." A large, formidable woman, who has borne and married off five sons, worries about her youngest son's treatment of his wife. "Imagine! He won't even let her go out to go to the grocery store. Even to me he says I shouldn't go out. 'If you need anything, mother, just tell me and I'll bring it to you.' But I tell him it's not right to lock a young girl like that up in the house. She'll get bored and then who knows what will happen." The other women murmur in agreement.

EMINE:

In the fall of her sixteenth year, the year Emine told me her secret wish, Emine, her family, and I were waiting in the street outside the house for a neighbor's car to take us to a wedding. The child Metin became impatient and began to hit Emine's legs, since that was all he could reach. Emine pushed him away again and again but he persisted. He spit at her and pulled at her clothes. Finally, Emine gave him a shove. As he stumbled backward, he let out a big yell of protest. Hatije, who had been at the curb watching for the car, marched firmly up to Emine and slapped her in the face. "Don't you ever hit your brother again." One evening a few weeks later, we were all sitting in the living room watching television. Metin began to tease Emine and some other visiting women, pushing them and running away. Hatije smiled at him indulgently and continued her knitting. Metin approached the television, looking back to see who was watching. On top of the television was an embroidered cloth under small ceramic statues of horses and dogs and a cheap vase. Metin grasped the cloth and yelled, "Look!" Hatije looked up from her knitting and uttered a half-hearted admonition: "Don't." She looked back at her knitting as, with a flourish, Metin pulled the cloth and the statues onto the floor, whooping. The women laughed. The statues and the broken vase lay on the floor until the next morning when Emine picked them up as she was sweeping the house.

METIN'S WEDDING:

Emine's cousin Ayshe has come from the village for Metin's wedding. She is wearing a yellow sweater over a long skirt under her voluminous Islamic-style coat, and one of the new-style Islamic head scarves I see everywhere—a print of black and white leopard spots within stylized gold loops. She looks very chic. She and I are at a tailor shop waiting for the tailor to put buttonholes into Hatije's blouse, part of her wedding outfit. Ayshe says she is unhappy in the village. Her mother and father lived in Istanbul twenty-two years, but couldn't make it financially and last year went back to their village. I ask if her mother is happy there. "Yes," Ayshe answers. "She loves being in the village where it's green and quiet and she is with her family. She has to work in the gardens and now they've bought some cows, but she still likes it. But I'm so bored. All my friends are in Istanbul and there's nothing to do in the village. At least my parents let me come to Istanbul often. I stay with my sister and then I visit my friends." Ayshe's sister is married to a truck driver and lives in Yenikent. We deliver the blouse to the women at Hatije's, one of whom will sew on the buttons. Ayshe disappears to visit a friend who lives two blocks away.

In late afternoon, we go to the henna party, put on by the bride's family. On the night before the wedding, the women of the groom's and the bride's families gather to celebrate. The women's hands are stained red with henna paste. A bus has been arranged but no one is sure when it will arrive. Suddenly there is a mad rush; everyone flies down the stairs. "The bus has arrived and will leave without us if we don't hurry." At the house door, I put on my shoes and run to the street. There is no bus in sight. The women stand around looking anxious and puzzled. Who will take them? How will they get there? It seems no bus has been ordered. Several people have come in cars, their husbands driving. Other cars arrive and finally we are off. It is a long drive, all the way out to the bride's home. Her family is considered relatively well off. They have a large apartment in Istanbul a ten-minute drive from Metin's family and another apartment in a building they own in a village just outside of Istanbul. In the basement is a hall that can be rented out, and on the ground floor is a cafe and roadside restaurant, where the men will wait for us. Above this is their apartment. The bride's family is from eastern Turkey and Hatije told me that people in her family are angry that she gave her son to "strangers." There are quite a few eligible girls in Hatije and Osman's village and in the extended family who would have been suitable matches. Metin is considered a good catch since his family lives in the city and they own their own house.

The hall is in the basement of the building: a large room painted on all sides with renditions of folk dancers and landscapes. In the middle of the wall is a painted heart enclosing a young man and woman in wedding attire. There are long sturdy tables and chairs, a cleared dance area, and a raised platform at one end. On the platform is a man playing the organ and singing. We seat ourselves, clustering haphazardly as people go around the room greeting each other and kissing the hands of elders. It doesn't take long for people to realize that the musician is a man and that there are men (including the brother of the bride) walking in and out of the room. There is a ripple of concern. Hatije is angry and exclaims to the others at her table, "How dare they have a man here! Don't they know that means no one can dance!" The whispers spread through the crowd. After all, the bride herself is veiled; her white satin gown has a matching turban that covers her hair and her bosom. She pays great attention to not being in the presence of unrelated males, even when she is completely covered, they whisper, so she should know better. The musician doesn't leave and the situation worsens. As the evening wears on, the bride's male relatives come in carrying the food and drink, plastic cups of sweet red punch and plates of sweet and salty cookies, and take away the empty plates and cups. Two lean, muscular young men in tight black jeans and white t-shirts lounge about most of the evening brandishing cameras with large flash attachments but rarely taking pictures. They look like wolves in a pen of sheep.

Ayshe and another girl from the village tell me they are going to put on makeup and ask if I want some. I am surprised, since many of the women are firmly opposed to the use of makeup and nail polish. We crowd into the bathroom and put on eyeliner and lipstick and a bit of foundation base. Without their coats, slim in their tailored outfits and long golden scarves, they are very attractive. Ayshe pulls a photo out of her handbag that shows her in jeans with makeup and long, loose black hair. She looks completely different. "I dress like that in the village sometimes among friends," she explains. Ayshe dances with the other young girls, mostly friends of the bride. Some have uncovered hair, but most wear their head scarves, although they have removed their coats to reveal modest but fashionable suits and slacks. Most of the women from the groom's family don't get up to dance. Hatije tells her niece Ayshe not to dance, but Ayshe ignores her and dances the entire evening. It is one of the few fun things she can do now that she is stuck in the village. The bride, Songül, looks upset and mutters to a friend, "Let whoever wants to dance. It's not my fault." She is near tears.

Finally it is time for the henna. Songül and her closest friends are in the small "bride's room" off the hall. Male staff cluster across the hall trying to catch a glimpse when the door opens. Songül has taken off her wedding dress but has left on the white corset. She is short and pudgy, with a generous white bosom and strong arms. Her face is flushed but she looks calm and in control of things as she brushes out her long brown hair and gives directions to her friends. There are five young women in the room, along with her aunt, her father's sister, who has never left her side all evening. Her aunt has on a black and gold scarf intricately caught at the nape of her neck in a big roll that shows off the luxurious material. She is wearing a black lace caftan over a long black jersey dress. The girls help Songül into a traditional Ottoman-style maroon velvet sheath and drape a gauzy red scarf over her head so that it obscures her face. One young woman leans over a tin tray and kneads a big pile of henna powder with water to make a paste. Another distributes small candles from a paper sack. Emine and Ayshe come in, then other young women. Each receives a candle. The lights are turned out in the hall and the women line up in the dark, in two rows facing each other, both arms raised. Their hands, holding candles, are clasped in the middle. The bride, her face obscured, is led out under the candles. The girls sing, a sweet plaintive song: "You will leave your mother and father and never see them again." The bride sits on a chair surrounded by her singing friends. She is weeping under her red veil. Hatije, her future mother-in-law, comes into the circle. Songül makes a fist, and Hatije pulls at it, showing her a gold coin as encouragement. When Songül loosens her fist, Hatije opens it, puts a ball of henna in the palm, presses the coin in it, and binds the closed hand in a cloth. The girls sing; Songül cries. The red veil is removed. Suddenly the girls pull Songül onto the platform where the musician is playing his organ. The lights go on and the girls dance around her, singing a new, more joyous song, about how they are giving her to Metin. The women in the audience begin chatting again and many begin to leave. Some people are bored and annoyed because they couldn't dance.

EMINE:

At eighteen, Emine was engaged to a young man her parents found for her among relatives of neighbors who had also migrated from the Black Sea coast. The wedding date was set for when he returned from military service. One day a girl from the neighborhood showed Emine a photo of her fiancé with his arm around another woman. "This is what your fiancé is doing while he's in the army," she said. When Emine saw the photograph she decided to get back at him for his disloyalty. Besides, she wanted to leave Yenikent. Once she was engaged, her fiancé's family had forbidden her to work in her father's workshop anymore. They argued that sometimes the merchants would come themselves to pick up their orders and so she would be exposed to the view of strange men. Emine was bored and willful and scared of the restrictions that she could already feel encircling her like a noose. Haluk, the young man in the lighted window, the man who loved her but whom she didn't love, now seemed more interesting. They spoke a few times by telephone. She told him she was breaking her engagement. They met early one morning and eloped to Izmir. When they returned three weeks later, Emine was pregnant. They were married but did not have a wedding celebration.

METIN'S WEDDING:

Emine and Haluk's apartment is up a long hill of struggling wooden houses and shabby new two- and three-story cement squares. Haluk is a thin, dour man with a face deeply lined despite his young age. He works with his father in a shop on the ground floor, making rough wooden cabinets. The couple lives above the workshop in a tiny and ill-furnished apartment. The living room has a cheap stuffed cloth couch, which folds out into a guest bed, and some end tables, but few decorations. Since Emine eloped, neither the groom's nor the bride's family, nor the wedding guests, provided the furniture, gold, cloth, money, and other items that would have been given during the series of ritual occasions leading up to their marriage. Theirs is a household with absolutely no extras. Since there is no space in the living room for a table, a small square table has been set in the hall outside the kitchen. Instead of separate hall space for shoes, customarily removed at the entrance, there is only a square of newspaper inside the entrance door. All the rooms are tiny, the kitchen with only a sink, a small counter, one cabinet, and a small refrigerator. The refrigerator is empty except for a plate of green beans and a pitcher of water. The bedroom is just barely big enough for their bed, a wardrobe, a vanity table, and a small bed for their daughter Serap. Haluk's parents live in the apartment above theirs.

The next morning Emine is working in her kitchen, and Serap is ironing. "I can do this *very* well. I have a talent for this sort of work," Serap announces brightly. We call Hatije to find out when we are leaving to get the bride. She says to come right away. Emine puts on a long pink dress, then a coat and scarf. We scurry down the stairs, dragging a reluctant Serap, and clamber onto a minibus. When we arrive, several women are in the garden. One old woman sits by the door, a pot and two knives in her hand. She explains that this is for the door-crossing ritual: as the bride crosses, she steps on the mother-in-law's pot three times. The women also hold crossed kitchen knives above her outside the doorway, to symbolize the cutting off of her old life from the new. There is another Black Sea custom called "tongue cutting": a woman uses a knife to raise the bride's veil to her mouth three times to signify that the bride should hold her tongue in her new home.

Across the narrow street, a space has been cleared and a table set up, decorated with vases of flowers. Behind the table sits Metin, getting the ritual prenuptial public shave. Around the table on chairs sit a few of the local men. A tape deck blares Turkish pop music. When half his face is done, he gets up and dances in the street with his father and one of the other men. Cars weave around them and honk congratulations. When the other half of his face is done, he dances again, then runs around the corner to try to convince his friends at the coffee house to come and dance. He is very upset that they refuse him this request on his wedding day. "They're involved in their own activities," he grumbles when he returns. "Some are eating and said they couldn't come, but some said they wouldn't come because there were women watching." A line of chairs set up along the street slowly fills with women gathering for the trip to get the bride.

Upstairs Hatije bustles around the house, occasionally breaking into a silly impromptu song and dance. We walk around the corner to a backyard with a giant rotating spit in the corner being worked by three sweating men who shave off flakes of meat onto plates of rice. Grapes are handed around. The women sit at a long table and eat, then leave to wait in front of the house. The men eat elsewhere. Finally cars arrive, but again no bus. People complain and ask how they are supposed to get there. Osman stands red-faced in his shirt-sleeves in the street and demands to know why everyone thinks they should be able to go. Eventually, enough cars arrive and we drive off in convoy back to the place where the henna party was the previous night. At the rise in the road before the village, we stop to let the rest of the convoy catch up, then descend en masse on the village. We park and move quickly toward the house. A plastic ribbon has been stretched across the lot just before the entrance stairs. The men and most of the women stay behind the ribbon but close relatives of the groom go through. I follow and watch as Hatije goes up the stairs alone and negotiates at the door with the bride's brother and aunt. A woman whispers to me that the mother-in-law has to give money or gold to the bride's relatives to unlock the door and let her in. She keeps giving them more until they turn the key. Another woman whispers that where she comes from they do it in reverse—the mother-in-law has to pay to get out of the building with the bride. Meanwhile more women leak past the ribbon barricade. The men remain behind and out of sight of the events at the head of the stairs. Metin's father also ascends the stairs to negotiate at the door, then comes back to stand among the men.

Finally, we are given the signal to come up and a great rush of women ascend the stairs into the strange house. I am in the vanguard and follow Ayshe as we career through corridors looking into large empty rooms, searching for the bride. "Where is the bride?" "What a large house!" Finally, we barge into a small room at the end of a corridor and seem to surprise Songül sitting in her gown on a chair, being tended by her aunt and a couple of friends. The other members of her family are nowhere in sight. She looks startled and upset. A crush of breathless women swarm into the room. In a second someone has pulled the bride to her feet and hustled her out. I can hear her cry out, "My shoes! My shoes!" and I rush back into the room, grab the high-heeled white satin platform shoes, and pass them into the crowd, where they make their way to the bride. A cascade of women pour down the hallways and stairway carrying the bride with them, the women like a single organism. There is no noticeable pause even at the lowest landing, where people have to retrieve their shoes and put them on. The shoes are scattered and trampled by the crowd. The women seem to run into their shoes and continue without breaking stride. I find mine under the feet of a bewildered child standing like a still rock in the raging torrent.

The bride is sluiced down the outside stairs to a waiting car. Her aunt gets in with her, her brother in the driver's seat. The men wait behind the plastic band. Everyone stops to pray for a moment, then people run for the cars and the entourage pulls onto the highway to the sound of rifles being shot into the air. Just over the rise, out of sight of the village, the cars pull off the road onto the shoulder where a second wedding car is parked. In this car waits Metin; his father is the driver. The bride is hustled into the second car and we continue into town to the government Wedding House where a state official will marry them in the required civil ceremony. The bride and groom wait in a small room on the second floor until it is time for their ceremony. In the meantime, the wedding guests watch a series of other marriages take place in the main hall. Songül's brother comes into the small waiting room and helps her tie the red ribbon symbolizing virginity around her waist. He hangs a gold bracelet from it before tying the final knot. Metin and Songül sit side by side, occasionally whispering and smiling and laughing at one another. Songül's aunt is there, and some of her friends. The official photographer comes in and takes pictures of the couple.

EMINE:

There are no photographs of Emine's wedding in Hatije's family album. Unlike Songül, who at every step is cajoled and rewarded for giving up her parental home, her virginity, and perhaps her voice in her husband's home, Emine received no gold bracelets or coins, no jewelry from the groom just before consummation, no furniture sets, no appliances except a second-hand television. Her mother-in-law pressures her to wear a head scarf, but Emine refuses, and also wears jeans beneath her coat. Her mother-in-law also wants her granddaughter to wear a head scarf, arguing that Serap needs to cover her hair and not mix with boys because "if you have girls together with boys in school something is bound to happen. People have no brakes. If you put them in a situation like that, something bad will happen." Emine wants to keep her daughter uncovered, but every day there is friction with her mother-in-law, who lives upstairs.

METIN'S WEDDING:

An attendant calls Metin and Songül and they hurry downstairs into the hall. Women cram every available space. The men fill out the background. There are over a hundred people there—a sea of colorful scarves, waves of pastels and intricate patterns flecked with gold that glint in the light, a bright and cheerful sea of churning heads, the men a dark promontory defining the rear. Metin and Songül sit on the stage behind a large table next to an official in a crimson robe. When the official asks, "Do you take this woman . . . ," Metin says not "Yes" but "Yes, with all my heart," loudly and firmly. A murmur of delighted approval ripples through the pastel sea. Then, as if a drain has been opened, the sea of women sweeps out of the room, slowing to a thick, viscous flow, body pressed to body, in the clogged hallway and stairwell. Metin and Songül hold court at one side of the hall, Songül still flanked by her aunt. People jostle and push into an amorphous line to shake the bride's and groom's hands, wish them happiness, and perhaps pin money or gold coins on the ribbons hanging from their necks. We collect our wedding remembrance from a man by the door passing them out from a cardboard box: a tiny white plastic basket swathed in white tulle and containing two sugar-coated almonds. Then we spill out the door into the sunshine and down the stairs to the parking lot below. The Bosphorus gleams just beyond the road.

Finally the couple emerge and sweep down the stairs into the waiting wedding car. We go ahead to Hatije's house to wait for the bride. The old women are waiting with their pot, but the couple don't come. One woman surmises, "They've probably gone to the park to stroll around. It's understandable for a bride to want to take this opportunity to go out—-it may be her last and only chance to get to do something like that." But soon a call comes—they are only at the photographer's. Finally they arrive in a flurry of activity at the door. I try to photograph Songül stepping on the pot but her dress fills the doorway and hides the pot. The old women cannot do the tongue-cutting ritual because, instead of the more common veil, the bride is wearing a more modest turban which fits tightly to her neck and is pinned to her bodice. The couple sweep in and upstairs to their own apartment.

In the lower apartment, the women continue as before, sitting, eating, chatting. The bride and groom are upstairs with Songül's aunt, eating from a round tray set on a low stool in the living room. Metin comes downstairs alone and sets up a portable cassette recorder with lively pop music. He and his mother dance together as the women clap. When he leaves, the young girls dance. There is much joking around. An hour later, Hatije and the others demand to see the bride and an unhappy-looking Songül and her aunt are brought downstairs. Songül is still tightly bound into her heavy white satin wedding dress. She sits next to her aunt, looking very uncomfortable. The women insist that she dance. She doesn't want to but is pulled to her feet and made to dance with Hatije. Songül drags her long, heavy train around and becomes twisted up in it, then tries to carry it looped over her arm, but this causes the hoop underneath to swing up crazily. She is made to dance a long time before she is allowed to sit down again. I take my leave, leaving the bride still sitting sweating and silent and unhappy on the couch in the small room full of women from Metin's family. Later the men will participate in a religious marriage ceremony with an imam upstairs in the new apartment.

EMINE:

The next day is the first day of school, and Emine and I take her daughter to the opening ceremonies of a local public school. It is a forty-minute walk. We spend a couple of hours milling in the courtyard of the unassuming cement building with other parents, the children corralled in a big group in the middle, herded by several teachers. When the principal announces the school fees, Emine winces. We go to the desk set up in the parking lot to pay the registration fees, but Emine doesn't have the money. The man at the desk tells her she can pay later, so she takes the forms and we wait in the hot sun for Haluk to arrive with the money. When he comes, she takes him aside and tells him what the fees are. "Where will we find that kind of money?" He answers softly, "We'll find it." But they leave without paying.

SONGÜL:

When I visit Hatije for the first time after the wedding, two weeks later, there is already friction in the house. Emine and I had called to say we were coming to visit, but Hatije told us Songül had invited some of her friends over so we should come another day. A few minutes later she called back to say Songül had canceled her friends' visit and that we should come. We find Songül at Hatije's dining room table stuffing grape leaves, looking disgruntled. Whenever Songül goes out of the room, Hatije looks at us meaningfully and whispers, "Oh, what am I going to do? Do you see?!" Songül looks grumpy but defiant. She stops stuffing grape leaves after we arrive and spends the next hour vacuuming her apartment upstairs, particularly the stairs coming down to her mother-in-law's apartment, making a great deal of noise. While she is doing that, Hatije confides in me that she heard Songül shouting at Metin, "Don't leave your things there. Can't you see I've cleaned there." She says she took Songül aside and told her there would be no yelling at her son in her house. But Songül didn't pay any attention to her. Songül had canceled her friends' visit when she heard we were dropping by unexpectedly, even though Hatije had told her she could go ahead. "After all, she has her own rooms upstairs." As we are leaving later in the afternoon, we say goodbye to Songül. She is just going up the stairs to her own place and pauses to say goodbye, adding, with a long look at Hatije, "And I hope the next time the plans don't get changed at the last minute." Hatije looks shocked and says to us sotto voce, "You see? You see how she talks to me?"

EMINE:

Emine sells Mary Kay cosmetics to the women in her neighborhood. "It's so hard to make any money doing this. Nobody uses makeup in this neighborhood; all you can hope to sell is face cream." She looks in the battered briefcase behind the couch for money her husband was supposed to have left her. There is no money there, so she borrows it from a neighbor. "I can't stand Haluk," she whispers to me furiously. "I hated him from the moment we got married." She pulls on a coat but leaves her hair uncovered. We share a public minibus downtown; she is going to get more face cream from her supplier. She looks out of the minibus window pensively, her face reflected against the skyline of Istanbul.

NOTE

1. In order to protect people's privacy, I have given pseudonyms to the neighborhood and to the people themselves, and have changed details of their life histories that were not essential to this essay. I have also combined events from the lives of several different people.

6. Editing *al-Fajr:* A Palestinian Newspaper in Jerusalem

Bishara Bahbah

Running a daily newspaper can be a harrowing experience under the best circumstances. Bishara Bahbah served as editor of al-Fajr *(The Dawn), a Jerusalem daily newspaper published in both English and Arabic, for the year 1983–1984. In that post he had to balance his Palestinian nationalist beliefs with the political realities of running a newspaper under occupation. Government-imposed media censorship is a fact of life in most of the Middle East, and often ordinary citizens learn more from what the newspapers do not print than from what they do print. It took Bahbah only a short time, however, to discover that the Israeli censor was but one of the many obstacles he faced. What follows is an account of the experiences of a Western-educated editor, the challenges confronting him, and the reasons why he resigned after one year on the job. —Eds.*

At the age of twenty-five I received my doctorate degree in political science from Harvard University. I was under the illusion that if I was able to earn my Ph.D. from one of the best universities in the world within a relatively short period of time, I could then take on the most challenging of jobs. I had not realized how pleasant (and relatively unchallenging) it was to be a student even at one of the toughest universities in the world. Of the job opportunities I had, I picked the one that had the most exposure and that provided me with the means to influence events on an almost daily basis in nowhere else than my birthplace, Jerusalem. Rather than settle into a teaching position at one of the universities, I decided to accept a position as the editor-in-chief of the Jerusalem-based *al-Fajr* Palestinian Arabic daily newspaper.

Al-Fajr newspaper was founded in 1972 by Yusef Nasr, a Palestinian schoolteacher educated in the United States. During his tenure at the news-

paper, Nasr was often very criticical, thus creating for himself many enemies among the Israeli authorities as well as among other Arabs, including
some Palestinians. In 1974, Nasr was kidnapped and presumed dead after
an extensive search, during which his family offered huge rewards for information leading to his whereabouts. His brother-in-law, Paul Ajlouny, a
self-made millionaire residing in the United States, took it upon himself
to finance the newspaper and to run it from the United States. He dele-
gated daily management of the newspaper to the Jerusalem-based staff,
who often manipulated the power associated with running a newspaper
to suit their political ideologies. In a ten-year period the newspaper had
more editors-in-chief than any other paper in the occupied territories.

By the time I was appointed editor-in-chief, the political line of the
newspaper was associated very strongly with the Palestine Liberation Organization, particularly with Fatah, the main faction within the PLO,
which is headed by Yasser Arafat. Although I had not set *al-Fajr*'s political
position, it was in agreement with my own political beliefs. I wanted *al-Fajr*
to become a model newspaper to be emulated in the Middle East. I wanted
it to be professional, non-factional, thought-provoking, responsible, and
credible in all eyes.

It took a short time for me to realize that my goals were idealistic and,
unfortunately, somewhat impossible. On one hand, the restrictions on the
freedom of the press in the occupied territories were stifling. We were
forced to submit all the materials to be printed in the newspaper to the Israeli military censor on a daily basis prior to publication. The censor would
determine what was to be published and what was not. Quite often our
hottest news items were censored and our best news analysis and feature
stories never went beyond the censor's desk. Under Israeli law, if we vio-
lated instructions given to us by the censor, then we were liable to various
punishments, including the closure of the newspaper (which did occur
on various occasions) and the suspension of our license to distribute the
newspaper, particularly in the occupied territories, where our largest read-
ership lives, in addition to a host of other punitive measures. Therefore, no
matter how hard we tried to provide our readers with analysis and up-to-
date news, we had to accommodate ourselves to the whims of the censor,
who in my opinion, because of the powers given to him by the Israeli government, was the actual editor-in-chief not only of *al-Fajr* but of the entire
Palestinian press in the occupied territories. Censorship was not the only
restriction imposed upon us by the Israeli authorities. Many of our best
journalists were imprisoned, others were put under town arrest, and sometimes some were even physically abused while trying to cover a story.

Being forced to deal with the Israelis and to survive under their harsh
and undemocratic regulations were only part of the challenge of trying to
produce a good newspaper. The other part originated in no other source
than the Palestinians themselves. The fact that I was educated in the West

and trained to value efficiency was part of the problem. I went to Jerusalem with expectations and visions that were difficult, if not impossible, given the circumstances, to attain.

First, many of the paper's employees had been hired for reasons other than excellence, efficiency, and qualifications. On numerous occasions some employees were hired because of their political affiliation and commitment, others because they needed a job—any job—others because they just happened to be there at the right time and in the right company. There were even those who were hired because they were persistent or willing to accept a modest salary for their services. In other words, most of the staff was hired irrespective of qualifications and productivity.

Thus my first challenge was to cope with a staff that I found inadequate. To quietly replace staff members was close to impossible. If fired, many of them would not have been able to find other jobs. Such an action would have cost such a nationalist newspaper supporters and readers. Then there were the political appointees whose patrons were so powerful that any action taken against the employees would have been viewed as an unfriendly political gesture. My only recourse was to help the staff develop and leave them no option but to work and produce. In the meantime, I was determined to replace any employee who resigned with people I believed were well qualified. I also began to hire people that I felt were assets to the paper. I hired a photographer, a translator, a political cartoonist, and a host of field reporters.

In addition to having staff problems, the newspaper needed a new printing press to replace the one of 1940s vintage that not only broke down almost daily but also was time-consuming to operate and difficult to supply with spare parts. Worse yet, our competitor had one of the most advanced printing presses in the Middle East. We tried to convince the publisher to buy a new press. The publisher insisted he would import one only if the Israelis allowed him to construct a building to house the entire newspaper operation. The Israelis naturally refused to permit the newspaper to build new offices and thus obtain a new press. From their perspective, why should they? We were a constant pain in their necks, criticizing their actions against our people and calling for the establishment of an independent, sovereign Palestinian state.

These restrictions made me realize quickly that it would be a hundred times tougher to carry out my original goals than I had earlier anticipated. In self defense, I sorted out matters over which I had no control whatsoever and those over which I had. Censorship and Israeli-imposed limitations were beyond my control, as was the acquisition of a new printing press. Other matters, however, seemed more within reach.

Although my relationship with the employees was very rocky at first, after a few months they began to recognize the purpose behind my course of action. Investments made in the newly-hired employees paid off spectacularly. They motivated the others to improve their performance. Improving the quality of the newspaper moved slowly. Part of the problem was the fact that I was a trained political scientist, not a journalist. I therefore had to learn how to run a newspaper and how to administer over one hundred employees. I also had to become acquainted with the political realities and sensitivities among both the Palestinians and the Israelis. After all, I had not been in my homeland for more than six years while I was studying in the United States.

To sort out internal problems within the newspaper and to introduce changes were tough enough for any editor. However, there were other job hazards. A little over a month after I started work, I decided to fire one of the secretaries, after several warnings, for what I felt was unprofessional behavior. The same day I fired the secretary, her brother forced his way very close to my office with the intention of "beating the hell out of me." Given my small stature and the fact that he was big and furious, if he had reached me, I would have ended up with a few broken bones. In the traditional Arab manner, many people, including my own eldest brother, who had nothing to do with the newspaper, tried to intervene on the secretary's behalf and dissuade me from firing her. I told everybody that the issue was strictly an internal administrative matter and that it was not their business to interfere. I stood firmly by my decision partly because I wanted the employees to realize that things would be different from then on. An interesting twist in the case was my brother's demand, as the eldest in our family, that the family of the would-be attacker apologize to our family for having threatened me. Some of the notables in the community intervened and arranged for a *sulha* or conciliation. During the sulha, the uncle of the young man who threatened me apologized for his nephew's behavior by kissing my brother's forehead. I was flabbergasted by the whole incident. In any case, I did not rehire the secretary.

On December 12, 1983, only a few months after I took the job, I left work about 8:30 p.m. to go home to celebrate my wife's birthday only to discover that my brand-new Volkswagen had been vandalized. Somebody had slashed the tires. A few days afterwards, somebody smashed the trunk with a big rock and broke a few lights. After fixing that damage, the car was hit again in various spots. All in all, within a two-month period, the car was vandalized at least six times. On one of those occasions, the rear windshield was entirely smashed while the car was parked in front of my house. I was suspicious and decided to call the police and have them check for possible bombs. Within minutes they arrived and discovered no bombs or clues as to who could have done it. I filed a complaint with the police department and, in a typical manner, I was informed that they were too busy to do anything and that if I discovered who did it then I should let them know. On that note, I realized that I would never find the vandalizer.

My personal safety was also at stake. My family and I received numerous telephone calls threatening to kill me. At that time, the publisher of the newspaper decided to hire a bodyguard for me. My entire family suffered because of constant threats hovering over my life. Nevertheless, such intimidations never hindered me from going on with my work as I saw fit. In fact, I refused to have any information about the vandalism and threats published in the newspaper so as not to give my enemies cause to rejoice or to give them the impression that I was intimidated in any way.

Despite all that, there were many positive aspects to the job. I remember my first day on the job, when the French television came for an interview on Jerusalem municipal elections. An earlier *al-Fajr* editorial had called on Palestinians in Jerusalem not to vote for the Israeli municipality of Teddy Kolek since as Palestinians we do not recognize Israel's 1967 annexation of Jerusalem. Later in the day I granted Israeli television an interview on the same subject. I quickly discovered that I had become the spokesperson for the Palestinians on many issues of the day. In the one-year period that I was editor-in-chief, I had interviews with hundreds of visiting reporters from all over the world, including live interviews for radio stations in the United States, Canada, and the United Kingdom. It seemed that my most important success at the newspaper was in dealing with foreign reporters and, quite often, foreign diplomatic dignitaries. Our role at the newspaper was more than reporters and opinion formulators. We were also newsmakers.

Our public noted improvements in both the structure and the content of the newspaper fairly quickly. Our local news reporting quadrupled and, ironically, we became a free source of news for the foreign press as well as for the Israeli press. About six or seven o'clock in the evening we customarily received calls from Israeli journalists in charge of covering the occupied territories inquiring about the day's news events. We were always happy to assist since, more often than not, the Israeli military censor refused us permission to publish many of the news items while the Israeli press, which had an agreement to censor itself and to submit only military-related news items to the censor, could actually publish the news. We then routinely copied "our" news items from the Israeli newspaper the following day, quoting them as the source.

My decision to leave the newspaper, at the end of my first year on the job, came simply because I felt let down by the publisher, who refused to adopt my recommendations about the staff and the needs of the newspaper. I was willing to withstand all the hazards and difficulties associated with the job so long as I felt that I was moving the newspaper closer to my objective. Unquestionably, that needed support from the publisher. When I realized that it was not forthcoming, I decided to resign.

7. The Son's Return

Driss Chraibi

Driss Chraibi, a French-educated chemist from Morocco, writes in this passage from his autobiographical novel, Heirs to the Past, *of the cleavage between generations which can result from exposure to the West. As traditionally educated parents realized the importance of equipping their children to deal with the technologically oriented West, newly independent nations adopted British and French education systems wholesale, and many talented students were sent to study in France and Great Britain. At times a byproduct of this education was the alienation of a native from his or her own culture. Chraibi, like many other Moroccans, admired French culture and technology although he had a strong emotional attachment to his home. When given a chance to attain the gloss of Western civilization in France, he left his home and sought education and work abroad. —Eds.*

A seat away from me, in front, there was an Arab with a European woman. The man was young, outwardly at least, with black frizzy hair, all shiny, a moustache as thin as mending-cotton, and an array of pens clipped to his breast pocket. He was talking in a loud voice, describing poetically the vast domain owned by his father; selecting an orange and peeling it with his thumbnail, he exclaimed, "O-la-la, these are sold by the heap in Morocco, practically given away. You'll see, my pet, you'll see." The woman was laughing. I heard the laugh, I could not see it. Behind her gold-rimmed spectacles her short-sighted eyes were timorous. She was what psychoanalysts call phobia-obsessed, like the kind of women I had known and loved during my long stay in Europe—a dread of people mocking at sex, a fear of change, a fear specially of death, taking all possible precautions against it. Orderly and methodical in their work as in their private life, conscientious and realistic, they were symbolic of the West which had brought me

Adapted from *Heirs to the Past*, trans. Len Ortzen (London: Heinemann, 1972).

to manhood. She had hands which would have inspired a Rodin, breasts straining forward like a pair of greyhounds on the leash, and hair that was very long, falling over her shoulders, on to the seat and her husband's arm like a flow of molten bronze. The man was talking and she was laughing bleakly, without the slightest sign of merriment on her face. Just her hands, now and again, closed over and kneaded her husband's hand, while he looked at her with the face of a worshipper prepared to wipe out a whole tribe for love of a woman.

I was surprised to find myself smiling. Perhaps it was her that I was smiling at. Through the window and seen from thirty thousand feet up, when the clouds thinned out and became like watered silk full of holes, this country I had believed in and still did believe in, and which was slipping past under my feet at five hundred miles an hour, appeared as no more than a map with waterways and sprawls of green that my ancestors had dreamed about in the course of centuries.

The moment I stepped out of the plane I was almost blown over. It was a free, wild wind, straight from the desert. My lungs were suddenly filled almost to bursting with warmth, oxygen, and light. For more than twenty-four hours I had been dead to all feeling except that one—the call to life.

Slowly, and shivering all over, I went down the steps. And just then came the sound. The long-drawn-out call rose from behind the white barrier, crossed the airfield, and burst behind me like a grenade at the feet of the Arab and his wife, who were descending the steps. But it seemed to have come from the depths of the past.

"Ooohoo! Bou-chaib. Ooohoo! My son!"

It was frightening to hear: a hymn to joy. And the man who had uttered it was even more frightening. He was an old peasant, dark and withered like a burnt stick, barefooted, bareheaded, wearing just a shirt, with muck up to his knees and the colour of dust up to his eyes. He was not so much astride his mount as lying along its back—a little donkey that was the very image of its master: ragged and shorn, mouth open and tongue lolling, eyes starting out of its head, lifting all four legs at a time and spreading them in all directions, and galloping, galloping in the wind straight for the white barrier, as no other representative of its breed had ever galloped before, in the memory of donkey-man. And the old peasant was urging the animal on with kicks and blows, stroking its neck, shouting fond names, calling it little jewel, God's blessing, hell's motor-car. He was promising it a she-ass, a bale of hay, some green peapods—lovely green peapods, oh so good—the whole of his coming harvest of barley and oats, if only it would gallop faster, faster still. And the donkey shook its ears madly and seemed to leave the ground altogether. And the old peasant, welded to his mount, shaded his eyes with his hand, opened his toothless, cavernous mouth and gave his long-drawn-out call of joy.

"Ooohoo! Bou-chaib. Ooohoo! My son!"

We were standing there in our clothes of civilized men and probably

with our problems of civilized men—passengers, policemen, customs officials and loafers, all of us fascinated by this stampede of primitive man
and beast—we had eyes for nothing else. The Arab with the thin moustache was standing among us in his expensive suit, which was flapping in
the wind. He kept looking at his wife, and she stared back with scared
eyes, as though afraid to understand. The wind was catching at her long
copper-coloured hair and making it stream round her head like a banner.
She tried to hold it down, but her hands were trembling and the wind was
stronger than any human sentiment.

She said: "What is it all about, darling?"

"If only I knew," he replied in a wary tone.

Then he shouted: "But-I-do-not-know!"

She took his arm and they began to walk on again. We who were there,
we bestirred ourselves and set off too. She said, and it was only a murmur,
yet even amid the roaring of the wind and the shouting of the old peasant,
we heard the murmur like an explosion, "But I'm sure there's something
the matter, darling. Everyone's looking at us."

"Well," he shouted, "it's a confounded habit in this country!"

And he began to walk faster, as though the only hope was in flight,
dragging his wife along on his arm.

And it came to pass: the donkey could not stop its headlong flight and
crashed into the barrier, the old peasant toppled to the ground, picked
himself up and prepared to jump the obstacle. We who were watching, we
all saw him and can bear witness: it was a man overcome with joy who was
trying to take a leap, a man whose trembling hands were stretched out to
the person he kept calling his in the voice of the damned; an old man with
a face as small as a child's, and so wrinkled as to appear seamed, a dog-
like face bathed in tears. When the policeman caught hold of him and said,
"Hey, granddad, where d'you think you're off to? Keep away from this barrier," the old man answered in a voice that trembled as much as his hands:
"But that's my son!"

"All right, all right," said the policeman. "That's your son, I'm not saying he isn't, but keep away from this barrier."

"Very well, sir," said the old man politely, "But you see, that's my son.
His name is Bouchaib."

"Bouchaib," repeated the policeman. "Bouchaib. All right, I'm not saying it isn't, but keep away from this barrier."

"But do you see, sir? I've been waiting for him for five years. That's my
son, my son Bouchaib. That's him, over there. I'd know him with my eyes
shut."

He started calling again. "Ooohoo! Bouchaib! Ooohoo! My son!"

"Take it easy, granddad," said the policeman. "Don't do anything silly.
I'm a peaceful sort, I am, and I shouldn't like you to spend the night in the
cells at your age. So stay quiet and keep off this barrier."

The old man seemed to understand; he calmed down, contenting himself with blowing a kiss to his son over the policeman's shoulder and calling to him: "I'll wait for you. I'm here. I shan't budge. You've only to go round the customs shed and you'll find me here. I shan't go away. Just tell them that you're my son and they'll let you through first. They all know I've been waiting for you a long time."

He explained to the policeman: "That's my son. He's just come back from France. He's highly educated. I say, sir, when you come off duty this evening, will you be one of our guests? There are couscous, a roasted calf, and honey cakes."

"This evening, you say? With pleasure, dad. There'll be a roast, you say?"

"Oh, only a little calf. Not very big, but I'm not rich. I've sold everything—"

"Ah, yes, that's the way of things. With pleasure, uncle, but keep away from this barrier . . . "

We were still walking across the airfield towards the customs shed when I heard the young woman ask her husband: "Do you know him, dear?"

"Know who?"

"Why, that man, of course! Anyone would think you were blind!"

"What man?"

"There was a short silence between them. I saw her slow down, on the point of stopping, and all of us who were following prepared to come to a halt too.

"I don't understand Arabic," she said, "But that man seems to me to have been calling to you for some time. Everyone has noticed it except you. Are you trying to tell me that it's not you whose attention he's been trying desperately to catch?"

He turned round, and it was as though he was seeing his father for the first time—the first time in his life. I was watching him, and I can bear out that his face became distorted with rage. Then he looked at his wife, and it was as though he was seeing her for the first time, too. But his face had fallen, all the muscles were sagging.

"Yes, you're right," he said. "It's an old servant." And he added quickly, "An old servant who has known me since I was born. I really hadn't recognized him. Of course, it's five years since I last saw him."

And he gave a friendly little wave to the old servant. She let go of his arm and looked him straight in the face. There was nothing of the phobia-obsessed about her now. She was no longer bothering about her hair streaming in the wind, and one would have said that we who were there mattered no more than a swarm of flies.

"But he recognized you straight away," she cried in a shrill voice. "He's over there, weeping and calling you by your name. I may not know Arabic, but I don't need anyone to translate for me. I know how you pronounce your name."

"What do you want me to do?" he exclaimed, exasperated. "Go and throw my arms round his neck?"

"And why not? If he'd been able to, he would have come and thrown his arms round the plane."

"Now look, my pet, you don't know what you're saying."

"I may not know what I'm saying, but I know what I'm feeling. And it's my impression that you're hiding something from me."

"Look, dear." His voice had gone all tender. "You don't know anything about this country . . . "

"He seemed to swoop down from the sky," she said vehemently. "If he'd had a car, he would have stamped on the accelerator to get here long before us. But all he had was his donkey, and if you didn't see that donkey galloping, then you didn't want to see anything. He's come a long way, just to meet you. Look at him, he's covered in mud, he was so afraid of being late. I wish I were like that old servant."

"All right," said the man wearily. "Wait for me here."

When the old peasant saw his son coming, he made no attempt to break away from the policeman. He merely said: "There you are, sir, you see? I told you he's my son. I haven't led you into error."

"All right, granddad, all right. I'm very glad, I'm sure. But keep off that barrier. I don't want to see you trying to jump it again, d'you hear?"

"He's my son, and he's been away for such a long time. He's the only one I've got now. I thought I'd lost him for ever. Ohoo! Bouchaib! Ohoo! My son!"

"Quiet, I tell you. Calm down. Otherwise, I'll be obliged to deal severely with you, and I don't like tackling old men. So be sensible."

"Now I can die in peace," said the old man. "I didn't want to die before he came back."

"You seem to me like one of those wholemeal loaves that aren't made any more," said the policeman. "But do, please, keep off that barrier. If it gets broken, I shall have to take you to the station, and I'm much rather help you eat that roast this evening."

"Bouchaib!" yelled the old peasant. And when at last he was able to grasp his son's hand and raise it to his lips, he stood there kissing the fingers one by one and saying over and over again, "Bouchaib, Bouchaib, Bouchaib."

"Steady, steady now," the policeman was saying. "Don't get excited. Be philosophical. Breaking barriers and spending the night at the station isn't at all the thing for a man of your age. Steady, I tell you!"

"Are you all right, son?" the old peasant was saying. "Are you eating well? You're not ill? Is that your wife? Why didn't she come and speak to me? Ah yes, of course, she's shy. But she mustn't be shy, I'll do all I can to make her feel at home. Tell her that in her own language. Your old mother has been busy beating up the couscous since dawn, and she hasn't been to bed all night. You know her; she always does what she pleases."

And he started laughing, but his laugh was assuredly a sob.

"Go back to your village," said Bouchaib, "and wait till I come. It may be tomorrow or the day after. I have to get my wife settled in a hotel. Good-bye."

I was so close to Bouchaib's wife that I could have touched her. She was watching the scene intently, aching to understand what was being said. For a moment I was tempted to translate her father-in-law's words into French for her, and the answer her husband had just given. But I refrained, and it was a relief to me. It was up to her to discover the truth in her own way. All I did was to raise my right hand and clap her on the shoulder. She must have cried out, but I couldn't hear very well as I was laughing into the wind. I went on my way, and when I met Bouchaib he did not even glance at me and I said nothing to him; I was still laughing. It was only when I had almost reached the barrier that I stopped and my laughter stopped, strangled in my throat—the old peasant had tossed the policeman over his shoulder like a sack of logs and had started to break the slats of the barrier. He was just breaking off the tops, giving each one a sharp little pull, steadily and unhurriedly, as though he had plenty of time and was counting them as he went. And he threw them over his shoulder, one after the other, with a leisurely, casual gesture, as if nothing mattered any more. As he did so, he intoned a kind of litany that I had difficulty in catching, not because his voice was soft (it rose above the wind) but because he rattled it off at great speed.

"In the name of God, the Compassionate, the Merciful, I sold my father's field, amen. And my brother's field, amen. And the one I robbed my neighbour of, my neighbour of, my neighbour of. The sheep, the billy-goats and the nanny-goat, the hens, the mattress, the army rifle, all sold. Amen. Thy will be done, O Lord, in this century of science, decolonization, and independence. Money-order, sixty money-orders, plus the postage. So that he might be worthy of my unworthiness. And three of my sons have died at their work, wretched are we, and turned to dust shall we be, amen. And now he is ashamed of his father. The road is long, so very long, back to the village, and I am weary, so very weary, Lord, I no longer even wish to die, I no longer wish for anything."

"And now, come along with me," said the policeman, getting to his feet. He spoke gently, as though to a sick child; but he was looking surly. "Come on, I'm taking you to the station. I told you to keep away from that barrier. Come on, granddad, come on."

Just then the donkey appeared, seemingly from nowhere. It finished chewing a blade of grass and then raised its old man's head to the sky and started to bray.

8. The Funeral

Driss Chraibi

Muslim burials are conducted as soon after death as is feasible. The deceased is washed, wrapped in a shroud, and carried to a cemetery. A coffin may or may not be used. The body is placed in the grave with the face oriented toward Mecca. Either at the deathbed or the grave, the shahada *(witness to God's oneness) is whispered in the ear of the deceased. The funeral prayer may be said at graveside, in the home of the deceased, or in a mosque. The memorial service held forty days after the death is as important as the funeral. Friends and relatives gather to mourn the deceased. Below, Driss Chraibi describes the chanting of the Qur'an at his father's grave. —Eds.*

The wind had changed and was now coming off the sea, a fresh, soft breeze that was bringing a flight of coppery clouds. Whether it was a yew or a cypress, whether young or old, I could not say, but a tree stood there that was so covered with dust from the graves that it had assumed the color of death and of time. Somewhere in the tree, a bird was singing—a canary. Except for its trilling note, nothing could be heard, nothing beyond the pickaxe digging into the rocky ground.

Those who were sitting there, those who had found places on the flat tombstones or on the walls, and were bunched along the paths, had probably been there since dawn. When the funeral procession came through the cemetery gates, there they were, their arms folded across their knees, with lifeless eyes, as though they had no other abode on earth. The only clear space was the main path, and when we had reached the grave-digger, when he had said "In the name of Almighty God" and spat on his hands and lifted his pickaxe to start digging his hole before us all, and when, bent beneath his burden, Nagib had placed it on the ground (he had carried it himself, across his shoulders, and the idea of offering to help had occurred to no one), when he had straightened up, sweat streaming from

Adapted from *Heirs to the Past*, trans. Len Ortzen (London: Heinemann, 1972).

his armpits, his body and his brow—I turned round and saw . . . that the main path had never existed and that someone had shut the gates from which traditional gnomes were hanging.

All the time the grave-digger dug and shoveled up soil, the bird sang. And when the grave was long and deep, when the man who had dug it climbed out, himself the color of the earth, flung away his tools and announced in a solemn voice, "Wretched are we, and turned to dust shall we be"—then the bird fell silent. It seemed to have flown off to another cemetery. A tidal wave of voices repeated, "Wretched are we, and turned to dust shall we be."

Then a man stood up. He had been sitting in front of me, his hands on the stretcher made of poles on which my father was lying. The man was of medium height, with no distinctive features, clad in a gray overall and wearing sandals. He got up and began to chant.

What he chanted was of no importance. It was not the words nor the meaning, nor even the symbolism, which moved our hearts, the men, women and children who were there. We forgot why we were there the moment he began to chant. It was the incantation, and the end of our woes and miserable little problems, the aching and yet serene longing for that other life which is ours and to which we are all destined to return, the victors and the defeated, the fully developed and those still at the larva stage, the faithful and the atheists, through God's great compassion. There was all of that in the voice of the man who stood chanting in the sun, and we were in his voice, I was in his voice despite the vast legacy of incredulity that I had received from the West. When he reached the end of a verse, he paused, and so it came about—an outburst of fervor. And while he chanted it was like a man in the wilderness chanting his faith. And the voice rose and swelled, changed in tone, became tragic, soared, and then floated down on our heads like a seagull gliding gently and softly, little more than a whisper. And so—never, never again will I go in search of intellectuals, of written truths, synthetic truths, of collections of hybrid ideas which are nothing but ideas. Never again will I travel the world in search of a shadow of justice, fairness, progress or schemes calculated to change mankind. I was weary and I was returning to my clan. That man who was not even aware of his voice of his faith was alive and held the secret of life—a man who could not even have been a dustman in this world of founts of knowledge and of civilization. Peace and everlasting truth were in him and in his voice, while all was crumbling around him and on the continents.

* * *

He stopped and sat down under a deluge. The clouds swept in by the wind had come to a standstill above the cemetery, thick, gray, and lowering, just over the tree where the bird had been singing, and they were sending down an autumnal rain on our bare heads. I had only just become aware of it. But not one of us moved. Long after the man had sat down, we remained as we were. The rain fell in torrents, and we let it fall.

It was Nagib who lowered the body into the grave. He jumped down, then stretched out his arms and quickly drew it towards him. Someone tried to help, but Nagib bared his teeth. I heard a moan, and knew that my mother had just fainted. Then Madini came forward and took me by the hand. He walked with his shoulders hunched and his head drooping. When we were at the edge of the gaping hole, when Nagib climbed out and nodded, Madini went and picked up the grave-diggers spade, then held it out to me.

"This was his last wish too," he murmured.

I took the spade and gazed at it. The handle was quite short and the blade was wide. It was the kind that he had used for sinking his wells, going off all by himself with that and a pick, a bucket, and a rope-ladder. He did not just dig where there would have been the best chance of coming upon water. He used to say: "Sometimes God causes water to fall from the sky—and a few ideas. And people wait for all that to germinate. And that's the downfall of individuals and nations." He would stand on a small hillock, look slowly all round him from horizon to horizon, and say, "There, there, and over there." Then he took his tools and went off to dig for days or weeks, in clay, stony or rocky ground. And he never gave up. I never saw him give anything up. And therein lay his strength, the source of his authority.

PART TWO

Gender Relations

Middle Eastern gender roles have traditionally been governed by a patriarchal kinship system which was well entrenched in both pre-Islamic Bedouin tribal society and the Middle Eastern locales to which Islam spread. While men's rights are far-reaching, women's status is much more carefully delimited. In discussions of gender relations, Muslims note that Islam improved the plight of women in the seventh century C.E. by prohibiting female infanticide, limiting the extent of polygamy, and restricting men's unlimited power to divorce wives.

Islam considers women to be believers with full religious duties, including the duty to make a pilgrimage to Mecca. While Islamic laws prescribe gender-specific rights in areas such as divorce and inheritance, ultimately women's status varies from locale to locale, depending on the implementation of Islamic law and on local traditional and social custom, which are often more powerful forces than the letter of the religious law.

Men are expected to provide for their families; women, to bear and raise children; children, to honor and respect their parents and grow up to fulfill their adult roles. Sons are to become educated, marry, and assume steady employment; daughters are to become mothers and increasingly to work outside the home as well. Actions, whether honorable or shameful, do not reflect upon the individual alone, but on the entire family.

Clear gender roles mean less confusion about social expectations. A woman's traditional role is domestic: to bear children and raise them, to maintain the home, to cook, in the country to work in the fields, and in the city perhaps to run a cottage sewing or vending business. A childless woman, as well as one who never marries, is somewhat socially marginal. Children are important, but not as central to a mother's life as they once were. Christine Eickelman observes that the status earlier earned by bearing children has subtly changed focus, and that a woman's status now depends on her husband's job, her home, and the hospitality she offers rather than on the number of children she bears. In Oman, this has led to smaller families.

Women's special status is reflected in the term for women of the household, *harim*, which is derived from the verbal root *harama*, to forbid. The requirement of proper behavior falls heavily upon female shoulders. An unmarried woman avoids sitting in a room alone or being seen in public with an unrelated male. She frets if she is accidentally thrown into the company of strange men, for she knows the consequence of improper behavior, no matter how innocent it may be.

Honor, an important cultural theme, includes social decorum, keeping one's word, and providing for one's family. Honor can be collectively held —and lost, as when a woman's improper behavior besmirches her family's honor. In the past, such a woman might have been killed to wipe out the blot, and one can still read of isolated incidents of honor killing. Although, as the research of a Jordanian woman journalist (published in newspapers in Amman) has documented, honor killings are rare (but not rare enough) and generally restricted to lower socioeconomic levels (despite the media coverage given these issues in the United States), chastity remains a critical question; double standards apply everywhere, and women are held responsible for their honor.

Islam accords men a higher status than women ("Men have a degree above them" [Qur'an 2:228]), but men are also obliged to care for the women and children dependent upon them. For a man, being married or not, a parent or childless, is not as important as it is for a woman. A man's improper conduct blackens his reputation and reflects on his family, but he cannot disgrace his family in the way that a woman can. There is more room for the peccadillos of male youth than for those of females.

Women are simultaneously cherished and seen as dangerous—beings who must be protected, but also possessors of strange powers stemming from their fertility. This doubleness resembles the Western dichotomy of virgin and vixen. Traditional Egyptian beliefs suggest that rituals surrounding charged life events such as birth, circumcision, and death are interrelated within a symbolic complex of blood and infertility. Folk tales similarly reflect ambivalence about women's powers. The following proverb from the Aures mountains in Algeria suggests that women's demonic tendencies increase throughout life while men steadily become more righteous.

> The child of male sex comes to the world with sixty *jnoun* (spirits) in his body; the child of the female sex is born pure; but every year, the boy gets purified of a jinn, whereas the girl acquires one; and this is the reason that

old women, sixty years and with sixty jnoun are sorcerers more malignant than the devil himself. Blind she sews more material, lame she jumps over more rocks, and deaf she knows all the news. (Nelson 1973, 52)

Fatima Mernissi, a Moroccan sociologist, has suggested that Islam is responsible for restrictions on women because it defines women as emotionally dangerous. It is woman, in Mernissi's interpretation of Islam, who is "the embodiment of destruction, the symbol of disorder. She is *fitna*, the polarization of the uncontrollable, a living representative of the dangers of sexuality and its rampant disruptive potential" (Mernissi 1975, 13). This viewpoint suggests that women must be restricted to minimize their destructive potential, and that local standards for decorum and Islamic restrictions on women's behavior have been developed to contain women.

Whatever may have been the respective contributions of Islam and local custom, it is clear that the majority of social restrictions on Middle Eastern women originate in social patterns such as patriarchy and honor, which had little direct link to Islam. A case in point is veiling, which literally means covering the face, although it is often used as a gloss for conservative dress or for seclusion. Islamic law does not mandate veiling, but only requests that women dress modestly. Historically, in nineteenth-century Egypt, veiling and the physical seclusion of women signaled the upward mobility of agriculturalists who moved to town and no longer needed women's labor. In the twentieth century the veil has assumed political and social meanings. Muslim women of Algeria concealed bombs under their robes in the 1950s, while those of Iran used the veil to demonstrate revolutionary fervor and support for the Ayatollah Khomeini in 1978. Erika Friedl discusses the changes which time has wrought in the Islamic Republic of Iran for women of marriage age in villages and towns. According to her research, women in the Islamic Republic are confronting much the same problems and situations as women elsewhere in the Middle East in working out the conflict between marriage patterns and education. Modest Islamic dress, referred to as veiling or *hijab*, has become more widespread and is seen on Muslims in the United States as well. Such clothing is an individual statement about piety and about society. Elizabeth Fernea analyzes meanings which can underlie veiling: traditional understandings as well as new manifestations rooted in Islamic activism.

Islamic law discriminates between genders on such matters as inheritance law, which limits a woman's share to roughly half that of a man. However, since in Middle Eastern society the male is expected to provide for his female relatives, the difference in inheritance is somewhat mitigated. A peasant woman in Egypt who was the senior daughter-in-law in an extended family household was quite secure in her position. Nevertheless, in the back of her mind she knew that her natal family would shelter her should she ever be divorced. Her family of birth assumed a mythic status as her potential refuge: "My brother Abdul Monaim has an extremely productive farm with six *feddan* [about six and a quarter acres] and forty goats. He also raises water buffalo for investors. The grounds are green and succulent. If I went to my family, they would lift me up and care for me. . . . There is much goodness there with my brother."

The option of ending a marriage through divorce, which has traditionally been reserved for men, is now legally guaranteed to women in most of the Middle East under specified conditions. Islamic law accords women the right to divorce, but a woman must show just cause and contend with a sometimes unsympathetic justice system. Some more modern couples include a clause in their marriage contract giving the woman full right to divorce. Ziba Mir-Hosseini presents legal cases, observed in Iranian courts, in which women attempt to find justice for their unhappy marriage situations. She also presents data showing that women may also manipulate situations to their advantage. Dawn Chatty discusses the role of marriage in linking families as well as individuals, and the role of divorce in sabotaging those relations.

Even though gender roles are strictly defined, new forms of association, such as coeducation, have created ambiguous situations. Traditional mores prohibited male-female contact before marriage. However, when students began to attend coeducational secondary schools and universities, this prohibition began to break down. Among more progressive Middle Eastern families, young men and women can mix as long as they are in a group. However, most families forbid dating as a couple alone. A brother, sister, or friend chaperones any couple until they are engaged. Angel Foster's research in Tunisia, one of the more Westernized Arab countries, points out the conflict which young university women encounter between traditional family expectations for their behavior and the pressures male students put on them. It has been hypothesized that foreign film and television programs, with their depictions of looser sexual mores, have influenced Middle Eastern youth. Here Foster describes the sexual pressures which women themselves face, and the lack of support which their society provides for sexually active young women.

Although informal associations may cause problems, Middle Eastern professional women experience little difficulty in their associations with men in the public realm. In essence, they become gender-neutral and are seen as an "engineers" or "physicians" rather than as "women." Even among more traditional Middle Eastern women, interaction with non-kin males in the course of work is acceptable. Agriculturalists have almost never secluded women; in earlier times and today women worked in the fields, marketed in the villages, and even hitched rides to market with men who happened to pass with a horse and cart.

In considering the selections below, we must ask what these examples from such divergent geographic regions tell us about gender relations. Do we learn, for instance, that courtship is not always a simple traditional act, or that women's legal status is greatly affected both by local custom and by specific judicial actions? Has modern medical technology, which can furnish abortions and birth control pills and repair hymens, made the conflicts which university students face any easier? How does the conflict between traditional or rural and urban mores resemble similar conflicts the world over? Female genital mutilation and honor killings are featured in Western media, but do they represent the problems which young women and young men face every day, or do such problems get lost when we exoticize Middle Easterners?

REFERENCES

Mernissi, Fatima. 1975. *Beyond the Veil.* Boston: Schenkman Publishing.
Nelson, Cynthia. 1973. *The Desert and the Sown.* Berkeley: Institute of International Studies, University of California.

9. Young Women's Sexuality in Tunisia: The Health Consequences of Misinformation among University Students

Angel Foster

Angel Foster interviewed Tunisian women university students in the dormitories of the University of Tunis while working on a project on women's health and sexuality. She describes the dissonance these young women experience between the peer pressures they feel at university, their own needs, and the expectations of their families.

The conflicts between the mores taught in rural traditional families and the changing interpretations of sexuality found in urban areas and in university settings are very real and have an impact on individuals' private lives. Medical technology—birth control, abortion, hymen reparation—not only raises moral and social issues for young women but has also affected sexual behavior and the traditional emphasis on virginity. —Eds.

HAGER'S STORY

Hager is a twenty-five-year-old university student in Tunis. For her, sexuality is a problematic issue. Hager notes that in the past girls married young, and therefore enjoyed full sexual lives in their late teens, with their husbands. Now many university students like Hager anticipate marrying in their late twenties or early thirties, after finishing their studies and perhaps beginning a career. For Hager, this is a long time to wait to experience sexual intimacy. She is torn: she believes strongly in the longstanding cultural and religious tradition of abstaining from sexual relations until marriage, but she has sexual needs that she wants to meet. Hager feels pressure from her family, her fellow students, and society. She comes from what she calls a conservative family in Tunis, a family that expects women to preserve their virginity until marriage. But what if she never gets married? If she doesn't get married until her thirties, will she still be attractive? Will she still have sexual desires? Many of Hager's friends are sexually active and most will have their hymens repaired in a private clinic before their wedding nights. And though Hager believes that hymen reparation is one of the most important medical procedures to become accessible in Tunisia, she feels a great deal of familial and societal pressure to remain a virgin. This pressure became so extreme and her depression so severe that Hager sought counseling, a service not widely available to university students. The sessions were largely unhelpful; the psychologist did not seem to understand or appreciate her dilemma. Feeling judged and humiliated, Hager doesn't know whom else to talk with. Though she knows that many of her friends are suffering as well, she doesn't feel comfortable openly discussing the problem of sexuality with them or anyone else. She feels very alone.

By 1994 women's average age at marriage in Tunisia had risen to over twenty-six. Though rarely discussed publicly, there is a growing consensus among health service providers that the average age of women's first sexual experience in Tunisia is decreasing and that the percentage of girls engaging in premarital intercourse is increasing. Thus throughout the region, unmarried women's health needs, particularly those needs relating to reproductive health and sexuality, are becoming increasingly significant. Yet, as Hager's story indicates, the subject of sexuality remains largely taboo. My research shows that the lack of information and services available to young women has helped to perpetuate a great deal of misinformation regarding sexuality and reproductive health, misinformation that is contributing to behaviors with negative health consequences. Since this misinformation is compounded with the continued social expectation of virginity until marriage, it appears that many young women in Tunisia are suffering from depression, anxiety, and fear related to sexual behavior, which has serious implications for their health and ability to make decisions about sexuality.

For my dissertation on women's health care in Tunisia, I did nearly sixteen months of fieldwork throughout the country in 1998–2000. As part of this research, I surveyed seventy-five never-married female university students living in Greater Tunis, students who reflected both socioeconomic and geographic diversity.[1] Through focus groups and an oral history project, I spoke to many more young women about their experiences with and views on sexual health and sexuality; several of their stories have been included in this essay. Finally, this essay includes excerpts from a number of the more than 160 interviews I conducted with health service providers, government officials, and representatives of various organizations.

Although the Tunisian women's health program primarily targets married women, several programs focusing specifically on sexual health in adolescence were initiated in the late 1980s and 1990s. Curriculum reform to include sexual health and reproduction in secondary school natural-science courses, health activity clubs in secondary schools, and a prenuptial certification program (including reproductive health information and tests for some sexually transmitted diseases) were among the most significant policy reforms. Yet the programs and research largely focus on adolescents and secondary school students and are approached in an academic rather than a practical manner. In reflecting on her secondary school experience, Imen, a student from Hammamet, noted,

> When I was in the third year I was too young to know what kind of questions to ask; I was still a child. We were learning how the egg moves through a tube. It didn't occur to me to ask questions about hymen reparation or condoms or anal sex. But now that I want to know more about these things, where am I supposed to go? Who am I supposed to talk to?

Further, sexual-health issues are tied to marriage and address sexuality as it relates to marital life. Thus these programs provide only a limited amount of information and are generally not conducive to open communication and dialogue, as Reem's secondary school experience illustrates.

> I had so many questions about pregnancy and about how sex worked, but I couldn't ask. If I asked questions, people would judge me. People would think that I wanted the information so I could do those things. So I only listened and it wasn't until I came to Tunis [for college] that I realized there were a lot of things I didn't know.

It comes as no surprise that many young women obtain information about sexual-health issues through unofficial channels. University students generally exchange information about sexuality and sexual health with friends and peers. Although this transfer of knowledge can involve relatives from the same generational cohort (cousins, sisters, and young aunts), most of this information comes from outside the family. Although in some cases this intra-generational exchange is more open than conversations with adults, it is also prone to transmit inaccurate information. Some students are well informed and can disseminate accurate and practical information about sexual health. Many others, however, propagate myths and misinformation.

University students are poorly informed about pregnancy and sexually transmitted diseases (STDs). My discussions with students indicated that although they had a great deal of basic knowledge about HIV/AIDS and contraception, they lacked a more profound understanding. For example, although all respondents cited sexual relations and fluids as a transmission route for HIV and 85 percent cited infected blood or blood products, only 11 percent also knew that HIV may be transmitted by breast milk and from a pregnant woman to her fetus. Twenty percent of the students cited incorrect routes of transmission, including kissing, casual contact, and sharing objects (spoons and glasses) with infected persons. Further, only 13 percent were able to identify an STD other than HIV; almost all of them cited syphilis.

With respect to contraception, students demonstrated a significant amount of knowledge about the types of contraception available in Tunisia; nearly 70 percent were able to name three or more types of available contraception. And though students were well informed as to where contraceptives are distributed, 60 percent incorrectly reported that unmarried women are not able to obtain contraceptives in Tunisia, and nearly as many were unable to correctly describe how at least one method of contraception works or is used.[2] Students from central and southern governorates showed lower knowledge levels than their northern, more urban counterparts. Thus, though superficial knowledge is high, more profound knowledge of importance to sexually active students is limited.

In focus group discussions centering on sexual behavior and pregnancy, students consistently revealed a lack of profound knowledge. A great deal of misinformation exists regarding both the mechanics of pregnancy and the risks associated with particular sexual behaviors. Popular inaccuracies include the belief that pregnancy requires full penetration or multiple liaisons, that the hymen serves as a barrier to both pregnancy and STD transmission, and that oral and anal intercourse are risk-free alternatives to penile-vaginal contact. Students repeatedly indicated that they had learned the information from peers, primarily through discussions with others in the university and dorms.

It would be desirable for the university student population to be better informed, since an increasing percentage of female students are sexually active. When asked to assess the level of sexual activity within the female university student population, 85 percent of the students stated that many or some female students are sexually active.[3] Only two students, both from the south, stated that there are virtually no sexually active female students. However, 44 percent stated that few to none of the sexually active women are using contraception, due to misinformation, embarrassment, a partner's refusal, and lack of access.

Students' attitudes toward premarital intercourse vary widely. I asked students how they would respond if a close friend were considering having sexual relations with her boyfriend. Forty percent stated that they would advise the friend not to engage in premarital sexual relations under any circumstance. As one student from the south remarked,

> In our religion [premarital sex] is forbidden. I would tell her not to do it. Even if the man loves her, after she sleeps with him he will leave her. He won't marry her because he will judge her, he won't be able to trust her. No man deserves a woman's virginity, it is very precious. Now there are some girls who make themselves virgins before their wedding night. I think this is very bad, it's forbidden. If my friend decided to have sex I wouldn't speak with her, I would shun her.

Approximately 45 percent of the students stated that it would be acceptable for a friend to have sexual relations before marriage as long as she was prepared for the risks, both societal and medical. Half of these students went on to say that she should only engage in sexual relations with her boyfriend if she was confident that they were going to get married. Amel, from Béja, explained,

> She has to be aware. She has to be sure that he loves her; she has to know that he will marry her. If they have sex and she gets pregnant, neither her family nor society will forgive her unless she marries this man. So if she knows this man well, if she trusts him, I think it's okay. But I would advise her to use protection. Condoms.

Finally, 15 percent of the students indicated that she could engage in sexual activity with her partner but must keep her hymen intact and thus preserve her virginity. Thus not only do female university students see themselves as a highly sexually active population, they are also becoming more accepting of premarital intercourse.

In spite of this perception of a high level of sexual activity amongst the female university student population, overwhelming social pressure against premarital sexual intercourse remains. A 1993 study of Tunisian couples concluded, "[V]irginity at marriage is still an important factor in Tunisian society, even if many young people deny it and even if many young people engage in premarital sexual relations" (Toumi-Metz 1993). Indeed, the attitudes and experiences of female students in Tunisia suggest a dissonance between sexual realities and societal expectations with regard to premarital sex. This division places significant pressure on many young women, both those who choose to abstain from sexual activity and those who engage in it. As Noura explained,

> Sex is a problem in Tunisia. It is a problem because of the dilemma that girls face. There are options, including hymen reparation, but this doesn't address the core problem. The core problem is the double standard that exists and the lack of open discussion about sexuality and women's sexual desires.

As Hager's story illustrated, many women are torn between acting on their sexual desires and adhering to social expectations. Some of those who choose not to engage in sexual relations question their attractiveness and their femininity, which harms their self-esteem. And while there is familial and societal pressure on young women to remain virgins, individual men often pressure them to be sexually active. Fétiha, a student from Gafsa, noted,

> Men want to date women who will have sex with them but they only want to marry virgins. Men break up with me because I won't sleep with them and it makes me feel awful. I feel ugly and sad. I can't concentrate on my studies. I failed my exams last year because of this. It's not fair. No one asks men if they are virgins before they get married, but for people in my town a woman's virginity is very important. I'm twenty-six years old and I'm still a virgin, but I don't want to be. I want to be able to express myself, but I can't. I think about my family and how they would respond and I just can't.

Yet in spite of the stress and depression many women go through, there are almost no counseling services dedicated to young women. Young women perceive that, in general, health service providers are unsympathetic to this dilemma, and many women continue to feel isolated. The persistent social pressure on women to remain virgins not only affects women's mental health and self-esteem, but also restricts the public discussion of sexuality and sexual behavior. As a physician working in health policy remarked, "[Female] students are sexually active. Now the average age of marriage for Tunisian women is over twenty-six. What are these girls supposed to do between the ages of fifteen and twenty-six? Many of them are going to experiment. It isn't responsible for us to just close our eyes and hope that problem will go away. It won't."

Societal expectations also place a significant psychological burden on many of the young women who decide to engage in premarital sexual activity. Indeed, as members of the Tunisian Mental Health Association wrote in 1998, "The taboo of sexuality remains effective, above all outside of the ties of marriage, evidenced by the too high frequency of suicidal conduct among female adolescents who 'sinned' and lost their virginity" (Douki 1998). The depression, anxiety, and fear associated with the loss of virginity are depicted in Samira's experience.

SAMIRA'S STORY

Samira and her boyfriend began dating in secondary school. Though they were sexually intimate, they refrained from penetrative intercourse because Samira wanted to preserve her virginity. However, one evening he penetrated her, and Samira was afraid that she had torn her hymen. She was terrified that her family would find out, so she constructed a story about falling on the lip of a toilet bowl. Her family was supportive and suspected nothing, but as a result of the incident her boyfriend broke up with her.

As Samira prepared to leave for the university, her family began to pressure her to become engaged. Her parents had already chosen a suitable man, a distant relative, who was working in Tunis. However, his family required that Samira produce a certificate of virginity before the engagement. Samira was terrified and sank into a profound depression. She had no one to confide in and she was afraid her secret would be revealed. Her mother accompanied her to the gynecologist.

Samira's first visit to a gynecologist was traumatic. The doctor refused to examine her and told her that she should come back a week before her marriage. Only then would he examine her and repair her hymen, if necessary. Samira tried to explain that she had fallen, but the doctor refused to listen and sent them out of his office. Samira began to contemplate suicide.

Samira and her mother then went to a second gynecologist, a woman, who was much more understanding. Again Samira was accompanied into the examination room by her mother, so she was unable to speak frankly. She explained that she had fallen. The gynecologist examined her and pronounced her still a virgin. She explained that Samira's hymen had suffered a small tear but that it was self-repairing and completely consistent with the accident she had described. Samira felt an incredible sense of relief. The gynecologist issued Samira a medical certificate attesting to her virginity, which her mother promptly took, and explained to Samira that she should return in the weeks before her wedding to make sure that her hymen had completely healed. If not, the doctor would be able to perform a reparation at that time. Samira became engaged later that year. She is not sure what she would have done if this doctor had not been so understanding.

The pressure on Samira to obtain a certificate of virginity is not unique. Indeed, suspicion is often cast on young women when they leave their hometowns for the university, and thus the number of university students requesting these certificates has been steadily increasing. Further, the last ten years have witnessed an increase in the demand for hymen reparations.[4] A growing number of physicians in Tunis work in the public sector but provide hymen reparations through a private-sector office, sometimes on a sliding fee scale.[5] One physician reflected on his work in this area: "Though I think it is a form of deception, I reconstruct women's hymens. I don't believe that a girl's life should be ruined because of an adventure.

Tunisian mores are conservative and there is a double standard, so I don't feel any guilt about my work."

Many young women in Tunisia seek a compromise between the desire to be sexually active and the societal pressure to remain a virgin. For some students the solution is to refrain from sexual activity that would rupture the hymen, as Miriam's remarks illustrate:

> Don't have sex. Even if you love him, even if you are sure that you are going to marry him, you must wait. What if he dies? What if something happens? What if you get pregnant? No, virginity is a gift to your husband and to your family. But that's not to say you can't do other things. You can be sexual without losing your virginity. Do not let him penetrate you, sleep with him but do not lose your virginity. Or anal sex, my friend does this with her boyfriend. You can do that and still be a virgin.

Obviously, significant risks accompany these types of sexual activity, notably of pregnancy and STD transmission. However, many female university students appear unaware of these risks. My discussions with students, both individually and in groups, revealed that they were surprised by the fact that a woman could become pregnant without full penetration. A former professor of medicine at the University of Tunis confirmed,

> I found that there was a very high level of ignorance with respect to women's bodies and reproduction, especially among young women. Girls would come to me, pregnant, without knowing how they got that way because, technically, they were still virgins. Many young women just do not know how pregnancy works and they think that you must have complete penile penetration and ejaculation to become pregnant.

There appears to be a widespread belief that the hymen acts as a barrier method of birth control. Therefore many women engaging in non-penetrative sexual activity do not use condoms or other types of contraception, which has led to increasing numbers of pregnant "technical virgins." As one student from the northwest explained,

> A good friend of mine became pregnant when she was still a virgin. She is from Gafsa and she had never learned about sexual intercourse or pregnancy. She thought that she could not become pregnant unless her hymen was broken. And she did not understand that she needed to use contraception even though she was not having full sex. She was so scared. I went with her to a private clinic to get an abortion. The doctor was very patient with her and explained how she became pregnant. I'm sure she will be more careful now, but it was awful.

Although there are numerous physicians who try to use these consultations to communicate information about sexual health, the timing of such talks makes this difficult. A gynecologist who performs private-sector hymen reparations and abortions noted,

> I find this aspect of my work [technical virgins] the most difficult. So many times educated girls have come into my office not knowing how their bodies work. I ask them who they have had intercourse with and when and they stare at me. They tell me that they have not had sex, even though they are three months pregnant. I have to coax them into giving me the full story and many of them still do not know exactly what type of act led to the pregnancy. I try to use the consultation as a way of educating the young women, but when they are scared and under pressure they do not absorb a lot of this information. I doubt that it affects their behavior.

Thus ignorance and misinformation, combined with the social pressure to remain virgins, have led to an increase in high-risk behaviors among young women.

The social pressure to refrain from premarital sexual relations also affects students' attitudes toward out-of-wedlock pregnancy. When I asked students how they would advise a friend who became pregnant when she was not married, they overwhelmingly stated that they would recommend that the friend have an abortion. Nearly 70 percent stated that she should abort the fetus under all circumstances, and an additional 11 percent stated that she should have an abortion if the father refused to marry her. Kauther, a second-year student from Bizerte, noted,

> As long as she is in her first trimester, she has to get an abortion. There is no question about this. Life in Tunisia would be too difficult as a single mother. Her boyfriend, her family, the society, no one will accept this. And it would be too difficult for the child. She has to have an abortion.

Fifteen percent of students would recommend that she carry the child to term.

Students were well informed as to where an unmarried woman could obtain an abortion in Tunisia. Eighty percent cited private clinics, 23 percent cited public health facilities, and 4 percent cited traditional healers. Only 8 percent of students were unable to name a place or believed that it was illegal for unmarried women to obtain an abortion in Tunisia. Many of the students who cited private clinics noted that though it is possible for an unmarried woman to obtain an abortion at a public health facility, they would not recommend it because they believe that unmarried women are mistreated, humiliated, or judged in public facilities. Sonia spoke from personal experience:

During my first year at university a close friend of mine became pregnant. Eight weeks into her pregnancy I went with her to get an abortion. The man was not going to marry her and she couldn't tell her family. . . . She didn't have a lot of money so we went to a public hospital. It was terrible. The staff were rude to her, they embarrassed and humiliated her. They talked about her condition and her marital status in front of other patients and amongst themselves. My friend was humiliated. In the future, I would only advise a pregnant friend to go to a private clinic, even if I had to lend her the money. She would have been treated so much better.

Students were also concerned that services in public health facilities are not confidential and thus the woman's family could learn of the abortion.

Young women's experiences with abortion indicate a great deal of misinformation regarding pregnancy. Physicians and researchers have reported that because young women do not understand the mechanics of pregnancy, they are often unaware that they have become pregnant, particularly if they have an intact hymen (Ben Rejeb 1993). In concert with shame and embarrassment, this confusion has led to women either being unable to obtain abortions or obtaining them late in the second trimester. As one woman explained,

I have a friend who did not realize she was pregnant until she was in her sixth month. I guess she was in denial. It is almost impossible to find someone to perform an abortion in Tunisia this late in the pregnancy. I encouraged her to get money together and go to a private physician. Her family would never accept her if she had the baby. She was finally able to find someone to give her the abortion, but it was very expensive.

Young women's personal experiences with abortion reveal a significant amount of confusion and fear, fear related to societal pressures for virginity and the taboo on single motherhood. Fatma's tragic story is but one example of the degree of desperation and fear some young women experience.

FATMA'S STORY

Fatma had never been to Tunis before she came there to study. When she arrived she felt lost and conflicted. She had never left her southern governorate or her conservative family before. Fatma wore traditional dresses and a head scarf, a rare form of attire for young women in Tunis. She also started to see someone. After dating for a couple of months she became pregnant. Her boyfriend would not take responsibility for the child and he refused to marry her. Fatma was desperate. She decided to have an abortion, but she didn't have the money to go to a private clinic. And she was afraid that the services in a public hospital would not be confidential and that her family would be informed of her condition. So she decided to abort the fetus herself.

Unlike some students who induce abortions with herbs or detergent, Fatma decided to use scissors. She waited until the weekend because she knew that most of the women in the dorm, including her roommates, would be home with their families. Fatma performed the abortion in her dorm room. In the process she punctured her uterus and began to hemorrhage. Another student found her body later that day, after she had bled to death.[6]

Fatma's experience dramatically illustrates how fear and misinformation contribute to high-risk activities with serious health consequences. This experience had a profound impact on other women studying at the university. As one student living in the dorm at that time noted,

> The dorm never acknowledged her death; it was as if she did not exist. Girls in the dorm were scared and it was all we talked about for weeks. No one wanted to live in the same wing as the one in which Fatma had died, like there was a curse on that part of the dorm. And [the administrators] did not do anything, they did not even offer us counseling. I think this would have been a perfect opportunity to talk about sexuality and pregnancy. There are a lot of girls here who do not even know how pregnancy works. But the university chose to ignore it. I was disgusted by the way the situation was handled so I decided to live in a private dorm the following year. A number of other students did this as well.

Many students are aware of high levels of misinformation at the university and the impact this has on student behavior. Nearly half of the surveyed students suggested that young women's health could be improved through programs designed to communicate openly about sexual health and increase student awareness.

> There are a lot of things that aren't being discussed right now. I am a journalism student and I know how important it is to communicate with people directly. But with issues involving sexuality, people don't feel comfortable talking about this publicly. Many girls at the university are becoming pregnant and contracting STDs but we don't have programs that focus on this. I think we really need them.

Efforts to make information and services more available to the university population would be overwhelmingly welcomed by female students. Making health service providers more accessible, establishing counseling services, and facilitating open discussions on issues of sexuality through health activity clubs or the dormitories are but a few of the reforms they often suggested. Many of them see programs to provide students with accurate information as ways of improving young women's health. Numerous physicians concur. One explained,

> Young women's health issues are gaining priority in Tunisia, in terms of both information and services. However, this movement is somewhat tentative because the subject is a delicate one. . . . Many of us in health promotion feel that it is important to protect young people. There are others who want to make sure that the program doesn't encourage young people to become promiscuous. But I think that a [young women's health] program is very important. . . . the curiosity about sexual issues is enormous among young people.

NOTES

I would like to thank the American Association of University Women, the American Institute for Maghrib Studies, and the Rhodes Trust for their generous funding and support of this project.
    1. "Greater Tunis" in this context refers to the governorates of Tunis, Ariana, and Ben Arrous.
    2. Students were asked to choose a method of birth control and explain how it works or is used. Twenty-five percent did not answer the question, and 32 percent incorrectly described the use of their chosen method. The remaining 43 percent were able to accurately discuss at least one method, with the majority choosing to speak about birth control pills.
    3. The majority of these students (73 percent of the total sample) stated that "many" female students were sexually active.
    4. It should be noted that "hymen reparation" is, in fact, a misnomer. Hymenoplasty is an outpatient surgery generally performed during the week prior to the wedding. The physician creates a small membrane from either hymen remnants or the posterior vaginal wall with dissolvable sutures. Upon intercourse this simulated hymen is ruptured.
    5. The reported cost of a hymen reparation ranges from forty to three hundred dinars.
    6. Fatma's story was first revealed in an interview with a student from Béja on October 21, 1999. This student was Fatma's neighbor, worked in the administrative office of the dorm, and was present when Fatma's father came to collect the body. The basic elements of the story were later confirmed in three interviews with others.

REFERENCES

Ben Rejeb, R. 1993. "Grossesse hors mariage et maternité provisoire: À propos du vécu psychologique de vingt mères célibataires." *IBLA* (revue de l'Institut des Belles Lettres Arabes) 56, no. 171: 65–72.

Douki, S., et al. 1998. "Femmes et santé mentale." Paper presented at the Seminaire sur Femme, Santé Mentale et Société, Tunis, March 28.

Toumi-Metz, L. 1993. "Le couple tunisien." Paper presented at the Seminaire de Sexologie Humaine et de Gynecologie Psycho-Somatique, Fort de France, Martinique, February 16–21.

10. A Thorny Side of Marriage in Iran

Erika Friedl

Until recently in Iran a twenty-year-old unmarried girl was said to be an old maid. The remark implied that something was wrong either with her or with her parents, who were shirking the important responsibility of providing their children with spouses in a timely manner. "Timely" meant to make a daughter a bride when she was around thirteen at the latest, shortly after or even before the onset of puberty. At around that time girls were considered to be "ripe," like ripe fruit, ready for adult responsibilities. Unmarried, they soon would dry up or spoil. However this custom may have developed, it necessitated that adults arrange marriages: a ten-year-old girl cannot possibly decide whom to marry, and neither can a very young man. In fact, child-betrothals were quite common. Because of the top-heavy male-female ratio in Iran, the difference in marriage age between spouses tended to be large. In the Iranian village I have studied for the past thirty-five years, for example, parents frequently looked for a future bride for their teenage sons among the girl toddlers and sought to arrange a betrothal early, for there might not be a girl left for their son if they waited too long.

According to the government census, there still is a slight surplus of men in Iran in all age groups. Usually when there is a surplus of men, women's marriage age drops. Nevertheless, over the past two decades more and more young men and women have married late, in their thirties, or have not married at all. More and more demand a voice in whom they are going to marry, or else they choose a marriage partner themselves. More and more young unmarried women are living not at home but in dormitories as students or, if they are working, on their own or with female roommates. Finally, more and more young women who don't have jobs live at home with their parents throughout their teens and beyond. Divorce is becoming more frequent, as well. These trends worry the older folks; they rightly see in them a profound shift in the meaning of marriage, even a crisis in what being a woman is all about. They also worry the young people themselves, but for different reasons.

One of the reasons for the deferment of marriage in Iran lies in the depressed economy, with its high inflation and very high rate of unemployment, especially among young people. Young men cannot provide for a wife and children. In earlier times, when sons brought their wives to live in the paternal household and worked alongside their brothers and their father, often as farmers, the costs of living were shared. Now, with households predominantly neolocal (newly founded at marriage), a young husband needs to get bread on the table by his own efforts alone, and if his income is insufficient he cannot afford a family—he will not even find a woman willing to marry him. In addition, wedding expenses have become so great that years may go by before a young man has the financial power to set a wedding date, even if his father and brothers are pitching in, and even if he goes deeply into debt. A thirty-two-year-old government employee in a small town, with an annual salary of about 1.2 million *toman* (in 2000, this was about US$1,500) planned to spend over two million toman for his wedding. He had already been forced to postpone the wedding for two years because inflation meant that prices were rising faster than he could save and borrow money.

In the urban middle class, which sets trends often later followed in the countryside, a proper wedding in a teacher's family cost nearly one and one-half years' salary in 2000. Just getting glittery makeup and a fluffy hairdo at the beautician's, renting a lacy white bridal gown, and hiring a professional to video the ceremony may cost up to six weeks' salary. But even in Iran people must keep up with the Joneses, and so a young man has very little choice in the matter: either the wedding is done properly or it is not, and if it is not, a social price has to be paid. The white gown, by the way, is a fairly recent import from the West. People explained that their expatriate relatives and foreign movies and television shows (which are widely available in Iran) are teaching them how to turn a plain girl into a beautiful bride. In the village a young woman expressed it differently: "The paint on her face was so thick that her own mother didn't recognize her," she said of a cousin.

As if this development were not financially worrisome enough, events leading up to the wedding that were formerly handled quietly and cheaply increasingly have to be honored with gifts and feasts in towns and villages alike. For example, the writing and signing of the ʿaqd, the marriage contract, in which conditions of the marriage and allowable reasons for divorce are spelled out, formerly was part of the wedding, but now it can happen any time after the engagement and is more and more often elaborated into a feast with scores of guests.

But a weak economy and rising expectations are not the only aspects of the crisis of marriage Iranians talk about. There is another, more complex aspect to consider, which has to do with gender philosophy.

Members of the urban upper middle classes in Iran had already started to change marriage customs and expectations of marriage two generations before the revolution of 1979. These classes modeled their social relations after those they saw in the European and U.S. middle class. They included what we would call emancipatory husband-wife relationships in which both partners, the husband and the wife, are more or less equal and independent. Housework was done by servants; wives spent their own money, especially if they were working, without consulting their husbands; children were sent to boarding schools or brought up by nannies; women could travel; and both men and women had a say in whom they were going to marry. For other Iranians, conditions of marriage started to change with the rapid so-called modernization of the country that began in 1970: the proliferation of schools, the opening of universities to women of all walks of life, the expansion of public transportation, the opening of the job market to women, and a marked shift in parents' attitudes toward children. In the wake of development the marriage age for girls rose almost everywhere to about sixteen before the Revolution, and it has reached that level again and is still rising in the Islamic Republic after making a steep dip right after the Revolution. (The legal minimum marriage age for girls in Iran is nine, according to Islamic law. The wisdom of this law is increasingly debated and doubted in Iran.)

The increase in marriage age led to the unprecedented appearance of a completely new social category, that of unmarried female teenagers who live at home and help their own mothers rather than being married, living with their in-laws, and being at the beck and call of their husbands and their mothers-in-law. Older married women remember without fondness the days when they worked "like servants" in their in-laws' house, enduring hard work, unwanted sex, insufficient food, and many pregnancies while still in their teens. But for all its advantages this new stage in a woman's life cycle has a downside. It is so new that no culturally and socially acceptable and meaningful way of living has yet developed for these young women. While their teenage brothers have the run of their village or town, the young women cannot go out unchaperoned without risking their reputation; they have no income and are therefore entirely dependent on the generosity of their father and brothers; they have very little to do at home because housework is shared among all female family members; their social circle is extremely limited; and outside work is not to be had. Most of them simply sit, bored, in front of the television. They "sit at home waiting for a good suitor," people say. And as the days of early arranged marriages are over in most families, this "waiting for a suitor" is more dependent on chance than ever before.

Young women who go to school and aspire to higher education and a profession have the burden of escaping unwanted suitors, who might derail their education by insisting on the wedding as soon as possible and then on full-time housekeeping services, no matter what they might have promised before the marriage. "My right to finish high school is even in the marriage contract," a young wife said bitterly, "but my husband and his family did not honor it. As soon as I was married they turned over the whole household to me because my mother-in-law was ill, and so I had to quit school." There are so many stories circulating in Iran on this theme that marriage, for young women, is often linked with abandoning studies, and seems to mean putting an end to any chance of "getting somewhere" or gaining "freedom" through formal education, as people say. Study and marriage are seen as an either/or proposition. The mother of a seventeen-year-old high school student who was not doing well in school angrily said, "She gets bad grades in school but she doesn't have a suitor either! What are we going to do with her?" Young women who are considered beautiful have the opposite problem: they have a hard time staying unspoken-for long enough to get through high school and a university curriculum. They are married out of the classroom to their cousins, to their brothers' friends, to male teachers, to young men who hear of their beauty through female relatives, to young men who glimpse them by chance in the street or in somebody's house. "By the time I met girls at the university, all the pretty ones were long gone," complained a male student. And a beautiful village woman in eleventh grade said, "Boys ogle, they phone, they send messages through my little brother. I don't go out at all any more, only to school, for fear that a dirty-minded guy will tell his mother about me and she will come here as a matchmaker. I want to finish high school."

A young woman has the right to reject a proposal of marriage. But if she rejects—and thereby humiliates—too many suitors she will scare the good ones away and in the end will be an "old maid" or will have to settle for an undesirable husband, one who has only a small income or is not handsome or comes from an unimportant family. In such a case, her own family might not even back her up. A thirty-year-old professional single woman in a small town who was getting impatient with what she called her own choosiness was considering the proposal of a somewhat younger man from outside the town who had a manual, but well-paying, job. Her brothers and sisters objected vehemently on grounds of social incompatibility.

Professional young women who earn their own money and probably have risen above their families in terms of status now tend to take matters of marriage more into their own hands. Although I have learned of only a few cases where a woman actually looked for a husband and proposed— not directly to him, but in one case through his mother, and in another through his sister—quite a few got acquainted with their future husbands through their work or, more likely, through the efforts of a friend or a co-worker. To take the initiative in dating is still out of the question for most young Iranian women, especially the millions living in small towns and villages, as are premarital sexual relations. Direct contacts are often established via the telephone. In the posh quarters of Tehran the game of exchanging telephone numbers in cars and taxis and then of checking each other out over the phone has become a popular sport among young people. It does have its advantages. A busy young woman physician said, "A woman patient kept asking me to give her son, who is also a physician, a chance as a suitor. I finally gave her my phone number, and he called. His first question was, 'Well, Doctor Amini, how good is your cooking?' and I said, 'What?! Are you in the market for a cook?' and slammed the phone down. That's what I have to put up with! At least I didn't waste much time on him."

Six short cases will illustrate various instances of young women who remain unmarried until they are "old and dry."

- I met Amene, a seamstress from a small town in southern Iran, when she was in her mid-twenties. She was supporting her father financially and also running a six-person household: her mother and a widowed aunt were ill, her father feeble, her youngest brother timid, and his new wife shy and inexperienced. She felt that the household would break down if she moved away. But to bring a husband to her house was unthinkable—no honorable man would consent to such an arrangement. By the time she was thirty-seven, however, her parents and aunt had died; her brother had assumed household management duties, and her sister-in-law now resented what she called Amene's "bossiness." Amene had lost her reason for staying at home—helping her family—and so she married a well-to-do widower in Tehran, far away from her brother's now inhospitable house.
- Sima remained unspoken-for during her teens in order to study. This was hard because she is considered extraordinarily beautiful and had "suitors banging on our door every day," says her mother. During her last year in high school, however, her mother became nervous about her old-maid status and paraded suitable young men for her to choose from. By then Sima's cousin Zahra, a very talented young woman who on her own and over the objections of her mother had decided to get married when she was a twenty-one-year-old student, was struggling with her household, two babies, and a demanding husband while trying to finish medical school. Her widely discussed predicament served as a warning to Sima. In fact, so determined did Sima become to avoid the matrimonial pitfall that she summarily refused all advances. "Iranian husbands are too selfish and demanding for me," she said. At the age of twenty-seven she is working as a physician and living at home.
- Maryam is a twenty-five-year-old graduate student from a prominent, religiously conservative family of teachers in a small town. Her elder sister was married against her will and became a mother at the

age of seventeen, and despite being very bright only managed enough higher education to become a grade school teacher. Even this minor achievement brought her great hardship, a long bout of depression, and ill health, according to Maryam. Maryam's mother feels she committed a sin by forcing her daughter into marriage early. She now is determined to spare her second daughter this hardship, although Maryam had "a dozen" suitors from the best families and it was socially awkward for her father to refuse them. Now word has spread that Maryam is "not for sale." Maryam's brothers say that this means that she won't find a husband at all and will die an ugly dried-up apricot. Maryam is not worried. "We will see what God has in mind for me," she said. At the university she lives in a dormitory for women students, closely watched and chaperoned, and this is just as well: she feels safe that way, she said, because otherwise men would make life very uncomfortable for the girls—men are that way. Besides, most of her female classmates are in the same position as she is—unmarried, even unspoken-for—and are having a good time, carefree and without a worry, while those who are married are harried, juggling husbands, in-laws, household duties, and studies.

• Fateme, Hakime, and Mina are high school teachers, all in their late twenties, living in a town far away from their own families. They met in the school where they are teaching and decided to rent an apartment together to share costs. The apartment consists of two small, dingy rooms and is ill equipped. The three women, however, are glad to have it because it gives them "freedom." Rooming together means that they can chaperone each other and thus prevent gossip. They go out only in pairs, but they pointed out that they go out whenever and wherever they want (within reason), without having to ask a husband's or father's permission. They explained their unmarried status as "fate," which includes their refusal of several suitors they did not think good enough. "Men want from a wife services and sex. Women are much better off staying single and working for a living," they declared. But their salaries are too small to make independent life possible—they have to pool their resources to make ends meet. All three said that their parents were understanding enough not to force them into marriage but that they were unhappy with their daughters' living far away from home. One mentioned a family home so crowded that it is impossible for her to move back. The others said that in their home towns they would not have any freedom of movement and would be gossiped about.

• Leila, twenty-eight, is working as an engineer with a fairly good salary, several hours away from her hometown. Her father insisted on the best possible education for all his seven children, sons and daughters, and went deep into debt in order to make this possible. He also alienated many local families by refusing proposals of marriage for his daughters in order to prevent the girls from becoming mired in homemaking and childrearing before they had, in his words, "amounted to something." For a few years around the age of twenty, Leila was unhappy about her spinster status, about the gossip and the taunts. When she was at home she hardly ever left the house. She remembers crying bitterly at the wedding of a cousin six years her junior. This cousin now has three children, while Leila isn't even married. But the title by which she is addressed, "Madam Engineer," has replaced all references to dried-up prunes and old hags, and the financial and social freedom the title implies compensate for her spinsterhood. Leila wants children, though, and says she wouldn't mind a "good" husband, but she won't compromise her standards.

- Masume broke off an engagement she had agreed to in twelfth grade—she was "too dumb then to know any better," she said—when on closer inspection she found many faults with the young man and his family. Ten years later, working as a college teacher in a city, she met and came to like the brother of her closest girlfriend, a well-to-do businessman, who was unhappily married and proposed to her with the promise to divorce his wife. After serious and lengthy deliberations on the pros and cons she decided against it. "All my friends and relatives were relieved," she said. All had distrusted the man's promise to divorce his wife and were afraid she might end up being a second wife in a polygynous household. She, too, is waiting to see what fate has in store for her.

What do these cases tell us about how young women have come to see marriage?

The rising number of unmarried women challenges several traditional popular assumptions about women and matrimony. These are, first, that women's uncontrolled sexuality will become a force that destroys the community—so God ordered early marriage for women in order to prevent this and to promote order in the world. Second, that women's moral and intellectual fiber is weaker than men's—God provided marriage for women's protection. Third, that women naturally long for children and a husband.

The young women I talked to unanimously declared that sexual urges were not a big deal at all; that, in fact, women's desires are much easier to control than are men's. Yet, women say, men always had to wait longer for marriage than girls, which means that they had to deny their desires much longer, and that apparently didn't hurt them. Young women said that they worry about marriage, the likelihood of getting a "good-looking, tall, rich" husband, but that sexual deprivation is a very minor irritant in their lives as single women. Sexual urges are exaggerated by moralists, they said. For years dormitory managers all over Iran were said to mix camphor into cafeteria food in order to diminish sexual urges in their students. Although we could not confirm this rumor, the students believe it.

The traditional beliefs about female sexual desire, however, together with the theory of a natural and general female weakness of rational mind, are used to keep unmarried young women under tight social control. In most places in Iran a wise unmarried woman will not go out alone unnecessarily, speak to strange men, dress provocatively, or maintain eye contact with men. Girls walk to and from school in groups; dormitories have guards around the clock and are locked at 9 P.M., and for good reasons. Women, especially young women, out alone are routinely harassed. A thirty-year-old single woman in Tehran said, "I leave for work in the morning only after my downstairs neighbor has left because if he hears me on the stairs he opens his door and makes advances at me." Women say that restrictions such as segregated seating on overland buses, and even the long cloak or a veil-wrap, help them to go about their business unmolested. Men's desires, women conclude, are the problem, not women's desires. Men's moral fiber is weak, not women's. Women no longer accept beliefs about their sexuality as a good reason for early marriage. Their successes in school, where they perform better than their brothers, disprove the weak-intellect argument. It is clear, women say, that a bright and able woman does not need to get married to secure her survival.

The (supposedly natural) longing for children can easily become an obsession in a social environment that contains so many. (In Iran, 50 percent of the population is under the age of sixteen.) To see sisters and cousins becoming pregnant and cradling their babies is hard for unmarried young women. Yet several young women I know declared that children are such a burden that they wanted none, or one at the most. One, a physician who married at the age of thirty-four, successfully insisted on remaining childless as a condition of marriage. She did not want to interrupt or curtail her work, she said. An unmarried professional woman in her forties said that she remained single because none of her suitors had agreed to a no-children stipulation in the marriage contract.

Modernization has brought new notions about children's needs and child development that make proper child care much more time-consuming and expensive than it was a generation or two ago, even in villages. In upwardly mobile families children are said to need good food, good clothes, entertainment and educational devices, ample personal space, a good (and expensive) education, and leisure to study. No longer are children supposed to be servants for the adults in the house. It is chic now to have a small family and to attend to the children lavishly. For young mothers, having either many children ill-kept or a few children well-kept means the same amount of engagement: in the absence of help with housework, and given the scarcity and reportedly low quality of paid child care in Iran, children and outside work are conflicting demands. Indeed, relatively few Iranian women participate in the labor market. Female students' main reason for deferring marriage until they have finished their studies is to avoid the burden of child care. Many broken engagements are blamed on the delaying tactics of the girl's family. "Girls who study are haughty and don't want a family," young men complain. Such opinions are based on the tacit expectation that a normal woman will get pregnant soon after marriage. Postponement of the first pregnancy is nearly unheard-of even in the urban middle class and among physicians, although birth control devices are available freely.

Folk psychology insists on young women's innate desire for a husband at the same time that it makes a contradictory but almost universal claim of young women's distaste for and fear of men. Both attitudes can be mobilized to explain particular conditions. For example, a young, hardworking, unmarried village woman's frequent bouts of depression were ascribed by her neighbors to a presumed unfulfilled wish for a husband and children, while an uncommonly cheerful twenty-year-old unmarried woman in the same village declared that her good mood was due to the fact that she did not have to be a servant to some "disgusting, ill-tempered husband" but was "free" in her father's friendly house.

For most young women in Iran, marriage implies doing nearly all housework unaided (save for appliances in well-appointed households), catering to the husband as a matter of course, preparing time-consuming meals daily, being dependent on the reasonableness and generosity of the husband in regard to provisions and social life, and being in danger—however remote it is in reality—of being saddled with a co-wife, being divorced, being trapped. When in-laws reside nearby, responsibilities and restraints can easily double. A sixteen-year-old girl said, "I have not seen my married sister in ten months because her in-laws won't let her out of the house. And now one of their relatives wants to marry me—ha! I am not going there." Under such circumstances marriage becomes a chore, if not a threat, and avoiding suitors becomes a strategy for self-preservation. Stories of broken promises of help with housework, of time for study, and of travel, as well as stories of outright mistreatment, are so familiar by now that they turn up in stories, in newspapers, and in television shows, not to mention family courts. "Marriage is good and necessary," said an older married woman (who got married at the age of ten), "but it has a thorny side to it. In my generation we didn't know and we didn't have a choice. Nowadays girls know and they do have a choice."

Although Iran has no official forum for rethinking restrictive assumptions about men's and women's nature and about marriage, these assumptions have come under scrutiny. Despite harassment in the streets by men, pressure at home to get married, the need for circumspection in public, sexual urges, and the wish for children, young women now press for what we would call "autonomy" and they call "freedom," a freedom they don't easily find in marriage. The casting of marriage as confinement and as antithetical to work and study and to "getting somewhere," as they say, amounts to a critique from within of this fundamental institution. This trend toward a critical evaluation of women's fate, as it were, meets with resistance from a great many conservative men and women, who see it as the beginning of the end of life as they think it ought to be lived. But it also meets with hopeful encouragement from many others, who say that their religion implies equality of the sexes and liberation from unnecessarily confining marital practices.

11. Harasiis Marriage, Divorce, and Companionship

Dawn Chatty

Marriage is almost universal in the Middle East. It is valued as a source of company, as the means of forming a family and having children, and as a resource for managing all the demands of life. If you think it is difficult to be on your own in the West, among laundromats, microwaves, and take-out, try it in the Middle East, where you wash heavy cotton sheets in bathtubs and cook meals from scratch. A solitary individual in the Middle East finds it difficult to survive, so those who are single, divorced, or widowed must try to find a niche among relatives with whom they can share homemaking tasks and income. Even today, and even in large cities, it is not common for individuals to live alone. Divorce is permitted by Islam, although it is not recommended. Divorce rates in the Middle East are far below those in the West (national rates in Egypt and Syria run just over one divorce per thousand married couples annually; the U.S. rate is about four times as high). Marriage between cousins has traditionally been preferred because it keeps resources within the larger family. It also allows the bride to retain the protection of her birth family, which can continue to watch out for her interests. Families avoid marrying their daughters to strangers who may not protect her well. —Eds.

Men and women among the Harasiis tribe in the central desert of Oman face the same difficulties in their relationships to each other as do people anywhere else in the Muslim world. Marriages are often arranged to link families together, and weddings of first and second cousins are very common. The primary aim of such arrangements is childrearing and companionship. These marriages bring together not only the individual man and woman but also their entire families. The individual thus has the support of an extended kin group in times of crisis, discord, and strife. The

Harasiis' solutions to conflict, breakup, and reconciliation are in keeping with the barriers and limitations which the physical environment they inhabit imposes upon them: flexibility and adaptation, individuality and compromise.

For most of the 1980s and early 1990s, I lived and worked among the Harasiis, a nomadic pastoral tribe of about three thousand people inhabiting the Jiddat-il-Harasiis, the central desert of Oman, which borders the great Rub^c-al-Khali (Empty Quarter) of Arabia (Chatty 1996). The Harasiis survive in this desolate land by raising herds of camels and goats, and rely on the herds' milk for most of their sustenance. Men own and look after the herds of camels, and women own and manage the goats. Only men are permitted to milk camels, although both men and women milk the goats. Occasionally a woman inherits a camel or two from her father or another male relative, which she then gives to a man to herd and look after for her.

From 1981 to 1983 I had as my assistants a young Peace Corps couple, and the three of us, along with our Harasiis guide and driver, moved continuously, visiting one family campsite after another in the vast forty-thousand-square-kilometer rock and gravel plain. We often tried to camp on our own a short distance from a family, but these efforts were firmly disallowed time and time again. We would be brought into the campsite and shown where to set down our sleeping bags, close to the campfire. Within a few months of this routine, we knew the families well and moved about with an ease that belied our discomfort at the vastness and emptiness of the land the Harasiis called home.

One late afternoon as our two four-wheel-drive vehicles approached the campsite of Merzooq, one of the most respected Harasiis elders, we came upon Samgha, the young wife of Merzooq's son Luwayhi. She was with her small herd of forty goats. It was an odd time to be taking goats out to graze. Most Harasiis would be calling the goats to come back to the campsites for water and some feed supplements at this time of day. We stopped and asked her how she was and where she was going. "Home," she said. "To my father's home." A bit surprised by this short, terse statement, we didn't ask any more and bid her a safe journey. It was bound to be a walk of several hours, if she was lucky. We carried on slowly to the campsite she had just left. On arrival we turned off our engines, set down our sleeping kit, and then joined the few adults sitting in the shade of a parked vehicle. A subdued family awaited our news.

Merzooq and Luwayhi greeted us, as did Luwayhi's mother. Had we passed by Samgha, they asked? Had Samgha told us anything? We recounted the events of the past half hour and asked them to tell us what was going on. Why was Samgha walking her goats away from the campsite at a time when she should be bringing them in? Did she make any explanations before she set out on what was going to be a walk of several hours? Merzooq's wife explained to us that she was leaving her husband. She was initiating a divorce proceeding. By taking her goats and walking back home she was signaling her wish to end the marriage. It was now up to Luwayhi and his father to try to persuade her to come back. If they did nothing they would be signaling that they agreed the divorce should be final. However, if in a few days' time they set out to visit Samgha and her father, Mohammed, at their home, then a reconciliation might be begun.

Merzooq was not only Samgha's father-in-law; he was also her uncle. Merzooq and Mohammed were brothers and they had married their children to each other. Labeled "parallel-cousin marriage" in the West, this *bint amm* (daughter of uncle) arrangement is very popular in the Middle East, among nomadic pastoral tribes in particular (Barth 1973; Kressel 1986; Murphy and Kasdan 1959). The Harasiis give a number of reasons for preferring this form of marriage: to keep property and capital within the patrilineal family; to know what kind of person one's family is taking in; and to provide better security for the bride, since her father-in-law is also her uncle. Samgha and Luwayhi were first cousins who had known each other their entire life. Their fathers had camped close together whenever possible and helped each other look after their herds of camels, and their wives and children worked the goat herds together. When grazing was plentiful, the two camps were often less than ten kilometers apart. Since the appearance of four-wheel-drive vehicles on the Jiddat in the mid-1970s, however, they occasionally camped some distance apart in their search for natural graze for their livestock. Fortunately for Samgha, her decision to leave with her goats and return to her father was made at a time when the campsites were only several hours' walk (or a half-hour's drive) across the Jiddat.

Merzooq waited a few days before visiting his brother Mohammed to discuss a reconciliation between Samgha and Luwayhi. These two young people had only been married a few months and had no children, nor did Samgha appear to be pregnant. Before he left to attempt to heal this rift, I asked Merzooq what he thought were his chances of success. "Not good," he said. "Not good, because she has not stayed long enough with Luwayhi to come to know him and feel contented with him. They are cousins, they know each other well, but only on the outside. The deeper knowledge has not yet been made." Merzooq spent a week with his brother and with Samgha. He spoke with her and listened to what she had to say. He spoke with his brother and heard him out, as well. And at the end of the week he returned to his home alone. Samgha had refused to return. She did not wish to be Luwayhi's wife any longer.

We often visited Merzooq's campsite and saw Luwayhi there too. As the oldest son, he was the most physically able and was always busy bringing water in tankers to the campsite, looking after the herds of camels, gathering up goat manure to sell in the desert border towns. He was his father's right-hand man. And, for months, he remained hopeful that Samgha would change her mind and return to him.

When we visited Mohammed's campsite we would also sit and talk with Samgha in the evenings when she had returned from herding her goats and those of her mother. Samgha was not averse to talking about her cousin. He was a nice enough person, she said, but she didn't want to live with him. She made no effort to cast any doubts upon his character, or to tell any tales of abuse. It seemed that we, the outsiders, were more interested in finding a reason for her return home than her family. They accepted her return with equanimity and got on with their business. One day, when she was ready, they all said, she would marry again and have children.

For the first few months after her return there was a quiet expectation in both families that she might be pregnant and her action in returning to her natal home was somehow related to a confusion she might have felt in such a state. But once it was established that she was not expecting a child, and her period of waiting was over (in Islam, a waiting period of four months is expected of a divorcée or widow before remarrying), her actions were accepted. She was not chided, nor was there any sense that she was somehow a used commodity.

Within a year she married again, this time successfully. She remained in her father's home for the first three years of this new marriage, before moving into her husband's family's camp. There she had children. Once they were old enough to start helping with some of the herding tasks, Samgha and her second husband set up their own household, which moved location in close association with her husband's extended family group.

Samgha's marriages reflect two very common patterns among the Harasiis: cousin marriage and delayed separation from natal households. One common feature of marriage to the very young bride—among the Harasiis girls are often engaged, given a face mask, and married at puberty, around age fourteen—is a form of "bride service." The family of a very young bride often insists that she remain in her natal family, with the groom coming to visit and provide services to the family regularly, helping to look after the family's herds, providing it with water, or bringing vital supplies from the distant towns. Such bride service often lasts for four or five years, after which time the young wife is expected to become pregnant with her first child. During the 1980s, I only once came across a case of a young bride's becoming pregnant before it was socially considered appropriate. This was talked about at numerous evening campfires throughout the Jiddat-il-Harasiis, with a certain amount of sniggering by the older generation. The mature husband who was taking this young girl as his second wife—a very rare occurrence among the Harasiis—was considered to have acted inappropriately, showing impatience and lack of respect.

The Harasiis maintain that an extended period of bride service is very important to make the bride feel confident and to give her time to learn all the additional skills she will need to run her own home. At the same time, the Harasiis are protecting the interests of the young bride vis-à-vis the groom. While the couple learn to interact and live together, the bride has her own family around her to help her through any difficulties and to give her the support she may need. Only as the couple begin to raise children and they, in turn, begin to provide some help with the daily chores does the new nuclear family consider splitting off and either joining the husband's extended family or setting up on its own with another elderly relative. Once she has left to join her husband's family or to set up on her own, the Harasiis wife needs to be totally self-sufficient and confident that she can cope with all the demands which a young family, a growing herd of goats, and an inhospitable and harsh physical environment may demand of her.

Cousin marriage, bride service, and delayed separation from the natal home are all common features of Harasiis society. These institutions serve to help men and women establish long-lasting relationships within which to raise their families and live out their lives. They provide the young bride with the protection, support, and companionship she requires until she is able to do so for others younger or less experienced than herself. They guide the young groom into his role as husband, father, and companion. In the vast, wide-open spaces of the Jiddat, living within a large extended family with many visitors and kin is an important survival strategy. Such an existence requires tolerance, adaptability, and flexibility in order to reduce conflict, and the Harasiis almost always try to reconcile misunderstandings.

Polygyny, marriage to several wives at once, is permitted in Islam but rarely practiced among the Harasiis. Considerations of survival, rather than any religious or ethical consideration, keep the Harasiis to one spouse at a time, or serial monogamy. The only case of polygyny that I recorded in the early period of my fieldwork was one in which the first wife had been unable to conceive. A second wife was taken, who conceived a number of children. The first wife remained within the household and became a herbalist. She provided the family with medicinal treatments and soon became renowned throughout the area as a healer. In more recent years, a few older and wealthy Harasiis men have begun to take much younger second wives. For the most part they are establishing separate family units, and they hire laborers to help each unit manage in the unforgiving environment of the Jiddat.

The solitary individual cannot survive in the Jiddat-il-Harasiis. Hence the separated, divorced, or widowed person is quickly assisted in finding new conjugal arrangements or in joining an existing extended family. Divorced or widowed men and women rarely remain on their own. Remarriage or cohabitation is the rule rather than the exception. It happens that occasionally an unlucky man or woman will have had three or four spouses in succession. In cases where children are born to these serial marriages, the mother's name becomes an important part of the children's. For example, Salim bin Hamad (Salim the son of Hamad—the father's name) would also be known as Salim bin Huweila (Salim the son of Huweila—the mother's name). This device, quite common in the Jiddat-il-Harasiis, is an indicator of the flexibility and adaptability of conjugal relations among the Harasiis. It is also a testimony to the extreme harshness of the physical environment and the all-too-common early deaths of Harasiis adults. We discovered, when trying to make out the kinship ties which bound households together, that extended family groups in the Jiddat often included long-term, unrelated visitors. Most of these visitors were older men who had never married or whose offspring had emigrated or died young. The local gold dealer was one such guest whom we got to know well. He was staying with a family we were visiting and we noticed him because he couldn't be parted from the pink acrylic blanket that he kept beside him at all times, in his special place by the campfire. It was filled with gold, we were told. He made the circuit, our host informed us, traveling slowly around the Harasiis campsites, delivering gold ordered on previous trips and taking new orders and payment. He was never sure where he would be going next or how long it would take him, since his progress depended entirely upon the movements of others. Over the year he would move among various Harasiis households, make a trip to the gold *suqs* (markets) of Dubai, and then return to continue his slow amble among families living in the Jiddat.

Occasionally we came across other old men, many very weak and hardly able to move. One man was a mute who had never married and had spent his entire life looking after the camel herds of his brothers. Now he moved from one household to another as a guest rather than a family member. Another was a widower whose two sons had emigrated to the United Arab Emirates. He didn't want to join them there and so he moved from one family to another, staying a few months or until transportation could be arranged to carry him to another willing host.

Only once did we come across a very old woman staying at a campsite made up of people unrelated to her. She had married and raised two children, but they had died and she was now on her own, too feeble to look after herself or her herd of goats. Her vision was very limited and she wore glasses which magnified her eyes and made it impossible for her to wear a face mask. She was perhaps the only unmasked woman on the Jiddat (for the importance of face masking, see Chatty 1997). She stayed with families for as long as they would have her before being moved on. Her survival depended upon such hospitality and generosity.

Harasiis men and women face the same problems of existence as any other society in the Muslim world. This small population of about 250 extended family units spread out over an area the size of Scotland has learned, however, to modify and adapt institutions in order to survive in the harsh and hostile physical environment of the Jiddat-il-Harasiis. Cooperation, support, and flexibility are the keys to the ways in which the Harasiis manage their marriages, divorces, and need for companionship. Relations between men and women, nurtured and strengthened by institutions such as cousin marriage, bride service, and delayed separation from the natal family, help explain the ways in which living units are formed, structured, and recreated to accommodate the births and deaths of new members of their society.

REFERENCES

Barth, Fredrik. 1973. "Descent and Marriage Reconsidered." In *The Character of Kinship*, ed. Jack Goody, 3–19. Cambridge: Cambridge University Press.
Chatty, Dawn. 1996. *Mobile Pastoralists: Development Planning and Social Change in Oman*. New York: Columbia University Press.
———. 1997. "The Burqa Face Cover: An Aspect of Dress in Southeastern Arabia." In *Languages of Dress in the Middle East*, ed. Nancy Lindisfarne-Tapper and Bruce Ingham, 127–48. London: Curzon Press.
Kressel, Gideon. 1986. "Prescriptive Patrilateral Parallel Cousin Marriage: The Perspective of the Bride's Father and Brothers." *Ethnology* 25, no. 3 (July): 163–80.
Murphy, Robert, and Leonard Kasdan. 1959. "The Structure of Parallel Cousin Marriage." *American Anthropologist* 61 (February): 17–29.

12. Oil, Fertility, and Women's Status in Oman

Christine Eickelman

Fertility has traditionally been highly valued in the Middle East. A woman's social identity is derived from bearing children, especially male children. Social events marking childbirth encompass all parts of life. Women visit each other and sell and buy perfume, clothes, and kitchen utensils. They compete for the largest number of visitors, who all bring gifts—usually coffee and fruit, which are served to subsequent guests. The present population explosion in the Sultanate of Oman is due to people's conscious choices as well as the decline in infant mortality. Oil wealth has led to considerable social mobility, and the cultural emphasis on women's fertility and hospitality has transformed women's postpartum visits into a means of testing the social order and building a public image. Because families are more dispersed than formerly, public transportation is not dependable, and individuals' time is taken up with work, children's school needs, and other tasks, visiting is less common and visits are shorter. But the pattern of women's visits is still an invaluable source of information on shifts in household status. —Eds.

The birth rate in the Sultanate of Oman has soared since the 1970s, and is now one of the highest in the world. Omani women bear on average 7.1 children (Population Reference Bureau 2000). The climbing birth rate is linked to the oil economy. New economic opportunities, social mobility, improved health care, and a cultural role for women that links fertility and hospitality are some of the factors that are contributing indirectly to the present population explosion.

When the present ruler of Oman, Sultan Qaboos, came to power in 1970, he used oil revenues for economic development and rapidly transformed

An earlier version of parts of this chapter appeared as "Fertility and Social Change in Oman: Women's Perspectives," *The Middle East Journal* 47, no. 4 (1993): 652–66.

both the country's landscape and virtually all aspects of its citizens' lives. Within less than thirty years, public education and health care became available in all parts of the country. A network of paved roads linked regional centers to the capital area and other parts of the Arab Gulf. Electricity, piped water, modern housing, telephones, televisions, cars, banks, computers, and shopping malls transformed everyday life.

Before 1970, many Omani men worked outside the country, often illegally, in Kuwait, Saudi Arabia, and the United Arab Emirates. After 1970, they sought jobs as drivers and guards in the rapidly expanding government bureaucracy, police force, and army of their own country and, more recently, in the private sector. Some men moved their families close to their work in the capital area, but a more common pattern was for a husband to leave his wife and children in the various oasis communities of the country and to commute back on weekends, an arrangement that enabled women to maintain the multiple overlapping social ties that linked families together in their home communities.

A society's past and its values affect the ways its members respond to economic and social transformations, and the effects of economic development cannot be reduced to statistics on employment and education. Until the mid-twentieth century, virtually all aspects of peoples' lives in inner Oman revolved around the tribe. A tribal elite monopolized economic and political resources as well as religious learning. Everyone else was linked to the tribal elite by patron-client ties, which afforded them protection.

After 1970, the provision of jobs and increased literacy led to considerable social mobility. People were no longer solely dependent on tribal elites for protection, and they developed new social aspirations and perceptions of relationships. Social mobility is a state of mind, a process, that cannot be measured by a single factor and that involves all adult men and women of a family cluster working as a unit. In post-1970 Oman, social mobility depended upon acquiring an education, obtaining a good government job, having a lot of children, having a wide network of acquaintances, providing favors and services to the less fortunate, and ensuring that one's family cluster had a reputation for being large, cohesive, economically autonomous, generous, and hospitable. Before that time, only the tribal elite could successfully present themselves as possessing all these qualities. The present baby boom in Oman needs to be understood within this climate of intensive social competition, image-building, and transformation of social expectations.

THE IMPACT OF TIME

My husband and young daughter and I first lived in al-Hamra, an oasis in the interior of Oman, in 1979–80, when oil revenues were just beginning to transform the social and geographical landscape. When we returned with our two children for a visit to the oasis in the spring of 1988, the change that surprised me the most was how large families had become. The fact that both our daughters are adopted and their features do not resemble ours made it easy to begin discussions of fertility and children with our former neighbors. A subtle but significant change in attitude toward family size had taken place: more and more people were bent on having as many children as possible. On occasions, the subject of fertility triggered openly passionate responses, a rarity in Omani sociability.

Many women I knew had given birth to four, five, or six children in eight years. Women told me they pitied a person who stopped giving birth after four children. Several astonished me by talking of having twenty children, although they could not explain why it was so important to keep on giving birth. I told a woman whom I knew well that I loved children but that I could not understand how twenty children was a good thing for any woman to have. I asked her if there did not come a time, after four or five children, when a woman thought that she had enough. My question made her furious and she vented her anger by mocking my comment in front of guests who arrived soon after. Her startling reaction—Omanis go to great lengths to avoid airing disagreements in public—indicated how explosive the topic of fertility had become. Two brothers, former neighbors, who had lived together for years with their wives and children in a single household—a common practice in inner Oman at the time—had been obliged to form separate households because their wives quarreled. Neighbors told me in scornful tones—a public quarrel is shameful in inner Oman—that the split took place because one wife, who had three healthy sons but was no longer giving birth, was overcome by jealousy of her fertile sister-in-law.

Omanis in the interior perceive children as signs of social strength. Children fill emotional needs and care for aging parents later in life. People need sons to work outside the community and help them cope with an increasingly complex world, and daughters to build and maintain social ties within the community. But these reasons for having children do not explain why it has become so important to many Omani women to prolong their years of fecundity. Bearing twenty children was unimaginable in the late 1970s in inner Oman. While some women at the time told me they wanted "as many children as God gives me," it was not uncommon for younger women to openly say "four is enough." By 1988 women no longer articulated such thoughts out loud.

THE OMANI CONCEPT OF FERTILITY

The term "fertility" does not have the same meaning for everyone. Americans associate fertility with "having a family," with "choice," and with birth control. For an Omani woman, fertility means a long period of life during which time she hopes to give birth regularly to live offspring. During my first stay in al-Hamra, when I asked a woman how many children she had, she usually gave me two answers: the number of times she had given birth to a live child followed by the number of children who were alive as we spoke. Postpartum visiting took place even when an infant died a few hours after birth—such deaths were still commonplace in the late 1970s. Neither guests nor hosts mentioned the death of the child during the postpartum visit, and parents mourned the infant only when they were alone.

The Omani concept of fertility means *regularly* giving birth to a live child, which is acknowledged in the community by postpartum visiting, and nurturing the child to adulthood, which has its own set of social rewards. I stress the word *regularly* because regular sequences of births were valued most of all; it was common to hear women ask a mother with a child not old enough to walk whether she was again pregnant.

The birth of a child is a rite of passage that transforms a woman into a social adult who may then visit households that are neither kin nor close neighbors in the community. Infertile women and women who do not marry begin visiting in the community at a later age and visit less often. Unable to reciprocate postpartum visits, they are at a considerable disadvantage socially.

The relation between birth and hospitality is firmly embedded in the taken-for-granted, practical routines of women's daily activities in Oman. Giving birth and providing hospitality go hand in hand, like the roles of wife and mother in some segments of Western society. However, the Western role set of "wife and mother" does not exist in Oman, because the two roles belong to different categories. The role of wife belongs to the private world of family life, never disclosed to outsiders, while the role of mother is one that a woman easily displays in public.

The ways Omanis present themselves in photographs demonstrate these cultural differences. In al-Hamra in the late 1970s it was impossible to take a family snapshot that included a husband and a wife surrounded by their children. This is not because the nuclear family was not a familiar concept; indeed, a significant percentage of households in al-Hamra were nuclear. Rather, it was unthinkable for a woman to be photographed next to her husband, because it implied her private role as wife. Husband and wife never visited in the community as a couple and men and women went to great lengths to avoid being in the same room when a non–family member was present. The occasions when husband, wife, and children interacted were rarely shared with non–family members of either gender.

In contrast, women displayed with ease their public roles as mothers, both in the community and to strangers. In al-Hamra, women willingly allowed themselves to be photographed with a child and often placed themselves next to coffeepots or trays of fruit to suggest hospitality to anyone viewing the photograph. In this respect, they were representing themselves in the two roles that usually went hand in hand—as mothers and as persons who received guests generously and networked formally in the community. Indeed, fertility affected even coffee-drinking among neighbors, who avoided gathering in the households of childless women. One of my neighbors in the late 1970s, a respected midwife who had never given birth, drank coffee daily in households in the immediate vicinity. Her own house, however, was never used as an informal gathering place.

POSTPARTUM VISITING

Postpartum visiting occurs in a climate of intensive social competition, image-building by family clusters, and testing of the social order. Over a period of three weeks, women from the community and the surrounding countryside are obliged to visit at least once if their households have any kind of tie to the family of the woman who has given birth. Close family members who live in the oasis visit for several hours every day. Family members who live in the capital area commute back to visit on weekends. No other social occasions except for mournings—not even weddings— bring so many people together for so long. The gender of the infant and the number of times a woman has given birth do not affect the public aspects of postpartum visiting in any significant way.

Until recently, birth was a private occasion and a woman who was about to begin labor did not speak of it to anyone except her closest relatives and the midwife. Today most women go the hospital to give birth. Once the child is born, the news spreads quickly throughout the community and the three-week visiting period ensues. The new mother lies on a steel cot at the head of a room and receives visitors from morning until sunset. A woman who is descended from a *khadima* (slave) is hired to serve guests and help with housework during the entire period.

The postpartum visiting period (*murabiyya*) lasts for three weeks. The focus of postpartum visits is the woman who has given birth, her immediate female relatives, and those of her husband, not the child. Indeed, at an earlier period, guests rarely saw the newborn infant, who was left, swaddled, in a side room. By 1988, women had begun using plastic bathtubs as cribs and mothers kept their newborn child, no longer swaddled, at their side so that they could better tend to the infant's needs as they received guests. The guests, however, did not speak about the child and left gifts unobtrusively at the entrance of the guest room. These gifts, often coffee beans or fruit, were served to subsequent guests. Never were the gifts items for the mother or the newborn child. In general, postpartum visits are not child-oriented and can be very difficult for young children. Toddlers who live in the household where the birth took place are often sent to a relative's house for the duration of the visiting period to prevent loud and disruptive behavior.

Men claim to have nothing to do with postpartum visiting and other birth-related activities, although this is not wholly truthful. Men from the household in which a birth has taken place buy the food, incense, and perfume used in offering hospitality, and they stay away from their homes until women visitors have left. The use of pickup trucks and automobiles has complicated the choreography of gender separation. Although women in Oman are permitted to drive, few women in the interior do so, and most households have only one vehicle. Thus, men are enlisted to drive women to visits and maintenance of the strictly segregated men's and women's visiting networks requires careful coordination on the part of both men and women.

Many women take advantage of postpartum visiting to sell to guests items such as clothes, perfumes, or even pots and pans. These objects lie on shelves around the room and guests can ask to see them, although they are under no obligation to buy. Women of the tribal elite cannot sell items because of their social position, but in 1988, when I returned to al-Hamra, I saw a client woman selling items in the household of her patron, a member of the tribal elite. The young elite woman, who had given birth, recorded each sale in a small notebook for her client because the woman was illiterate. At another time, in the same household, another client used a room adjacent to where the guests sat to perform medicinal branding, a traditional form of medicine that was still practiced in the Arabian peninsula at the time.

The number and range of persons who visit a household during a postpartum visiting period reflect that household's social standing. The size of the room where visitors are received, its decor, the quality of the food and perfumes that are offered and of the incense that is burned, the number of women of slave descent serving guests, the presence of clients offering a variety of services—all these factors reflect how generous the host household is and how accustomed to receiving and pleasing guests. Other factors—seating arrangements, greeting etiquette, and the demeanor of the hosting women and the guests—can change rapidly. If all the women present know each other well, the atmosphere is relaxed and casual. However, when there is a wide discrepancy in the social status of the women present—if, for example, a group of elite tribal women, who generally visit in fours or fives, enter the room—women who were earlier conversing in earnest lapse suddenly into silence or offer monosyllabic responses to direct questions. Some women, in deference to such guests, move immediately to the least prestigious seats in the room. Likewise, coffee, fruit, and perfume may be served in a relaxed manner amidst laughter and joking, or their distribution may be rushed and tense.

The women of the tribal elite now indirectly compete with other families to attract large numbers of guests. The physical dispersal of cement housing away from the original mud-brick village has made frequent visits to show respect and acknowledge status much more difficult than when most members of the community lived less than a twenty-minute walk from the edge of the oasis. Women's need to arrange for transport as well as childcare sometimes cuts the number of visitors to well below what hosts may be expecting. Likewise, women seeking to enhance their social standing—such as women of slave descent or clients of the tribal elite whose husbands or brothers have become officers in the police, army, or security services—avoid visits that place them at a social disadvantage. This is because even if their men are accorded respect at formal gatherings for state and religious holidays, earlier understandings of client status prevail at women's gatherings, and women thus seek to avoid them.

Social competition now occurs in two interconnected arenas: the local community, where many more women than men live full-time, and the cosmopolitan urban setting of the capital area, where many men work and to which some households have moved from the oases of the interior. People need local ties, however, to present themselves to their best advantage in the capital area, just as some try to use the status acquired in the capital to manipulate and improve their standing in their oasis of origin, although they may be unevenly successful. People who have moved to the capital area return regularly to al-Hamra to maintain their land and houses, to oversee small local businesses, and to sustain their extended family ties and those of their visiting networks. Most women return to the oasis regularly to participate in postpartum visiting networks.

Women's need to network has increased, and hospitality has become more elaborate as the tribal elite competes with other upwardly mobile families. The large guest rooms for women in the newly constructed cement-block houses in al-Hamra indicate the value placed upon women's visiting networks. In 1988, in one household, men used an old mud-brick guest room adjacent to the new cement-block house used by women for their visiting. Its bare simplicity stood in sharp contrast to the women's luxurious setting. An older woman from the tribal elite described to me how full the new, modern house had been at a recent wedding: "Fifty cars were parked outside." Weddings, which were generally restricted to the family in the late 1970s, are now public occasions for large-scale hospitality as well.

GOVERNMENT RESPONSE

Oman's population has risen from an estimated 435,000 in 1970 to 1,480,000 in 1993, the year of Oman's first official census. By mid-2000 the population had reached 2.4 million (Population Reference Bureau 2000) Demographers predict that if growth continues at the same rate, the population will double every fifteen years (Range 1995, 131).

Until recently, the Omani government saw the high population growth as satisfactory. Contraceptives were available from pharmacies and from private doctors but no government-sponsored population planning program existed. Some educated Omanis privately expressed concern over the skyrocketing birth rate, but Oman's reliance on large numbers of noncitizen migrant laborers (approximately one-quarter of Oman's total population) and the need to develop a skilled Omani labor force made population a sensitive topic.

In 1994, a year after the completion of Oman's first official census, Sultan Qaboos began encouraging Omanis to cut their average family size to five children (Range 1995, 131). A year later, the Omani minister for development said Oman hoped to lower the rate of its population growth through "improved education, greater participation of women in the labor force and family programs underway" (Curtiss 1995, 51). These family programs are attempting to lower the birth rate by convincing women to space births more widely. Hopefully, these efforts will sensitize people to the subtle relations between fertility and other aspects of culture and prompt them to articulate issues related to fertility, potency, and family planning.

Social prestige in the late twentieth century is linked to family size, although a large number of children in itself is not enough to allow an Omani family to be upwardly mobile. The highest status comes to people with a good number of children, access to well-paid government jobs, and the means to behave like *shaykhs* (respected leaders) in the community. This means being able to provide favors, gifts, and services to those who need them, having a wide network of acquaintances, being lavishly hospitable, being able to settle disputes, having good judgment, and finally, ensuring that one's large family presents a harmonious front to outsiders. For a final touch of elite status, people fiddle with their genealogy to provide themselves with illustrious family connections. Social mobility is a process that reflects a state of mind, not any concrete status indicators. Status can change also with territory. Some families are perceived as shaykhs in the capital area (usually because of resources which originate in their home town) but are not considered successful in their home town. Children are one part of the process of changing conceptions of status, an important part of the equation for women, but not the whole.

REFERENCES

Curtiss, Richard H. 1995. "Oman: A Model for All Developing Nations." *The Washington Report on Middle East Affairs* 14, no. 2 (July): 49–57.
The Population Reference Bureau. 2000. *World Population Data Sheet*. Washington, D.C.
———. 1999. *World Population Data Sheet*. Washington, D.C.
Range, Peter Ross. 1995. "Oman." *National Geographic* 187, no. 5 (May): 112–38.

13. Tamkin: Stories from a Family Court in Iran

Ziba Mir-Hosseini

While making a documentary film on Iranian family law, Ziba Mir-Hosseini collected case studies of marriage and divorce. She reports in this article on the conflicts between marriage as represented in law and marriage as lived in reality. Marriage, especially the tensions which can lead to divorce, pits the wife's understanding of the spouses' obligations against the husband's. When these differences erupt, spouses may resort to a judge to untangle their affairs. Islamic law is often seen as remote, rigid, and biased against women, but although it favors men, many protections are built in for women. In reality, much of the interpretation of Islamic jurisprudence is left to the judge. As in the West, law can work for or against whoever enters a courtroom. —Eds.

In Iran, as elsewhere in the Middle East, the law defines the institution of marriage and the relationship of a married couple in ways that do not conform very closely to the experiences of ordinary people. The legal and the popular understandings of marriage are neither mutually exclusive nor necessarily in conflict, but they can be seen as distinct and opposed forces, particularly when a marriage is under strain or breaks down, when one or both of the partners have recourse to the law in order either to repair the marriage or to bring it to an end.

This chapter tells the stories of three women, each of whom is going through a difficult phase in her marriage. I came to know them while working on a documentary film about women and family law.[1] We meet them in court and learn how they confront the legal understanding of marriage. But first, we need some background on the main ways in which the legal and the popular understandings of marriage differ.

MARRIAGE IN LAW AND IN PRACTICE

In Muslim societies, marriage is not so much a sacrament as a contract regulated by a code of law rooted in religious precepts—in the shariʿa. The Islamic Republic of Iran, which is ideologically committed to the shariʿa, has codified it and grafted it onto a modern legal system.[2] It is based on a strong patriarchal ethos imbued with religious ideals and ethics.[3] This ethos defines marriage as a contract of exchange, whose prime purpose is to render sexual relations between a man and woman licit. Any sexual contact outside this contract constitutes the crime of zina, and is subject to punishment. The marriage contract is patterned after the contract of sale, and its essential elements are (i) the offer (ijab) made by the woman or her guardian, (ii) its acceptance (qabul) by the man, and (iii) the payment of dower (mahr), which is a sum of money or any valuable that the husband pays or pledges to pay the wife on consummation of the marriage.[4] Polygamy is a man's right; only a man can enter more than one marriage at a time, and he is permitted up to four permanent unions and as many temporary ones as he desires or can afford.[5]

The contract establishes neither commonality in matrimonial resources nor equality in rights and obligations between spouses. The husband is the sole provider and the owner of the matrimonial resources, and the wife remains the possessor of her mahr and her own wealth. The procreation of children is the only area the spouses share, and even here a wife is not legally obliged to suckle her child unless it is impossible to feed it otherwise. With the contract, a wife comes under her husband's ʿisma (a mixture of authority, dominion, and protection), entailing a set of defined rights and obligations for each party; some have legal force, others depend on moral sanctions, though the boundary between the legal and the moral is hazy and shifting. The main legally sanctioned rights and duties are tamkin (submission, obedience) and nafaqa (maintenance). Tamkin, defined as sexual submission, is a husband's right and thus a wife's duty; whereas nafaqa, defined as shelter, food, and clothing, is a wife's right and a husband's duty. A wife is entitled to nafaqa after consummation of the marriage, but she loses this right if she is in a state not of tamkin but of nushuz (disobedience).

The patriarchal emphasis and inequality of men's and women's legal rights in marriage are sustained through the rules regulating the termination of the contract. Talaq (repudiation), the unilateral termination of the contract, is the husband's exclusive right: he needs no grounds, nor is the wife's consent or presence required. Although a wife cannot obtain release from marriage without her husband's consent, she can offer him inducements to agree to *khulᶜ* (divorce by mutual consent). According to Muslim jurists, the wife may ask for khulᶜ on the grounds of her extreme aversion to her husband; in return for his consent, the husband should receive compensation. This can mean the wife's forgoing her right to mahr (dower), or returning it if it has already been paid. Unlike talaq, khulᶜ is a bilateral act, as it cannot take legal effect without the husband's consent. If the wife fails to secure her husband's consent, then her only recourse is to the intervention of the court. If she can establish valid grounds, the judge may pronounce talaq on behalf of the husband.[6]

This, in a nutshell, is the shariᶜa understanding of marriage in Iran. But the law is liable to be modified as a result of both manipulations by the state and conflicts with social practice and custom.[7] Marriage, as ordinary people live and practice it, involves a host of customary obligations and social relationships that go far beyond its legal construction. Some of these are rooted in the ideals of the shariᶜa and enjoy its moral support, though not legal sanctions. Marriage in practice not only has a more egalitarian structure than the law allows, but varies greatly with individuals, their social origins, and their economic resources. In particular, men's unconditional legal rights to divorce and polygamy are checked in practice by the mores and pressures of the extended family, the social stigma commonly attached to both divorce and polygamy, and above all by the practice of mahr. In Iran, a wife's right to mahr provides her with a strong negotiating card. She does not receive it upon marriage, but can demand it whenever she wants. Its value varies with social class and the wealth of the family, but it is always beyond the husband's immediate means to pay. In this way, the unclaimed mahr acts as insurance: a wife can, by forgoing her mahr altogether, persuade her husband to consent to a khulᶜ divorce; or, by threatening to claim her mahr, she can dissuade her husband from either divorcing her or taking a second wife; or she can claim substantial material compensation if an unwanted divorce goes ahead.[8]

In most marriages, couples find ways of accommodating or circumventing the legal requirements. Yet the tension is there, and it surfaces when the marriage breaks down or is under strain. It is then that many women first come to learn what their marriage contract entails, and how their rights and duties are defined in law. How do women relate to this legal reality? Do they accept it? Can they defy it? As the following extracts suggest, there are no simple answers. Their responses depend on their force of character, their socioeconomic condition, and the options available to them.

These extracts are drawn from my transcripts of three cases that appeared in a court in central Tehran in November 1997. Judge Deldar, a cleric, ran his court in an informal way, so that at times we (the film crew) were involved in the procedures. All three cases are typical of marital disputes that come to court in that they revolve around tamkin, nafaqa, and mahr, the main elements in the legal understanding of marriage that have been translated into positive law and can be enforced.[9] All three, moreover, betray the tensions between the different understandings of marriage and of gender relations. The only understanding that can be articulated in court is that of the law; the popular, everyday understanding of marriage cannot be articulated directly. As in all other court cases, the tensions between these understandings emerge in the form of two distinct agendas. As we shall see, while these agendas and understandings interact with and redefine each other, there is a wide gap between them, which has deepened in recent years. This is because women's position in society and their expectations of marriage have changed radically, while Iranian family law has remained some way behind these changes.[10]

EXTRACT 1. MS. AHMADI, DO YOU KNOW WHAT TAMKIN IS IN LAW?

Ms. Ahmadi[11] stands in front of the judge. She is small, and probably in her early fifties. He is busy reading a file. She waits for some time for him to raise his head. When she gets the chance, she starts to talk to the judge, handing him her file. Her voice is low, and her tone hesitant. She says that her husband recently took another wife, a sixteen-year-old girl. For the past five months he has not paid her any nafaqa; she made a petition for it, which was rejected. She has come to ask the judge why, and to ask what to do next. She adds that she has been married for twenty-eight years and has five children, two of them still at home. The judge looks at her file and tells her, "Here it says that you weren't in tamkin." She looks lost. I know that look; I have seen it many times. She is unfamiliar with the court and its language. I ask her, "Ms. Ahmadi, do you know what tamkin is in law?" "No," she answers.

Judge: Then why did you say [probably in a previous session] you weren't in tamkin, if you didn't know what it is? It says here [in her file] that you said you weren't in tamkin; when you neglect your duties in marriage, you lose your right to nafaqa.

Ms. Ahmadi: I never neglected my duties, I kept house for him, raised five children. Isn't that enough tamkin?

Judge: No, tamkin is more than that. When he wants to sleep with you, you must agree. At night when he wants to come and sleep with you, you must let him. That is tamkin. Are you prepared to do this or not?

She reddens, lowers her head, and answers, "No."

Judge: Why not?

Ms. A.: I can't . . . I can't. . . .

She must have reacted similarly in the previous session, which might explain why her petition was rejected. I am now convinced that she is new to the intricacies of the law. She is too honest, too naive. She doesn't know that legal facts are not necessarily about truth. She has now given the judge a reason to blame her for her husband's action.

Judge: Why can't you? He's gone and taken another wife, you say he's married a sixteen-year-old. It's a wife's lack of tamkin that causes such a thing. Why aren't you prepared to be in tamkin?

Ms. A.: Wasn't I in tamkin for twenty-eight years? Where have all these children come from?

Judge: Yes. You must always be in tamkin. It was your lack of tamkin that caused him to take another wife. Encourage him a little, entice him back. If you are not in tamkin then you are not entitled to anything for yourself, and you can demand nafaqa only for the children.

She looks at the judge in horror. I can see the hurt in her face. I have to come to her aid once again, and tell her how the court defines tamkin. I address the judge: "I know the court's presumption is that a wife is in tamkin as long as she stays in the marital home. But what happens, for instance, if a wife says she is in tamkin but her husband says she is not? Whose word does the court accept?" The judge replies, "The wife's, of course." To make it crystal clear, I turn to her and say, "A wife can demand nafaqa when she says she is in tamkin, and she is still in the marital home. This is the meaning of tamkin. So you can file a new petition for nafaqa, and this time make it a penal one." She sighs and says, "Now I understand, but what can I say?"

We did not see Ms. Ahmadi again, which means that she did not take the course I suggested, to file a penal petition for nafaqa. If a wife submits such a petition at her local police station, it is dealt with that very day. If her husband is found, then he is brought to court, where he faces two options: either to pay the nafaqa calculated by the court, or to receive the penalty of a maximum of seventy-four lashes. Most men choose the first, and pay up then and there. But such radical action takes the dispute to a different level and almost always puts an end to the marriage, a step that many women of Ms. Ahmadi's generation and situation, lacking economic independence, cannot afford. A wife who takes this step is likely to be intent on teaching her husband a lesson, or exacting revenge after he has taken a second wife.[12]

Probably Ms. Ahmadi chose the softer option: to make a civil petition for nafaqa, to which she is entitled if she has not left the marital home and declares she is in tamkin. When her case duly appears in court (usually within three months), if the husband comes but refuses to pay, or if he fails to appear, then the court will issue a nafaqa order. With this order, she can take legal action to recover past nafaqa (if he is salaried, a sum is deducted monthly). But Ms. Ahmadi could obtain a divorce at any time, since her husband's taking a second wife without a court order constitutes valid grounds. Whatever she does, she needs knowledge of the law, or a lawyer, but above all she needs the financial means to survive outside marriage.

For many women like Ms. Ahmadi, tamkin is a way of life, going far beyond its narrow legal mandate. This is reflected in the dictionary definitions of tamkin: "giving power," "empowering someone to attain something," "accepting a situation." The word itself is seldom used in everyday language, and many women do not know its meanings, legal or popular; but it rules their lives, as they have little choice other than to be in tamkin—to submit to their husband.

But some women, as the next extract suggests, are able to refuse tamkin as a way of life and to challenge its legal link with nafaqa, the provision of food, shelter, and clothing. A wife with independent means and somewhere to go can circumvent the legal understandings of nafaqa and tamkin and assert her own. One of her options is to rewrite the terms of her marriage contract. She can obtain the right to choose her place of residence, either through a stipulation in the marriage contract or by a court order following a dispute. It is common, when a wife demands both nafaqa and a separate place of residence, for her husband to make a counter-petition for tamkin, though when she no longer resides in his house his power over her is substantially reduced and it is hard for him to insist on her submission, sexual or otherwise.

EXTRACT 2. MS. BEHROUZI: I WAS IN MY HOUSE, IT WAS
UP TO HIM TO COME TO ME FOR MY TAMKIN

Ms. Behrouzi, middle-aged and wearing a *chador* (full-length veil covering the body and hair) and glasses, enters the courtroom with her lawyer, a younger woman wearing just a head scarf. Her husband follows them. They exchange greetings with us and take their seats. We have already met in the corridor, and they have agreed to be filmed. Ms. Behrouzi told me that two of her sons from her previous marriage live in London, and she wants them to see her in the film. She is more or less the same age as Ms. Ahmadi in the previous case, but unlike her is cheerful and full of confidence. We are delighted: very few cases that come to court involve lawyers, and we have been invited to film this one.

The lawyer starts to present the case to the judge.

"Your Honor,[13] I would like to inform the court that fifteen years ago my client contracted a permanent marriage with this gentleman. Both had children from their previous marriages. For six years, she lived in his house with his four children. But his children resented her, could not accept her taking their mother's place. There were frequent quarrels. Finally she went to the court and made a petition, demanding a separate residence and payment of nafaqa. The court found her demand reasonable, and issued an order to that effect. He too made a petition for tamkin [her return to his house] but it was rejected by the same court. You will find both orders in the file, which states that his house was not a suitable place for her to reside, and continuation of that situation could have caused her spiritual, psychological, and physical harm. In this way, she obtained the right to choose her place of residence and the husband was required by law to provide for her. At present she lives in a house in which she has a small inherited share. By law, this gentleman is required to pay her monthly nafaqa, and visit her there. But since New Year's Day [21 March 1997] he has failed to comply with his marital duties."

Ms. Behrouzi's husband, Mr. Amiri, is on the edge of his seat, looking more and more agitated. Several times he tries to get a word in, but the lawyer does not let him. Now, unable to contain himself any longer, he leaps up and approaches the judge's desk to tell his own side of the story.

"God be my advocate! This lady received nafaqa regularly until the New Year. In that court she used my children as an excuse. The court said, 'Provide her with a separate room.' I did that. But she said she wanted to go and live in her own house. I said, 'Fine, as you like.' I even increased her nafaqa, and paid until the end of last year. Just before New Year, I telephoned her and said, 'New Year is approaching, husband and wife should be together, either you come to me or I come to you.' She said, 'I won't come, nor will you.' You yourself are a man, Your Honor. You know that we men work from morning to night, in hot or in cold weather. Is this how a wife should reward us? I was offended and had no intention of going to her for New Year. But she has a brother with whom I have lunch every other day. He said, 'My sister is not well, go and visit her, ask how she is doing.' I said, 'Just as you say.' So I went to see her on New Year's Eve. I swear by God, I am not lying to you. I bought two kilos of the best almond cookies that I could find in the bazaar, and I went to see this lady. It's 9:30 in the evening. I tell her I haven't eaten. She says, 'There's no food prepared in the house.' Then she goes and fries two eggs, and puts them in front of me. I say nothing. Eleven-thirty comes. I tell her, 'Aren't we going to bed?' She says, 'Are you going to sleep here?' I say, 'Yes, my children are away; and you are my wife in law and in religion. It is also written here [i.e., in the marriage contract].' She says, 'Not any more! If you want to spend the night here, I'll go downstairs to my son's flat, and sleep there.' So I said, 'Well, then, go and get your nafaqa from your son!' and I left. After all these insults, I asked her brother and others to mediate, and offered to send her money. But she told them she didn't want money, and she didn't want me to go to her. A wife who doesn't do tamkin is not entitled to any nafaqa."

The lawyer gets up and hands the judge two documents, saying, "Here is a copy of the nafaqa petition this lady made, and here is the summons sent to him claiming nafaqa, which he ignored." This infuriates Mr. Amiri.
Mr. Amiri: Your Honor, I swear to God I telephoned and said, "My girl, my

lady, the light of my eyes, your nafaqa is ready, stop this nonsense."
She said, "We'll talk in court." I said, "Fine, we'll see each other in
court."

Ms. Behrouzi: Please, [let me say] only one word, please, Your Honor, let me.
He telephones and says he wants to come at seven in the morning
and then leave at seven-thirty [i.e., for quick sex], I said I wouldn't
do such a thing.

The judge tries to calm them down, without success.

Judge: No marriage can carry on with arguments and things like this. No
one can be forced; there must be agreement. Madam, you must also
be in tamkin, it's your duty.

Ms. Behrouzi: When this gentleman says he wants to come for half an hour,
what does this mean? This is an insult to me.

Mr. Amiri: What insult? We agreed in court that I could go to her once a
week, and have breakfast.

Ms. Behrouzi: This gentleman wants to come to my house on Friday mornings.

Mr. Amiri: That was our arrangement.

Ms. Behrouzi: He has breakfast, and half an hour later . . . he knows what I
am talking about, this is shameful, really! One wants a husband for
companionship; I've been ill for two years, going to hospital, and he
doesn't even know which hospital I've been to, where I go.

Mr. Amiri: You didn't want me to come!

Judge: How long since you last paid nafaqa?

Mr. Amiri: Since New Year. If she's entitled to anything, by God, I'll give it
to her right now.

Lawyer: It's no good. The fact is that the condition for divorce has been fulfilled. In the previous court, they agreed that she could divorce herself if he failed to pay nafaqa. It's here in the court order. Whatever
you do now does not change the past.

Mr. Amiri: I won't give her a divorce, under no circumstances. From now
on, I won't give any money; I'll go and buy whatever she needs; if
she needs medical treatment, I'll take her to the doctors.

Judge: Was she in tamkin to you?

Mr. Amiri: No.

Ms. Behrouzi: I was in my own house, Your Honor. It was up to him to come
to me for my tamkin.

Mr. Amiri: I come there, and at twelve at night, you tell me to go away. What
sort of tamkin is this?

The session ends with the judge requiring Mr. Amiri to pay the nafaqa
due to his wife. I do not know what happens later, but I learn that the un-
derlying problem is Mr. Amiri's children, who, egged on by their mother,
resent his remarriage to Ms. Behrouzi, refuse to let him visit her as often
as she would like, and are determined to ruin their marriage. He is ada-

mant that he will not give her a divorce, but if she is intent on it, he has little option but to agree to one or to try to accommodate her wishes. Legally he is bound to pay her nafaqa every month, but since she is living in her own house he has little chance of being able to enjoy what he is legally entitled to in return, i.e., his wife's tamkin, sexual and otherwise. The new court order has further improved her bargaining position, so that she can now negotiate her release from the marriage or insist on her own terms if it is to continue. For her, like most women, what is important in marriage is companionship and sharing; for her husband, like most men, it seems to be little more than sex, cooking, and personal services.

If older women like Ms. Behrouzi, with financial means and previous marital experience, can evade and subvert the legal mandate of tamkin, younger women are now challenging it in the name of religion and questioning its legal justification, as our third extract shows.

EXTRACT 3. MINA: DOES ISLAM SAY I MUST BE IN TAMKIN TO SUCH A MAN?

Mina and Javad, a young couple in their early twenties, sit next to each other. Throughout the court session, they never look at each other, and they speak only to the judge. Mina is wearing a black chador. Her face is pale, and her voice husky. Javad is wearing a sports jacket; his voice is rough and impatient.

Judge: You say here that she left your house several times. Why? What is the problem in your marriage?

Javad: From the very beginning of our marriage, I found certain things unacceptable. If I came home and objected to something, for instance, "Why is the food like this?" she would just say, "I have no duty to cook for you, to take your orders, or to raise your children." I found this too much to bear. Naturally, I would get upset. You can keep quiet for a day or two, but finally you say something, you do something. Anyway, we went on like this for a while; and she left me four times.

Judge: What was the latest dispute about, this last time?

Javad: She's completely self-obsessed in her life. I think she has no respect for me—I mean, for her husband. She wants everything for herself: she goes wherever she wants, and she doesn't go anywhere she doesn't want. She does as she pleases, and then claims that I beat her. I came to the end of my tether, two or three times. Then she made a row, shouting and crying. Now I want her tamkin.

Judge: Your husband has petitioned for a tamkin order [for return to the marital home]. A wife must be in her husband's tamkin; if she leaves home it must be with his agreement, with his permission. A wife must have understanding, and not let things get to the point that her husband has to come here and petition for a tamkin order. Now tell me, why did you go back to your father's house?

Mina: From the very beginning—only three days after our wedding—he raised his hand at me. I was horrified. I am the last child of my family [usually the favorite] . . . I came to his house with hope. I did not expect that, only three days after the wedding, I'd get beaten because the food was not ready. He doesn't have the right to raise his hand at me because I didn't prepare the food. Islam doesn't give him that permission. A man can't compel his wife to do housework, according to the religion (*shar*) that we have. God knows, since I went to his house, I've been beaten every three or four days. Once he hit me so hard that my eardrum was damaged, my thumb was broken. He insults me, he calls me names like—begging your pardon—"bastard." Does Islam say I must be in tamkin to such a man? What religion, what law allows this? This man does whatever he wants to me, he hits me. Your Honor, I fear for my life. He gives me assurances of safety, so I return to our marital home. He tells me, "In the court I say I love my wife and my marriage, and then at home I break your bones." This is his position, as I see it . . . What guarantee do I have if I remain in his house? Has the Prophet said I must do tamkin to such a man?

Judge: You must live together in peace. You, too, you cannot order your wife to do things. She should do certain things in the house, from moral obligation; but a husband should not give orders . . . If [she] works on the husband's orders, she can demand wages . . . the domestic wages that women are entitled to [as part of a divorce settlement] are about this: the wife has done work and can demand wages for it. You, madam, if you do things on your husband's orders, you can demand wages. Does he give orders?

Mina: He does, but I am not the type to demand wages for what I do at home. Every woman cares for her home. But he is unreasonable. For instance, one day we did not have hot water, so I couldn't do the washing up. Because of this I was badly beaten. Does Islam allow such a thing?

Clearly Mina has been following current debates over women's rights in parliament and the journals, particularly over what a wife's duties in marriage are, as well as the issue of wife-beating. Since the Revolution and the return to the shari'a there have been attempts to give legal sanction to shari'a moral injunctions. She knows the judge is referring to the 1992 amendments to the divorce laws, which enable the court to put a monetary value on women's housework, and to force the husband to pay *ujrat al-mithl* (like wages) for the work she has done during marriage. She also knows that this law is of no use to her, as it only applies when divorce is not initiated by the wife or is not caused by any fault of hers.[14] So she invokes the sacred, by appealing to Islamic ideals of justice and fairness. Is she alluding to the Quranic verse commonly interpreted as an endorsement of wife-beating (4 [Nisa]: 34)?[15] Has she been reading the women's magazines in which alternative Quranic interpretations and equality for women are aired and debated? Whatever the case, the judge does not react but avoids her question, dismisses her concern as trivial, and continues his attempt to make peace between them. Mina now reveals why her husband actually beats her: he wants her to give up her claim to mahr in return for a divorce.

Judge: It is a shame to ruin your marriage for such trivial things. Now what's your problem with returning to your marriage?

Mina: I don't want to live with him any more. He wants a divorce too. Two months ago, he agreed to give me a divorce by mutual consent; we discussed all this in my father's house. He signed it [the terms of the divorce settlement]; he agreed to pay the mahr in installments. The very morning we were to go to court for him to give me my divorce, he changed his mind and tore up the agreement. Then he filed a petition for tamkin, in order to put pressure on me to give up my claim to mahr. If I go back, he will make life hell for me. He puts his foot on my throat to suffocate me, he pulls my hair; all this is causing me bodily harm.

Judge: If such things happen, you can file a report and he will be prosecuted.

Mina: I made a petition a month ago, and a hearing was set for six months ahead.

Judge: The petition you made was for divorce. If he insults you, or if he causes you bodily harm, you should make a penal petition and your case will appear in court the same day. Civil cases, such as divorce, take a long time to appear. Young man, will you give her a guarantee here that, if she comes to live with you, there will be no insults, no maltreatment?

Javad: Of course! I am not that type, Your Honor!

Judge: He will give you a guarantee not to insult you under any circumstances, not to cause you bodily harm. Will you agree to go back?

Mina: No! He has given such promises many times; the last time, when I came back from my father's house, he swore by Fatemeh Zahra,[16] but as soon as we got into the car, he started insulting me, and two days later he hit me.

Judge: OK, you have no special problem, so go off and live together; God willing, nothing else will happen.

Javad: If I insult her, she can come here and make a petition; but what can I do if she continues to paralyze my life and leaves for her father's house?

Mina: Why does she leave? Ask him, Your Honor. He hits me, and I have to leave. Tell him he's gone too far. He damaged my eardrum, he broke my thumb; he admits all that. Tell him there's a law, that no man can do just what he wants even within the four walls of his house.

The session ends with Javad signing a document guaranteeing to respect his wife and not to maltreat her. Both leave the courtroom in silence. I follow them, wanting to talk to her. I want to know whether she is going to return to the marital home and give him another chance, and to tell her that if he beats her again, she can bring a penal case against him by going to the police: they will send her for a medical examination, and if there is any physical injury, such as bruises or broken limbs, then a certificate will be issued and Javad will be summoned to court and forced to pay compensation. If she refuses to accept compensation, he will be imprisoned. Such a court order can strengthen her case later, if she chooses to apply for a divorce on the grounds of harm.

Outside the courtroom, I see Mina with her father, and tell them about the options. Her father says, "I'll never let her go back to that madman. I'm now going to make a petition for her mahr. He will pay for what he has done to my daughter, for ruining her life." They know that Mina's mahr—set at 140 gold coins—is their only negotiating card. Javad is legally obliged to pay it on demand, either in full or in installments, depending on his financial situation. Since the amount involved is substantial, he will probably agree to give her a divorce or to mend his ways, if they give up the claim. By law, there is nothing Javad can do to bring Mina back to the marital home, even if he succeeds in obtaining a tamkin order. A wife who refuses to comply with such an order merely loses her claim to nafaqa.

I never saw Mina or Javad again, and I don't know what the outcome was. But Mina's pale face and husky voice will remain with me forever.

What do these glimpses into the breakdown of three marriages tell us about law and social practices in post-revolutionary Iran? How do wives relate to the inequality inherent in their shari‘a marriage contracts? What are their strategies to overcome it?

Like other marital disputes, these three stories must be interpreted in the context of different understandings of marriage and gender relations. By the time a marital dispute appears in court, it has already become a war of attrition. What causes and then fuels this war in Iran is the tension between the legal and the everyday understandings of marriage. While the marriage contract as defined by law concedes neither a shared area of ownership nor equality and reciprocity in conjugal rights and duties, marriage in social practice assumes all of these.

When this sharing and reciprocity is jeopardized by either spouse, the marriage comes under stress, and may end up in court. Each spouse will do whatever is possible to create a new balance. Husbands appeal to their shari῾a prerogatives and demand their legal rights, especially the wife's submission; wives appeal to social practice and custom and try to offset their husband's legal power. Whatever the dispute, whatever her circumstances, a wife tends to resort to similar kinds of strategies, with the objective of making her husband pay for what she sees as a denial of her conjugal rights.

Men often retaliate with neglect and violence. A man can avoid confrontation with his wife and withstand social pressure by neglecting her. As our first two stories show, when confronted by his wife's demand for reciprocity in conjugal rights and duties, a husband tends to neglect his legal duty to provide for her. The more guilty he is in the eyes of his wife and of society—for example, if he takes a second wife—the more he stays away. Our third story shows how a man may try, through violence and physical domination, to assert an authority which the law bestows on him but which has little basis in social expectations of marriage. Physical violence then becomes a measure of the erosion of a man's authority in marriage: it is more frequent when a marriage is under stress, exactly because he feels a more acute need to assert his authority.

The wife then reacts by making financial demands. In this way, she makes her husband pay, both literally and figuratively. The very elements in the marriage contract that give men power can now be turned against them. The husband's authority over his wife, legally sanctioned and enforced through nafaqa, becomes a double-edged sword. A man who is unable to pay, or whose wife has her own income, can exercise little power over her, and he has no choice but to negotiate terms for either continuing or terminating the contract. The ways in which these negotiations take place, and women's choices and options, are shaped by their personalities, their conjugal circumstances, and the socioeconomic context in which marriage is embedded.

Thus a woman with no financial security outside marriage, like Ms. Ahmadi in our first story, comes to court either to get nafaqa from her straying husband or to preempt a divorce. Ms. Ahmadi's case was at an early stage of its court career. Soon she will learn that the most effective way to bring her husband to his senses is to take as much as she can. She can make one petition for nafaqa and another for mahr, but she can waive rights to these in return for a share of the marital home or custody of the children together with a set nafaqa payment for looking after them. A 1997 law requiring mahr to be revalued in line with inflation has put her in a better negotiating position. Now she can count on her mahr as an insurance in marriage.

Other women, like those in our second and third cases, come to court to negotiate the terms of a divorce. They have either economic means, like Ms. Behrouzi, or the support of their natal families, like Mina. By refusing to grant his wife a divorce, a man can hold on to his power, even though

he knows that the marriage is over. This is often the only way he can realize his legal prerogatives if she leaves the marital home. She retaliates by
bringing the case to court, and thus takes the marital dispute to another
level. Her strategy is to resort to the contractual side of the marriage and
to demand fulfillment of its terms. As we saw with Ms. Behrouzi, whose
case had been in the courts for a good while, a wife can make the husband
fulfil his legal duty (reduced to nafaqa) while evading her own (reduced
to tamkin). But in most cases, like Mina's, a wife's main negotiating card
is her mahr, since by leaving the marital home she has already lost her
claim to nafaqa.

A large majority of divorce cases initiated by women never reach a decision; they are abandoned after two or three hearings. Either the couple
succeed in reaching an out-of-court agreement or they give up, realizing
the futility of their efforts. More than 70 percent of all divorces registered
in any given year in Tehran are khul⁽ (by mutual consent). Most if not all
of these will have involved the wife waiving her claim to mahr in exchange
for the husband's consent. As a Persian saying has it, *Mahram halal junam
azad:* "Let my mahr go and my soul be free."

NOTES

1. *Divorce Iranian Style,* a film by Kim Longinotto and Ziba Mir-Hosseini
(1998, distributed in the U.S. by Women Make Movies, in the U.K. by the Royal
Anthropological Institute). We did not use any of the cases discussed here in the
final version of *Divorce Iranian Style.* For the story behind the making of the film,
see Ziba Mir-Hosseini, "Negotiating the Politics of Gender in Iran: An Ethnogra
phy of a Documentary," in *The New Iranian Cinema: Politics, Representation, and Identity,* ed. Richard Tapper (London: I. B. Tauris, 2001).

2. The Iranian state's appropriation and selective enforcement of the shari⁽a
predates the establishment of the Islamic Republic in 1979, and it is not unique to
Iran. Iran, however, is the only Muslim country in which the custodians of the
shari⁽a (the *ulama*) now control the machinery of a modern state and are able to
pass and enforce laws in the name of the shari⁽a. For the impact of this on gender
rights, see Ziba Mir-Hosseini, *Islam and Gender: The Religious Debate in Contemporary Iran* (Princeton: Princeton University Press, 1999).

3. Ten percent of all Muslims adhere to Shi⁽a Islam; Iran is the only Muslim
country in which it is the official religion. Family law in Shi⁽a Islam shares the
same inner logic and patriarchal bias as Sunni schools of law. For differences
among the schools of Islamic law, see John Esposito, *Women in Islamic Family Law*
(Syracuse: Syracuse University Press, 1982).

4. Despite the uniformity that exists among all schools of Islamic law on the
rules governing mahr, Muslim societies vary greatly with respect to its practice.
In many societies mahr has a "prompt" portion, which is paid before marriage,
and a "deferred" one, which is paid only upon divorce. In some countries, such
as Morocco, the prompt portion constitutes the bulk of mahr, and is used by the
bride's family to provide her with a trousseau; in others (including Iran), as we
shall see later, mahr is prompt in form but deferred in function. See Ziba Mir-

Hosseini, *Marriage on Trial: A Study of Islamic Family Law: Iran and Morocco Compared* (London: I. B. Tauris, 2000).

5. Temporary marriage, or *mutʿa*, exists only in Shiʿa law; see Shahla Haeri, *Law of Desire: Temporary Marriage in Iran* (London: I. B. Tauris, 1989).

6. For the different shariʿa modes of termination of marriage, see Mir-Hosseini, *Marriage on Trial*, 36–41.

7. For changes in Iranian laws relating to marriage and divorce, see Ziba Mir-Hosseini, "Family Law iii. In Modern Persia," *Encyclopaedia Iranica* 9 (1999), 192–96.

8. For ways in which women use mahr in Iranian courts, see Ziba Mir-Hosseini, "Women, Marriage, and the Law in Post-revolutionary Iran," in *Women in the Middle East, Perceptions, Realities, and Struggles for Liberation,* ed. Haleh Afshar, 59–84 (London: Macmillan, 1993).

9. Most files contain a wife's petition for nafaqa or mahr, and a husband's counter-petition for tamkin. I have been doing research in Tehran family courts since the early 1980s. For court procedures and the content of files, see Mir-Hosseini, *Marriage on Trial*, 28–31.

10. See Mir-Hosseini, "Women and Politics in Post-Khomeini Iran: Divorce, Veiling, and Emerging Feminist Voices," in *Women and Politics in the Third World,* ed. Haleh Afshar (London: Routledge, 1996), 142–70, and "Iran: Emerging Feminist Voices," in *Women's Rights,* ed. Lynn Walter (Westport, Conn.: Greenwood, 2000), 113–25.

11. All the names used are pseudonyms. In Iran, a woman does not take her husband's name on marriage, so although she may be addressed as *khanum Ahmadi,* Mrs. Ahmadi, this is her father's, not her husband's, surname.

12. See Mir-Hosseini, *Marriage on Trial,* 63–65.

13. The term most people use when addressing clerical judges, like this one, is "Hajji Agha."

14. For the 1992 amendments and gender debates, see Mir-Hosseini, "Women and Politics in Post-Khomeini Iran" and *Islam and Gender.*

15. For an alternative interpretation of this verse, see Ziba Mir-Hosseini, "Stretching the Limits: A Feminist Reading of the Shariʿa in Post-Khomeini Iran," in *Islam and Feminism: Legal and Literary Perspectives,* ed. Mai Yamani (London: Ithaca Press, 1996), 285–319.

16. Daughter of the Prophet and wife of ʿAli, the first Shiʿa imam, from whom the other Shiʿa imams are descended.

14. The Veiled Revolution

Elizabeth W. Fernea

Since the early twentieth century, patterns of women's work and dress have moved closer to the western model. However, as Elizabeth W. Fernea shows, those patterns are beginning to shift again as young, educated women return to conservative "Islamic" dress, not for the reasons their grandmothers veiled, but to define their identity as Muslim women in a changing world. (This article was written to complement Fernea's film, The Veiled Revolution, *part of her film trilogy,* Reformers and Revolutionaries: Middle Eastern Women.) —Eds.*

"The feminine veil has become a symbol: that of the slavery of one portion of humanity," wrote French ethnologist Germaine Tillion in 1966. This view of the veil appears again and again in the West, partly, of course, because the veil is indeed a dramatic visual symbol. It attracts us to a face that may not be seen and at the same time signifies a boundary that may not be crossed.

Such a barrier or boundary between men and women exists in some form in all societies. But the veil as a visible barrier calls up in the viewer a complex reaction. We tend to believe that those who look out (through the veil) suffer from the same exclusion as those of us who look at the veil and its hidden contents. However, we have no right to make such an assumption. Much depends on who makes the decision to veil—whether it is imposed or self-selected.

Until recently, veiling and conservative dress had been declining steadily in all parts of the Islamic world. Walking on the streets of Turkey, Lebanon, Iraq, Tunisia, Morocco, Algeria, Jordan, and Egypt, a visitor would find a veiled woman the exception rather than the rule. Yet it has continued to be the rule in Saudi Arabia, North Yemen, and some areas of Afghanistan and Pakistan. And now patterns are shifting again.

Western and Middle Eastern rejection of, or outrage against, the veil has been seen as rejection of, and outrage against, the values believed to be associated with the veil. These values include that of chastity, a prescribed role for women in the family, and, above all, unequal access to divorce, inheritance, and child custody. If these problems are reformed, many Middle Eastern women say, the use or non-use of the veil will become unimportant.

But as the veil has been used over the centuries for political, religious, and social purposes, it is a symbol within the society itself that can find new uses, "an outward sign of a complex reality." The donning of modest dress or, as some women call it, "Islamic dress" is a personal statement in response to new and changing social conditions in Egypt.

The first thing that must be stressed, however, is that the contemporary use of conservative dress is a new phenomenon. Women are not "returning to the veil," for the garments they are designing for themselves and wearing on the streets of Cairo are not of the style worn since before the turn of the century—the *milaya*, the head scarf, the long, full black dress. The modest garments of today constitute a new style, developed only in the past ten years. The head scarf, the turban, the fitted long dress or the loose full dress are variations on an old theme—with new expressions and new implications.

The second point is that Islamic dress today is a middle- and upper-middle-class phenomenon, found mostly among educated working women. The majority of those taking up modest dress are young, in their early twenties, and many are in the universities and professional schools throughout Egypt. As a medical student at Tanta put it, "I think of Islamic dress as a kind of uniform. It means I am serious about myself and my religion but also about my studies. I can sit in class with men and there is no question of attraction and so on—we are all involved in the same business of learning, and these garments make that clear."

The young women who are wearing Islamic dress are often the daughters and granddaughters of women who wear Western dress. Some sociologists in Egypt suggest that the adoption of conservative dress is a form of rebellion, a rebuff to a parental generation whose efforts have not, as expected, improved conditions in Egypt. Economic conditions in Egypt are indeed better for a small percentage of the population, but for at least half of Egypt's people, the bright future promised in the 1950s has not materialized. In this sense, the new garb carries a political message: it is a dramatic, nonviolent protest against the establishment and its policies, as well as against the West.

But political statement, in Islamic countries, cannot be separated from religious statement. For Egypt is a society which still considers itself a Muslim state, where religion and politics have never been separated. A small minority of Christians (Copts, Armenians, Nestorians, Eastern Orthodox Catholics, Roman Catholics) live in Egypt, but nearly 90 percent of the population is Muslim. The Qurʾan is the basis for family law still, though some modifications have been made in recent years, and the criminal and civil codes are amalgams of European and Quranic laws. Thus religion is part of everyday life, and religious affiliation is part of one's social identity, whether or not one is a practicing Muslim or Christian.

Therefore, far from being a simple statement of religious affiliation, the wearing of Islamic dress is related to the very basis of social life in Egypt and in other Muslim countries, where the wearing of Islamic dress has also been observed (Jordan, Lebanon, and Libya are recent examples). The wearing of Islamic dress also relates to the individual's sense of belonging to a group, and to the individual's sense of her own identity. Although some men also wear a form of Islamic dress (a long, loose homespun shirt, a white skullcap and beard), their numbers are not nearly so high as are found among women. Such apparel may even be politically risky these days as it suggests sympathy with Muslim "extremists," as their critics call them.

A third important point to be made, and one that women stress repeatedly, is that the choice to wear Islamic dress is one that they make themselves, and it must come "from inner religious conviction." Although stories of organized Muslim groups paying women to wear Islamic dress are told by Westerners in Egypt, these seem generally to be unfounded. Women make their own choice, but of course they are influenced by their peers, and the decision is one hotly debated within families and among different groups of friends.

Finally, the wearing of Islamic dress has, in addition to the genuine religious motives avowed by many young women, many practical advantages. As one young woman put it, "My family trusts me implicitly, and now that I wear this dress, they are not worried if I stay out later than usual or mingle with friends they do not always approve of. In this dress, my reputation remains intact, for everyone knows that it is a respectable garment. People thus respect you if you wear it."

In crowded conditions, such as the streets of Cairo and the packed public buses, Islamic dress does offer some protection against importuning and aggressive sexual advances by men. Further, the new phenomenon of women working outside the home places many men and women in new situations—close to each other for long periods of the day—that place a strain on the traditional boundaries between men and women, and may also place strains on the public reputation of the young women. It is true that many of the outward signs of the older Egyptian society—veiling, seclusion of women, segregation of women from public work places, education institutions, and so on—have disappeared, but traditional attitudes are slower to change. The wearing of Islamic dress is a practical, simple way of stating publicly, "I am a respectable woman. Leave me alone."

A small number of women cover themselves completely. They take the Quranic injunction "and tell the believing women to draw their garments close around them" to its logical extreme, and describe themselves as "devout, devoted to God and unwilling to enter the public workplace."

The majority of women wearing Islamic dress do not seem to feel this way, however, but see themselves as making a statement or taking action that strengthens their own position with the society. They continue to attend colleges and universities, work outside the home, mingle with men in the classroom and on the streets. They also attend study groups in mosques and private homes to learn more about their own faith and law. Many have taken the "service" aspect of Islamic teaching seriously, and, under the direction of persons like Dr. Zahira Abdine, director of the Giza Children's Hospital, do volunteer work among the poor. Two young medical students and one doctor spend one day a week at the Sayyida Zeinab mosque, where they have opened a people's free medical clinic. Others teach and offer services as social workers.

The veil, then, is a complex symbol that can have multiple implications and different impacts. Manipulated in one way, it can become a symbol for conservatism or for reaction against modernization; utilized in another way, it can become a symbol for an Islamic approach to the solutions of both old and new problems. However it is used, it means different things to different people within the society, and it means different things to Westerners than it does to Muslim Middle Easterners.

PART THREE

Home, Community, and Work

Traditional institutions such as the family or the mosque educate and socialize their members in values and roles which preserve a cultural heritage and ensure social stability. At the same time, a society must adapt to new institutions, such as those created by secular education or corporate business. Each affects the other. Traditional ties can dilute crisply impersonal business dealings, benefiting interpersonal relations but sabotaging efficiency. Students may spurn tradition, but in doing so they may scandalize their grandparents with their views or their style of clothing. Institutions are not much thought of until they seem threatened; then there is great consternation and self-examination. Consumerism and obsession with material objects have been highly visible sources of conflict with traditional society—and they have been widely criticized by Muslim activist movements.

The family, the most important traditional institution, filters children's experience of the world and conveys cultural values. Adults become involved in the everyday affairs of community and marketplace, where individuals fashion their identities. They do this in various ways: through sponsoring the modern or the traditional, through education, through their looks, and through the political and religious groups they associate with. Susan Ossman describes the relation between images of beauty and people's construction of their identity. Although women's displays of beauty were traditionally reserved for home and husband, women who dress in a Western fashion now find inspiration in foreign sources such as magazines, television programs, and movies. Women once retreated to the *hammam*, the steam bath, for beauty treatments; now they go to salons, where they analyze their looks feature by feature in an attempt to fashion an image that shows the outside world whether they are contemporary or traditional.

In many villages today, village elders retain their influence, and the central government is hard pressed to implement programs which these elders oppose. Tayeb Salih's story of a Sudanese village proposes institutional adaptation, the idea that new technology need not destroy old social forms. The coexistence of old and new allows constructive change. But the modern and the traditional are seldom able to coexist easily. Generally one replaces the other, and the tension between the two generates friction between generations about how to live. Probably nowhere is the conflict between modern (often interpreted to mean Western) and traditional more noted than in moral questions such as abortion. As Donna Lee Bowen shows, although Muslim theologians oppose abortion on principle, they leave room for exceptions to their general rule, most notably when the health of the mother is endangered. The debate over abortion has not yet hit the Middle East with the force it has attained in the West, but a desire to safeguard moral values and avoid the deterioration of morals seen in Western countries underlies much of the concern over increased abortion rates.

In the past, religion reinforced the family as another vital institution of socialization. Islamic brotherhoods, as discussed in W. Stephen Howard's article about education in Sudan, were originally guiding spiritual and moral forces throughout most of the Muslim world. They governed the croplands and provided spiritual and social guidance as well as education for the community. Over time, secular education has replaced religious schools, but the moral force of teachers and their position in the community remains strong today.

Education is the critical necessity for modern careers. Literacy in the Middle East averages 40 to 60 percent, but is as low as 28 percent in some countries. Female literacy ranges from 15 or 20 percent to 60 percent and higher in Jordan, Palestine, and the United Arab Emirates. Girls in urban areas of the Middle East have improved access to education. The newly independent Middle Eastern nations have recognized that education is a major challenge and have poured resources into facilities, teacher training, and rural education. But with populations growing rapidly, schools simply cannot be built nor teachers trained fast enough to keep up, except in the oil-rich states. Governments do go to great lengths to train and retain teachers. Education, seen as the most important key to social mobility, has been eagerly sought.

The tragedy for young graduates in Egypt, Morocco, Algeria, and other labor-exporting countries is that few opportunities exist for employment. The roadblocks which restrict young men from getting on with life push some to migrate and others to join Islamist groups, which promote conservative Islamic revival. Youssef Ibrahim quotes a young Algerian who was asked in June 1990 why he had supported the Islamic Salvation Front (FIS) in recent elections: "In this country if you are a young man . . . you have only four choices: you can remain unemployed and celibate because there are no jobs and no apartments to live in; you can work in the black market and risk being arrested; you can try to emigrate to France to sweep the streets of Paris or Marseilles; or you can join the FIS and vote for Islam" (Ibrahim 1990).

Many families sacrifice enormously to educate at least one son. A peasant family in a mountainous area of Morocco is typical. The parents planned to educate as many of their sons as possible. The first son remained to work with his father in the family fields. The second son joined the army and began to contribute part of his salary to support son number three, who was in secondary school in the nearest provincial capital. Son number four took a baccalaureate and became an air traffic controller with the military. Son number five attended a university, then became a government bureaucrat. Sons six and seven were expected to become engineers. The youngest two sons—numbers eight and nine—had the combined financial support of every older brother and groaned under the weight of family expectations.

In some countries, swelling university populations have created a huge number of unemployable white-collar workers. While white-collar jobs may bring prestige, skilled and unskilled labor are in higher demand and in many cases bring higher salaries than positions as clerks, professionals, or bureaucrats. Diane Singerman describes how Middle Easterners obtain precious commodities like education, training, and jobs. Perhaps to a greater extent than in the West, where families matter but the individual is expected to be self-sufficient, families mobilize networks to obtain jobs or education for their children.

In bedouin and agriculturalist societies the family or household produced most of what it needed, and little was purchased. With industrialization and urbanization, a job or career became important to support a family. As some Middle Eastern nations grew wealthy in the oil boom, overpopulated poorer nations furnished them with skilled and unskilled workers. Rapid urbanization pushed housing, transportation, and service infrastructures past the breaking point. The oil-rich nations imported workers, but in labor-rich, capital-poor nations such as Egypt, Morocco, Algeria, and Tunisia unemployment is over 30 percent and around 10 percent of the work force works overseas.

Brian Barber, writing about adolescent men in Gaza in the aftermath of the first Intifada, emphasizes how politics underlies all aspects of young people's lives. For Palestinians, national identity and its economic and social ramifications are the focus of individual lives. Despite the violence and chaos these young men experienced as adolescents, individually they are stable and secure, responsibly pursuing career options as their situations permit. This concern with politics is reflected in Quintan Wiktorowicz's article on Islamist activism. When most Westerners think of Islamist activism, which they often call Islamic fundamentalism, they think of terrorist cells and plots against governments. Wiktorowicz discusses how prominent activists contribute to the community by training young people, teaching them about Islam, and organizing their political input. Nowhere is the collision between old and new, between tradition and the present, more dynamic than in questions of religion. Islamists and all Muslims who phrase political questions in religious terms play into this dynamic.

The Middle Eastern community, then, is a scene with many contradictions. There are close-knit extended families and migrant laborers living alone. There are old-fashioned water wheels and modern electric pumps. There are mules and metros. But the real story is told in the lives of individuals who fashion a family and a career, who form a community. All the customs and ceremonies—greeting, visiting, eating, exchanging—are a means of getting through the daily grind of raising and educating a family and, quite simply, of surviving. As these everyday rituals unfold, many conflicts between tradition and modernity are expressed. Some are resolved, and others are laid aside to dissolve in time as the problems are coped with from day to day.

REFERENCES

Ibrahim, Youssef. 1990. "Militant Muslims Grow Stronger as Algeria's Economy Grows Weaker." *New York Times*, June 25. Quoted in Mark Tessler, "The Origins of Popular Support for Islamist Movements: A Political Economy Analysis," in *Islam, Democracy and the State in North Africa*, ed. John P. Entelis (Bloomington: Indiana University Press), 93–126.

15. The Doum Tree of Wad Hamid

Tayeb Salih

"The Doum Tree of Wad Hamid" by Sudanese author Salih, is a classic story of accommodation of the old and the new in a village. It offers lessons best heeded by developers, city dwellers, and national leaders. Although the story pits the villagers against outsiders, the opposition is far from clear-cut. Wad Hamid is not a simple, stick-in-the-mud village; it is a place that will always endure. —Eds.

Were you to come to our village as a tourist, it is likely, my son, that you would not stay long. If it were in winter time, when the palm trees are pollinated, you would find that a dark cloud had descended over the village. This, my son, would not be dust, nor yet that mist which rises up after rainfall. It would be a swarm of those sand flies which obstruct all paths to those who wish to enter our village. Maybe you have seen this pest before, but I swear that you have never seen this particular species. Take this gauze netting, my son, and put it over your head. While it won't protect you against these devils, it will at least help you to bear them. I remember a friend of my son's, a fellow student at school, whom my son invited to stay with us a year ago at this time. His people come from the town. He stayed one night with us and got up next day, feverish, with a running nose and swollen face; he swore that he wouldn't spend another night with us.

If you were to come to us in summer you would find the horseflies with us—enormous flies the size of young sheep, as we say. In comparison to these, the sand flies are a thousand times more bearable. They are savage flies, my son: they bite, sting, buzz, and whir. They have a special love for man and no sooner smell him out than attach themselves to him. Wave them off you, my son—God curse all sand flies.

And were you to come at a time which was neither summer nor winter you would find nothing at all. No doubt, my son, you read the papers daily, listen to the radio, and go to the cinema once or twice a week. Should you

Adapted from *Modern Arabic Short Stories*, ed. and trans. Denys Johnson-Davies (London: Heinemann, 1967, 1976).

become ill you have the right to be treated in a hospital, and if you have a son he is entitled to receive education at a school. I know, my son, that you hate dark streets and like to see electric light shining out into the night. I know, too, that you are not enamoured of walking and that riding donkeys gives you a bruise on your backside. Oh, I wish, my son, I wish—the asphalted roads of the towns—the modern means of transport—the fine comfortable buses. We have none of all this—we are people who live on what God sees fit to give us.

Tomorrow you will depart from our village, of this I am sure, and you will be right to do so. What have you to do with such hardship? We are thick-skinned people and in this we differ from others. We have become used to this hard life, in fact we like it, but we ask no one to subject himself to the difficulties of our life. Tomorrow you will depart, my son—I know that. Before you leave, though, let me show you one thing—something which, in a manner of speaking, we are proud of. In the towns you have museums, places in which the local history and the great deeds of the past are preserved. This thing that I want to show you can be said to be a museum. It is one thing we insist our visitors see.

Once a preacher, sent by the government, came to us to stay for a month. He arrived at a time when the horseflies had never been fatter. On the very first day the man's face swelled up. He bore this manfully and joined us in evening prayers on the second night, and after prayers he talked to us of the delights of the primitive life. On the third day he was down with malaria, he contracted dysentery, and his eyes were completely gummed up. I visited him at noon and found him prostrate in bed, with a boy standing at his head waving away the flies.

"O Shaykh," I said to him, "there is nothing in our village to show you, though I would like you to see the doum tree of Wad Hamid." He didn't ask me what Wad Hamid's doum tree was, but I presumed that he had heard of it, for who has not? He raised his face, which was like the lung of a slaughtered cow; his eyes (as I said) were firmly closed, though I knew that behind the lashes lurked a certain bitterness. "By God," he said to me, "if this were the doum tree of Jandal, and you the Muslims who fought with Ali and Muᵓawiya, and I the arbitrator between you, holding your fate in these two hands of mine, I would not stir an inch!" and he spat upon the ground as though to curse me and turned his face away. After that we heard that the Shaykh had cabled to those who had sent him, saying: "The horseflies have eaten into my neck, malaria has burnt up my skin, and dysentery has lodged itself in my bowels. Come to my rescue, may God bless you—these are people who are in no need of me or of any other preacher." And so the man departed and the government sent us no preacher after him.

But, my son, our village actually witnessed many great men of power and influence, people with names that rang through the country like drums, who we never even dreamed would ever come here—they came, by God, in droves.

We have arrived. Have patience, my son, in a little while there will be the noonday breeze to lighten the agony of this pest upon your face.

Here it is: the doum tree of Wad Hamid. Look how it holds its head aloft to the skies; look how its roots strike down into the earth; look at its full, sturdy trunk, like the form of a comely woman, at the branches on high resembling the mane of a frolicsome steed! In the afternoon, when the sun is low, the doum tree casts its shadow from this high mound right across the river so that someone sitting on the far bank can rest in its shade. At dawn, when the sun rises, the shadow of the tree stretches across the cultivated land and houses right up to the cemetery. Don't you think it is like some mythical eagle spreading its wings over the village and everyone in it? Once the government, wanting to put through an agricultural scheme, decided to cut it down: they said that the best place for setting up the pump was where the doum tree stood. As you can see, the people of our village are concerned solely with their everyday needs, and I cannot remember their ever having rebelled against anything. However, when they heard about cutting down the doum tree they all rose up as one man and barred the district commissioner's way. That was in the time of foreign rule. The flies assisted them too—the horseflies. The man was surrounded by the clamoring people shouting that if the doum tree were cut down they would fight the government to the last man, while the flies played havoc with the man's face. As his papers were scattered in the water we heard him cry out: "All right—doum tree stay—scheme no stay!" And so neither the pump nor the scheme came about and we kept our doum tree.

Let us go home, my son, for this is no time for talking in the open. This hour just before sunset is a time when the army of sand flies becomes particularly active before going to sleep. At such a time no one who isn't well accustomed to them and has become as thick-skinned as we are can bear their stings. Look at it, my son, look at the doum tree: lofty, proud, and haughty as though—as though it were some ancient idol. Wherever you happen to be in the village you can see it; in fact, you can even see it from four villages away.

Tomorrow you will depart from our village, of that there is no doubt, the mementos of the short walk we have taken visible upon your face, neck and hands. But before you leave I shall finish the story of the tree, the doum tree of Wad Hamid. Come in, my son, treat this house as your own.

You ask who planted the doum tree?

No one planted it my son. Is the ground in which it grows arable land? Do you not see that it is stony and appreciably higher than the river bank, like the pedestal of a statue, while the river twists and turns below it like a sacred snake, one of the ancient gods of the Egyptians? My son, no one planted it. Drink your tea, for you must be in need of it after the trying experience you have undergone. Most probably it grew up by itself, though no one remembers having known it other than as you now find it. Our sons opened their eyes to find it commanding the village. And we, when we take ourselves back to childhood memories, to that dividing line beyond which you remember nothing, see in our minds a giant doum tree standing on a river bank; everything beyond it is as cryptic as talismans, like the boundary between day and night, like that fading light which is not the dawn but the light directly preceding the break of day. My son, do you find that you can follow what I say? Are you aware of this feeling I have within me but which I am powerless to express? Every new generation finds the doum tree as though it had been born at the time of their birth and would grow up with them. Go and sit with the people of this village and listen to them recounting their dreams. A man awakens from sleep and tells his neighbor how he found himself in a vast, sandy tract of land, the sand as white as pure silver; how his feet sank in as he walked so that he could only draw them out again with difficulty; how he walked and walked until he was overcome with thirst and stricken with hunger, while the sands stretched endlessly around him; how he climbed a hill and on reaching the top espied a dense forest of doum trees with a single tall tree in the center which in comparison with the others looked like a camel amid a herd of goats; how the man went down the hill to find that the earth seemed to be rolled up before him so that it was but a few steps before he found himself under the doum tree of Wad Hamid; how he then discovered a vessel containing milk, its surface still fresh with froth, and how the milk did not go down though he drank until he had quenched his thirst. At which his neighbor says to him: "Rejoice at release from your troubles."

You can also hear one of the women telling her friend: "It was as though I were in a boat sailing through a channel in the sea, so narrow that I could stretch out my hands and touch the shore on either side. I found myself on the crest of a mountainous wave which carried me upward till I was almost touching the clouds, then bore me down into a dark, fathomless pit. I began shouting in my fear, but my voice seemed to be trapped in my throat. Suddenly I found the channel opening out a little. I saw that on the two shores were black, leafless trees with thorns, the tips of which were like the heads of hawks. I saw the two shores closing in upon me and the trees seemed to be walking toward me. I was filled with terror and called out at the top of my voice, "O Wad Hamid!" As I looked I saw a man with a radiant face and a heavy white beard flowing down over his chest, dressed in spotless white and holding a string of amber prayer beads. Placing his hand on my brow he said: "Be not afraid," and I was calmed. Then I found the shore opening up and the water flowing gently. I looked to my left and saw fields of ripe corn, water wheels turning, and cattle grazing, and on the shore stood the doum tree of Wad Hamid. The boat came to rest under the tree and the man got out, tied up the boat, and stretched out his hand to me.

He then struck me gently on the shoulder with the string of beads, picked up a doum fruit from the ground and put it in my hand. When I turned around he was no longer there."

"That was Wad Hamid," her friend then says to her. "You will have an illness that will bring you to the brink of death, but you will recover. You must make an offering to Wad Hamid under the doum tree." So it is, my son, that there is not a man or woman, young or old, who dreams at night without seeing the doum tree of Wad Hamid at some point in the dream.

You ask me why it was called the doum tree of Wad Hamid and who Wad Hamid was. Be patient, my son—have another cup of tea.

At the beginning of home rule a civil servant came to inform us that the government was intending to set up a stopping place for the steamer. He told us that the national government wished to help us and to see us progress, and his face was radiant with enthusiasm as he talked. But he could see that the faces around him expressed no reaction. My son, we are not people who travel very much, and when we wish to do so for some important matter such as registering land, or seeking advice about a matter of divorce, we take a morning's ride on our donkeys and then board the steamer from the neighboring village. My son, we have grown accustomed to this; in fact, it is precisely for this reason that we breed donkeys. It is little wonder, then, that the government official could see nothing in the people's faces to indicate that they were pleased with the news. His enthusiasm waned and, being at his wit's end, he began to fumble for words.

"Where will the stopping place be?" someone asked him after a period of silence. The official replied that there was only one suitable place— where the doum tree stood. Had you that instant brought along a woman and had her stand among those men as naked as the day her mother bore her, they could not have been more astonished.

"The steamer usually passes here on a Wednesday," one of the men quickly replied. "If you made a stopping place, then it would be here on Wednesday afternoon." The official replied that the time fixed for the steamer to stop by their village would be four o'clock on Wednesday afternoon.

"But that is the time when we visit the tomb of Wad Hamid at the doum tree," answered the man. "When we take our women and children and make offerings. We do this every week." The official laughed. "Then change the day!" he replied. Had the official told these men at that moment that every one of them was a bastard, that would not have angered them more than this remark of his. They rose up as one man, bore down upon him, and would certainly have killed him if I had not intervened and snatched him from their clutches. I then put him on a donkey and told him to make good his escape.

And so it was that the steamer still does not stop here and that we still ride off on our donkeys for a whole morning and take the steamer from the neighboring village when circumstances require us to travel. We content ourselves with the thought that we visit the tomb of Wad Hamid with our women and children and that we make offerings there every Wednesday as our fathers and fathers' fathers did before us.

Excuse me, my son, while I perform the sunset prayer—it is said that the sunset prayer is "strange": if you don't catch it in time it eludes you. *God's pious servants—I declare that there is no god but God and I declare that Muhammad is His Servant and His Prophet—Peace be upon you and the mercy of God!*

Ah, ah. For a week this back of mine has been giving me pain. What do you think it is, my son? I know, though, it's just old age. Oh, to be young! In my young days I would breakfast off half a sheep, drink the milk of five cows for supper, and be able to lift a sack of dates with one hand. He lies who says he ever beat me at wrestling. They used to call me "the crocodile." Once I swam the river, using my chest to push a boat loaded with wheat to the other shore—at night! On the shore were some men at work at their water wheels, who threw down their clothes in terror and fled when they saw me pushing the boat toward them.

"Oh people," I shouted at them, "what's wrong, shame upon you! Don't you know me? I'm 'the crocodile.' By God, the devils themselves would be scared off by your ugly faces."

My son, have you asked me what we do when we're ill?

I laugh because I know what's going on in your head. You townsfolk hurry to the hospital on the slightest pretext. If one of you hurts his finger you dash off to the doctor, who puts a bandage on, and you carry it in a sling for days; and even then it doesn't get better. Once I was working in the fields and something bit my finger—this little finger of mine. I jumped to my feet and looked around in the grass, where I found a snake lurking. I swear to you it was longer than my arm. I took hold of it by the head and crushed it between two fingers, then bit into my finger, sucked out the blood, and took up a handful of dust and rubbed it on the bite.

But that was only a little thing. What do we do when faced with real illness?

This neighbour of ours, now. One day her neck swelled up and she was confined to bed for two months. One night she had a heavy fever, so at first dawn she rose from her bed and dragged herself along till she came—yes, my son, till she came to the doum tree of Wad Hamid. The woman told us what happened.

"I was under the doum tree," she said, "with hardly sufficient strength to stand up, and called out at the top of my voice: 'O Wad Hamid, I have come to you to seek refuge and protection—I shall sleep here at your tomb and under your doum tree. Either you let me die or you restore me to life; I shall not leave here until one of these two things happens.'

"And so I curled myself up in fear," the woman continued with her story, "and was soon overcome by sleep. While midway between wakefulness and sleep I suddenly heard sounds of recitation from the Koran and bright light, as sharp as a knife edge, radiated out, joining up the two river banks, and I saw the doum tree prostrating itself in worship. My heart throbbed so violently that I thought it would leap up through my mouth. I saw a venerable old man with a white beard and wearing a spotless white robe come up to me, a smile on his face. He struck me on the head with his string of prayer beads and called out: 'Arise.'

"I swear that I got up, I know not how, and went home, I know not how. I arrived back at dawn and woke up my husband, my son, and my daughters. I told my husband to light the fire and make tea. Then I ordered my daughters to give trilling cries of joy, and the whole village prostrated themselves before us. I swear that I have never again been afraid, nor yet ill."

Yes, my son, we are people who have no experience of hospitals. In small matters such as the bites of scorpions, fever, sprains, and fractures, we take to our beds until we are cured. When in serious trouble we go to the doum tree.

Shall I tell you the story of Wad Hamid, my son, or would you like to sleep? Townsfolk don't go to sleep till late at night—I know that of them. We, though, go to sleep directly the birds are silent, the flies stop harrying the cattle, the leaves of the trees settle down, the hens spread their wings over their chicks, and the goats turn on their sides to chew the cud. We and our animals are alike: we rise in the morning when they rise and go to sleep when they sleep, our breathing and theirs following one and the same pattern.

My father, reporting what my grandfather had told him, said: "Wad Hamid, in times gone by, used to be the slave of a wicked man. He was one of God's holy saints but kept his faith to himself, not daring to pray openly lest his wicked master should kill him. When he could no longer bear his life with this infidel, he called upon God to deliver him, and a voice told him to spread his prayer mat on the water and that when it stopped by the shore he should descend. The prayer mat put him down at the place where the doum tree is now and which used to be wasteland. And there he stayed alone, praying the whole day. At nightfall a man came to him with dishes of food, so he ate and continued his worship till dawn."

All this happened before the village was built up. It is as though this village, with its inhabitants, its waterwheels and buildings, had become split off from the earth. Anyone who tells you he knows the history of its origin is a liar. Other places begin by being small and then grow larger, but this village of ours came into being at one bound. Its population neither increases nor decreases, while its appearance remains unchanged. And ever since our village has existed, so has the doum tree of Wad Hamid; and just as no one remembers how it originated and grew, so no one remembers how the doum tree came to grow in a patch of rocky ground by the river, standing above it like a sentinel.

When I took you to visit the tree, my son, do you remember the iron railing round it? Do you remember the marble plaque standing on a stone pedestal with "The doum tree of Wad Hamid" written on it? Do you remember the doum tree with the gilded crescents above the tomb? They are the only new things about the village since God first planted it here, and I shall now recount to you how they came into being.

When you leave us tomorrow—and you will certainly do so, swollen of face and inflamed of eye—it will be fitting if you do not curse us but rather think kindly of us and of the things that I have told you this night, for you may well find that your visit to us was not wholly bad.

You remember that some years ago we had Members of Parliament and political parties and a great deal of to-ing and fro-ing which we couldn't make head or tail of. The roads would sometimes cast down strangers at our very doors, just as the waves of the sea wash up strange weeds. Though not a single one of them prolonged his stay beyond one night, they would nevertheless bring us the news of the great fuss going on in the capital. One day they told us that the government which had driven out imperialism had been substituted by an even bigger and noisier government.

"And who has changed it?" we asked them, but received no answer. As for us, ever since we refused to allow the stopping place to be set up at the doum tree, no one has disturbed our tranquil existence. Two years passed without our knowing what form the government had taken, black or white. Its emissaries passed through our village without staying in it, while we thanked God that He had saved us the trouble of putting them up. So things went on till, four years ago, a new government came into power. As though this new authority wished to make us conscious of its presence, we awoke one day to find an official with an enormous hat and small head, in the company of two soldiers, measuring up and doing calculations at the doum tree. We asked them what it was about, to which they replied that the government wished to build a stopping place for the steamer under the doum tree.

"But we have already given you our answer about that," we told them. "What makes you think we'll accept it now?"

"The government which gave in to you was a weak one," they said, "but the position has now changed."

To cut a long story short, we took them by the scruffs of their necks, hurled them into the water, and went off to our work. It wasn't more than a week later when a group of soldiers came along commanded by the small-headed official with the large hat, shouting, "Arrest that man, and that one, and that one," until they'd taken off twenty of us, I among them. We spent a month in prison. Then one day the very soldiers who had put us there opened the prison gates. We asked them what it was all about but no one said anything. Outside the prison we found a great gathering of people; no sooner had we been spotted than there were shouts and cheering and we were embraced by some cleanly dressed people, heavily scented and with gold watches gleaming on their wrists. They carried us off in a great procession, back to our own people. There we found an unbelievably immense gathering of people, carts, horses, and camels. We said to each other, "The din and flurry of the capital has caught up with us." They made us twenty men stand in a row and the people passed along it shaking us by the hand: the Prime Minister—the President of the Parliament—the President of the Senate—the member for such-and-such constituency—the member for such-and-such other constituency.

We looked at each other without understanding a thing of what was going on around us except that our arms were aching with all the hand-shakes we had been receiving from those Presidents and Members of Parliament.

Then they took us off in a great mass to the place where the doum tree and the tomb stand. The Prime Minister laid the foundation stone for the monument you've seen, and for the dome you've seen, and for the railing you've seen. Like a tornado blowing up for a while and then passing over, so that mighty host disappeared as suddenly as it had come without spending a night in the village—no doubt because of the horseflies, which, that particular year, were as large and fat and buzzed and whirred as much as during the year the preacher came to us.

One of those strangers who were occasionally cast upon us in the village later told us the story of all this fuss and bother.

"The people," he said, "hadn't been happy about this government since it had come to power, for they knew that it had got there by bribing a number of the Members of Parliament. They therefore bided their time and waited for the right opportunities to present themselves, while the opposition looked around for something to spark things off. When the doum tree incident occurred and they marched you all off and slung you into prison, the newspapers took this up and the leader of the government which had resigned made a fiery speech in Parliament in which he said:

" 'To such tyranny has this government come that it has begun to inter-fere in the beliefs of the people, in those holy things held most sacred by them.' Then taking a most imposing stance and in a voice choked with emotion, he said: 'Ask our worthy Prime Minister about the doum tree of Wad Hamid. Ask him how it was that he permitted himself to send his troops and henchmen to desecrate that pure and holy place!'

"The people took up the cry and throughout the country their hearts responded to the incident of the doum tree as to nothing before. Perhaps the reason is that in every village in this country there is some monument like the doum tree of Wad Hamid which people see in their dreams. After a month of fuss and shouting and inflamed feelings, fifty members of the government were forced to withdraw their support, their constituencies having warned them that unless they did so they would wash their hands of them. And so the government fell, the first government returned to power and the leading paper in the country wrote: 'The doum tree of Wad Hamid has become the symbol of the nation's awakening.'"

Since that day we have been unaware of the existence of the new government and not one of those great giants of men who visited us has put in an appearance; we thank God that He has spared us the trouble of having to shake them by the hand. Our life returned to what it had been: no water-pump, no agricultural scheme, no stopping place for the steamer. But we kept our doum tree, which casts its shadow over the southern bank in the afternoon and, in the morning, spreads its shadow over the fields and houses right up to the cemetery, with the river flowing below it like some sacred legendary snake. And our village has acquired a marble monument, an iron railing, and a dome with gilded crescents.

When the man had finished what he had to say he looked at me with an enigmatic smile playing at the corners of his mouth like the faint flickerings of a lamp.

"And when," I asked, "will they set up the water-pump, and put through the agricultural scheme and the stopping place for the steamer?"

He lowered his head and paused before answering me, "When people go to sleep and don't see the doum tree in their dreams."

"And when will that be?" I said.

"I mentioned to you that my son is in the town studying at school," he replied. "It wasn't I who put him there; he ran away and went there on his own, and it is my hope that he will stay where he is and not return. When my son's son passes out of school and the number of young men with souls foreign to our own increases, then perhaps the water-pump will be set up and the agricultural scheme put into being—maybe then the steamer will stop at our village—under the doum tree of Wad Hamid."

"And do you think," I said to him, "that the doum tree will one day be cut down?" He looked at me for a long while as though wishing to project, through his tired, misty eyes, something which he was incapable of doing by word.

"There will not be the least necessity for cutting down the doum tree. There is not the slightest reason for the tomb to be removed. What all these people have overlooked is that there's plenty of room for all these things: the doum tree, the tomb, the water-pump, and the steamer's stopping place."

When he had been silent for a time he gave me a look which I don't know how to describe, though it stirred within me a feeling of sadness, sadness for some obscure thing which I was unable to define. Then he said: "Tomorrow, without doubt, you will be leaving us. When you arrive at your destination, think well of us and judge us not too harshly."

16. Abortion and the Ethics of Life

Donna Lee Bowen

Muslims hold that Islam was ordained for every place and every time and that it gives guidance to those facing contemporary problems. The Muslim stance on abortion has received attention as abortion has been legalized in a handful of Muslim countries, and as more women quietly seek abortions. Despite publicity to the contrary, Islam permits abortion under certain well-defined circumstances, but it does discourage it. Personal ambivalence about abortion means that it is rarely discussed publicly, and when abortions are sought, they are generally sought in secret. Bowen's article emphasizes the flexibility of Islamic law when looking at personal circumstances. —Eds.

Middle Easterners find the question of abortion as thorny and conflict-laden as Westerners do, for life is strongly valued both in Islam and in Arab culture. In the Middle East, as in much of the world, ethical values are grounded in religion. Islam, Christianity, and Judaism all emphasize preserving and valuing life and the importance of children. For Muslims, as for most people, love of children makes the idea of terminating a pregnancy traumatic. Muslims believe that children are a joy, an adornment of life, and a gift from God, who bestows children on their parents with the responsibility to raise them righteously. They quote from the Qurʾan: "God has made for you mates from yourselves and made for you, out of them, children and grandchildren" (16:72).

Much of the worldwide debate over abortion boils down to a question of which alternative is worse, abortion or carrying the pregnancy to term. Few societies present abortion as a social good, for it denies the major need of all communities: children which are their future. Women in the Middle East—along with Muslim religious scholars—hold that abortions, however undesirable, are nonetheless at times justifiable. Despite Islam's emphasis on valuing life, Islamic teachings do not prohibit abortion, and teachings on abortion differ greatly. While most schools of Islamic law prohibit abortion as a general rule, a minority are more permissive and permit abortion within a generous window of time. However, women seldom speak openly about obtaining abortions, and there have not been political movements to promote access to abortion. This hesitancy can be attributed to two major factors which are mutually reinforcing: the value of life and the value of community welfare and morality. While the West emphasizes the individual and individual rights, the Middle East puts primary value on the community and family. Muslims, and in particular Muslim religious scholars, consider any action which threatens community welfare and morals dangerous both for the individual and for the group.

The fact that Islamic law permits abortion under certain conditions does not mean that Muslims approve of abortion. The Muslim stand on abortion could be summarized as a soft "no." While Islam allows abortion under certain conditions, it also strongly regulates those conditions. In Islamic law (*shariᶜa*), actions are assigned one of five values, ranging from obligatory (prayer, fasting during Ramadan) through recommended (marriage), neutral, and disapproved (divorce) to, finally, forbidden (adultery, murder). Abortion is not a recommended action, or even a neutral action on the Muslim legal scale. It is qualified as *makruh*, disapproved, detested, or reprehensible in some cases. In other cases, abortion is considered *harram*, prohibited. Abortion is a particularly sensitive area because it denies life where life is possible. Because of this, women generally approach abortion with caution and usually only when caught in a serious dilemma which involves life, health, family relations, or honor. A woman resorts to abortion after pitting the loss of potential human life against whatever human difficulty or tragedy looms in the future if the fetus comes to term.

Abortion on demand (social abortion) is legal in only two Middle Eastern Muslim countries, Turkey and Tunisia. Iran, responding to high birth rates, began in 1994 to allow abortions to be performed again, but has not formally legalized the practice. Even in these countries, abortions can be difficult to obtain in rural areas or in certain hospitals. In Tunisia, women caution friends that some hospitals refuse to perform abortions, or require more medical documentation than other, more permissive hospitals. In other countries, such as Jordan, Kuwait, Saudi Arabia, Iraq, Algeria, and Morocco, although therapeutic abortion (to preserve the mother's health) is legal with the signature of the wife, the husband, and the physician, abortions are performed by physicians in private clinics. Public health hospitals do not like to perform abortions, and acknowledge that the political fallout of doing so can be heavy.

HAVING AN ABORTION IS A SERIOUS AFFAIR
IN MUSLIM CULTURE

A Jordanian woman, Maha, described the climate for abortions in Amman.

> Abortion is a big deal culturally, so women have to have abortions secretly
> with the help of a very good friend. They go to the hospital, stay a couple
> of hours, and then their friend takes them home to relax. A few months ago
> one of my friends called and asked me to pick her up at the hospital. When
> I arrived she was dizzy and weak. I asked her why the doctor had let her
> go, why he hadn't kept her until she had recovered. A few weeks later when
> I put everything together I realized that she had secretly had an abortion.
> She didn't even dare tell me.

Maha went on to explain that abortion in Jordan is a very sensitive issue.

> Abortion is just like honor killings. No one wants to talk about it, although
> it goes on. Abortion exists, but no one wants to disturb it. People say, "it is
> not a human yet so it isn't killing." Bit by bit in Jordan we're beginning to
> work on social issues. My cousin is a social worker and she tells me about
> what is really going on in Amman—child abuse, rape, children running
> around with no parental supervision—things I had no idea about when I
> was growing up. But like honor killings, abortion hits at something deep
> in our culture, and it reflects things we are not ready to face.

People's belief that abortion is serious, something they hesitate to speak
openly about, is apparent when individuals tell stories about abortions. A
few typical ones follow.

- An American professor working in Rabat, Morocco, tells of drinking
  cola in his apartment with a young family friend, a male lycée student. After some discussion of school matters, the student confided
  what was on his mind. "I go around with a group of friends, all sixth-
  year students [the year before the baccalaureate]. One of the girls just
  told us that she is pregnant [by one of his male friends in the group].
  We've been working for the past two weeks to collect as much money
  as we can. We need $250 to pay for her abortion."
- The fashionable, middle-aged Egyptian wife of a demographer who
  works on population issues brags about her two sons. Then, over
  drinks before dinner, she quietly tells me that she has had four abortions as well.
- A middle-aged traditional housewife tells me that abortion is com-

mon in Salé, Morocco. "I'm done having my family; they're growing up, and I'm far too old to have any more children. When I get pregnant I go to the doctor. I don't tell him I want an abortion. I tell him my period hasn't come. He performs a D and C [dilation and curettage], and I'm back to normal. I've probably done this four or five times. The doctor doesn't ask questions, and I don't say anything."

• A young army wife, in her early thirties with four small children, is horrified to discover that she is pregnant again. She confides in me that she has heard people talk about abortion, and sometimes she thinks she should have one. She says, "I don't think I can handle another pregnancy right now." She stops, then looks at me, and says, "But everyone tells me I cannot have an abortion. It is against Islam."

For the past twenty years, I have interviewed women, men, religious scholars at all levels, and government officials about different aspects of family planning. Most of the interviews have taken place in Morocco, which is the primary focus of my research, but because of my interest in family planning in general, I've talked to people about it all over the Middle East. Whenever I ask religious scholars (ʿulama, singular ʿalim) about abortion, the answer has been the same: "Islam forbids abortion." Then after a short pause, the ʿalim continues, "Of course, if the mother's life is in danger . . ." and proceeds to outline exceptions to the religious prohibition. Lay Muslims do not necessarily know about the exceptions. Many Muslims— young and old, educated and uneducated, in the United States and in the Middle East—have told me that abortion is totally prohibited, no matter what the situation, having never heard that Islam permits it in some cases.

When I went back through my notes looking for data on abortion, I was struck by the cursory nature of entries on abortion. The brevity of the stories quoted above reflects how little people talk about abortion, how few details they give about arranging or having one. Their brevity may be partly due to their discomfort at speaking about a practice with which they are not culturally or morally at ease. Under certain circumstances, people may judge abortion to be necessary, but this does not necessarily mean that they advocate or are comfortable with the practice. The affirmation of life, expressed by having children, is a prime cultural and religious value. That abortion negates life, a primary cultural value, may explain Muslims' hesitation about it. For Muslims, asserting the value of life is as natural as breathing.

WHAT MUSLIM RELIGIOUS SCHOLARS SAY ABOUT ABORTION

In Islam all religious law begins with what the Qurʾan says on an issue. Failing a reference in the Qurʾan, one looks to the *sunna* of the Prophet and to the *hadith,* which are accounts of the Prophet Muhammad's actions and conversations. The sunna are verbal accounts; the hadith are written versions of the sunna. Part of the explanation for the scope of opinions on abortion stems from the fact that the Qur²an does not mention it; neither do the sunna and hadith. The Qur²an forbids infanticide in several forceful statements, and the Muslim religious scholars draw parallels from the Quranic prohibition in ruling on abortion.

Before the coming of Islam, the tribes of the Arabian peninsula routinely rid themselves of unwanted newborns by leaving them outside to die of exposure to the elements. The children victimized were generally girls, for girls were considered a drain on family resources rather than an asset. This practice was condemned in the eighty-first *surah* (chapter) of the Qur²an. There, in a description of Judgment Day, a verse mentions the time "when the infant girl, buried alive, is asked for what crime she was slain." Other verses in the Qur²an caution, "Do not kill that which God has made sacred except for just cause" (17:33) and instruct parents, "You shall not kill your children because you cannot support them; we provide sustenance for you and for them" (6:151); "Kill not your children for fear of want, we provide sustenance for them and for you. Their killing is a great sin" (17:31).

The revulsion felt in Islam at this practice has continued to the present day. By extrapolation, these verses became the basic text forbidding the killing of infants still in their mother's womb, and ²ulama use them as a juridical parallel to rule against abortion. One should not kill a newborn; neither should one kill an unborn child. This protection extends to both sexes, for Islam guarantees to both men and women the same protection of life. In pre-Islamic times the majority of infants killed were female, and the Prophet's prohibition of infanticide protected baby girls, but the principle protects boys as well. This is not the case in all cultures in which girls are less valued than boys. In Bombay, India, in 1992, a study of parents who had determined the sex of their fetus by ultrasound examination found that, of eight thousand abortions performed, only one fetus was male (Holloway 1994, 80). Neither Islam nor Middle Eastern culture tolerates such discrimination against females in the womb. I have listened to Middle Eastern women discuss the practice of sex-selective abortion in India and China, and their reactions reflect horror that a mother would abort solely because the fetus was female.

The question Islam asks is whether aborting a fetus is the same as killing a child. Some Muslims believe that it is. For example, Dr. Shahid Athar, a physician, writer, and speaker, speaks to Muslims and non-Muslims seeking answers to everyday questions in his booklet "Twenty-five Most Frequently Asked Questions about Islam," which is also on the Internet. Defining the Islamic position on abortion, he says, "Islam considers abortion as murder and does not permit it except to save the mother's life

(Qur²an 17:23–31, 6:151)" (Athar 2001). I have heard a few ʿalims in Morocco use the same words. Other scholars take a different approach to analyzing the situation. They first make the point that aborting a fetus is not a neutral action, for the fetus has, if not life itself, the potential for life, and the survival and strength of the Muslim community depends on multiplying and replenishing its numbers. Muslims are commanded to do so in a hadith of the Prophet: "Marry and multiply, for I shall make a display of you before other nations on the day of Judgment." Beyond this, most legal scholars recognize that an early-stage pregnancy is not the same as a newborn child. The critical point for Muslims is whether the fetus has been ensouled. Differences of opinion arose in the early Muslim community, and scholars put the soul's arrival at a variety of times, from conception to 120 days later.

When Muslim jurists use the term "abortion" (*ijhad*), they mean the killing of a created entity. If the spirit has not entered the fetus, then the act is not killing, for the fetus has not yet received the breath of life. The difference between the English term "abortion" and the reference term Muslims use is that, to religious scholars, abortion is the killing of the created fetus. So although "abortion" is forbidden, some schools of Islamic law allow the termination of pregnancy before a given period of time. The maximum period is 120 days or four months. The sheikh of al-Azhar University in Cairo stated in a newspaper article about abortion written just before the Cairo Population Conference in 1994 that "according to religious legislation, abortion is not available after the first four months, and then would be considered the same crime as killing a human being." The only exception he allowed to this was when the mother's life is in danger. Otherwise, even congenital defects are not sufficient reason to allow an abortion after four months. The fetus at that point "is a human being and you must not kill a person for his sickness." He goes on to state that "modern science can often compensate these days for such defects. . . . they are not a valid reason for abortion, unless the defect is critical, assuring the child's death, or threatening the mother's life, in which case abortion could be permitted" (*al-Ahram* 1994, 4). Over the last twenty years, scholars have differed on whether abortion of deformed fetuses is allowable—whether a fetus may have a right not to be born. In 1982, Kuwaiti jurists gave permission to abort deformed fetuses in the first three months of pregnancy. Another scholar permits abortion of deformed fetuses before forty days of pregnancy have elapsed. Other scholars forbid it, among them Jad al-Haqq, a late sheikh of al-Azhar, who pointed out that "an illness that cannot be cured today might be cured in the future." A major question here, which scholars are still debating, is what qualifies as a severe enough defect to allow abortion (Rispler-Chaim 1999, 134–36).

The window of 120 days does not mean that abortions performed during this period have no legal consequences. For the schools which follow this reasoning, abortion, while not prohibited during this time, is nevertheless makruh. Only a religiously acceptable reason, such as the mother's serious health problems, can render the abortion a neutral action. Over the years I have talked with numerous Muslim religious scholars as well as local religious leaders. All emphasized that when the mother's life was in question, abortion ceased to be a religious matter and became solely a medical question. Unlike Roman Catholics, for whom the life of the fetus cannot be sacrificed to preserve that of the mother, Muslims hold that the mother is the origin of the child's life, and as such, cannot be sacrificed for the fetus.

ABORTION UNDERMINES COMMUNITY WELL-BEING

In the West, abortion is often debated in terms of individual rights rather than morality: the right of a woman to control the use of her body is pitted against the moral right of the fetus to be born or of the community to protect its moral well-being and the rights of its unborn. In Muslim communities, a critical argument against abortion focuses on the welfare of the community. This argument has two components: the duty of ensuring healthy progeny to populate the community, and the effect of abortion on the morals of the community.

Over the past twenty years, sexuality has intruded more and more into everyday life. Latin American soap operas bring adultery and open sexuality onto TV screens every afternoon. In the evenings, Conan O'Brien and Jay Leno tell vulgar jokes on satellite TV. The Internet puts pornographic sites within the reach of anyone with a computer and modem. Foreign films feature scantily clad actresses in compromising situations. Young men and women meet in parks, on campus, and at work. University students have always been ahead of the curve when it comes to relations with the opposite sex, but most professors and observers believe that sexual relations among unmarried students are becoming more common. Residents of middle-class suburbs tell of well-dressed prostitutes soliciting customers on street corners only a few blocks away from the main city mosque. Newspapers run editorials exposing the recent explosion in prostitution and articles by prostitutes telling how prostitution supports a lavish lifestyle. In the mid-1990s Morocco was galvanized by the publicity given to a sex scandal involving a school inspector, his female student victims, and officials who for a price protected him. While the punishment was swift and befitted the crime, one result was unexpected. A young woman journalist told me that she believed that the scandal had altered the customary Moroccan family silence on sexuality. She commented that suddenly her family was talking about sex over the dinner table. As they kept up with the story, they opened up discussion about related matters. Her father and mother had never talked openly about sex before, she said, and suddenly the whole family, parents and children, were discussing sex, abuse, and political corruption. The U.S. parallel is the public discussion of sexual behavior occasioned by the Bill Clinton/Monica Lewinsky scandal. While sexuality was discussed openly in homes and in schools, most parents did not welcome their children's new acquaintance with sexual practices, which resulted from media coverage and public discussion of the president's impeachment.

One Syrian scholar put the problem this way:

> The family, which but a few years back was still preserving within the sanctum of the home certain genuine principles of Islamic education, now stands bewildered before this sweeping onslaught. It can no longer act in accordance with its beliefs and convictions, except in very limited and rare cases, for radio and television inside the home have shared with movies, theaters and wanton entertainment haunts outside the home in infixing more firmly, the impression of this crushing overpowering invasion. (al-Khayyir 1974, 347–48)

When Muslims discuss morals (*al-akhlaq*), they refer to sexuality, not financial dishonesty or political corruption. Muslim religious leaders believe that their main purpose is to safeguard community order, to prevent Muslim society from lapsing into chaos, and they believe that sexual permissiveness is one of the worst dangers. The worst examples of social disorder they can point to are public homosexual behavior and abortion on demand. Their criticism of the West focuses on sexual decadence, and particularly on open access to abortion.

Few Muslim leaders today oppose the use of birth control pills or other family planning measures as destructive of community morality. A few extreme conservatives follow Abul Aʾla Maududi, the Pakistani religious scholar and head of the conservative Jamaʿat-Islami, in prohibiting family planning on the grounds that it "lead[s] to illegitimate sex relations on a scale unprecedented in the history of our society."

SOCIAL REALITIES OF ABORTION

Despite the room opened up by jurists for abortion in the first 120 days of pregnancy or when the health of the mother is in danger, Muslims seem to be highly conservative about abortion. In Tunisia, where abortion has been legal since the early 1970s, the latest statistics available (for 1996) record 19,000 abortions, so that 7.8 percent of pregnancies ended in abortion. In Turkey, abortions are more common; in 1993 (the only year for which figures are available) 20.5 percent of pregnancies were terminated. In the world as a whole, 22 percent of pregnancies end in abortion, 15 percent in miscarriages and stillbirths, and 63 percent in live births (Alan Guttmacher Institute 2001). Abortion is especially common in countries with high birthrates: in 1997 70 percent of Russian pregnancies ended in abortion (a 25 percent decrease since 1992), as did 59 percent of Romanian pregnancies (Galway for Life 2001). In the United States in 1997 the ratio was 30.5 percent, the lowest in two decades (*Salt Lake Tribune* 2000).

Women in the Middle East use much the same reasoning as the Muslim ʿulama in figuring whether abortion is permissible. When I ask women about abortion, they too immediately exclaim, "Islam prohibits abortion." Then, as we talk more, they add qualifying conditions. Many women believe what was accepted wisdom in the United States in the nineteenth century, that abortion before the child quickens in the womb is not killing, for the pregnancy is not "real" until it makes its presence felt. Since women generally sense the movements of the child between the tenth and twelfth weeks, the time span they allow for abortion is much the same as that permitted by the more lenient schools of Islamic jurisprudence. Once they feel the movement in their womb, the pregnancy becomes actual, and the child they will bear a real entity. Abortion after this point becomes, as the Chief Mufti of New Delhi phrases it, "a great sin, rather than the smaller sin it is considered before 120 days" (Dahlburg 1995, 5).

For many women, the smaller sin of abortion before 120 days seems preferable to bearing another child. In Tunisia, as in many other developing countries, older women tend to seek abortions at a higher rate than young women who are trying to establish their families; there the highest abortion rates are found among women between twenty-five and thirty-nine (Jacobson 1990). Many women seek abortions because they already have a good-sized family and they fear the physical and mental demands of another pregnancy. One older Jordanian woman with six children secretly went for an abortion when she found herself pregnant again. "We have enough children. I am old and don't want to risk it. If I had told my husband, he would have prevented the abortion; he would be so angry. My relatives would be angry."

The sense that having an abortion warrants divine punishment haunts some women. Marcia Inhorn relates the story of a woman who was forced by her husband to undergo three abortions following her marriage. Her husband subsequently divorced her, and she married again. When she found herself unable to become pregnant, she believed that her infertility was a punishment from God for the abortions. "I'm afraid from God that I'm going to hell. But I think that I was too young then, and I did as I was told by my husband" (Inhorn 1996, 81).

Women seeking abortions tap into networks of other women. They secretly pass along the names of doctors willing to perform abortions. Women needing abortions can choose an expensive abortion in a private clinic or try to abort by traditional means. Abortions in private clinics cost from $200 to $250 in most Arab countries. They cost up to $3000 in Iran before the regime relaxed its official pro-natalist policy, loosened restrictions on family planning, and allowed a limited number of abortions to be performed in public health facilities. The high cost has meant that poorer women risk injury and death in substandard illegal abortions. Physicians often work in small clinics, or in some cases in their homes. Recently, a case was publicized in which a woman living in Amman, Jordan, died during an illegal abortion performed at the doctor's house. Evidently these deaths are not uncommon, and a number of cases have been reported in Jordan where women died during abortions in small hospitals. Even in countries where abortions are legal, physicians may refuse to perform them, and hospitals in some areas refuse to allow them to be performed in their facilities. In Morocco, abortions can only be performed with the written permission of both the father and the mother, as well as a statement from a physician. Despite these precautions, the public health system—which is the major health service supplier for the majority of the country's citizens—hesitates to perform abortions because of the political sensitivity of the issue and prefers to have nothing to do with the practice.

Traditionally, Muslims have tolerated a high amount of ambiguity regarding abortion—some forbidding all abortion, others permitting abortion until the fetus was 120 days old. This ambiguity allowed Muslims to emphasize moral values while still granting room for individuals whose circumstances mandated an abortion. The general rule was that abortions were prohibited. This affirmed the value of life and community order. Exceptions to the rule were granted on the word of the attending physician, which relegated the problem to medicine, and not to religiosity or morality. Thus, the importance of life was never questioned; rather, exceptional individual dilemmas were bracketed for the exceptional solution of abortion.

During the 1994 Cairo Population Conference, Benazir Bhutto, then prime minister of Pakistan, gave a speech which disappointed many feminists and development experts. She noted that abortion "strik[es] at the heart of a great many cultural values, in the north and in the south, in the mosque and in the church," and that "Islam places a great deal of stress on the sanctity of life" (United Nations 1994, 30).

Abortion is controversial in the Middle East, as it is in the West, because its use pits values of life and morality against individual needs and individual rights. The fact that such a variety of Muslim positions exist may seem to muddle the issue rather than clarify it, especially to those not versed in Islamic law. However, the flexibility allowed by the absence of a hard and fast law allows some room for women caught in personal dilemmas, while at the same time emphasizing that abortion must remain exceptional rather than routine. Thus, Muslim thinking on abortion recognizes human needs while affirming that respect for life is fundamental in Islam.

REFERENCES

al-Ahram. 1994. "Abortion Is Not Permissible in Islamic Law Unless for Protection of the Mother's Life." September 7, 4.
Alan Guttmacher Institute. 2001. http://www.agi-usa.org/pubs/fb—0599.html. February 4.
Athar, Shahid. 2001. "Twenty-five Most Frequently Asked Questions about Islam." http://www.islam-usa.com/25ques.html. February 4.
Dahlburg, John-Thor. 1995. "Faiths Disagree on Morality of Abortion." *Los Angeles Times*, January 24, 5.
Galway for Life. 2001. http://www.galwayforlife.ie/global—figures.html. February 4.
Holloway, Marguerite. 1994. "Trends in Women's Health: A Global View." *Scientific American* 271, no. 2 (August): 76–83.
Inhorn, Marcia. 1996. *Infertility and Patriarchy: The Cultural Politics of Gender and Family Life in Egypt*. Philadelphia: University of Pennsylvania Press.
Jacobson, Jodi. 1990. "The Global Politics of Abortion." Washington, D.C.: Worldwatch Institute.
al-Khayyir, ᶜAbdul Rahman. 1974. "Attitudes of Islam towards Abortion and Sterilization." In *Islam and Family Planning*, ed. Isam Nazer, vol. 2, 345–61. Beirut: International Planned Parenthood Federation.
Rispler-Chaim, Vardit. 1999. "The Right Not to Be Born: Abortion of the Disadvantaged Fetus in Contemporary Fatwas." *The Muslim World* 89, no. 2 (April): 130–43.
Sahnoun, Ahmad. 1974. "Islam's View of Abortion and Sterilization." In *Islam and Family Planning*, ed. Isam Nazer, vol. 2, 371–86. Beirut: International Planned Parenthood Federation.
Salt Lake Tribune. 2000. "Number of Abortions Drops to Two-Decade Low." January 7.
United Nations. 1994. "Report of the International Conference on Population and Development." Cairo, September 5–13.

17. Fashioning Casablanca in the Beauty Salon

Susan Ossman

Looking good matters to Middle Eastern women and men, and they regularly spend time in beauty parlors and barber shops. The beauty parlor has replaced the hammam *as the place where women gather and work on their appearance. Images of beauty may come from foreign sources, such as magazines and films, but in constructing a self, images of beauty and "what's cool" are ultimately influenced by local standards. —Eds.*

If you walk through the door of "Salon Venus" you'll find your image reflected back at you from many mirrors, jumbled together with those of the actresses and models whose faces appear on the many fashion magazines scattered on coffee tables and on the posters that decorate the walls. You won't have to wait long at the door before being greeted by an elegant woman in a suit. She says, "Bonjour, Madame."

"Bonjour, avez-vous le temps pour me faire une petite coupe?"

"Of course, Madame, just wait here for a couple of minutes."

She gestures toward a couch and a stack of magazines: *Femme Actuelle, Nous Deux, Sayedati.* Then she turns her head to look at a woman dressed in white, with white shoes that look like those nurses often wear.

"Mina, jibha ila le shampooing."

She turns her head back toward you: "Here's Mina to take care of you; let me take your coat."

The manager leads you to an easy chair and you get a closer view of the room. A radio is playing a song by Vanessa Paradis. You pick up the magazines on the coffee table beside you, and glance at a little girl who cringes as the hairdresser trims her shoulder-length hair. The setting seems so familiar. What might let you locate this place? The song on the radio is in French. The mix of magazines includes titles in French and Arabic. You must be somewhere in North Africa, where magazines and television programs from France and the Middle East provide abundant resources to women in search of styles for their hair and for their lives. Still, only recognizing the portraits of the country's present and former kings on the wall lets you to locate this beauty salon more precisely in Morocco. You might begin to check out the magazines on another table and come across a glossy magazine called *Femmes du Maroc*—Women of Morocco. But before you get a chance to read it, Mina is ready to help you slip into a white smock and take you over to the section of the salon where lines of sinks are lined up to wash clients' hair.

It was in salons like this one, in Casablanca, that I began to study how beauty salons help women to "become themselves," or "become more themselves," by interacting with images, professional advisors, and each other. In a world of increasingly international fashion, where pictures of many beauties enter our homes each day on television, the faces women can assume might appear infinitely various. Yet such variety is not seen on city streets anywhere. Fashions are not simply imitated, and choices are not truly open. In order to understand how fashion and society are related, I visited many salons in Casablanca. I talked to hairdressers like Mina, and with my research assistant Fedwa Lamzal I interviewed women who go to salons to get their hair done, legs waxed, or nails manicured. We also met with women who never went to salons. And I asked men what they thought of such places, and noticed that although they were welcome in some salons, there were many others that they did not dare to enter.

The mixes of images from places like Paris, Cairo, and Milan in Casablancan salons might make salons seem like an institution without a sense of place. The pictures that line the walls and litter the coffee tables of salons throughout the city sport photographs of Egyptian actresses and French starlets. French terms, including English words already adopted into French, are universally used to describes styles and processes. "Un brushing" for instance, is the process of styling hair that in the United States is called a "blow-dry." Most conversation is in the Moroccan dialect of Arabic, but in upscale salons managers often converse with clients in French as well. Does this make the beauty salon French or universal, rather than Moroccan? What kind of body does it produce?

Some people that I met in Casablanca told me that I could only understand the "Moroccan" body if I abandoned my study of salons and instead focused on the *hammam*—the steam bath. The hammam immerses the whole body in steam, whereas the salon treats discrete parts of the body with chemicals. What might a comparison between the two institutions teach us? The answer to this question seems especially interesting because many women patronize both baths and salons—indeed, some of the more chic health clubs in the city propose various versions of both as part of their "total" body work.

THE HAMMAM

The public bath has a long history around the Mediterranean. Roman ruins consistently show the centrality of the public baths. In Europe, the institution languished after the Middle Ages, but along the southern and eastern edge of the Mediterranean the institution survived, coming to be referred to in English as a "Turkish bath." The collective steam bath, or hammam, sparked the imagination of many European men who traveled to the Orient. Artists and writers depicted it as a place of sensual abandonment: a meeting place for voluptuous women. These orientalist visions might have been shared by many European women, but when Suzanne Voilquin, a French Saint-Simonian who worked as a midwife in nineteenth-century Cairo, and Leonora Peets, a Finnish woman who lived in Marrakech in the 1930s, wrote about their experience of the baths they emphasized, not their sensuality, but their nature as a space of feminine sociability. Their descriptions focus more on the hammam as a place where women could meet and gossip. They do not forget that baths also had the practical aim of allowing people to thoroughly cleanse themselves. Men and women both go to the hammam—although, as we see in the Tunisian director Férid Boughedir's award-winning film *Halfaouine*, the moment when a boy must stop accompanying his mother to the hammam and begin washing with the men can be experienced as a rite of passage. Modern male writers in the Maghreb tend to focus on this separation from the world of women.

Most baths in Morocco have several bathing rooms—usually three—each progressively hotter. As you move through, the steam grows thicker. Hoses, fountains, or faucets supply hot and cool water with which to rinse yourself as you wash. Your entire body is immersed in this aqueous milieu. A single element, water, is altered and used to clean, relax, and purify your body. Often people come to the bath with friends. People are not rushed in the baths. Many women like to hang out there on Friday afternoon. Friday is the day of Muslim rest and prayer, when people have a little more free time.

When you go to a hammam, whether in a city neighborhood or in a smaller provincial town, you are asked to pay a fee. Then you hang up your clothes in a dressing room, usually stripping down to your underpants. You are given a mat and carry your shampoo, soap, comb, and other utensils and beauty products in a bucket as you enter the first room. As soon as you open the door you are engulfed in steam. Your eyes have to adjust to the shadowy room. You notice some women sitting in a circle. Some are scrubbing others' backs, and one is shampooing a friend's hair. You might notice how she lathers the long tresses, then uses her pail to rinse them off, then begins again. Water flows over the seated women, splashing over the floor and then toward the drain in the corner of the room. You notice that there is another passageway toward another room, so you move on to the second chamber, where you set your mat down and sit. Here the temperature is hotter, but the activities are similar to those in the first room. In fact, there are more women seated here—presumably the warmer atmosphere is more effective in making you sweat, getting your skin soft so that you can rub dead skin off with a gritty washcloth (something like a loofah). A third room offers a truly hot environment—you notice that many people go there to sit for a while, then return to the middle room.

As you move through the rooms of the bath, you can hear people talking and opening faucets. You hear women talking, laughing. You can watch them, but you cannot see yourself. There are no mirrors inside the baths. Their walls tend to be plain, with very small windows or, more likely, none at all. You might forget what you look like as a *gsella* washes your entire body, simultaneously giving you a massage. Your body is immersed, dampened, and purified. You don't examine yourself, though you do see others. At the hammam you treat your entire body with variations on a single element, water. Whether you carefully wash each part of your body or not, whether there is a woman whom you pay to wash and massage you or not, you cannot enter the bath without your body becoming totally immersed in some form of watery flow or rush of steam. Only once you have done a final rinse and moved back to the dressing room will you dry off.

Today, some people in cities like Casablanca continue to bathe at the hammam, since their homes have no bathrooms. But many men and women who do have bathrooms go to the hammam as a leisure activity, in the same way that the middle and upper classes frequent sports clubs to relax. The uses and meanings of the baths might be different for different groups or individuals. However, whether a bath is beside a shantytown, in a middle-class shopping district, or part of an upscale gym or club, it will share certain basic characteristics. Whether it has several rooms or consists of a simple plastic prefabricated box, it will engulf those who enter it. It implicitly treats the entire body. This implies a very different kind of experience, and a very different way of feeling one's body, than that made available by the hairdressers, aestheticians, and masseuses who work in beauty salons.

THE SALON BODY

Unlike the hammam, salons do not work with variations of a single element. Instead, they cut up the body: hair, nails, face, legs. Different body parts are approached differently and given different treatments. Salons use many bottled and boxed products involving myriad chemicals, soaps, and plant extracts. In Casablancan salons, a sign at the entrance to the salon usually indicates the price you will pay to have particular operations performed on given body parts. From the first, clients are encouraged to think about the parts of the body as separate. They are taught that different kinds of operations will involve various kinds of products and will be performed by specialists. The person who washes hair rarely cuts it. The manicurist is not always allowed to perform facials. Rather like doctors, those in beauty professions specialize in particular kinds of interventions; they get to know specific parts of the body. Moreover, like medical professionals, beauticians often wear white or pastel smocks. Adjustable chairs that resemble those in dentists' offices, complicated metal and plastic equipment, towels to cover clients; all of these elements recall the hospital or the physician's office. They remind us that the body in the salon is to be "operated on" by a knowing professional. They indicate that the salon is hygienic, not only stylish but scientific. Beauty salons, like mass-media images or modern doctors, help to establish ideas of modern, fragmented bodies.

So as you enter the salon you must break down the diverse operations that go into working on your hair or nails or legs. Often, the manager or beautician helps you in this process of differentiation; indeed, if you have calculated prices differently than she has, there may be misunderstandings at the end of the visit, when it is time to pay. So you carefully dissect your body, count your dirhams, and imagine how, after decomposing you into your component parts, the specialists of the salon will put you back together. So from the moment you walk into a salon beauticians take on the roles of both seer and judge. To get them to do their work well you must yourself conjure up visions of your own potential "look."

"But how do women choose what kinds of haircuts they want?" Fedwa asks Halima, a hairdresser in Casablanca.

> *Halima:* Each does it in her own way. Some ask us to cut their hair according to the shape of their face. Some bring in photos from magazines and ask us to copy the picture. But they never just have the cut done without asking our advice. They always ask us if the cut will look good on them or not. Some women have long, round, or thin faces and the cut they chose doesn't go with that face. We suggest that they get another kind of style.
> *Fedwa:* Do you think that a woman can chose her own hairstyle and makeup?
> *Halima:* A woman can choose her own model of hairstyle that she's seen others wear and she likes, but the choice of a model depends on many things—on the form of her face and the way she dresses. A person with a long face who wants to wear her hair long; this doesn't go at all, and we counsel her to get a shorter, blunter cut. For makeup too it depends on the form of the eyes, lips. If the lips are too full, you have to thin them a bit. If the eyes "fall" you have to pick them up with a little pencil.

The hairdresser went on to explain, "Women get information about fashion from television and radio. The magazines also help them to know how to dress and to wear makeup. Sometimes a woman can go to a hair salon to learn how to do her hair and makeup. Then, at home, she does what she learned there. Some [beauty] institutes give out information about how to use makeup."

While a woman can easily change clothes without lasting consequences, getting a new haircut or changing her hair color is a more permanent signal of her taste and propriety. In a world of frivolous, disinterested aesthetics, we might expect the creation of a self-image to be exciting; the salon, along with mass media, opens up an infinite possibility of participating in the world of international fashion. It should be fun, thrilling, playful: and yet, everywhere in modern cities, the issue of appearances provokes intense anxiety. People worry about the relationship of how they look to their "true selves." They must take responsibility for their choices and use them to point out who they "are." A high heel, a fold of the *hijab* (veil), a line under the eye, or color on the nails will indicate something about who a woman is and what others might expect her to do.

When women in Casablanca are asked about beauty practices in general, they may allude to a specifically "Moroccan" look. Leila, a student, speaks of how Moroccan women are "more natural" than Europeans or, especially, Egyptians. However, when Moroccan women describe themselves they usually use words like "classic," "traditional," "sportive," "modern" (*casriya*), and "feminine" more than national identifications. Indeed, many women draw attention to the fact that they don't fit the "Moroccan" idea as it is presented on television. Some turn to alternative national images for inspiration. Khaltoum, who has dark skin, says that she looks to American black models for ideas and ways of valorizing her own looks. Latifa is told by everyone that her "Chinese" appearance requires a straight, bobbed hairstyle. Hamid, who goes to a unisex "quick" salon, insists on wearing his hair long, in a "surfer" style, while Touria says she selected her hairstyle after watching a Mexican soap opera. Looks can be described in terms of nations or in terms of styles. Someone can be described as "sporty," or "Brazilian," or as resembling a well-known singer.

"How do Moroccan women learn about how to select their looks?" Fedwa again asks a salon owner.

"From magazines—but not everyone buys them. Even to get the information you have to have the means. There are magazines that do a lot of publicity for products, but if the woman doesn't have the means to buy them [the magazines] she is uninformed. I think that we should raise salaries so that women can allow themselves to [buy these magazines and be informed]."

This comment led me to think not only about how some poor women, or women recently arrived from the country, are unable to read magazines, whether about beauty or anything else, but also about how beauty and style are related to economic and social class, and even to regional origins. Amal, a wealthy Casablancan housewife of Fassi origin, remarks, "Ever since I got married in Casablanca I have noticed that people have changed a lot. There is an incredible competition among people to appear to be the best. Then there has also been this phenomenon of the ʿaroubiyya (rural, unsophisticated woman). The ʿaroubiyya always tries to imitate women who know how to dress and act. But you see, the problem is that everything that one does should be natural. If it's not natural to them, these classy styles can't look right on these people."

Girls whose grandmothers were ʿaroubiyya, peasants in the central part of the country, may very well have been brought up in Casablanca. Their parents may be educated, and they themselves may speak several languages, own a business, or hold a prestigious diploma and a steady job. When Amal exclaims at how ʿaroubiyya girls now have money and the ability to buy fashionable clothes, but "they just don't know how to wear them," she is expressing her anxiety at the mixing of what formerly were, in her mind at least, distinct sets of people. She seeks to maintain her status in "knowing how to wear" the clothes that are now available, if not to all, at least to a growing number of urban women.

Models in magazines, actresses on television, beautiful and smart but penniless girls parading down the boulevards of the city preoccupy Amal, as they do the columns of newspapers and the conversations of men at cafes. Often the accusation that women are imitating the images in the media leads to debates about morality. For isn't someone who is not playing her usual, expected social role, who is not learning to dress from her mother but is instead adopting "uppity" ways and pretending to be what she is not, a threat to social order? As definitions of status change, influence and good marriages become possibilities for "unattached" but alluring young women. The girl on the move is suspected by all, and yet all kinds of people, especially in the city, encourage their own daughters to pursue their education, find gainful employment, and, yes, make themselves beautiful.

Amal dreams nostalgically of the time before "they" took to the streets. But she cannot keep people from confusing "imitations" with originals. What she can do is attempt to develop stories that make sense of the changing society in which she lives. She explains things in terms of evolution. We learn from our mothers, and so, if our mothers were already more "evolved" than others of their generation, we must be "ahead" of those who are now trying to "copy" us. It sometimes sounds as though there is some kind of fashion evolution—or a race in which certain women claim to be so far ahead that the others can never catch up. Certainly, those ʿaroubiyya women might be imitating elite tastes, but nonetheless, they will always remain a bit behind when it comes to fashion. Amal tells a history of the "modernization" of the Moroccan woman which begins with women of urban families. She tries to place herself at the beginning of an imagined Moroccan modernity. So does Hind, a woman in her twenties, who says, "My grandmother was already wearing short skirts and bobbed hair" and notes, "It was my mother who insisted I go to the salon and wear makeup." The way that Amal and Hind express why they are different from other Casablancan women reminds me of how the famous anthropologist Marcel Mauss emphasized the importance of our family milieu to how we learn to walk, dress, or hold a teacup.

Yet a look at beauty salons shows the extent to which people can rework and remodel their looks and even the way they walk. Halima protests that not all women can buy fashion magazines, but those who cannot buy them can see them in shops and adopt some of the styles they see on their pages or on their television sets at home. With such easy access to the varied faces of fashion it becomes more difficult to keep clear distinctions between different "kinds" of women. But people still endeavor to make these distinctions. We can see this when we put aside the comparison between salons and baths, or modernity and tradition in terms of types of institutions, and instead focus on the different kinds of beauty salons in Casablanca.

Salons are not just places to read magazines or look at oneself. While the body they work on is different from that of the hammam, they have become comparable to that institution in becoming a space for women to meet, gather news, and try out ideas on one another. Salons in Casablanca are places women go to meet, talk, have coffee, and exchange information. In neighborhood salons a glance around the room shows women exchanging gossip. Several of those seated in the reception area are contributing ideas about how the client having her hair done ought to look. In salons downtown, on the other hand, well-known beauticians promise to transform women, not according to neighborhood ideas of beauty and propriety, but according to some magic, artistic formula that will reveal the "real" person. Relationships with the salon professional and with people not even in the salon, but present in imagination, become more important than relationships with family, friends, and acquaintances.

One of the things that interests me about salons is the way that they, like contemporary baths, developed in diverse ways. The social space of the salon is used in diverse ways, and we can see that what seems to be a single institution in fact integrates all kinds of moves for prestige and power. To go to a neighborhood salon or to a well-known hairdresser downtown involves not only conspicuous consumption but also different ways of determining who has the right to judge and shape your appearance. In neighborhood salons people tend to discuss their looks in terms of people they know. Downtown at fancy upscale salons, the reference group is made up of people one might not rub elbows with daily. *Haute couture* and *haute coiffure* promise, rather, to shape your looks to bring out the "very special you." Meanwhile, in what I call "quick" salons, menus of looks give you a choice of what kind of impression you want to make: you can be "classic" or choose a sporty cut called "Cindy."

Today the hammam is spreading to places like Paris and Sacramento, where it takes on new meanings and new forms. Salons are even more widespread: they exist in nearly every urban center throughout the world. We must not forget that any salon anywhere implies certain manners of cutting up the body, or that the steam bath inevitably drenches every inch of your skin when you enter it. But we must also remember that the two kinds of institutions emphasize different ways of thinking about hygiene and beauty, and they authorize different judges—people we know, or abstract pictures—to determine how we shape our looks. For if historical and ongoing exchanges have brought salons to many of the smallest Moroccan cities, and hammams to hotels and health clubs around the world, this does not mean that all faces get equal treatment before the mirror or receive the same shape in the hands of the masseuse. Differences arise neither simply because some are blessed with beauty at birth, nor from easily identified cultural differences. Instead they arise in the ways that different kinds of baths or salons involve their holistic or fragmented bodies in modes of judgment that involve, not only appearance, but also notions of whether it is the eyes of those we know or the distant eyes of fame that count.

18. Chalk and Dust: Teachers' Lives in Rural Sudan

W. Stephen Howard

Teachers in the Middle East still command respect from their students and community, much as they did in the U.S. in past years. In the non-oil-rich Middle East, education is the largest line item in the national budget. Even so, given the population explosion, few resources are spent on any one student. Teachers' salaries are very low, and class sizes are large. The majority of students drop out before reaching middle school. Teachers' effectiveness depends on their ability to incorporate community values into teaching. Rural teachers will of necessity reflect the religious beliefs of their locale.

Despite their low economic status, rural teachers are the vanguard of change in their communities and have to balance adherence to conservative traditional values with their attempts to advance student learning and respond to community needs. —Eds.

Societies organize themselves to teach their children how to become good members of society, and teachers are the agents of this task. In Muslim Sudan, the northern two-thirds of Africa's largest country, education has been closely associated with the religion of the people, even in state schools. Before independence from Britain in 1956, most boys and a few girls studied the Qurʾan at *khalawi* (Quranic schools) for a year or two, but during the colonial era Western-style education was limited to a few large towns. From independence, formal schooling became a government priority, but always an underfunded one in this, one of the poorest countries in the Arabic-speaking world.

Sudan is a religious country and a rural country. The Nile courses through Sudan from its southern borders with Uganda and Ethiopia to its northern border with Egypt, providing the cradle of ancient religions and the later Christianity and Islam, as well as the waters for the agricultural schemes that feed Sudan's people. Islam is now the religion of approximately 70 percent of the forty million people in the country, spread from the fifteenth century through the missionary work of Islamic teachers. And today Islam is a central part of the curriculum of all schools in northern Sudan. This chapter describes the life of teachers in rural schools and how they teach and demonstrate their religious culture to the country's children.

A story circulates in Sudan's cities and towns at the expense of the nation's beleaguered teachers:

> A young woman approaches her father with the news that a man has proposed marriage to her. The father asks, "What does he do for a living?" "Oh," she cautiously replies, "he's a teacher ... " and then adds hopefully, "but he has a cousin working abroad!"

Jokes can reveal much about attitudes in the society of their origin, and this bit of Sudanese humor may be evaluated on several different levels, all related to the decline in the status of the teaching profession in Sudan. Within this story we find commentary on young men's need to migrate abroad—usually to the Arab Gulf—in order to earn money for inflated dowries for themselves or their kin, and on the lack of confidence in teachers' ability to support a family on their salaries. Indeed, since most of the work available abroad is low-status manual labor, the joke reverses expected status relationships.

This chapter describes the Eastern Gezira, an area bounded on its western and southern sides by enormous irrigated agricultural schemes (Gezira and Rahad) that played an early role in the spread of Islam in Sudan. The Eastern Gezira, from Rufaʿa, Hilaliyah, and Um Duwumban to Abu Haraz and Tundub, was a center of *Sufi* (mystical) teaching from the mid-sixteenth century onward (McHugh 1994). The remains of this era are in the *kubab* (singular *kubba*), wonderful Turkish-style domed tombs found in many of the region's towns and villages. They are the final resting places of *awliya* or holy men, who were the first teachers in the region.

The economy of the region is dominated by subsistence production of *dura* (sorghum), the staple grain of Sudan, and by the out-migration of men, primarily to commerce in the cities or to work overseas, and some involvement in neighboring agricultural schemes. Commercial activity within the region is limited to permanent markets in the larger towns of Rufaʿa and Tamboul and three small markets held once every three days.

The two largest towns in the region have intermediate and higher secondary schools for both boys and girls. There are also intermediate schools in three smaller towns. Primary schools for both boys and girls are found in all but the smallest villages. The Central Region, including the Eastern Gezira, is better supplied with schools than any of Sudan's other political

subdivisions except the capital, Khartoum. But within the region, the politically powerful farmers of the irrigated schemes have taken the majority
of social service resources for their communities west of the Blue Nile.

THE CASE STUDIES

I will describe the lives of rural teachers at two schools: one of the boys'
intermediate schools in Abu Haraz, a town that is an important local pilgrimage site because of its collection of about thirty brightly painted tombs
of early holy men; and a coeducational primary school in Tundub, also the
site of an important tomb, but a town smaller and more remote than Abu
Haraz. Primary and intermediate schoolteachers have the same educational credentials and are on the same pay scales. Higher secondary school
teachers—who are not subjects of this study—are university graduates.
Higher secondary schools also tend to be centrally located in more urbanized areas.

At the school in Abu Haraz there are six teachers and a headmaster,
who also has a full teaching schedule. There is a dormitory, and about half
of the students are boarders from tiny villages in a twenty-mile radius of
Abu Haraz. The boarders must bring their own beds—usually an *angareb*
or traditional wood-and-rope bed brought in on a pickup truck. A common
sight at the beginning of the school year is a truck piled high with the beds
of all the boys from one village, and their male relatives unloading them
into the dormitory. One of the teachers at the school is expert in repairing
this type of bed; he also instructs students in the skill, encouraging some
degree of self-reliance in the boys.

Some people in the town says that the skills of this teacher and of one
of his colleagues, who can mend watches and radios as well as teach math,
are being wasted in rural Sudan. They both could make more money as
full-time sidewalk repairmen in a bigger town, according to the critics. The
regional capital of Wad Medani, a forty-minute truck ride to the opposite
bank of the Blue Nile, would give them such opportunities.

But the teachers express the view that their repair skills are part of their
negotiation with the community. They are originally from nearby villages
smaller than Abu Haraz, and as they are unmarried, they live together
with three other teachers in a house, "bachelors' quarters," in one corner
of the school yard. People in Abu Haraz come to them for help with simple
household problems, and in exchange the bachelors get home-cooked
meals and a comfortable position from which to participate in the community's social life. "I'm saving money for marriage," stated one, "and the
people in town know that, and make it easier for me to prepare for marriage. Besides, I am a terrible cook."

Teachers in schools like Abu Haraz Boys' Intermediate are frequently biding their time, waiting for acceptance from a university or building credentials to get a contract to teach abroad. There was much talk over meals about the prospects for teaching in nearby Yemen, which had recently taken nine thousand primary school teachers on secondment from Sudan. Apparently the Yemenis prefer Sudanese over their closest rivals, the Egyptians, because of the Sudanese reputation for patience and greater tolerance for rural life, as well as a higher moral standard. The salaries are good in Yemen, where a qualified Sudanese teacher can make many times what he is paid in Sudan. But while the Abu Haraz teacher faces an average class size of forty in this school, it is not uncommon to find ninety to one hundred pupils in one Yemeni classroom.

The teachers of Abu Haraz are all high school graduates, holders of the Sudanese School Certificate. Three of the younger teachers are studying to retake the school-leaving exam, hoping to improve their scores and gain admission to a national university. Obtaining a government scholarship to study in Egypt was a second option in recent years, when relations between the Nile Valley neighbors were not so strained. But the legitimacy that the Sudan government has given to radical Islam, conflict over border territory near the Red Sea, and Sudan's alleged support of a plot to kill Egyptian President Mohammed Hosni Mubarak have made it difficult for Sudanese to find places in Egypt.

Apprentice teachers—new high school graduates—have four years to practice in the classroom before getting a chance to enter a teacher-preparation institute. They do not teach the grades facing exams for promotion to the next level, those tough years being reserved for experienced teachers. After two years at the institute and four more years of service in the classroom, they are entitled to a certificate from the government which will allow them to seek secondment to a teaching post in one of the wealthier Arabic-speaking countries.

Alternatives to teaching, or to teaching in Sudan, are very much on the minds of the younger staff members. They know that they are "stuck" in teaching jobs because of their relatively poor performance on the high school leaving exam. It is common knowledge that a merely passing score on the exam leads to work in the primary or intermediate classroom instead of to university study. But there are more than twenty high school students taking the exam for every university seat available in Sudan, and teacher shortages are chronic.[1]

These realities and the rhythm of life in the Abu Haraz school create a strong community feeling among the teachers. The school building is perched on a hill overlooking a bend in the Blue Nile on one side and the cemetery where the holy men are buried on the other. While waiting for the mid-morning breakfast to be served in the teachers' room, the headmaster fills a space in the conversation by humming a popular Sufi *qasida*, a tribute to one of the best known *sheikh*s buried in the cemetery below. His colleagues quickly join in, with percussion provided by an appropriate thumping of the desks. An earlier disagreement that had surfaced among the staff temporarily fades as the melody rises.

The headmaster is a third-generation schoolteacher and his ancestors were noted Sufi sheikhs. He frequently visits the tombs of these holy men, alone, with students, or in the company of fellow teachers. I asked him what the difference was between him and Sufi teachers of the past. He thought for a long time and answered, "I can write Arabic very well and teach the language properly." While the teaching of Arabic may have improved—it is the most important subject on the syllabus—the role of the teacher as an intellectual resource in these small communities has changed little over the centuries. The headmaster's knowledge of local history, which is also important religious history, often enters the conversation. He also holds up the lives of the holy men as models for his students, urging them to "walk in the path of those who have walked before us." The material world, however, is never far away. The giant bottle of chloriquine tablets on his desk, to combat malaria among the students, attests to his readiness to intervene.

The Sufi pupil in a spiritual teaching relationship has intense loyalty to his teacher. The teacher is a role model, himself trying to follow a path toward spiritual perfection. Sufism, the mystical teaching aspect of Islam, is boundless, and the teacher needs to be ready to address any question from his followers (Howard 1988, 93). My North American presence in a geography class prompted a student to ask the teacher, "How do Eskimos fast during Ramadan when the sun never sets or rises where they live?" The answer was that an Eskimo Muslim would follow the fasting schedule of the nearest country with a distinguishable night and day.

Much of the bonding between student and teacher is through ritual: prayers, chants, readings, and songs, activities which in themselves are intuitive teaching techniques for mystics. Shah 1971 maintains that intuition is the teaching path of the Sufis, that something subliminal draws the student to the teacher. Certainly the members of a small rural community—schoolteachers and pupils alike—have shared hardships and experienced joys that cannot be discerned by outsiders, that remain unspoken between them. These teachers know how the children learn at home and are intimate with the their circumstances. While respect is a hallmark of the teacher-student relationship, one can also hear teachers addressing their pupils with the affectionate *yᵓahki* ("O my brother"). Such communication is a foundation for effective socialization and learning. The Sufi teacher travels the path to enlightenment with the seeker. The material world is the common ground of everyone in Abu Haraz; it is natural that the spiritual world be shared as well.

The religious atmosphere colors most aspects of the school curriculum. Group oral reading, *al-giraya al-jamaᶜiyya*, crosses over from the traditional

Quranic school to classes in Arabic language and religious studies at the intermediate school. When there is an English teacher available, the same mode of instruction is found in his class as well. Students and teachers engage in the secular exchange of the school during the week, and can participate in *dhikr,* the chanted rituals of "remembrance of God," at the tombs on the weekends—Thursday afternoon and Friday. In fact, students have been known to wander through the cemetery on the way home from school, stopping at the tombs of their families' favorite saints in search of *baraka,* God's blessing or grace, before the next day's exam.

The headmaster has introduced many of his pupils to his favorite saint, one whose modest tomb reflects the teacher's focus both on the non-material life and on obedience to God. He sometimes took me to visit this saint on my visits to the town and I, too, was impressed with the atmosphere of the place. Every saint buried there has a story or particular hymn dedication, and the one to this saint rhymed: *la ʿandi binaya, ma bedug tahiyya?* ("Just because I don't have a kubba, you're not going to salute me?"). The remains of this saint were said to be somewhere in the rubble of bricks that sat close by the bank of the Blue Nile.

Cooperation and Sudanese paternalism, both fostered by the intimacy of the surroundings, are seamless within the school community. The young headmaster is responsible for the school's finances, which are made complex by the existence of boarders, but he is able to make few decisions without some input from his staff. At meeting times, students will be found leaning in doorways or looking through windows until finally shooed away. The cooks and watchmen may also join in the fiscal debates, which can get quite noisy. The easy, cordial relationships that exist between the educated teachers and the older and often illiterate cooks and watchmen recreate an atmosphere much like Sudanese rural home life, which is particularly familiar to the boys from the town's hinterland. The teachers are often called upon to help the non-teaching staff write letters to sons abroad or solicitations to government agencies.

The teachers keep a careful collective watch over the school's financial affairs because they feel strongly that they are at the end of the long list of the Khartoum government's priorities. "The government abandons us," one of the teachers stated, "because social services are seen as draining the economy rather than building up productive resources. Why can't they see education as important to our country's future?" Another teacher adds, "We don't have time for second jobs, and they are hard to find in rural areas anyway." Here and in the town's other schools, the teachers talk of striking. The issues include the size of the annual wage increase and supervision of the dormitories. Since the 1989 takeover by the Islamist "Revolution of National Salvation," all talk of strikes has become dangerously illegal. But frustration is deep, and some are disgusted with the government's shortsightedness and profoundly misplaced priorities.

TEACHING IN TUNDUB

The village of Tundub lies thirty miles to the northeast of Abu Haraz in the zone between the Eastern Gezira and the *butana* or arid plain of eastern Sudan. As one travels east from the market town of Tamboul, tiny villages, Tundub and others, appear out of the red dust of the horizon. Before the droughts of the 1980s, most of the inhabitants of Tundub raised sheep, goats, and cattle. Since then, this small community and its surrounding villages have experienced enormous out-migration of the male labor force. As a consequence, women have taken on greater responsibility for the family stocks of sheep and goats. Another consequence is the increase in local development projects funded by the expatriate sons of Tundub. A primary school and a new well system are examples of that effort, known as *al-ᶜawn al-zati* or "self-help." A small clinic has also been built, and the community is talking about trying to bring electricity to town, also through self-help efforts.

The schoolteachers, with their high school diplomas, are the educated elite of the resident community. In this capacity they also provide leadership for self-help projects, which involves a considerable amount of their time as well as their organizational skills. The literate teachers are essential to the progress of the projects in that they travel to the region's cities or Khartoum in search of information from or to negotiate with government agencies. They also take charge of the finances, writing to overseas members of the community to solicit contributions and following up on rumors of assistance from relief- or development-oriented non-governmental agencies working in the area.

The school constructed through self-help is beyond the eastern edge of the village and consists of two four-room brick buildings facing each other across a yard that has been decorated with a border of rocks. The staff is young, which is characteristic of self-help schools. Fully trained teachers are usually assigned to schools that have more support from the Ministry of Education. The teachers at the Tundub school have assessed their resources and have decided to emphasize reading skills with the children.

The headmaster's assistant told me, "I spent two years in the [primary teaching] Institute just learning how to teach this hard language." The children come to school fluent in spoken colloquial Sudanese Arabic, a language that most Sudanese assert is remarkably close to the language of the Prophet. But Standard Arabic, the language used in mass communications throughout the Arabic-speaking world, requires years of schooling for its mastery, a task that can begin in the Tundub school.

During the era of British-Egyptian colonialism, the older teachers contend, teachers were better prepared for the difficult challenges of rural schools. The Bahkt-e-Rhoda Teacher Training Institute, founded by the British in the 1940s, was deliberately established in the White Nile town of Dueim, five hours over unpaved roads from Khartoum's bright lights, in order to promote the notion that learning can take place even in electricity-less rural Sudan. Today Dueim has electricity and a paved road, and Tundub's teachers complain of some graduate teachers bribing doctors for medical excuses in order to avoid rural assignments. "Teachers should be ready to teach and serve the nation anywhere," the head teacher told me, "but now urban schools are well staffed and equipped while we are empty here."

While nationally more than 50 percent of Sudan's primary teachers are unqualified, the head teacher in Tundub does his part in the training of the next generation of teachers. Every year he takes on several young women who are studying at home to retake the high school leaving exam and places them—supervised—in his classrooms as additional staff. These women primarily lead reading and writing drills and have developed some creative visual aids to help with them. They are paid so little that if they do join the teaching profession once they earn their school leaving certificates, it will not be for the salary. But under the current regime in Khartoum, women are encouraged to restrict themselves to primary school teaching and nursing if they must work outside of the house.

As we observed the pupils hurrying toward the school buildings one morning, I asked the head teacher what he thought that he was preparing children for. He responded, with great enthusiasm, "National participation." He went on to explain how important it was to instill ideas about the purposes of Sudan in the young.

Details of Sudan's history, culture, and religion, the importance of cotton to the economy (students have been trucked about sixty miles to the cotton fields of the Gezira in order to help with harvests), and both the evils and benefits of Britain's colonialism were all on the head teacher's agenda. I asked him what he thought would become of these children when they finished their Tundub schooling. "Everyone moves to the big towns today," he said. "I just hope that they can communicate well in our language and be good neighbors and workers, good people, good religious people. And I know that they will remember us here—sending home their money for our projects!"

We watched as the students took care in opening the classrooms to sweep away the night's accumulation of blown sand from the floors and desks. Before they left for the day, the children lined up in front of the head teacher to be given a dose of tetracycline eye drops, a gift of the World Health Organization's campaign to eradicate dust-related conjunctivitis. He steadied each student with a hand on the shoulder and spoke their names as he applied the medicine. The small school seems to serve many purposes beyond its basic teaching function; it is a convenient and comfortable place from which to reach a large proportion of the community.

The ubiquitous sand not only endangers the children's health; it can also serve as an educational tool. Small children practice their alphabets by writing in the dust, their first attempt at composing this tough language. A teacher with some free time may be observing as well, and when the child makes a mistake the teacher will take the child's finger and press it gently into the dust, marking the spot. The neophyte writer will always remember the tactile aspects of this language.

Other members of the school community get involved with the children's education as well. The part-time "guard" employed by the school, an elderly villager who is related to the head teacher, will bring water from the well to children playing outside so that they can make mud animals for art class. Or he will bend in the dirt himself and dig a series of small holes, showing the children how to play *mankalla*, a game found all over Africa that uses seeds or stones as counting pieces.

Almost all teachers in this area supplement their small incomes by engaging in subsistence farming of rain-fed dura. Teachers at this school seldom produce more than twelve bags of dura, the amount consumed by a family in a year. In the past, one type of communal or self-help activity was the construction of storage pits for grain, called *matamora*. The decline in grain production—replaced by manufactured foodstuffs—and in the number of working farmers has brought matamora construction to a halt in this area.

It is difficult to know to what extent teacher-farmers might inspire respect for rural occupations among the schoolchildren. When the schoolchildren were asked about local agricultural practices they had ready answers and indicated that farming was as natural a part of their lives as school. The teachers' farming is limited to sowing and harvesting dura, but their knowledge of agricultural issues is extensive. Because of this, schools often become centers from which the non-governmental agencies begin their agricultural extension projects. Horticulture and poultry projects, particularly, can easily involve students, their parents, and their teachers.

In Tundub School we see different modes of teaching coexisting: experiential, spiritual, and teacher-centered "chalk and talk." The village is also the site of an important *zawiya*, or religious school, associated with the Khatimiyya Sufi sect, where perfect rote memorization is the major goal. The government primary school's pupils, parents, and teachers all avail themselves of the spiritual strengthening that the presence of such an institution provides, and the zawiya's Sufi teachers supported the self-help efforts to construct it.

The poorly paid and poorly trained teachers of Abu Haraz and Tundub are doing their best, with some degree of enthusiasm, to teach the children of their communities under daunting circumstances. Books, facilities, and curricula are inadequate or poor and relief is not in sight. But genuine learning does seem to be occurring in these rural sites. The closeness of the teaching staffs, with younger teachers serving as apprentices to those with more experience, appears to mitigate some of the harsher assaults on teacher motivation.

Granted, the structure and much of the content of education in the Eastern Gezira originates in the center, the militarized government's Ministry of Education in Khartoum. But a significant part of the content, as well as the philosophy of teaching, has its roots in this rural area, as when teachers discuss local social life, agriculture, and religion with their students. Teachers certainly feel estranged from the state center, now more than ever, and look to their local roots for inspiration, spiritual sustenance, and the bonds of community. In these distant rural towns the teachers do have some autonomy in the educational atmosphere they create, but that atmosphere is, in fact, a product of centuries of proud religious tradition.

NOTE

1. The 1990s have seen an explosion in the establishment of new "universities" in Sudan, with high schools and high school teachers all over the country being transformed into institutions and personnel for higher education. The quality of these institutions is much in doubt.

REFERENCES

Howard, W. Stephen. 1988. "Mahmoud Mohammed Taha: A Remarkable Teacher in Sudan." *Northeast African Studies* 10, no. 1: 89–100.

McHugh, Neil. 1994. *Holymen of the Blue Nile: The Making of an Arab-Islamic Community in the Nilotic Sudan, 1500–1850.* Evanston: Northwestern University Press.

Shah, Idries. 1971. *The Sufis.* New York: Anchor Books.

19. Networks, Jobs, and Everyday Life in Cairo

Diane Singerman

Jobs are hard to find in present-day Cairo. Family and neighbor-hood networks help facilitate all kinds of efforts, from finding jobs to getting permits from government agencies. For lower- to middle-class Egyptians, a network of contacts who can help clear a way through miles of tangled red tape is a necessity. Informal networks facilitate access to scarce information, resources, and po-litical and social capital. They are very common in everyday life and supplement the multiple ties of kin, class, neighborhood, oc-cupation, gender, and rural origins. —Eds.

In Cairo, earning a living is a complex process, particularly among the working and lower middle classes. An abundance of unskilled and semi-skilled workers compete for the limited number of secure positions in the public and private sectors. For many years after the Free Officers Revolution in 1952 that brought Gamal Abdel Nasser to power, the Egyptian government was the largest employer in the nation, expanding employment in public-sector industries, government services, and the civil service to build a new middle class and a more skilled and educated working class. Government and public sector employment constituted 59 percent of all wage labor in Egypt even as late as 1984, and 68 percent of all labor in urban areas (Zaytoun 1991, 220).

When Anwar Sadat came to power after Nasser's death in 1970, he began to turn Egypt away from a socialist-oriented strategy of state-led development that had relied largely on investment from public resources. The Open Door Policy launched in 1974 encouraged private-sector development, foreign investment, and reduced government expenditures. At the same time, Egypt shifted its strategic alliance from the Soviet Union to the United States and other Western nations.

After Anwar Sadat's assassination in 1981 by Islamist activists angered by the Camp David Accords, political repression, and Western influence, President Hosni Mubarak continued Sadat's campaign of privatization and structural adjustment. International financial institutions such as the World Bank and the International Monetary Fund insisted on further deep cuts in Egypt's expenditures to offset the nation's escalating foreign and domestic debt, and wages for public-sector professionals and clerical workers fell. Unemployment rose in the 1980s, and those who worked in the public sector often supplemented their income through part-time employment or second jobs as taxi drivers, private tutors, plumbers, or construction workers in the private sector or the informal economy. (Informal activities, whether economic or political, are those which escape licensing, regulation, and even enumeration by the state and thus have an illegal or quasi-legal status [Hopkins 1991; Abdel-Fadil 1980; Zaytoun 1991; Singerman 1995].)

Whether they are seamstresses, schoolteachers, janitors, grocers, clerks, metalworkers, taxi drivers, shop clerks, accountants, or lemon wholesalers, people rely on their repertoire of personal, familial, and communal networks to find employment or obtain better positions, since good, secure, well-paying jobs are few and far between, particularly for those in the working class and lower middle class, who have less education and technical skill. In Egypt, it is not only individual effort, skills, and capabilities that secure a job, but also knowing the right people, who can intercede on one's behalf. To find a job, secure an apartment, or open a business, Egyptians must negotiate the pervasive government bureaucracy, complex social norms, and the material struggles of everyday life. At the same time, rather than dismantling old yet still powerful bureaucracies or regulatory practices, the Mubarak government in the last twenty years has installed new layers of bureaucracy and competing regulatory frameworks on economic life, often complicating the average citizen's effort to secure essential needs and services such as schooling, employment, or housing while staying on the good side of the law.

Egypt's position in the changing global international economic and political order poses complicated questions for its citizens, who must balance many different interests and factors in their lives and hopes. Should a married woman work outside the home to finance private tutoring for her children's education or work within the home and rely solely on her husband's income, which cannot cover expensive tutoring for her children? Should young people leave their families to work abroad or should they remain in Egypt and live more modestly? Should a young father launch a new business that is financially risky or should he stay in his safe and secure, but low-paying, civil-service position? Should families construct an apartment on land that is zoned for agricultural use, which is technically illegal, or wait years to secure a subsidized government apartment?

As new economic policies are promoted by the state, everyday life is shaped by limitations, opportunities, and a certain measure of ambivalence about not only the choices that women and men must make, but whether those choices are right, appropriate, moral, and proper. As international alliances, global alignments, and the economic and political foundations of the state shift, the meaning and morality of everyday life are affected as well, in myriad different ways. Through informal networks, ordinary citizens not only seek access to public goods and services, but also promote the rules, order, and public and private morality of the community. Networks are designed not only to obtain more frozen chicken or soap from food cooperatives, but to solve intra-family and intercommunal conflicts and promote morality in the community. A constant articulation and refinement of right and wrong and propriety pervades daily discourse and serves as a backdrop to citizens' perceptions of and attitudes toward their government, as well.

Building networks that link together kin, neighbors, or colleagues allows women and men to pursue their objectives by finding out information, exchanging services or labor, or providing access to important officials or businessmen. Despite differences in status, wealth, education, piety, and property, people can "work" their networks to further their personal and familial goals. The logic of the system promotes the proliferation of one's networks in an ever-widening web, including more and more people. Networks become stronger as they become denser: as more and different types of knowledge, resources, people, and information are incorporated within the network. Knowing local officials in police headquarters, schools, or courts potentially means points of access and assistance for members of networks. Parents curry favor with local schoolteachers, employing them as private tutors to ensure that their children pass important examinations that determine promotion and graduation. Relatives and neighbors who work in the local food cooperative or subsidized grocery store can direct more food to their networks, or at least minimize the time that friends have to spend in long lines in the summer heat of Cairo.

Obtaining basic necessities is made more difficult for the young by high unemployment. More than three-quarters of all new entrants to the labor force were unemployed in the mid-1980s. Women and educated young people had higher unemployment rates than men: 24.2 percent as opposed to 10.4 percent (Handoussa 1991, 6). Under these conditions, a young female university graduate would have to exploit her family's networks to find a job, unless she wanted to wait at home for five to seven years for a position in the civil service or public sector. Networks help businessmen negotiate their way through complex and, at times, maddening tax and industrial regulations, which they must abide by to practice their trade or operate their small workshop. Sharing such things as information, an introduction to an employer, a loan, a tip on a cheap apartment, and assistance in filling out applications and welfare forms lies at the heart of networking, and these countless exchanges and services vary widely in importance, direction, and function.

Because informal and formal networks are routinely utilized to accomplish a wide range of mundane and exceptional tasks, people constantly enter into relationships of mutual exchange. Frequent reversals in the direction of exchange maintain the reciprocity of networks and discourage exploitative and manipulative behavior. The roles of giver and receiver are constantly shifting. One day a woman may receive a loan from a friend, and the following week she may launch an informal savings association, or *gam^{c}iyya* (plural *gam^{c}iyyat*), on the friend's behalf. A respected teacher in the community whose father suddenly dies and who does not have the money to host a proper funeral turns to her friends, who start a savings association on her behalf. Everyone agrees, at the outset, to the size of the monthly contribution and eleven friends decide to join the association, giving the first lump sum that is collected to the teacher and arranging a payment schedule for the remaining eleven months of the year (gam^{c}iyyat may also operate daily or weekly). These associations, largely organized by women, operate on trust within networks of family, neighborhood, or occupation. No fee or interest is charged to any participant. Gam^{c}iyyat offer credit to those who do not typically have the collateral to qualify for loans from banks. These associations are also popular because they conform to Islamic law, which forbids interest (Singerman 1995; Baydas, Bahloul, and Adams 1995). Women's and men's ability to count on a wide range of associates for help and assistance in both good and bad times mitigates fears of slipping into poverty and financial insecurity. Obviously, extending informal networks to different sectors and fields of Egyptian society enhances their usefulness.

Maintaining extensive networks that penetrate deeply into the community, local markets, occupational networks, financial and religious institutions, and local and national governmental offices can be as important as income, property, or status as people try to meet their goals. Illiterate men can be power brokers in their community because they know everyone and have friends in high places. Wealthy people who have not cultivated a complementary system of networks may still be thwarted by bureaucratic obstacles, lack of knowledge, and little access to those with connections (*wasta* or *mu^{c}arifa*). Wealth alone, particularly new wealth, can be disarming to the educated class and the civil servants, who have status as educated people but little wealth themselves, due to government retrenchment. It is not uncommon, for example, for poorly educated or even illiterate nouveau-riche businessmen to endow local mosques and charitable associations in order to enhance their networks and status in the community. Others might engage in local politics or provide loans to broaden the depth and reach of their networks (and their business activities, of course). Investments of time, labor, and money oil the machinery of networking, and some of the poorest and least skilled members of the community may be excluded from networks because they cannot afford to reciprocate exchanges of information, cold sodas, food, or labor.

The following story, relayed by a young woman from a centrally located, very old, popular area of Cairo, describes most forcefully the ways in which Egyptians must negotiate both the informal and the formal faces of the bureaucracy and labor market to find a job. Amina had just taken her final secondary school exams for the second time and doubted that she had passed them. She was supposed to marry after graduating—if she passed the national exam that is a requirement for graduation. Entrance to universities and technical institutes depends on the results of this exam, and young people enter more or less prestigious fields of study and degree programs according to their score on it. High school students cram throughout the entire school year and parents spend considerable sums on private tutors. Throughout Egypt, when results are posted outside secondary schools, there are many dramatic responses from students and their parents as they view the final results. The year before, Amina had failed the exam and her mother had refused to allow the marriage to proceed unless she passed, arguing that her diploma would provide security, the opportunity for public-sector employment, and social status. The mother had spent considerable sums on her daughter's private lessons, books, school clothes, and fees and worried that all her money and effort had gone to waste. Her fiancé had graduated from a vocational high school, and Amina agreed that she needed a diploma to match her prospective husband's status. Her commercial diploma would be more prestigious than his vocational school diploma, which she and her family felt was important and would allow her to demand a higher bride-price (*mahr*) from her fiancé's family.

During the summer, however, she had little to do but worry over her exam scores, which would be published soon. Bored by the prospect of remaining at home under the watchful eyes of her brothers, who felt compelled to guard her "honor," she agreed with her mother that she would work at a local daycare center. She was only able to find this summer job because her mother ran the daycare center that was attached to a local women's vocational training center established by the prominent female member of parliament from her district. She made numerous visits to government offices to register as an employee with the private voluntary organization which administered the daycare center. One cannot work in Egypt without obtaining a security clearance (*fiish w-tashbiih*) from the local police station that confirms residence in an area and the lack of an arrest record. Although her mother was a master at creating and using informal networks for many purposes, and she had picked up many of her mother's skills while growing up, only as she matured into her new adult role as an official member of the labor force was she given an education in the importance of informal networks.

First, in order to prepare the papers in order to work I had to have a fiish w-tashbiih. I went to get a copy of my birth certificate at the civil registry within the police station, because I had learned this was needed. The employee there said to come back tomorrow. I took the paper and returned the next day. He said to come back tomorrow again. I went the next day and he said my papers could not be processed because the date of birth was wrong. It was correct, but he was just lying to me, laughing at me. So I went the next day and told him the date was correct. He said to return tomorrow because he was about to leave. He told me to arrive at 1 P.M. the next day, which I did, but when I found him he said that he was turning out the lights and leaving and to return the next day. When I returned he told me that he couldn't find my name in the file and to come back the next day to see the person who specializes in birth certificates.

I went the next day and he said that my mother's name was in the dossier but that my name was torn off. By the time the papers had come from the health unit [where births are initially registered] he said that my name was missing and that the form had been thrown away years ago. "There is only your mother's name." "Is that my fault?" I asked. "It's the fault of those employees, not mine, *mish zambi, ana maali* [it is not my fault, why should I care]. After all this effort and work, you can't find the names?" He said that it wasn't his fault either and that he would prepare other papers that I had to purchase from the post office first.

I stayed home for two days, realizing that he wanted money before he would process my papers. But I didn't know how to offer him money. Perhaps he would take the money, perhaps not. If he didn't and was insulted he could make my life difficult and send me to hell [*yiwaddiini f-dahya*].

So, I asked my friend Iman, who was the sister of my brother's fiancée, if her father knew anyone at the police station. She said he did, a police officer named Ustaaz Ahmed. I went to the station the following day, but he wasn't there. Iman's father had tried to find me to go to the station together the next day, but I wasn't home. He told my older sister that I should yell up to him the next morning so that he would come with me. The next morning I called for him and he went with me to the office and introduced me to his friend who told me to get another copy of my birth certificate. After I copied it, I returned and gave it to him. He told me to buy several forms from the post office and to make a copy of my I.D. card (which all Egyptians must carry and which lists their official occupation) and my mother's. He put them with another paper and asked me to get it stamped at the civil registry, which I did.

When I came back he said that only one stamp was missing. I asked if I could take care of it now, he said no, but that I should take the papers home (so they would not get lost or misplaced) and return with them in the morning.

At 8 A.M. I returned and he stamped the paper to send it to the Ministry of Health for approval. Then he said that I should come back in twenty-five days. Nearly a month! I asked what I was supposed to do in the interim. He said that the law requires this. I said, is that my fault, those are your laws and your regulations. He said, "It's not in my hands, what do you want me to do?" I had made all that effort, all those visits, and tired myself out [this occurred during the July heat], and all of this was because he wanted money out of me. The paperwork could have taken an hour to finish but they want your money.

This young woman had visited these offices nine times over a period of eleven days. Despite her best efforts to exploit informal networks at the police station and registry, and to enlist others in her struggle, she was unsuccessful and still had to wait for some time for her papers to be processed so that she could receive payment in her new job. (Rather than sitting idle, she began her job nonetheless, working without compensation, which was quite low anyway, until the papers were processed.) She had few expectations of government efficiency or due process, but still blamed herself for not mastering the art of informal politics. She admitted her inexperience and admired her older sister's skill in knowing how to deal with (*biyitsarraf*) bureaucrats and merchants. Her family often asked this older sister to deal with bureaucrats and bargain with merchants on behalf of her extended family because she was so skillful and shrewd.

Seeing to the material needs of one's family involves complex interactions with governmental, economic, and social forces. The Egyptian state is a large employer, producer, provider, and rule-maker that also closely supervises civil and political society. Because the state controls immense resources, people strive for autonomy to gain some independence of movement, but do not want to cut themselves off from state benefits or isolate themselves. Informal networks strive for both autonomy from and integration with the bureaucracy and political elites, because the ultimate goals of networks are diverse. At times people try to escape the state, and at other times to exploit it. What they do gain is a modicum of political space, which comes with the requirement of extensive organization and intricate webs of association. Building an organizational grid in a society where associational life is tightly controlled and repressed by the state, and where citizens have little ability to upset powerful constituencies with far greater resources at their disposal, still allows these communities room to pursue their interests and expand their political space. Again, the dimensions of this space may be narrow and constantly shifting, but the institutional framework of networks remains in place, responding constantly to changing material and political circumstances.

As James Scott has argued, informal networks remain intentionally invisible, underground, and informal because publicizing them might attract unwanted attention and perhaps retribution from the powerful (Scott 1990). Women who organize and exchange food ration cards to obtain more food are thieves in the government's eyes. Families who get friends in the Ministry of Education to transfer their children to better schools may expose their contacts to charges of corruption. Producing pots and pans in the informal sector lays businessmen open to fines and retroactive penalties from the tax authorities, social affairs ministry, or labor department. Talking with neighbors and friends about politics and organizing community activities and services without obtaining the proper licenses and permissions can lead to government intimidation and harassment. (Examples include the repression during the 1980s and 1990s of the Muslim Brotherhood, a long-established Muslim reformist movement that calls for the imposition of Islamic law and values, as well as government campaigns against more militant Islamist groups such as the Islamic Group and al-Jihad, who call for the violent overthrow of the Egyptian state.) Depending on the political winds of the moment, the stability of peace in the region, and the state of the economy, the Egyptian government either tolerates, re-presses, or intimidates formal, organized political opposition and civil society.

Informal networks and strategies to obtain goods, services, or political preferences are often not strong enough to withstand government bulldozers that tear down informal housing, or the police who arrest young men during indiscriminate sweeps of coffee houses, or the tax authorities who seal up businesses with red wax seals because they are operating "informally" in one fashion or another. Informality has costs, as loosely organized networks that rely on trust and personal ties maintain fragile leaderships that fall apart, fragment, or become atomized in the face of government intimidation and violence. They are not open to all comers, but only to those who can reciprocate exchanges, and so in some sense they are exclusionary. However, because people have multiple identities (family, work, gender, religion, neighborhood, reputation, etc.) and multiple skills and resources to offer their associates, many people can participate in networks even if they remain at the lower end of larger hierarchies of class, gender, or status.

The polarization and factionalism of opposition political forces in Egypt, such as Islamist activists, the left, and human rights organizations, and their inability to forge solidarity against the government, is a legacy of the government's tight rein over associational life. Fundraising, outreach, agendas, publicity, leaderships, internal rules, and principles are all tightly controlled and limited by government bureaucracies. It seems that only the organizations that have turned to violence and do not bother to seek the approval of the Egyptian state, but operate informally outside the law, manage to grow and remain a threat to the government.

On the other hand, we can no longer afford to dismiss or denigrate the personalistic, clientelist, or episodic nature of informal politics and informal networks, because they do provide a voice and a structure, however wanting, with which people can act collectively. Understanding the presence, meaning, and capabilities of informal institutions may help us to understand how seemingly marginalized communities may be able to organize social forces when, or if, political opportunities and openings arise (Tarrow 1994).

Within the context of significant economic and political uncertainty and change, informal networks remain a tool with which many Egyptians meet their everyday needs and organize their activities without attracting the scrutiny of government authorities. Under certain conditions, informal networks can become more public and visible and turn into a more conventional trade association or political organization. At the minimum they deserve more attention and analysis in the explanatory frameworks of social scientists who are trying to understand everyday life in Egypt within its larger political, economic, and cultural context.

NOTE

This chapter is based on field research largely conducted in the mid-1980s in a centrally located, very old, mixed residential and commercial neighborhood in Cairo, Egypt, and is informed by further research trips in the 1990s. For further detail and theoretical arguments, see Singerman 1995 and Singerman and Hoodfar 1996.

REFERENCES

Abdel-Fadil, Mahmoud. 1980. "Informal Sector Employment in Egypt." *Series on Employment Opportunities and Equity in Egypt,* no. 1. Geneva: International Labour Office.
Baydas, Mayada M., Zakaria Bahloul, and Dale W. Adams. 1995. "Informal Finance in Egypt: 'Banks' within Banks." *World Development* 23, no. 4 (winter): 651–61.
Bouis, Howarth E., and Akhter U. Ahmed. 1998. "The Egyptian Food Subsidy System: Impacts on the Poor and an Evaluation of Alternatives for Policy Reforms." International Food Policy Research Institute, Food Security Research Unit of the Agricultural Policy Reform Program in Egypt in collaboration with the Ministry of Agriculture and Land Reclamation and the Ministry of Trade and Supply, March 31, 1998. Washington, D.C.: International Food Policy Research Institute.
Handoussa, Heba. 1991. "Crisis and Challenge: Prospects for the 1990s." In *Employment and Structural Adjustment: Egypt in the 1990s,* ed. Heba Handoussa and Gillian Potter, 3–21. Cairo: The American University in Cairo Press.
Hopkins, Nicholas S., ed. 1991. "The Informal Sector in Egypt." *Cairo Papers in Social Science* 14, no. 4 (winter).
Scott, James C. 1990. *Domination and the Arts of Resistance: Hidden Transcripts.* New Haven: Yale University Press.
Singerman, Diane. 1995. *Avenues of Participation: Family, Politics, and Networks in Urban Quarters of Cairo.* Princeton: Princeton University Press.

Singerman, Diane, and Homa Hoodfar, eds. 1996. *Development, Change, and Gender in Cairo: A View from the Household*. Bloomington: Indiana University Press.

Tarrow, Sidney. 1994. *Power in Movement: Social Movements, Collective Action, and Politics*. Cambridge: Cambridge University Press.

Zaytoun, Mohaya A. 1991. "Earnings and the Cost of Living: An Analysis of Recent Developments in the Egyptian Economy." In *Employment and Structural Adjustment: Egypt in the 1990s*, ed. Heba Handoussa and Gillian Potter, 219–57. Cairo: The American University in Cairo Press.

20. Politics, Politics, and More Politics: Youth Life Experiences in the Gaza Strip

Brian K. Barber

If political realities inform adolescent experience in Jerusalem and the West Bank—both locations that have been greatly influenced by the West through tourism and international interest in Jerusalem and other religiously significant towns—youth experience with politics in Gaza is more intense and comprehensive. This is true for a variety of geographical, historical, economic, and political reasons. Indeed, a brief but sufficient description of the difference between Palestinian life in the West Bank or East Jerusalem and Palestinian life in Gaza is that all things—culture, hardship, politicization, devotion, etc.—seem more intense in Gaza.

Gaza has been so isolated for so long that very little is known about it, even by Palestinians from the West Bank or Jerusalem. Since the early days of the Intifada, Palestinians have generally not been permitted to enter or leave Gaza (especially from or to East Jerusalem or the West Bank), so even non-Gazan Palestinians know little of life there. As for the broader world community, virtually all that is known or remembered about Gaza is the footage of conflict during the six years of the Intifada (1987–1993). Not surprisingly, therefore, the image the outside world has of Gaza is of a rather pitiful, violent place. This was evidenced in a recent content analysis of U.S. media exposure to Gaza from 1980 to 1997 that showed that 69 percent of all references to Gaza described conflict and violence.[1]

Currently, 77 percent of Gaza's 1.2 million Arab inhabitants are refugees from the 1948 war or their descendants, two-thirds of whom live in the eight refugee camps. The other third live in towns and villages that were in place before the influx of refugees. Approximately four thousand Jewish settlers live in nineteen settlements sprinkled throughout the Strip, occupying thirty-five percent of the land. The settlements are heavily guarded by Israeli soldiers, military equipment, and fencing. All are made of modern building materials, with conveniences that in some cases include

watered lawns. Some of the settlements sit on or near the few ma-
jor traffic arteries in the Strip; others are clustered together in a
large bloc on the southeastern coast.

Brian K. Barber's first exposure to Gaza was in 1994, when
he began preparatory work with colleagues for a research project
on Palestinian family life. —Eds.

I was alerted to the role of politics in the lives of youth when, during my first set of interviews in Palestine, I asked four youths from East Jerusalem to identify a Palestinian man they respected and to tell why they admired him. All of them identified a political figure; two named Yasser Arafat and the other two named members of the Palestinian negotiating team at the 1991 Madrid conference. They did not refer to sports figures or TV or movie actors, as their Western counterparts tend to do. However, another question revealed much more profoundly and poignantly how politics can penetrate the everyday experience of youth.

This later question asked each youth when he is most happy. All of them immediately responded politically, saying things like "I am happy when the peace negotiations are going well," or "I will be happy when we achieve a Palestinian state." I had to probe several times before they grasped that I was after a personal answer, the likes of which—for example, "when things are going well with my girlfriend or boyfriend," "when my parents buy me something," etc.—come so readily to the minds of many American teens. Finally, Tareq understood what I was after and replied, "I am happy when I run. I love to run." But with the same breath he added, "But whenever I run the soldiers [Israelis] want to arrest me." Thus, even the momentary diversion to a personal issue was regulated immediately by a political reality. This was my first indication that for Palestinian youth there is no separation between the personal and the political.

Perhaps the central, defining characteristic of being Palestinian is the inescapable role of the political in personal and collective identity. This is so regardless of where a Palestinian may live because of enduring controversies about the basic elements that make up a person: home, heritage, nationality, culture. What is a Palestinian? Where is Palestine? What are its borders? Who has sovereignty over it? Is it a country? A culture? An occupied territory? A future state? For U.S. citizens, as well as for other Western cultures, politics is largely the concern of the adult community, and only a portion of adults are interested enough to cast a vote, at that. Children and youth do not typically have much to say about politics, because their everyday circumstances, needs, resources, or achievements are not directly influenced, at least in their minds, by political realities.

Palestinian children and youth in the West Bank, and particularly in the Gaza Strip, live a life that contrasts starkly with this apolitical Western stance. For them, every facet of their lives is informed and shaped by political history and current political dynamics and realities, of which they are very aware. This pervasive influence of the political in the lives of young people is certainly fascinating, considering its dramatic contrast with the experience of children in many other parts of the world, and it may also help us understand the capacities of children and the course of their development.

This essay centers on the role of the political in the lives of young people as one way of illustrating the life of children in the Gaza Strip as I have come to know it as a U.S. social scientist who has spent considerable time there during the past six years. My time in Gaza (I have also spent substantial time throughout the West Bank and in East Jerusalem) has consisted of fifteen visits, many of which have extended for several months, and during which I have lived primarily with families in or near refugee camps in the Strip. I wanted to immerse myself in the culture in order to investigate the current psychological, social, religious, and political functioning of youth who have grown up in the shadow of the six-year-long Palestinian popular struggle against the Israeli military occupation: the Intifada.[2]

DAILY LIFE IN GAZA

Ahmed, nineteen, and I spent last night on the roof of Mohammed's home. Mohammed is Ahmed's uncle and one of my first contacts in Gaza. His home has been my headquarters on research trips for the past four years. The house is a three-story cinder-block structure, the outside of which, like virtually all other buildings in Gaza, shows a variety of stages of completion: plastered and painted at the first level, plastered and unpainted on the second level, and bare cinder blocks on the third level. From the roof protrude clusters of steel reinforcing bars, anticipating future expansion. The building houses fifty-year-old Mohammed, his mother, three married brothers with their wives and children, one single brother, and one single sister. This sister, one brother, and Mohammed have jobs; the others are looking for work. Mohammed's Bedouin father, who died twenty-five years ago, owned this orchard land before the 1948 Arab-Israeli war that resulted in the influx of hundreds of thousands of refugees from the northern coastal and interior portions of Palestine, now Israel, to Gaza. A portion of the land was given by Mohammed's father to the United Nations to help establish the Maghazi refugee camp, which is just to the south of Mohammed's home.

Just behind the house is Ahmed's home, where he lives with his parents and eight younger siblings. The house is a single-story structure built ten years ago. It remained completely unfinished, but still inhabited by the family, until this year, when the rough concrete floors were tiled, the cinder-block walls plastered and painted, and windows and doors installed in the bare openings in the walls. The second story will be constructed when Ahmed is ready to marry, some five to ten years in the future.

Sleeping on the roof has become a tradition for us. We often held English lessons there to help him pass his college entrance exam, which he took earlier this year. We sleep on two-inch-thick foam mattresses laid on the concrete roof and under thick acrylic blankets, because even in Gaza's Mediterranean climate November mornings are chilly. Ahmed left the roof at six this morning in order to get ready for the twenty-minute ride in an old Mercedes seven-seater public taxi to Gaza City, where he attends the Jerusalem Open University. There are two major universities in Gaza, Islamic University (religious) and Al-Azhar University (secular). Each currently has a student body of about ten thousand, but is expanding far faster than construction, staff, or faculty can keep pace with. There are also a few smaller institutions, such as the Jerusalem Open University, either for specialized training or for those like Ahmed who didn't do especially well on the exam. Ahmed's decision to pursue a university education after passing the entrance exam marked a major shift in his plans. Up until just a few months ago he had planned to join one of the several police or security forces of the Palestinian Authority after completing high school. These forces were established in 1994 when Yasser Arafat was permitted to set up a governmental authority in Gaza and Jericho, and they are virtually the only source of reliable employment for youth, especially those worst off economically.

Anticipating precisely when I would be ready for breakfast, Tarik, twenty-five, Mohammed's single brother, emerges from irrigating the citrus groves into my room downstairs with a tray of fresh-baked Bedouin bread, olives, boiled eggs, *zatar* (ground oregano), olive oil, and tea. Just last month he finished a two-year degree in public relations at Al-Azhar University, unable because of Israeli regulations to complete the bachelor's degree he had begun at Hebron University in the West Bank. He hopes to marry, but not until he finds a job. Along with the breakfast tray, he has with him the local daily newspaper and shortly asks with feigned excitement, "Do you know what today is? It is the anniversary of the Balfour Declaration." Of the many documents that have shaped the political future of the Palestinians, this brief and informal 1917 letter from Arthur Balfour, the British foreign secretary, to Lord Rothschild, the head of the Jewish community in Britain, has likely done more than any other document or process to justify and solidify the Jewish presence in this part of the world, a presence that is the most recent and problematic source of challenge and confusion about Palestinian identity. And thus the day begins with a political memory.

Tarik returns to the fields and I set up to continue writing, only to be reminded of how many interruptions there will be. There is no such thing as privacy in Gaza, both because of the sheer concentration of people and because of their social nature. When a foreigner is around, there is all the more interest. Any number of family members find their way eventually to my room, ignore the closed door, and enter to greet me on the new day, bring tea, or arrange a time to talk later; the children run their fingers through my straight hair or ask whether there are any sweets or gifts for them that day. Last year, one friend from Maghazi tried to keep a trip to Cairo private, only to be approached about the visit by several community members. He complained with humor and exasperation, "There is simply no privacy in this camp!"

Soon it is time for Hazim's English lesson. Hazim is Ahmed's next youngest brother, who faces the *tawjihi*—the college entrance exam derived from the Egyptian educational system—next summer. (Egypt controlled Gaza most recently from 1948 until 1967.) He is nervously preparing with the hope that he can follow Ahmed's lead and get into a university. Education has long been the key to any type of meaningful employment or social mobility among Palestinians. It is particularly critical in Gaza because of the deteriorating economic conditions, with unemployment rates regularly above 50 percent. Gaza youth such as Tarik are still forbidden by Israel to travel to the better universities in the West Bank, and places in the local universities are becoming scarce. Hazim recites in well-practiced English phrases his daily schedule: up at 5:30, tea, to school by 6:30, four classes, home for lunch, nap, studying in the orchard, tutoring lesson, dinner, to bed at 10:00. I can't remember when or how, but politics emerge in the lesson and Hazim proclaims, "I am for peace. All people want peace."

Tarik, Yehyie (the next oldest brother), Ahmed, and I drive to Gaza City to deliver boxes of my research questionnaires to the DHL office for shipment to the U.S. After reaching the main road, we drive straight north to the metropolitan center of the Strip. We weave around wooden carts pulled by donkeys and modern construction vehicles installing a drainage system that may finally solve the winter flooding problems that often make this, the only main thoroughfare, impassable. The road constrution is being financed by the government of Japan, recently a heavy donor to infrastructural improvements in Gaza.

At the DHL office I ask the proprietor how his work is going, as one of a string of pro forma questions one asks upon greeting—"How are you?" "How are your children?" "What is new with you?" "How is your father? Your mother?" "How is your health?" "How is work?" He isn't fifteen seconds into his response when the political questions began to flow. With real bewilderment and some anger he asks, "Why does America give so much economic aid to the Israelis? I don't understand this. I really don't understand this. We have nothing and they have everything. Tell me, please tell me, why does America do this? This office used to have six employees out front. Now, you see, there is my wife, that is my daughter, that is my son. That is all. We have nothing. Maybe two or three packages a day. No business. We need help." He and Tarik and Yehyie switch to Arabic and continue to discuss the political and economic conditions over spiced coffee.

I go back to Maghazi for lunch with Mohammed, who has just returned from his day supervising English instruction in UNRWA schools in the southern part of the Strip. UNRWA (the United Nations Relief and Works Agency) was established in 1950 to deal with the Palestinian refugees, seeing to their education, relief, and health needs. Immediately upon arriving home, Mohammed turns on the TV news, something he will do several times before the day is over. News broadcasts in Gaza, whether from the local Palestinian station, the Egyptian channel, or the Israeli channel, are 95 percent politics and 5 percent weather. Today the top stories are the clashes between Jewish settlers and Palestinian officials in Jerusalem; these are followed by appraisals of the peace process, with reports from Palestinian, Israeli, Jordanian, and Egyptian officials. The weather will be warm again tomorrow.

The meal of grilled fish, rice, salad, and guavas is followed by an afternoon nap and the evening program of social visits. There is little to do in Gaza but visit family and friends—there are no theaters, bowling alleys, concert halls, shopping malls—so it isn't clear how much of this socializing is cultural and how much is a function of the absence of other diversions.

The social program for the day begins with an unannounced visit from Abu Husein, an elderly camp neighbor, who stops by to chat. During tea he begins to reminisce about the village he lived in before 1948, when his family fled the war to become temporary, and then permanent, refugees in Gaza. Abu Husein talks of having taken all his sons to visit his village, not more than a fifteen-minute drive from the current borders of the Strip. He remarks that the village has been renamed in Hebrew, and none of them are allowed to visit now. Our conversation is interrupted a number of times by the roar of Israeli fighters streaking overhead to or from their bases. I can only recall a few days in Gaza when I haven't heard them. The locals seem oblivious to them, despite the fact that at times they fly so low that the din drowns all conversation. I once asked about them and a friend cynically remarked, "Israeli music."

Then it is off to visit some of Mohammed's colleagues and friends in Gaza City, the major urban and commercial center of the Strip. On the way, a passenger asks to hear the radio news to get another of several daily reports on political conditions. Mohammed points out the site of a recent suicide bombing, an uncommon event in Gaza itself. Contrary to U.S. stereotypes, Gaza is calm and quiet, and has been so since the Intifada, when admittedly it was a war zone. Rarely is there violence. Periodically, Palestinian security forces clash with Israeli soldiers at checkpoints and near settlements. This settlement was built in 1971 and sits directly on the main thoroughfare. Twelve families live in modern apartments behind the barbed-wire fences and machine-gun turrets that are the only separation between the settlement and the main road. A pedestrian bridge spans the main road to the Jewish school across the thoroughfare. I note that a new addition to the bridge is a large menorah, under which all the Palestinian traffic flows. As we pass through the military checkpoint near the settlement, Mohammed remarks, "I envy your life, your freedom; no checkpoints."

Sometime during the socializing at our destination the hosts bring out the freshly acquired Arabic and English versions of the Wye River Memorandum, the result of the conference that was held last week. They are very cautious in discussing their criticisms of it. Before leaving, Mohammed fills a five-gallon plastic container he brought along with water filtered through the host's new five-hundred-dollar purifier. The local water is heavily salinated because the aquifers, the only natural source of water for the Strip, are depleted. The water is also dangerously high in nitrates because of the percolation of raw sewage from the refugee camps. Arabs have not been allowed to dig any new wells since the Israeli occupation of the Strip began in 1967. Israeli settlers have dug between thirty-five and forty new wells for themselves since 1971, when the settlement program began.

As we arrive back home that evening, Mohammed points out that the gate we are entering to his property is bent out of shape because during the Intifada an Israeli tank plunged through it to the orchard after the camp youth had blocked the road with stones and burning tires. He can't believe that it has already been ten years since it happened.

And so the very unremarkable day ends. The days are long past since this string of references or recollections of political issues would have been displayed for my education. This is simply life in Gaza, an assembly of daily, even hourly, physical reminders, social and economic conditions, and current events that maintain an existence forged and scripted by political controversy and conflict.

ADOLESCENTS

Given the degree to which politics saturates the daily life of Gaza, it is not surprising that children incorporate it into their own worldview. They, after all, travel daily past the settlements, hear the news reports, and listen—

either by invitation or through eavesdropping—to the adults' constant discussions of political history and current affairs. And though adolescents, the focus of our original study, were too young to be very directly involved in the conflict, they have clear memories of the intense days of the Intifada.

Our research has taken us to nearly a hundred different schools in the West Bank and the Gaza Strip. Because of the volume of students, school buildings—some quite old, some very new—often have two or three shifts per day, with the first group of students coming as early as six A.M.. Boys dress in uniforms of blue denim, girls slip striped or solid-colored dresses over their denim pants, and all sport square backpacks that are sometimes half the size of the children carrying them. Ninety-seven percent of children in Gaza complete high school.

The walls of the classrooms and hallways are covered with student artwork and with the three standard political icons: maps of Palestine, pictures of Jerusalem's Dome of the Rock mosque, and portraits of Yasser Arafat. By Western standards, the children are exceptionally well behaved. Except during recesses, when their energy is expressed in spirited games of soccer or basketball, the hallways and classrooms are generally quiet and orderly, with students responding to a strict and authoritarian teaching style. As part of our school visits I would often ask to spend some time talking with a classroom of adolescents. Most often these were classes of eighth or ninth graders (the subjects of our research), often English classes so the kids could show off their English skills. English language instruction is compulsory beginning in the fifth grade in all schools.

My visits were unannounced. The teacher would introduce me and I would say a few words about our research project and then ask for questions from the students. These discussions became quite predictable. The students, invariably fascinated and excited by the visit of a foreigner, would always begin, at first shyly and then with quickly growing confidence, by asking my name, my age, and whether I was married. And then the political questions would begin, always gentle and respectful but nevertheless direct. "Why does America give so much money to the Jews?" "Why doesn't America give us any help?" "Why do Americans hate us?" "What do you think about the peace process?" "Do you think we should have a state?" "Do you think Jerusalem should be our capital?"

After struggling through these questions, students asked about my reaction to Gaza and to them as people. "Why did you come to Gaza?" "Will you come back?" What do you like about Gaza?" "What do you think about us?" During one twenty-minute discussion with a class of college-aged students, this last question, "What do you think about us?" was asked at least six different times, in the same words, as if the hunger for acceptance was insatiable. This sentiment was illustrated poignantly in a letter to me from Ibtisam, a student from Ramallah, West Bank, who was then a graduate student in the U.S. I had recommended that she write her own story of growing up Palestinian. In the letter she suggested that her working title would be "Marked for Destruction,"[3] and in response to a comment I had made about admiring her people, she wrote, "That simple statement was an intense contradiction to all the messages I knew the world to ascribe to my people. It was magical and healing to hang on to that when distressing news from home reinforced the old messages that my people were not worthy of all things human." That the source of such feelings is political was illustrated by the plea from a fourteen-year-old boy from Rafah, in the very southern part of the Gaza Strip. As I was preparing to leave the room after the typical classroom discussion, he raised his hand and pleaded, "Please go home and tell your people that we are not all terrorists."

It is the youth who were adolescents during the Intifada whose lives have been most completely and dramatically shaped by the political. This is so because of their heavy involvement in it. The Intifada began in the Gaza Strip, and it was more intense there than in the West Bank or East Jerusalem[4] because of the density of the population (the Jabalia refugee camp, where the Intifada began, is the most densely populated place on earth), higher rates of poverty, and stricter forms of occupation that endured over the twenty years since the Israeli occupation began in 1967. Gaza has always been the home of fundamentalist religious groups and of Palestinian attempts to form resistance governments.

The adolescent population's heavy involvement in the Intifada can be explained by several factors. At the time of the Intifada fully 50 percent of the population of Gaza was fourteen years old or younger. Their economic condition had worsened, because the Gulf oil crisis dried up many employment opportunities for youth abroad. Further, since these adolescents had been born after 1967, they knew nothing but military conflict and had been witnesses to and victims of extreme treatment by the occupiers. It is not surprising, therefore, that youth participated heavily in the popular revolution. Indeed, 80–90 percent of them took part in demonstrating, throwing stones, etc., far overshadowing the rates (15–20 percent) at which youth have participated in other social movements, such as those in South Africa and Northern Ireland and the U.S. student protests. Accompanying their activism were very high rates of exposure to trauma. For example, 90 percent experienced late-night home raids by Israeli soldiers, 65 percent witnessed their father or a neighbor's father being beaten or humiliated in front of them, etc.

HUSSAM

Hussam is typical of Gaza youth who were adolescents during the Intifada. I first met Hussam in May of 1996, when Mohammed recommended that I include him in my interviews. Mohammed drove me from his home at the edge of Maghazi (with a population around 20,000), the second smallest of the eight refugee camps in the Gaza Strip, to Nuseirat (with a population around 51,000), the fourth smallest camp, where twenty-three-year-old Hussam lived with his parents and eight siblings. The drive only takes about ten minutes, but it reveals much of the uniqueness of Gaza. These camps are two of the four called Middle Camps, because they are in the middle of the Gaza Strip. The Strip is twenty-five miles long, running north to south, and averages five miles wide. Israel borders the north and east; Egypt borders the south. Maghazi is set toward its eastern border; Nuseirat sits just off the Mediterranean Sea, the western border of the Strip. The northern, eastern, and southern borders are fenced with barbed wire, which is why locals refer to the Strip, even during these times of greater Palestinian political autonomy, as "The Big Prison."

With the exception of a couple of entries for produce trucks, there are only two entrances to the Gaza Strip for Palestinians (there are others reserved for Jewish settlers). The southern one, equipped with Israeli, Egyptian, and now Palestinian border stations, is used by Gazans for occasional trips to Egypt, if they have enough money. The northern one, the Erez Crossing, is the major entry point from Israel. It was here in 1998 that Nasser, a seventeen-year-old from Maghazi, was three times refused exit to the international airport in Tel Aviv, an hour's drive from the crossing. He had lived for the last three years in Florida with his father and brother and had come to Gaza to visit his mother. Despite the fact that Nasser carries a U.S. passport he was refused exit from Gaza and entry into Israel. The Israeli soldier's comment: "I don't care what kind of passport you have. You are a Palestinian and will always be a Palestinian."

Through Erez pass the twenty-five thousand married Gaza men over thirty-five who work in Israeli agricultural fields or help build Israeli settlements in the West Bank. (Younger, unmarried men fit the profile of suicide bombers and are not allowed out of Gaza.) They make this trip six days a week, except when the border is fully closed by Israel for political reasons, such as in response to Palestinian bombings in Israel, or for a variety of Jewish holidays. As many as seventy-five thousand people worked in Israel before the Intifada, when their passage was unrestricted. Now they pass through elaborate security checks on their early-morning departures and late-afternoon returns. They are funneled through a narrow concrete corridor along the eastern side of the half-mile crossing. Foreign visitors walk through two Israeli checks in an adjacent corridor. Those who arrive when most workers are returning home, around 5 or 6 P.M., hear the surreal clamor of thousands of workers noisily funneling unseen through the corridor. Ahmed's father and two uncles work in Israel, two roofing settlement homes and one laboring in the olive orchards.

We drive to Nuseirat in Mohammed's rickety U. N. Peugot that cramps the legs of even the shortest of people. We leave through the warped gate through the cinder-block wall that separates the orchard property from one of Maghazi's main byways on the east. Spray-painted on the interior of the wall in red Arabic letters are congratulations to Mohammed from Ahmed for having recently completed his M.A. in educational leadership at a U.S. university. The statements are reminiscent of the thousands of slogans painted on Gaza walls and homes during the Intifada—many are still visible—as a primary means of communicating about the progress of the resistance. Surely this is where Ahmed got the idea.

Paralleling the two-kilometer-long partially paved road leading west to the main north-south thoroughfare is a two-foot-wide open channel of raw sewage draining from Maghazi. It is separated from the road by a natural, two-foot-high hedge of cactus. At certain times of the year it is common to see college students escape the hectic atmosphere of the camp to stroll along this road, book in hand, studying for their exams. At the main road the channel feeds into a larger one running north to an open field, where the sewage drains into the soil. During the twenty-six years it has formally occupied Gaza, Israel has built sewer systems for two camps; both systems were undersized at their completion. The other six camps have no sewer systems. Those close to the sea drain their sewage directly into the Mediterranean.

After going a few kilometers north on the main road we turn west into Nuseirat along an asphalt road, and then south at the pharmacy—the site of some of the Intifada's heaviest fighting between Gazan youth and Israeli soldiers—onto the sand road leading to the sector of the camp that Hussam lives in. His house is on a relatively wide street that contrasts with the narrow alleyways that make up the rabbit warren of the camp. This camp, like the rest, is largely a maze of four-foot-wide alleys, and youths' familiarity with them helped them avoid capture in the often daily confrontations with Israeli soldiers during the Intifada.

Hussam's home is older than Mohammed's and Ahmed's, and is typical of a basic camp home. Originally, in the 1950s, the camps consisted of tent dwellings, but when it became clear that the refugees would not be permitted to return to their homes, UNRWA built simple, solid structures in the 1960s. Most of these have been replaced with updated cinder-block versions over the years. We enter through the standard heavy metal door into a narrow, polished concrete corridor and are shown by one of Hussam's younger brothers into the sitting room. The room, with its sparse furnishings—a couple of sofas, some chairs, several small tables for tea, and a spare bed—looks old but is good-sized. The corrugated asbestos roof channels lie atop the cinder-block walls about nine or ten feet above the concrete floor. From the ceiling hangs a simple electric fan that provides some air flow during the sweltering summers. In my first several visits to Hussam's home, this was the only room that I saw.

I didn't know what to expect of Hussam before this meeting. To that point, I had intensively interviewed only four boys in East Jerusalem and Tarik, Mohammed's brother. I had nevertheless formed an opinion about the personality of Palestinians, especially Gazans, from the less intensive exposure I had already had to thousands of youths at the schools we had visited. My judgment that Gazan youth tended to be very quiet and respectful had been confirmed some months earlier, when as I walked from my hotel on the coast toward the city I passed a group of teenagers huddled together off the pathway. They were far enough away that I did not greet them, but they saw me and, recognizing immediately that I was an English-speaking foreigner, began shouting, sarcastically, a few English words: "Hamburger, hot dog."

I joined the group. My discomfort increased when they began criticizing Gaza and sneering at its poverty. Rather proudly, they revealed that they were newcomers to Gaza and were not at all pleased to be here. They had been raised in Tunisia as part of the large diaspora Palestinian population that developed there after the 1948 Israeli-Arab war, and had come to Gaza in 1994 as part of the contingent that accompanied Yasser Arafat. They talked of the pleasures of Tunisia, emphasizing particularly how women went to the beach there in bikinis. (Gazan women who go to the beach wear ankle-long robes that they pull up to mid-calf while wading in the sea.)

With the group of teens—the fact that both boys and girls were there should have told me they were not Gazans—were two boys, a few feet apart, whose dress was less fancy and whose speech was quieter and more shy. I could tell immediately from their dress and demeanor that they were native Gazans. The substantial gentleness and deference of Gazan youth contrasts with the vigorous role Gazan teens played in the Intifada, defiantly initiating confrontations with Israeli soldiers, taking extreme risks, and witnessing and experiencing extreme forms of victimization.

I had been told that Hussam had been one of the leaders of the youth resistance in the Middle Camps, and I was uncertain what to expect from him at this first meeting. He joined us after we had waited for a few minutes. His very slim, even gaunt, frame was clothed in pressed dress slacks and a dress shirt. His hair and moustache were neatly trimmed, and his glasses helped present a scholarly air. His voice was very soft, so much so that I needed to ask him to speak up on occasion. His English was excellent, if not polished, and it was occasionally punctuated with unusually sophisticated words that seemed to indicate a careful study of English dictionaries. (At the end of the interview he proudly showed me some of the poetry he had written in English.) Hussam's manner was extremely respectful and deferent, expressing a sense that it was an honor to meet me and welcome me into his home.

Hussam sat rather rigidly on the edge of the spare bed next to my chair, and as the interview began he seemed nervous but clearly eager to express himself. His mind seemed to be flooded by memories and experiences that he shared with relish or passion but always with a kind of scholarly erudition. Like the dozens of other Intifada youth I interviewed later, he seemed to relax quickly, and though he became more comfortable, his expressions maintained a seriousness, sincerity, and intensity. His justification and explanation for youth involvement in the resistance was obviously centered on his appraisal of the historical and political conditions under which his and his parents' generations grew up during the occupation:

> The Intifada was a public reaction against the Israeli hardness and inhuman actions against Palestinians; especially killing, harsh circumstances, bad economical situations, and other actions. I can't describe them exactly [the behaviors]. To them we were subhumans.

He described a moment that crystallized his own action:

> I saw a soldier hitting and kicking a woman in the street here. We could do nothing because there was a huge number of soldiers in the street. They began to besiege us so we couldn't do anything but flee. . . . We felt that our immortality, our supremacy was no more. In the eyes of the soldiers, we were animals that they wanted to hunt. So this created feelings of anger and revolution inside each one of us.

His serious presentation was occasionally tempered with a more youthful animation, particularly as he described details of his resistance. His recollections revealed a clear sense of pride and self-respect in his role in the resistance, as well as the passion and commitment of the youth in general.

> In the memory of [someone who had been killed by Israeli soldiers], we planned to make a demonstration against the Israelis. It was not to be an ordinary demonstration, but a real revolution in the camp. So during the night of the day before, almost fifty persons hurried to plan for this. They put up barricades, they prepared tires [for burning], they put up Palestinian flags, some people arranged firebombs, cocktail bombs. By the next morning, we were all prepared for this day. Some people went to the soldiers here near the camp in order to entice them to come inside the camp. The soldiers refused. It continued until almost three o'clock in the afternoon. But the people accumulated and increased and the soldiers were obliged to come into the camp. Attacks began soon—severe attacks. It was a day of which we are still proud.

For adolescents in Gaza, the Intifada was not a momentary foray into risk and danger, but a sustained and intense exposure to the exciting but sobering realities of political conflict. Speaking for his age-mates in his camp, Hussam said,

> It was our life, every day. . . . Almost every day we were sitting in one home here or in another friend's home thinking about how to face the occupation: how, when to wait and how to wait, and what were the most certain ways to crush them [the soldiers] from the camp. . . . Sometimes I walked in the street peacefully and calmly with my friends, laughing and remembering past moments . . . suddenly a jeep would emerge from a street and begin to chase us. The soldiers would be laughing and shooting. Sometimes we were sitting in a home like this, drinking tea or coffee, and watching TV or exchanging opinions on the occupation. The soldiers would violate the house and begin to chase us on the roofs. . . . I can't remember everything, but actions or experiences like this would happen every day—one time, two times, three times, ten times, every day.

If there is any exaggeration in this characterization, as one Gaza adult suggested after reading it, it only reflects the depth to which the commitment to the cause and the fervency of association with it still pervades the consciousness of young men whose developing years were steeped in political struggle. So much of current identity and self-evaluation seems to have been influenced by these experiences. Like others, Hussam commented on his own psychological and civic development:

> Before the Intifada we were children. The only thing we thought about was football. Sometimes we studied, or watched TV, or did many things which were not so important. But during our actions or involvement in the Intifada, we began to think in another way. We began to have a role in our society. We changed the way people thought. We became leaders when we were children, so we began to think that we had a great role to perform. . . . By this we achieved self-satisfaction, self-assertion. . . . We thought we could do something against the Israeli occupation. . . . I am proud of myself to have lived such a life. Because what kind of life can a child have during the occupation? I think I lived my childhood in the kindergarten in the [refugee] camp. They were happy days. I also felt happy during my study in preparatory school. But during the Intifada it was our task to rebel and to fight, or to be engaged in conflict against the Israelis. . . . Yes, in fact, it was a good life. It was a good opportunity for us to become self-made men.

Approximately one-quarter of Gazan adolescent males were imprisoned during the Intifada. Hussam was imprisoned three times. During our discussions he has never shown an interest in detailing his treatment in prison—only once, after some probing, did he discuss the various forms of torture he endured—but he sees the prison experience as fundamental to his growth. His friends, he says, agree.

Some of my friends often tell me nowadays that when I was arrested and went to prison my behavior changed. I mean older friends . . . friends who are now maybe twenty-nine years old. They tell me that before I went to prison I was an ordinary child. But they say that when I came out of prison, they thought I was another man, another person; one who had exceeded his age.

Hussam's letter to me after our first interview in 1996 reveals the freshness of his optimism and how easily it is stimulated by attention from someone from the outside. The letter arrived by fax three days after he had received a letter from me:

Thank you very much for your nice letter of September 10, which has given me the greatest pleasure. Hardly can I find words to express my feelings toward you. I have asked about you many times since your last visit to Gaza. I wish I could meet you soon to exchange opinions and thoughts. Really, your visit was an epoch-making in my life as it made my potentials sparkle, and reinforced my confidence in my abilities and skills.

I am so pleased to hear that you are going to spend October, November, and part of December in Palestine. It gives me the greatest honor to read your words regarding my interviews as facilitating and contributing to understanding the experiences of the Palestinian youth. I owe you this opportunity which makes me share in transferring and introducing real images and experiences of my people to your community and the world so that they may have a clear-cut idea about my people's circumstances. I am strongly willing to speak with you about my experiences and recollections of the Intifada, and my personal life. I am looking forward to meeting you and spending much time discussing these matters. I really love recalling the recollections of the past. I think that no assistance should be spared, and lots of effort should be made.

Since this initial interview I have spent considerable time with Hussam, in formal interviews, in increasingly personal discussions, and in observing his day-to-day life. The political is a thread that runs through every facet of his life. Our conversations reveal what is on his mind, and usually it is something political, incorporating the latest blip of the never-ending erratic pulse of the peace process into his evolving political philosophy. But beyond philosophy, his daily life and future are affected by the current political dynamics—now intra-Palestinian political dynamics—as demonstrated by his Gaza university's rejection of his application for an overseas scholarship because he is not registered as a member of the Fateh, the predominant political faction in Gaza, despite his superior qualifications. Even more telling, however, is the depth to which political history has permeated his psyche. The substance of his personal involvement in the Intifada surfaces in his English grammar lectures to students at a junior college, where he will illustrate grammatical points with sentences like "The soldier killed the woman" or "The man killed the soldier." And the overall political conditions of Palestinians in Gaza surface in his humor. In a recent phone conversation he was worried about the lack of rain this winter. Referring to the frequent Israeli closures of the Gaza Strip that bar the transport of workers and goods, he said with good humor and resignation, "We are also under closure from the sky."

Gazan youth's extensive political involvement means that they identify political concerns as their personal concerns. Careful study of the world's literature and history reveals that youth have on many occasions been engaged in political events and conditions, but usually only a small percentage have engaged themselves in relatively short-term bouts of activism; more often than not children and adolescents have been passive victims of turmoil. Not so for the Gazan youth. Large majorities participated over an extended period with precocious awareness of political history and ideology. To a large extent their current identity as young adults was shaped by this immersion in the political struggle, an identity that appears now, several years after the Intifada, to be largely positive and supportive of personal and cultural well-being. An identity that is based on political history, however, is, by definition, also subject to future political conditions. Thus the future identity of Gazan youth can be read according to the constantly shifting dynamics in the political processes that continue to control life in the Strip—up and down, jockeying between hope and despair, but so far, at least, with a basic patience that things will work out in the end.

Such personal growth is not unique to Hussam. Recent findings from a study of a scientific sample of seven hundred men and women of the same age show that the more youth were involved in the resistance movement, the higher are their current levels of psychological well-being and social and civic functioning. Youth who were active in the Intifada feel good about themselves and their identity and are currently actively involved in political organizations and in volunteer services in the community. Contrary to predictions based on Western social science theories, such precocious involvement in protracted conflict and exposure to traumatic conditions has not resulted in any decline in values and practices in the central social contexts of family, education, and religion, and there has been no perceptible increase in the very low levels of social deviance. The trauma that was associated with the political resistance appears to have been buffered by the high levels of political and religious commitment to a cause the youth felt was necessary for the welfare of their people, and in which they felt they played an instrumental role.

Just yesterday, a conversation with Hussam echoed earlier discussions with Mohammed and Adnan and gave another illustration of the political seesaw on which the Gazans ride. President Clinton's visit in 1999 touched the Gazans deeply. That so important a figure would deign to visit Gaza soothed the pervasive insecurity Palestinians characteristically feel and enlivened their hopes dramatically. American flags were everywhere, even, according to Adnan, in people's living rooms. But then, just days later, came the U.S. bombing of Baghdad. Upon word of this the Gazans plunged into confusion and despair and found themselves forced to reframe Clinton's visit as a political strategy, with all of its attendant hypocrisy and self-serving motives. But Hussam said in closing, "But we know that people are different than politics, and so we continue to hope."

AN UPDATE

In the two years that have passed since this chapter was written, some things have changed and much has stayed the same in Gaza. Just recently a sewer system funded by the Palestinian Authority was completed in Maghazi. It rids the camp of the open channels of sewage, but still empties in the open fields outside the camp. All the roads in Maghazi will soon be paved. It feels so modern. The political currents shift predictably with negotiations for a final resolution to the conflict. Permit requirements are still oppressive; some Gazans are now allowed to visit the West Bank, but not Jerusalem. Economically, there has been no improvement in Gaza.

But, characteristically, individuals don't stay idle. Ahmed is now in the second year of his university education in Gaza. He is also working part-time in a cafeteria at the truck crossing. He is feeling the burden of sustaining his family, as his father has become less able to work. He also spent a memorable two months in the U.S. visiting and studying English at the invitation and with the funding of a U.S. friend. He was dazed with the size and culture of the U.S., but his culture shock seemed to have been worse on his return to Gaza. Hazim, his next youngest brother, did not pass the Tawjihi the summer after finishing high school, but he did pass just last month, when he retook it after a year. Amr, the next youngest brother, did not pass this year, on his first try. Mohammed has been promoted within the UNRWA educational system in Gaza, and serves now as the third most senior educational official. Yehyie currently has a job in a private hospital south of Maghazi, where his sister, Muteah, works as a nurse. Tarik graduated from Al Azhar University in Gaza and now is employed as a public relations official at the Khan Yunis branch of the Jerusalem Open University. With a steady job, he can now prepare to marry. Adnan finished his master's degree in the U.S., returned to Gaza for a year to resume his work as principal of two schools, and has recently returned to the U.S. with his wife and three young children to begin work on his doctoral degree in educational leadership. Hussam recently finished his master's degree in the same field in the U.S. He returned to Gaza to his job teaching English at a technical college and to marry his fiancée of five years, Mai. He has agreed to begin writing his life story.

NOTES

1. R. B. Bell and B. K. Barber, "U.S. Media Exposure to the Gaza Strip," unpublished manuscript, Brigham Young University, 1998.

2. Funding for the research projects on Palestinian families has been provided by the Social Science Research Council, New York; the Center for Studies of the Family, the Kennedy Center for International Studies, and the Department of Religious Education, Brigham Young University; and the Center for Policy Analysis on Palestine, Washington, D.C. The original research team consisted of Bruce A. Chadwick, Tim B. Heaton, Camille Fronk, Ray Huntington (still at Brigham Young University) and Brian K. Barber (now at the University of Tennessee). For more detailed treatment of extensive interviews with Gazan adolescents of the Intifada, see B. K. Barber, "Youth Experience during the Palestinian *Intifada:* A Case Study in Intensity, Complexity, Paradox, and Competence," in *Roots of Civic Identity: International Perspectives on Community Service and Activism in Youth,* ed. Miranda Yates and James Youniss (New York: Cambridge University Press, 1999), 178–204; Brian K. Barber, "Political Violence, Family Relations, and Palestinian Youth Functioning," *Journal of Adolescent Research* 14, no. 2 (April 1999): 206–30; B. K. Barber, "Political Violence, Social Integration, and Youth Functioning," *Journal of Community Psychology,* forthcoming; B. K. Barber, "Deeper inside a Youth Social Movement: Gaza's 'Children of the Stone,'" paper presented to the Kennedy Center for International Studies, Brigham Young University, December 1998; B. K. Barber, "Palestinian Children and Adolescents during and after the Intifada," *Palestine-Israel Journal* 4 (1997): 23–33; and B. K. Barber, "What Has Become of the 'Children of the Stone'?" *Palestine-Israel Journal* 6 (2000): 715.

3. The essay is now in print: Ibtisam Barakat, "Marked for Destruction," in *Children of Israel, Children of Palestine: Our Own True Stories,* ed. Laurel Holliday (New York: Washington Square, 1998), 165–76.

4. Certain locations in the West Bank also experienced very intense and prolonged conflict, such as the Balata and Askar camps, near Nablus, and the Deheshia camp, near Bethlehem.

21. Islamist Activism in Jordan

Quintan Wiktorowicz

The classic stereotype of a Muslim fundamentalist is a terrorist. The implicit assumption, however, that because a Muslim cares deeply about his religion and practices it fervently he is therefore violent and dangerous is both false and misleading. In fact, the term "Islamic fundamentalist" connotes a kind of fanaticism that does not accurately reflect the concerns and activities of those who seek to transform society into one governed by the precepts of Islam. The term "Islamist," used below, is a more neutral term that encapsulates the desire to apply Islam to all aspects of everyday life. This includes a desire to apply Muslim values to politics, much as many U.S. citizens want to include family and ethical values in U.S. political life. While radical Islamists dominate media coverage, there are many moderate Islamists active in political processes across the Muslim world. —Eds.

My first experience with Islamist activism in Jordan took place at a small cultural society in a poor section of East Amman. Three badly lit, sparsely decorated rooms in a dilapidated building were furnished with a conference table, folding chairs, and a bookshelf filled with leather-bound Islamic texts that seemed out of place, given the paucity of furnishings. On this particular day, twenty-five young Islamists with well-manicured beards, skullcaps, and white *jalabiyyas* crammed into a small room to hear an Islamic scholar lecture on the radical ideologue Sayyid Qutb. The scholar was a large, impressive figure whose physical and spiritual presence in the room commanded respect. After a brief introduction, he sat silently as the audience waited for him to begin . . . then he began to weep. No one in the room seemed surprised, and I quickly realized that his visible emotion reflected a deep and overpowering religious conviction. For Islamists, every act, even the mundane, is an act of worship if it is in accordance with God's commands. At that moment, he was not simply a scholar; he was a Muslim engaged in an act of worship through the transmission of Islamic knowledge.

After he gained his composure, his words were slow and deliberate, as if he was consciously striving for perfection to reflect his fervent devotion to God. As the lecture progressed, he became more animated and his tone reached a fiery pitch as the mood of the room transformed from pensive to excited. The audience of young men concentrated on every word, never interrupting the rhythmic pace of the speaker's erudite classical Arabic. They were captivated by an educational experience permeated by heightened religious sensitivity. This event was more than a lecture; it was an emotional and religious moment that united the audience in a shared purpose of Islamic learning.

This is an example of everyday Islamist activism. Despite popular media attention to acts of terrorism, the vast majority of Islamists do not engage in violence; they seek instead to peacefully transform society into one governed by the Qur'an and the *sunna* ("paths," the traditions of the Prophet Mohammed). While activities such as the one described above may not capture headlines, they constitute everyday reality for most Islamists in the Middle East. Typical Islamist activism includes such things as religious lessons, informal study groups, charitable activities, publications, and even political election campaigns. Through these actions, Islamists produce, articulate, and disseminate Islamic values and particular understandings of how religion should regulate all aspects of individual and social existence. Though Islamists may disagree over interpretations of religious precepts, they are unified by a desire to transform the rules and norms that guide society.

In this pursuit, Islamists in Jordan primarily use three strategies of social transformation. First, they believe that by changing individual beliefs through informal lessons and religious proselytization, they can create the foundations necessary for broader societal change. The norms and rules of Islam are thus internalized in individual Muslims, who follow them in their actions. This strategy aims to create a community of devout believers through individual transformations, in the hope that this devotion will eventually permeate the entire society. Second, a growing number of Islamists in Jordan mobilize through an assortment of civil associations in an effort to reach a wide audience through formally organized efforts. A myriad of grass-roots organizations are designed to provide goods and services while informing community norms. And finally, since political liberalization began in 1989, moderate Islamists have turned to the state as a possible vehicle of transformation. The state and governance are seen as powerful instruments for promulgating legal restrictions designed to encourage and enforce Islamic values and practices. From this perspective, control of the decision-making structure of the state is not an end in itself; it is only one of a number of possible strategies for social change.[1]

These three strategies should not be understood as mutually exclusive. Though many Islamist groups direct their energy to one of the three approaches because they believe it is the most effective avenue of change, they frequently use multiple strategies. These distinctions are meant as an interpretive device to illustrate the diversity of Islamist activism in everyday life, not as a rigid typology. By focusing upon each of these three strategies in turn, this essay maps the constellation of Islamist activities and provides a broad picture of how the majority of Islamists in Jordan pursue their shared goal of social transformation.

INDIVIDUAL BELIEF AS A VEHICLE OF CHANGE

In a conversation about social change, a Jordanian Islamist imam (prayer leader) commented, "To rectify our society, we have to bring the individual back to Islam. We need to start by returning to the Qur'an and sunna, and then expand the circle. This is the rational way. If the circle expands to others, then laws and regulations will be rectified and there will be a societal resurrection in all areas—politics, economics, administration" (Raoud 1997).

This statement reflects a belief that social transformation must begin with change in individual beliefs about the role of Islam. From this perspective, it is only when individuals view Islam as encompassing and guiding all aspects of their lives that broader societal change becomes possible. As more individuals make Islam central to their everyday life, religiosity spreads and permeates all aspects of society. Islamists hope that eventually these values will filter into the political system, as religiously oriented leaders and citizens emerge to govern according to Islam. Individuals thus serve as vehicles of societal resurrection. As 'Ali Hasan al-Halabi, a well-known Jordanian Islamist scholar, argues, "If the Muslims desire good, unity and establishment upon the earth, then they should make their manners and behavior like that of the *Salaf* [companions of the Prophet Mohammed] of this *Ummah* [Muslim community] and begin by changing themselves. However, he who is unable to change even himself, will not be able to change his family, not to mention changing the Ummah" (al-Halabi 1995, 16). Such statements are predicated upon Qur'an 13:11: "God does not change the condition of a people until they change what is in their hearts."

To change what is in a person's heart and eventually expand the circle to induce transformative social change, Islamists advocate *tarbiyya* (education and cultivation to encourage proper Islamic practices) and *da'wa* (calling people to Islam). In the past, Islamists in Jordan primarily pursued this strategy through lessons, sermons, and other activities in the mosques. As a community institution, mosques are powerful engines of socialization, and Islamists used the social space of the mosque to encourage Islamic behavior and practices. Lessons and sermons served as vehicles for disseminating Islamist understandings of religion and its application to everyday life.

Preachers and sheikhs in Jordan used these opportunities to routinely denounce Israel and its proponents as "enemies of Islam" because of Israel's occupation of the West Bank and Jerusalem (the third holiest city in Islam). Since this opposition coincided with the regime's own foreign policy at the time, these activities were openly encouraged. Following the 1994 Jordanian-Israeli peace treaty, however, the regime itself became a target of critique. Islamists decried the peace treaty as a betrayal of Islam, and the regime responded by limiting their access to mosques. A number of famous preachers and Islamist scholars were subsequently banned from delivering sermons and lessons in mosques. Since the government tightly controls all mosques in Jordan (there are no private mosques in the kingdom), this limited the ability of Islamists to effectively pursue a strategy of individual transformation through arguably the most important public religious institution.

As a result, most Islamist activities explicitly focused on tarbiyya have moved to informal settings and institutions, such as special prayer sessions, informal lessons, study circles where participants meet to discuss religious issues, and informal conversations among friends. All of these activities serve as institutions for the resurrection of society, one individual at a time. They are informal in the sense that, unlike the mosques, they are outside the juridical control of the state. The activities are frequently routinized at a particular time and place (though they may develop spontaneously when like-minded Islamists come together) and utilize the vast reservoir of Islamist publications in books, pamphlets, tapes, and videos. Such informal institutions depend upon the interconnected relationships among Islamists for communication and organization, since they are not tied to formal organizations. Because these kinds of activities are embedded in social networks that include friends and other Islamists, a personal dimension permeates the settings and the dissemination of Islamic values.

A good example of tarbiyya through informal activism is the lessons in private homes. These lessons are increasingly popular among a variety of Islamist groups and represent one of the primary strategies for change. The lessons are advertised by word of mouth through participants and their social networks, and the topics address a number of religious issues. The precise subject depends upon the expertise of the audience, but can include such things as rituals, history, behavior, *hadith* (reported traditions of the Prophet Mohammed), and *fiqh* (Islamic jurisprudence). Some lessons also address political issues, such as the peace process, the role of the United States in the Middle East, and human rights abuses in the region. Because the participants frequently bring friends to these lessons, they serve as an opportunity to expand the circle of moral resurrection. They also enhance personal relationships, thus creating a high sense of solidarity by linking religious activities to friendship circles.

The religious and social dimensions of these lessons became clear to me when I accompanied an Islamist scholar from Amman to a small, informal lesson on daʿwa in the northern city of Salt. This lesson was part of a weekly series held every Wednesday for a group of local boys ages twelve to sixteen. They were interested in learning more about their religion and attended the lessons without their parents. The hosts viewed the lessons as an opportunity to socialize the boys into proper Islamic manners and values, thereby creating the foundation for future social change. They were thus part of a conscious strategy of tarbiyya in an effort to indoctrinate the next generation of Muslims. The lessons frequently explained the basics of the religion from an Islamist perspective and were geared toward a receptive, but novice, young audience.

Before this particular lesson, we first met the Islamist hosts and a group of their friends at a house outside Salt. It is common for invited speakers to meet informally with other Islamists, not only to discuss complex Islamic issues but for social purposes as well. Especially when scholars travel to other cities to give lessons, such meetings offer an opportunity to reinvigorate social ties to Islamist communities elsewhere in the kingdom. We enjoyed a long, lavish meal that reflected traditional Jordanian hospitality, after which the group adjourned to the living room for tea and conversation. Most of the questions were about friends and family rather than religion. The context was characterized by friendly exchanges and socializing, which are important to the Islamist community, since it depends upon trust and personal relationships to conduct activities through informal institutions.

After this initial social call, we proceeded to another house for the lesson. As the neighborhood boys filtered in before the lesson, the adults discussed *jihad* (struggle or striving in the path of Islam). The visiting scholar argued that jihad is more than liberating Palestine from Israeli occupation; it means liberating human beings from constraining circumstances, whether repression, poverty, or religious ignorance. He also chastised King Hussein (d. 1999) for "fighting the Islamic movements" and spoke about historical examples of resistance to oppression. This conversation almost turned into a lesson in its own right before it was interrupted by the call to prayer from the neighborhood mosque. Rather than leave the house, the participants gathered for prayer in the lesson room, where a prayer rug was set up in the corner to indicate the direction of Mecca. The owner of the house served as the imam and his melodic voice led the others in the ritual.

After the prayer, the scholar moved to the front of the room, where he proceeded with the lesson. The lesson itself was on the psychology of daʿwa. It required extensive background in Islamic studies and was quite complicated, even for many of the adults. It was certainly too scholarly for the boys, but they listened patiently for two hours before returning home. After the boys left, the adults discussed a variety of political topics related to current events in the kingdom.

Other activities are more akin to informal study groups in which people discuss Islam. For example, a Syrian immigrant who fled the Asad regime in the 1980s opened his apartment in East Amman for meetings to explore and study Islamic topics. With a narrow kitchenette and small main room, the apartment was certainly not a comfortable place for meetings, especially considering that two people shared this space. The paint was chipping and worn away and the apartment was dark and damp. In the main room there were three mattresses, which served as both beds and cushions for sitting. A few throw rugs covered the cold tile floor. There were no chairs, shelves, closets, or tables. A large steel locker positioned against the far wall loomed over the room, dominating the empty space. Yet despite the discomfort of the apartment, three or four visitors typically stopped by every week to discuss Islam.

The meetings operated like a research seminar. Visitors were given research assignments on a variety of topics and would return with other Islamists to discuss their findings. When I visited the sheikh, he and his followers were searching for evidence to demonstrate what he called a "Moscow–Tel Aviv connection." He theorized that Israel was heavily tied to communism and that this force, and not the West, was the greatest threat to Islam. Though the evidence for his theory was weak at best, a number of people, including faculty from the Shariʿa College at the University of Jordan, stopped by to discuss his research. The meetings were an informal forum for the exchange of ideas and the search for answers to questions related to Islam.

These events may seem banal to the outside observer, but they represent ubiquitous examples of everyday Islamist activism. They are not designed to directly threaten the regime or mobilize people into violent activism; they are part of a strategy of tarbiyya. Tarbiyya is a gradual process that uses individuals as vehicles of Islamic social transformation. As one Islamist put it, "Resurrection is like ripening a fruit" (Ibn Hasan 1996). Such an approach takes patience, a virtue extolled in the Qurʾan. Activists argue that Islam sanctions this method of change because it reflects the Prophet Mohammed's primary emphasis when he built the first Muslim community.

CIVIL SOCIETY AND THE ORGANIZED EFFORT

At the Society of Islamic Science in Amman, the Islamist mission of religious transformation is juxtaposed with non-religious activities and friendship cliques. This juxtaposition is best represented by the decor of the main room, where Islamic symbols and books surround a new Ping-Pong table, which dominates the space. Prior to a general membership meeting, I watched as members filtered through the door to the main room, where the Ping-Pong table became the center of sociability. Islamists challenged one another to friendly games while the buzz of casual conversation filled the room. The Ping-Pong table and the surrounding symbols of Islam physically depict the dynamics of the organization. It was founded by a group of friends concerned about declining moral values in society who decided to provide a variety of services and activities to promote Islam. These include Quranic lessons, a program for young boys called Youth of the Prophet (similar to the Boy Scouts but within an Islamic educational context), an Islamic magazine titled *al-Shariʿa* (The Islamic law), and donations to the poor. The religious activities grew out of friendship cliques, and the sociability of the Ping-Pong table remained central to the organization's endeavor.

This cultural society represents a growing organized Islamist presence in civil society through Islamic non-governmental organizations (NGOs). These organizations provide basic goods and services to communities in a manner Islamists deem consistent with the *shariʿa*. They are non-profit, grass-roots organizations that serve as conduits for the Islamist message of societal transformation. As points of contact between Islamists and communities, Islamic NGOs promote religious values while serving the needs of the congregation and community. Islamic organizations, such as medical clinics, hospitals, charitable societies, cultural associations, training centers, and schools, have proliferated throughout the Middle East, including in Jordan. They are typically formed for three basic reasons: 1) to provide an example of Islam in practice and thereby garner support for the Islamist cause by demonstrating its efficacy in solving basic social problems; 2) to create formal institutions for promoting Islamic values through education and contact with communities; and 3) to provide practicing Muslims with greater opportunities for fulfilling obligations of the faith, such as charity and daʿwa. Though Islamic NGOs are also concerned with tarbiyya, they focus on institutionalizing Islamist activism through formal organizations and address a much broader range of activities. Some may appear more "Islamic" than others, but they are united in a concern for resurrecting the morality of society.

The largest Islamic NGO in Jordan is the Islamic Center Society, run by the Muslim Brotherhood (a moderate Islamist reform movement). Licensed in 1963, the Center provides a variety of charity programs and projects, including a network of some of the best schools in the kingdom. Additional services include orphanages, charity centers, and health care facilities. All of these are provided within a religious context designed to propagate Islamic values.

Although the Center offers a variety of programs and projects, its most prominent achievement is the Islamic Hospital in Amman. Following the 1967 war with Israel, members of the Muslim Brotherhood decided to establish a health care facility to serve the community and fulfill religious obligations of charity. Opened in 1982, the Islamic Hospital is similar to most modern hospitals and provides a number of specialties, including heart surgery. There are 1,100 employees, including doctors, nurses, and specialists. Most of the personnel are affiliated with the Muslim Brotherhood or sympathetic to its cause.

The hospital has a special fund for the poor, which distributes around $14,000 per month to patients who cannot afford treatment. A committee assesses whether applicants need assistance and determines the specific level of financial disbursements. The fund has provided thousands of poor patients with free medical care, thereby fulfilling Muslim responsibilities of charity and compassion, which are emphasized in the Qurʾan and the sunna. In addition, since the hospital is run as a non-profit charitable organization, all profits are reinvested, thus improving the quality of services.

The Islamic Hospital is more than a charitable organization; it is an instrument for promoting a Muslim society. First, hospital policy requires that employees adhere to Islamic norms, thereby reinforcing Islamic behavior and providing an example for patients and the community. Nurses, for example, must wear a standard *hijab* (head scarf and modest dress, though not the more restrictive full veil), which Islamists believe protects propriety. In addition, the hospital enforces gender segregation (of both employees and patients) where possible. In certain instances, such as when female patients must see male doctors because there are few female physicians, this rule is relaxed. Employees are also required to pray five times a day in accordance with accepted Muslim practice (though many doctors seem to ignore this policy), and the hospital offers voluntary activities, such as religious lessons on a variety of subjects. These are organized opportunities for employees to practice and deepen their faith.

Second, the hospital also directly exposes patients to Islamic values. Staff members discuss Islam with patients; televisions throughout the hospital broadcast religious programming; and the hospital provides free books and pamphlets on Islam. Though many patients claim they utilize the hospital because of its effective treatment, not because it is specifically Islamic, Islamists believe it allows them to propagate meaning within the context of health care provision.

Though the hospital is one of the best-established examples of Islamist institutions in civil society, the rising star of the Islamic NGO community is the al-Afaf [Chastity] Society. Al-Afaf is a charitable organization designed to promote marriage and family formation and prevent what Islamists view as un-Islamic practices, such as premarital sexual relations, abortions, and unwed motherhood. Marriage is encouraged in five ways. First, al-Afaf offers a series of collective weddings every year to lower the cost of marriage. It absorbs the entire cost of the wedding, including the ceremony, wedding festival, and gifts such as furniture, appliances, household necessities, and cash. Islamists hope that the collective wedding will remove the financial barriers to marriage that many Jordanians face. Second, the society offers interest-free loans to prospective grooms for marriage-related expenses. Third, a matching service helps men and women find suitable marriage partners. Fourth, the society organizes periodic seminars and workshops on marriage-related issues, such as the need for premarital medical screenings, and publishes the proceedings. And fifth, al-Afaf has launched a Web site in Arabic and English, which discusses the society, its activities, and marriage to propagate an Islamic message. All of these are intended to encourage proper marriage and family formation, which are central to Islam.[2]

Other Islamic NGOs deal more exclusively with cultural activities in an attempt to spread Islamic learning through formal organizations and an institutionalized presence. Organizations with names such as the Qurʾan and Sunna Society and the Society for the Preservation of the Qurʾan provide educational and cultural activities for ordinary Muslims and Islamists seeking further knowledge. They provide lessons on hadith, Quranic recitation and memorization, fiqh, and history. Many cultural Islamic NGOs provide forums for discussing Islamic thought and publish small booklets and magazines on a variety of subjects, ranging from general overviews of Islam to specialist material addressed to scholars.

Since the 1970s, Islamists have also mobilized through non-religious professional and university organizations in an attempt to usurp their structure for Islamist agendas. Appealing to the mood of change that swept Jordan after the advent of political liberalization, Islamists took advantage of popular discontent and gained control of most professional associations in the kingdom during the 1990s. Islamists successfully won elections to the executive committees and leadership positions of these associations, thus placing themselves at the helm of well-organized civil institutions. This included the Engineer's Syndicate, the largest and most influential association, with more than thirty thousand members and a budget that exceeds that of all political parties combined. Through elections, Islamists also successfully gained control of student leadership positions at a number of universities, including the University of Jordan.

Despite this success and the potential of these associations for activism, however, the Islamists' ability to manipulate these institutions for purely Islamic purposes has remained circumscribed, for several reasons. First, while these organizations have large memberships, their activities are limited. Most were founded by the state as a way of monitoring the professional class, and only provide basic membership services, such as notifying members of the effects of new legislation. Second, while there is certainly an Islamic tone at many organizational headquarters, it is typified by symbolic banners and scattered prayer meetings rather than a coordinated effort to transform society. These organizations are first and foremost responsible to their membership, and as a result the Islamists predominantly focus upon the membership's concerns rather than an intensive Islamicization program.[3] In addition, because the leadership is chosen by a vote of the membership, Islamist control could be lost. All of these factors indicate that although Islamists are working at these institutions, the organizations do not represent examples of specifically Islamic grass-roots organizations.

REFORM THROUGH THE STATE

In 1991, at the beginning of the Gulf War, King Hussein and his appointed prime minister invited five members of the Muslim Brotherhood to participate in the government. The new ministers were given some of the most influential domestic portfolios, including the ministries of education, health, justice, social development, and *awqaf* (religious endowment lands) and religious affairs. This was the first time the regime had incorporated such a large number of Muslim Brothers into the cabinet, and the Jordanian public was curious to see how they would use the power of the state to implement Islamic values. Not long after they assumed office, the Islamists issued a number of rulings designed to Islamicize society from above. Perhaps the most infamous of these rulings was the minister of education's decision to prohibit fathers from attending their daughters' sporting events at school. He reasoned that young girls dressed in tee shirts and shorts would feel self-conscious playing in front of men who were not relatives. In addition, fathers would inevitably see other girls immodestly dressed, thereby violating Islamic norms of propriety and gender segregation. Outraged parents circulated a petition against the ruling, getting thousands of signatures, and met with the prime minister to protest the decision. A few days later the prime minister resigned and the cabinet collapsed, rendering the Islamist promulgation powerless.

Though Muslim Brotherhood participation in the Gulf War cabinet lasted only six months, it reflected the changing political opportunities and concomitant Islamist strategies that followed political liberalization in 1989. In response to an economic crisis and riots in April 1989, King Hussein initiated political changes that eventually ended martial law, legalized political parties, enhanced civil liberties, and led to elections. Though these changes are still incomplete and authoritarian practices persist, many view the new political opportunities as possible means of societal transformation. A variety of Islamists believe that if they could effectively control decision making in the kingdom, they could promulgate laws that enforce greater adherence to Islamic norms and principles.

This belief leads moderate Islamists, especially the Muslim Brotherhood, to organize and compete in parliamentary elections. In the 1984 by-elections held to fill vacant seats in the Chamber of Deputies (the lower house of Parliament), members of the Muslim Brotherhood won three of the six seats reserved for Muslim legislators. In the 1989 kingdom-wide elections, the Brotherhood and other Islamists campaigned in full force. Islamist banners were flown throughout the kingdom with slogans such as "Islam is the Solution" and "The Qur'an Is Our Constitution." The slogans reflected their belief that if Islam were correctly applied to all aspects of life, many of the problems of society would be solved. The Islamist candidates articulated vague platforms with little policy substance or concrete plans, but they fared well in the election. To the surprise of many, independent Islamists and the Muslim Brotherhood won thirty-four seats and became the single largest political bloc in Parliament.

Shortly after the elections, Islamists formed the Islamic Action Front Party (IAF), which was licensed in 1992 after the legalization of political parties. Because Islamists eschew schisms in the Muslim community, the term "front" was carefully chosen to signify a broad political party, unified by a desire to advocate for a more Islamic political system but receptive to a variety of different Islamist groups and perspectives. This idealism quickly broke down after internal IAF elections to leadership positions indicated that the Muslim Brotherhood would, in reality, dominate the party. To protest the leadership elections, independent Islamists resigned en masse, rendering the IAF a de facto Brotherhood organization.

The Islamists, both independents and Muslim Brothers representing the IAF, entered the 1993 elections, but were hamstrung by a royal decree that changed the electoral system from bloc voting, which favored disciplined voting blocs such as the Islamists, to a one-person, one-vote system. Though the reforms hurt the Islamists' electoral prospects, they still won twenty-two seats and continued to seek reform through the state.

This strategy was halted in 1997 when the IAF decided to join other opposition groups in boycotting the parliamentary elections. To protest the electoral law, peace with Israel, corruption in government, and a host of other issues, the IAF decided not to participate in the elections. However, several prominent members of the Muslim Brotherhood defied the boycott and ran anyway. In total, six independent Islamists won seats. In addition, Bassam Umush, a former Muslim Brother who was expelled from the organization for participating in the election, was appointed minister of administrative development.

Despite the 1997 boycott, moderate Islamists believed transformation through the state was possible and reentered electoral politics in the 1999 municipal elections. They did quite well, winning all of the seats in Zarqa and Rusayfa, twenty seats in the powerful Amman city council, and six of the eleven seats in the Christian-dominated city of Madaba. The results sent mixed signals, since voter turnout was low, but the Islamists continue to seek influence through the state and are poised to reenter national politics.

In addition to participating in electoral politics, moderate Islamists in the IAF attempt to influence state policies through peaceful demonstrations. The IAF has used civil disobedience to protest a number of government policies and actions, including the press and publications law, the electoral law, and the peace process. In a recent example, the IAF held a rally in Irbid to protest a government crackdown on Hamas. Hamas has operated openly in the kingdom since the 1980s, but in August 1999 the government decided to close Hamas offices and arrest leaders to prevent the movement from opposing the continued Palestinian-Israeli peace process from Jordanian soil. During the thirty-minute rally of about four hundred protestors, IAF leaders called for the government to reconsider the crackdown. The government did not reverse its actions, but the rally provides a good example of Islamist civil disobedience—another mechanism for encouraging change through the state.

Islamist movements are complex and diverse. Just as there is no single interpretation of Islam, there is no one activity that represents the entire range of everyday Islamist activism. This chapter depicts the variety of activities designed to promote Islamic social transformation and points to three dominant strategies in Jordan—transformation through individuals, civil organizations, and the state. The Jordanian case also demonstrates that much of Islamist activism is peaceful . . . and personal. Individual activist Islamists create bonds of solidarity that unite them in a shared cause and a shared belief about the proper role of Islam in society. This personal dimension creates the trust necessary for Islamists to work together toward what they view as the ultimate goal of humankind—everyday life in accordance with God's law.

NOTES

1. It should be noted that violent Islamist groups do exist in Jordan and have become increasingly active in the 1990s. Unlike those in Egypt and Algeria, however, they are extremely few and are marginal to the thrust of Islamist activism in the kingdom. Indeed, even among radical Islamists, few support violence.

2. For more on the al-Afaf Society, see Quintan Wiktorowicz and Suha Taji-Farouki, "Islamic Non-governmental Organizations and Muslim Politics: A Case from Jordan," *Third World Quarterly* 21, no. 4 (summer 2000): 685–99.

3. When they are politically active, these Islamist-led associations typically join other opposition groups in civil society to protest for common concerns. For

example, the professional associations have joined other opposition groups in rallies to protest the normalization of relations with Israel.

REFERENCES

al-Halabi, ʿAli Hasan. 1995. "Tarbiyah: The Key to Victory." *al-Ibaanah* 2 (August): 16.
Ibn Hasan, Sheikh Mashhor. 1996. Interviewed by author, 12 November, Amman.
Raoud, Sheikh Mohammed. 1997. Interviewed by author, 1 April, Amman.

PART FOUR

Popular Expression of Religion

The Middle East is the birthplace of monotheistic religion: Islam, Christianity, Judaism, and Zoroastrianism all began there, and practitioners of each of these religions can be found throughout the area. The majority of the people, roughly 90 percent, are Muslims, believers in Islam.

The word "Islam" means to surrender oneself, to submit to another's will, in this case to the will of God. Islam teaches believers the meaning of this submission to God and how to conform to the Creator's will. Anyone who recognizes God and follows God's admonitions is a Muslim.

Islam's first principle is belief in one God. Arabs at the rise of Islam professed different faiths: some were Christian, some Jewish, the majority pagans worshiping numerous gods. The revelations to Muhammad, the first prophet of Islam, stressed that there is but one God (in Arabic *Allah*, literally "the God"). God created human beings, the world, and all that it contains; he guided the earlier prophets (whose records are also found in the Jewish Torah and the Christian scriptures), and revealed the Qurʾan to furnish believers with precepts to guide them on the proper path. The Qurʾan, the Muslim scripture, is revered as God's word; it is a compilation of the 114 revelations given to Muhammad. Two essential Quranic *surahs* (chapters) are presented here to give a sense of the Qurʾan's language and content. Kristina Nelson, in her article, emphasizes the vital significance of the sounds of the recited Qurʾan.

The worst sin that a Muslim can commit is polytheism: denying the unity of God or attributing God's powers to any other being. The muezzin emphasizes this acknowledgment of God's supremacy as he calls the faithful to prayer five times each day with "God is the greatest. God is the greatest. Come to prayer."

The Muslim *shahada*, or statement of belief, acknowledges the one God and Muhammad as the prophet of God. Each Muslim repeats this creed to testify that God is one, that he was not born, neither can he give birth, nor can he be compared to any other creature. In Islam God is defined by ninety-nine attributes: omnipotence, omniscience, mercy, beneficence, etc. Muslims repeat these qualities as they work their way three times around their string of thirty-three prayer beads. Religious posters list the ninety-nine traits in elaborate calligraphy. Every document, every meal, and many other things begin with an invocation of God's name—"In the name of God, the beneficent, the merciful."

The second line of the shahada affirms Muhammad as the final prophet of Islam. God spoke to humans through all the prophets, from Adam to Muhammad, and demonstrated his concern for people and his desire that they be led properly through the vicissitudes of life. If individuals follow God's commandments, they will be rewarded at Judgment Day. The Qur'an vividly describes the paradise of the believers and the hellfire of the wrong-doers.

God chose prophets to preach his laws to their people. Muhammad emerged as the leader of the Arab community and organized a community of believers which replaced the community of blood relations and wealth that was common in the Arabian Peninsula until that time. The Qur'an speaks of the *umma*, the community of believers which replaces all other types of community organization. Membership in the umma is based upon belief; all Muslims are equal in the umma whatever their birth, rank, nationality, or wealth.

Islam's second principle is the necessity of a just social and economic order in the community. Muslims are expected to follow the moral order outlined in the Qur'an. This moral order defines membership in the umma and the responsibilities of its members, such as caring for the poor, the orphaned, and the needy. Islam established a social and economic order inextricable from religious duties. It accomplished this largely through the institution of a system of Islamic law, the *shari'a* (literally, a path or way). Islamic law is derived first from the Qur'an and second from the example set by Muhammad and his early community. By following these sources of law (which have been combined with community standards and legal precedents into massive jurisprudential texts) in such areas of life as worship, family relations, social codes, and political regulations and laws, Muslims express their submission to God's will.

The Qur'an names five obligatory religious practices that form the essence of faithful life. These five pillars of Islam are the shahada, prayer, *zakat* (tithes), the fast of the month of Ramadan, and the *hajj* (pilgrimage to Mecca). Each speaks to two aspects of worship: the spiritual or transcendent side of Islam and the importance of the community.

The creed, "There is no God but God and Muhammad is the messenger of God," states the core beliefs of Islam. Muslims hear and recite it in Arabic repeatedly throughout their lives. Although it might seem to be a formula, repeated unthinkingly, every believer must at some point declare this phrase with full knowledge of what it means, thereby committing him- or herself to following the tenets of Islam. Conversion to Islam is accomplished simply by pronouncing it before witnesses with full knowledge of what is being said.

In Islam there are two types of prayer: *salat*, the ritualized prayer, and *du'a*, a personal plea to God. Each salat prayer incorporates a short du'a in its ritual. The salat prayer is performed communally five times each day. In the mosque the worshippers line up in rows, shoulder to shoulder, rich and poor, young and old, merchant and farmer. They bow and kneel together to acknowledge the greatness of God.

Originally zakat, tithes, provided the economic base of the umma. Rich and poor were to provide equal proportions of their resources to support the community, and specifically to care for orphans and widows, those with no family safety net to rely upon. Even though zakat is rarely paid as a tax these days, the obligation to care for the poor is graphically illustrated in Donna Lee Bowen's story of Abu Illya.

During Ramadan each Muslim fasts from sunrise to sunset to cleanse his body, recognize God's bounty, and feel kinship with the deprived. At the same time, community solidarity is never stronger than when Muslims worldwide await the signal that the sun has set and they may begin to eat. In Morocco, all break the fast with the same type of soup, so all Muslims, rich and poor, in cities or villages, break their fast at the same time with the same food.

All Muslims, circumstances permitting, are commanded to make the hajj or pilgrimage to Mecca, to the sites of the revelation of Islam, at some point in their lifetime. Close to a million Muslims arrive in Saudi Arabia each year by plane, ship, and truck, don *ihram*—plain white garments which they will wear for the duration of the pilgrimage—and follow the path pilgrims have taken for centuries. At this point, whether peasants or kings, all Muslims are dressed alike and follow the same ritual—all united in Islam. Michael Jansen, an American convert to Islam, explains both the ritual of the pilgrimage and the emotions evoked by her presence in Mecca.

Muslims view Islam as being both *din* (religion) and *dawla* (state). All actions, from ritual cleansing before prayer to the formulation of business contracts, are defined by Islam. Thus Islam becomes a standard for society as well as a standard for worship.

In the centuries following Muhammad's death, Muslims elaborated on the Quranic injunctions and incorporated other practices into Muslim religious expression. Scholars systematized Islamic jurisprudence, developed approaches to theology, and generated Islamic philosophy based on Greek sources.

A widely quoted *hadith* (saying) of Muhammad stated that his community would divide into seventy-seven sects, of which only one would be correct. While a variety of sectarian groupings have emerged over the centuries, the two major movements within Islam are the Sunni (*Ahl al-Sunna wal-Jama*ᶜ*a*, the people of the Prophet's sunna, or practice, and the community) and the Shiᶜa (*Shiᶜat Ali*, the Party of Ali). At Muhammad's death, the fledgling Muslim community divided over how to select a new leader. The Sunnis eventually settled on consultation among the community elders; the Shiᶜi claimed that Ali, the Prophet's cousin and son-in-law (husband of Muhammad's daughter Fatima and father of his grandsons, Hassan and Hussein), should succeed him by virtue of blood ties. Over the years, political conflicts exacerbated differences between the groups. While the two groups' basic theology and jurisprudence are very similar, there are instructive differences in their beliefs about community governance, derivation of juridical positions, ritual practice, and other subjects. Sunni Muslims, the majority (at around 85–90 percent) of the world's Muslims, consider themselves the mainstream of Islam. Shiᶜi Muslims compose a majority of the population in Iran and Iraq and around 40 percent of that of Lebanon. There are also significant numbers in parts of the Arabian Peninsula, Pakistan, and East Africa.

A highly significant development of Islamic belief was the formulation of Sufism (*al-tasawwuf*), or mysticism, as Islamic precepts were influenced by Christian, Jewish, Hindu, and Buddhist mysticism. Elaborate schools of mystical thought grew up around famous mystics, and branches of their *tariqa* (mystical order) spread throughout the Muslim world. Mystics like the poets Hafez, Rumi, Attar, and others wrote a world-famous body of poetry addressed to God and celebrating his glory.

Local peoples added their traditional holy spots to their new religion, and pious men or mystics were identified with sacred streams and trees and commemorated with shrines. While the formal Islam of religious and legal scholars seemed far removed from daily needs, the shrines made the religion responsive to individuals, serving as focal points for both locals and pilgrims requesting help. A shrine may be a humble, un-whitewashed mud house, a pile of stones, or an elaborate gilded edifice. Local saints are believed to respond to pleas, and all shrines exhibit scraps of cloth knotted to window grilles, folded papers shoved into cracks, or locks of hair which pilgrims have left as signs of their vows. Although many local saints were originally pious men or women from the village or neighborhood, the family of Muhammad—his daughter Fatima, son-in-law Ali, and grandchildren—are revered worldwide. Popular stories are told and written about their lives.

Both Sunni and Shiᶜi Muslims make minor pilgrimages to these shrines. A popular time for these visits is the *mawlid*, the anniversary of the saint's birth or death. The ritual practices of local pilgrimages mirror some of the Meccan pilgrimage. For instance, worshipers commonly walk around the tomb seven times counterclockwise, as is done at the Kaᶜba, the great shrine in Mecca. While pilgrims to Mecca always sacrifice sheep, pilgrims to other shrines may bring poultry, goats, or other foodstuffs as well as sheep to present to the guardian of the shrine or, as vowed, to the poor in return for help received. Anne Betteridge presents an account of women's visits to shrines in Iran. She notes that not only do women's religious observances differ from those of men, but the patterns of women's visits to shrines have changed since the Islamic revolution.

Other types of religious observance, practice, and expression include drama (such as the *ta ziyeh*, passion play, of the Shi a), the mysticism of the various Sufi orders, formal traditions of Islamic education, the elaboration of jurisprudence, architecture, and art, house paintings which tell the story of the resident's pilgrimage to Mecca, pamphlets which apply the lives and teachings of Muslim historical figures or prominent preachers to present-day concerns, treatises on the interpretation of the Qur an, and cassette tapes which record the sermons of popular preachers. All of these pull the individual Muslim into the larger context of Islam while at the same time answering an individual call for guidance, help, comfort, celebration, or spiritual sustenance.

Muslim holidays and feasts commemorate the Prophet's birthday, saints' birthdays, and significant anniversaries. Id al-Adha, the Feast of Sacrifice, which falls ninety days after the end of Ramadan and during the pilgrimage to Mecca, commemorates Abraham's willingness to sacrifice his son; it lasts three days and is the most important holiday of the year. The small feast called Id al-Fitr occurs at the conclusion of Ramadan. Observance of these feasts varies throughout the Middle East. As Bowen notes in the story of Abdul Qadar, a family's way of observing the feast sometimes eclipses the meaning of the feast itself.

Dale Eickelman notes that the practice of Islam is undergoing major change worldwide. As more and more Muslims become educated, their religion and the sources which govern the practice of Islam become more accessible. This, he posits, will have wide-reaching ramifications for the shape and content of Muslim belief and practice. Annabelle Böttcher writes about the boom in Islamic study groups held by Syrian women desiring to learn more about their religion. For these women, and for many other Muslims throughout the Middle East, religious activity has moved out of the mosque as individuals have taken responsibility for their own faith and have begun to study the sources of their religion. With the advent of the Internet, as Jon Anderson documents, the nature of religious knowledge is changing. On the Web, Muslims can sample religious writings by scholars in Canada and the Gulf as easily as they can listen to the neighborhood *imam*. Nationals living outside the country can interact with those in the country, and Muslims from different traditions can interact more easily.

22. Inside the Islamic Reformation

Dale F. Eickelman

*Levels of education are rising throughout the Islamic world, af-
fecting the approach that individuals take toward their religion.
Literacy makes the Islamic texts and arguments accessible to a
wide variety of Muslims. In the "Islamic Reformation," scholars
from secular backgrounds like engineering, medicine, and ac-
counting are writing books which are read by increasing numbers
of devout Muslims. This, coupled with developments in mass media and communications, challenges the traditional authority of
Muslim religious scholars. Writers who combine secular education with a strong background in Islam appeal to Muslims yearn-
ing to integrate their religious values with a modern technological
lifestyle. —Eds.*

Al-Hamra, a provincial capital in the northern interior of Oman, was remote even by that country's standards when I first visited it in June 1978.
Paved roads and electricity had not yet reached the oasis; only a few homes
had generator-powered televisions, and the nearest telephone was almost
an hour's drive away. It was much the same when I returned to the oasis a
year later to conduct field research. On this second visit, I spent a day in
formal discussions with local officials and tribal leaders, and then, having
missed my bus, was obliged to spend the night. The *shaykh* (tribal leader)
of the ʿAbriyin graciously invited me to stay in his guest house, along with
several men who were visiting from outlying villages.

Well before dawn, these other guests—observant Muslims to a man—
rose for morning prayer, and one of them called to me to ask whether I
intended to perform my ablutions. "Not yet," I replied, and went back to
sleep. Some minutes later, my host, Shaykh ʿAbdallah al-ʿAbri, gently prod-
ded me with the muzzle of a machine pistol. In Oman, it is bad manners

Adapted from the *Wilson Quarterly* 22, no. 1 (winter 1998): 80–89. © 1997 Dale F. Eickelman,
with revisions.

to touch a sleeping person with one's hands, and Shaykh ʿAbdallah was a model of politeness.

"Are you sick?" he asked. "You're not getting ready to pray."

Half asleep, I mumbled, "I'm Christian; we pray differently."

Shaykh ʿAbdullah looked momentarily puzzled, then went away.

His puzzlement was no mystery. The shaykh had naturally assumed that a speaker of Arabic with a reasonable command of Omani etiquette would also rise to pray. In the late 1970s, he and the other inhabitants of the oasis had no pressing reason to think about any faith beyond Islam. Such terms as "Muslim" and "Christian" scarcely entered their minds. The British army officers and oil company officials who regularly passed through the region rarely stayed for long and, in any case, gave the inhabitants of al-Hamra little reason to think about other religions. The South Asian construction workers at the oasis were mostly Muslim, as were the schoolteachers from other Arab countries.

Yet al-Hamra (pop. 2,600), a compact town of mud-brick buildings on a rocky slope next to an underground irrigation canal (falaj), was changing—just how profoundly, I did not then grasp. A decade earlier, the oasis's habitable limits, still defined by the watchtowers used to guard against rival tribes, had begun to push outward, as new diesel-driven pumps brought water from privately owned wells to new agricultural lands far away from the head of the town's falaj (where, the water being purest, the tribal aristocracy lived). By the late '70s, schools and government offices were being built beyond the marketplace, once the far end of the town. By then, too, nearly all school-age children in al-Hamra attended elementary school, and government jobs and wage labor had replaced date palms as the inhabitants' foremost source of income. The Beau Geste appearance of al-Hamra was fast being altered, and I had come—and would return again and again over the ensuing years—to study the transformation.

A few weeks after my overnight stay, I returned with my wife and daughter to spend a year in al-Hamra. Adjusting to a rhythm of life marked by the five daily prayers and, for men, the weekly congregational prayer, we soon learned to distinguish the voices of neighbors calling the faithful to mosques throughout the oasis. Islamic rituals were so thoroughly woven into the daily life of the community that everyone took them for granted.

That was why, on a return visit nearly a decade later, I was startled when a young relative of the tribal leader—a high school student when I'd first met him in 1979 but now a university-trained police officer—announced to me that the people of al-Hamra, his own relatives included, were "ignorant" of Islam and therefore acted "like animals"—that is, unthinkingly. "Sure," he said, "they pray and fast, but they can't explain why. Muslims must explain their beliefs."

His words came back to me in April 1997, when I gave a public talk in Istanbul. I had been invited by an organization connected with the Refah

(Welfare) Party, which had been running Istanbul since 1994 (it was banned in early 1998 and replaced by the Virtue Party). Although the Refah party is routinely described as "fundamentalist," the Turkish panelists who commented on my talk were anything but provincials cut off from the outside world. They invoked such figures as the German philosopher Jürgen Habermas and the French sociologist Pierre Bourdieu, and were at ease in English and other foreign languages. These, and other religiously minded young Turks I met, were not the "fundamentalists" of stereotype. The reality they represented—like that of the young Omani policeman—was far more complex.

Years hence, if my suspicion is correct, we will look back on the latter half of the twentieth century as a time of change as profound for the Muslim world as the Protestant Reformation was for Christendom. Like the printing press in the sixteenth century, the combination of mass education and mass communications is transforming this world, a broad crescent stretching from North Africa through Central Asia, the Indian subcontinent, and the Indonesian archipelago. In unprecedentedly large numbers, the faithful—whether in the vast cosmopolitan city of Istanbul or in Oman's tiny, remote al-Hamra oasis—are examining and debating the fundamentals of Muslim belief and practice in ways that their less self-conscious predecessors in the faith would never have imagined. This highly deliberate examination of the faith is what constitutes the Islamic Reformation.

Unfortunately, buzzwords such as "fundamentalism" and catchy phrases such as Samuel Huntington's rhyming "West versus Rest" and Daniel Lerner's alliterative "Mecca or mechanization" are of little use in understanding this reformation. Indeed, they obscure or even distort the immense spiritual and intellectual ferment that is taking place today among the world's nearly one billion Muslims, reducing it in most cases to a fanatical rejection of everything modern, liberal, or progressive. To be sure, such fanaticism plays a part—dramatically and violently—in what is happening, but it is far from the whole story.

A far more important element of the Islamic Reformation is the unprecedented access that ordinary people now have to sources of knowledge about religion and other aspects of their society. Quite simply, in country after country, government officials, traditional religious scholars, and officially sanctioned preachers are finding it very hard to monopolize the tools of literate culture. For example, when I first ventured into the field as an anthropologist in 1968, I routinely saw people in southern Iraq gather around literate members of the community, including shopkeepers, to have the newspapers read aloud to them; that same year, in rural Morocco, I was not infrequently asked to translate the formal Arabic of radio newscasts into colloquial Moroccan. By the mid-1970s, however, the need for such translation had dramatically decreased. And in 1992, during the Moroccan parliamentary election campaigns, I observed that young people, even in remote villages, were unafraid to ask the candidates probing questions, because they could now speak the public language of the educated. I also saw a *makhazni*, a low-ranking rural auxiliary policeman, politely but firmly refuse a questionable command from a local Ministry of the Interior official, pointing to written instructions he had received from provincial headquarters. Just a decade earlier, the same policeman would have been illiterate and therefore unable to challenge such an order.

In al-Hamra, when I first came to know it, people received "news" from Shaykh ʿAbdallah. In 1980, when he started his generator to run the electric fans in his guest house, everyone in town knew that visitors with "news" had arrived and that soon the shaykh would be relaying it to them (or at least as much of it as he cared to tell). Two years later, when I was again in Oman, families in al-Hamra saw the same TV images of the massacres in Beirut's Sabra and Shatila refugee camps that viewers in America did—thanks to a CBS news feed to Omani state television. Today, with paved roads, telephones, electricity, fax machines, and satellite television, al-Hamra is a changed place. "News" is no longer a monopoly of the few, and TV images bring people and places previously at the margin of awareness into the foreground. Among other consequences, this is helping to alter the way large numbers of Muslims, in al-Hamra and elsewhere, think about themselves, their religion, and their politics.

Mass education, the other major catalyst of change, has also gained momentum. In much of the Muslim world, it began to be introduced only after the 1950s, and in many countries considerably later. Morocco, for instance, committed itself to universal schooling after gaining independence from France in 1956. Though in 1957 only 13,000 secondary school degrees were awarded, and university enrollments remained low, by 1965 there were more than 200,000 students in secondary schools, and some 20,000 in universities. By 1992, secondary school enrollment topped 1.5 million, and university students numbered 240,000. While illiteracy rates in the general populace remain high—38 percent for men and 62 percent for women—there is now a critical mass of educated people who are able to read and think for themselves without relying on state and religious authorities.

The situation in Oman is more dramatic because the transformation has taken place in a much shorter period. In 1975–76, a mere twenty-two students graduated from secondary school. Little more than a decade later, in 1987–88, 13,500 did. In 1995, 60,000 graduated; more than 3,500 students were in post-secondary institutions, including the national university, which had opened in 1986.

Elsewhere the story is much the same, though the starting dates and levels of achievement differ. In Turkey, Indonesia, and Malaysia, mass education has reached every city, town, and village. In Turkey, for instance, adult illiteracy rates as of 1990 were 10 percent for males and 30 percent for females, down from 65 percent and 85 percent, respectively, four decades earlier. Secondary schools are now ubiquitous, and both private and public universities have proliferated. In Indonesia, university enrollment, only 50,000 in 1960, reached 1.9 million in 1990. Iran also has seen a significant expansion in educational opportunities at all levels. In Egypt (as, for that matter, in Morocco), population growth has outpaced educational expansion; yet even so, the number of people able to converse intelligently with religious and political authorities, and not just listen to them, has increased dramatically.

So has the market for books, including books about religion and society. One Arabic text that has figured centrally in the Islamic Reformation is the ground-breaking *The Book and the Qur°an: A Contemporary Interpretation* (1990), written by Muhammad Shahrur. a Syrian civil engineer. To date, it has sold tens of thousands of copies. Even though circulation of the eight-hundred-page book has been banned or discouraged in many Arab countries, photocopy machines and pirate editions (published in Egypt, among other places) have allowed it to travel across state borders.

Shahrur, who was educated in Damascus, Moscow, and Dublin, draws an analogy between the Copernican revolution and Quranic interpretation, which for too long, he says, has been shackled by the conventions of mediaeval jurists: "People believed for a long time that the sun revolved around the earth, but they were unable to explain some phenomena derived from this assumption until one person, human like themselves, said, 'The opposite is true: The earth revolves around the sun.' . . . After a quarter of a century of study and reflection, it dawned on me that we Muslims are shackled by prejudices, some of which are completely opposite the correct perspective."

On issues ranging from the role of women in society to the need for a "creative interaction" with non-Muslim philosophies, Shahrur argues that Muslims should reinterpret sacred texts and apply them to contemporary social and moral issues. Islamic inheritance law, for instance, which provides women a smaller share of any legacy than men, may have been an advance for women in an earlier era, but, he contends, it is discriminatory in modern society. "If Islam is sound for all times and places," Shahrur says, Muslims must not neglect historical developments and the interaction of different generations. Muslims must act as if "the Prophet just . . . informed us of this Book."

Shahrur's book may one day be seen as a Muslim equivalent of the ninety-five theses that Martin Luther nailed to the door of the Wittenberg Castle church in 1517. Luther quickly gained broad support within Germany, as well as widespread opposition, and eventually even steadfast opponents had to take his ideas into account and modify their ways of thinking and acting. The same may happen with Shahrur's ideas, though even more rapidly. Already, his views have been assailed in fourteen books (some longer than his own) and countless magazine articles and sermons.

Shahrur is not alone in attacking conventional religious wisdom and the intolerant certitudes of religious radicals, or in calling for an ongoing interpretation of sacred texts in their application to social and political life. Another Syrian thinker, the secularist Sadiq Jalal al-ᶜAzm, for instance, does the same. In May 1997, a debate between al-ᶜAzm and Shaykh Yusif al-Qaradawi, a conservative religious intellectual, was broadcast on al-Jazira Satellite Television (Qatar), and for the first time in the memory of many viewers the religious conservative came across as the weaker, more defensive voice. That program is unlikely to be rebroadcast on state-controlled television in most Arab nations, where programming on religious and political themes is generally cautious. Nevertheless, satellite technology and videotape render traditional censorship ineffective. Tapes of the broadcast are circulating from hand to hand in Morocco, Oman, Syria, Egypt, and elsewhere.

Other voices also advocate reform. Turkey's Ali Bulaç, a university-based theologian, has captured the imagination of the educated young with his call for authenticity and a reinterpretation of the first years of the Prophet's rule, applying Muhammad's precepts and practices to current controversies about pluralism and civil society. Fethullah Gülen, Turkey's answer to media-savvy American evangelist Billy Graham, appeals to a mass audience. In televised chat shows, interviews, and occasional sermons, Gülen speaks about Islam and science, democracy, modernity, religious and ideological tolerance, the importance of education, and current events. Because he regards Turkish nationalism as compatible with Islam, Gülen is said to have the ear of Turkey's senior military officers.

For a pan-Arab audience, Morocco's Saᶜid Binsaᶜid argues that a proper understanding of Islam leads to dialogue, a willingness to understand the opinions of others, adaptation, and a disposition toward good relations within a framework of civility. Indonesian and Malaysian moderates make similar arguments. So does Iran's Abdokarim Soroush, who, to the annoyance of more conservative clerics and the government, has captured the religious imagination of Persian readers. His work, in translation, also reaches Turks and others in the Muslim world. In Pakistan, a recent book making an argument similar to Shahrur's, *Qurʾanic and Non-Qurʾanic Islam* (1997), by Nazir Ahmad, a retired military officer, quickly went into a second printing.

The books of the Islamic Reformation are not all aimed at highbrows. Mass schooling has created a wide audience of people who read but are not literary sophisticates, and there has been an explosive growth in what a French colleague of mine, Yves Gonzalez-Quijano, calls generic "Islamic books"—inexpensive, attractively printed texts intended for such readers. Many address practical questions of how to live as a Muslim in the modern world and the perils of neglecting Islamic obligations, and not all appeal to reason and moderation. Many of these books have bold, eye-catching covers and sensational titles such as *The Terrors of the Grave; or, What Follows Death* (1987), while other, more subdued works offer advice to young women on how to live as Muslims today. Often based on the sermons of popular preachers, Islamic books are written in a breezy, colloquial style rather than in the cadences of traditional literary Arabic, and are sold on sidewalks and outside mosques rather than in bookstores. While Egyptian Nobel laureate Naguib Mahfouz is considered successful if he sells five thousand copies of one of his novels in a year in his own country, Islamic books often have sales in six figures.

Increasingly in the Muslim world, religious beliefs are self-consciously held, explicitly expressed, and systematized. It is no longer sufficient simply to "be" Muslim and to follow Muslim practices. One must reflect upon Islam and defend one's views. In Oman, one of the few places where all three Muslim traditions—Sunni, Shiʿa, and Ibadi—converge, the debates can be spirited indeed, as I learned from one young Omani, who recalled the late-night dormitory arguments he and other students had in secondary school.

Roughly 90 percent of the world's Muslims are Sunni or "orthodox" Muslim. Nine percent—mostly in Iran, but with significant minorities in southern Lebanon, Iraq, Syria, Pakistan, Bahrain, Saudi Arabia, and coastal Oman—are Shiʿa, or "sectarian," and believe that legitimate religious leadership of the worldwide Muslim community should remain in the hands of the family of the Prophet, Muhammad. The Ibadiyya, not as well known, believe that anyone who possesses the necessary piety and moral qualities can become head of the Muslim community. The Ibadiyya are few in number and clustered mostly in northern Oman (where they constitute nearly half the country's population), East Africa, southern Algeria, and Libya.

When I visited al-Hamra in 1979, many Muslims could practice their faith without reducing it to formal principles or comparing it with other Muslim or non-Muslim doctrines. Now, however, most of the younger inhabitants of the oasis are aware of what it means to be an Ibadi Muslim, and how Ibadi practices and doctrines—on such questions as whether or not believers see God on Judgment Day—differ from Sunni and Shiʿi ones. In the early 1980s, when Ibadi university students went to study abroad in places such as Tucson, Arizona, they were shocked to find other Muslim students describing them as kaffirs, or unbelievers, and asked Oman's *mufti*, an Ibadi religious leader, how to respond. One result was videocassettes and pamphlets explaining Ibadi doctrine and faith and arguing that Ibadi principles agree in most respects with Sunni ones.

The rise of literacy and the spread of communications—with tapes of popular preachers being played incessantly in taxis and other settings, and banned literature being copied almost everywhere—have prompted more Muslims to interpret Islam's texts, classical or modern, and apply them to modern life. They offer advice in popular "how-to" pamphlets: how to lead the life of a Muslim woman in a modern city, how to raise children the Islamic way, how to follow Islamic banking and business practices. In other pamphlets and cassettes, often clandestinely circulated, Muslims measure particular regimes by "Islamic" standards. Sometimes, as on the Arabian Peninsula, these standards are progressive, insisting upon governmental integrity and upholding human rights. Often they are reactionary, restricting women's public roles and advocating religious censorship and control of schools.

In Muslim-majority countries, many regimes court popularity by emphasizing their Islamic credentials and spelling out, in state-approved schoolbooks, standards that governments must meet. In Egypt, Saudi Arabia, and other countries, dissidents have succeeded at times in embarrassing the government by pointing out performances that fall short of such proclaimed standards. Some regimes try by various means to restrict what is said in public. In Oman, for instance, a special government department churns out model sermons for the "guidance" of approved preachers. In Morocco's large cities, mosques are kept locked except during hours of formal prayer, to prevent their use by unauthorized "study groups." In most countries, the regime carefully regulates broadcast and print media. But through alternative media, including cassettes and photocopies, the multitudinous voices of dissent and difference continue to be heard.

The situation varies widely among countries and regions, but everywhere there is a collapse of earlier, hierarchical notions of religious authority based on a claimed mastery of fixed bodies of religious texts and recognition by a prior generation of scholars. In Central Asia in the early 1990s, a Tajik garage mechanic became the leader of the most popular Islamic movement in the region. Even when there are state-appointed religious authorities—as in Oman, Saudi Arabia, Iran, Egypt, Malaysia, and some of the Central Asian republics—there no longer is any guarantee that their word will be heeded, or even that they themselves will follow the lead of the regime.

No Muslims—whether their outlook is deemed "fundamentalist," "traditionalist," or "modernist"—have been unaffected by the sweeping changes of recent decades. Islam has been democratized. Like Martin Luther at the Diet of Worms in 1521, more and more Muslims today claim attachment to God's unmediated word, as interpreted only by their conscience.

But that does not mean that Muslim tradition is simply being discarded. Rather, it is being examined and discussed. As the Syrian reformer Muhammad Shahrur well knows, the forces supporting conventional interpretations of God's word remain strong. And many debates are in progress.

This was evident the summer of 1997 in Damascus in what could be called the "duel of the wedding speeches" (subsequently available on videotape, of course). First, at the wedding of Muhammad Shahrur's daughter, some six hundred guests—including many officials of the state and the ruling Baʿth party and one non-Syrian (me)—heard Jawdat Saʿid explain Islamic beliefs and their relation to current events. Then, two days later at another Damascus wedding, Saʿid Ramadan al-Buti, a popular Syrian television preacher who strongly opposes Shahrur's views, spoke in response. After referring to the talk given at the recent wedding of the daughter of "a certain well-known engineer," he declared, "Just as one goes to a medical doctor for illness and an architect to build a house, for Islam one should go only to specialists formally trained in the religious sciences."

The Islamic Reformation is a protean phenomenon, its ultimate outcome far from clear. Shahrur maintains that democracy is a fundamental tenet of Islam, and his proposition seems to have growing appeal. But most Arab regimes remain authoritarian. In Algeria, where Islamist radicals employ terrorism against a brutally repressive military regime, and in certain other Muslim countries, the new Islamic self-consciousness and fervor may result in an even more severe authoritarianism, at least in the short run. Elsewhere—in Malaysia, Pakistan, Saudi Arabia and other Arabian Peninsula states, Morocco, and Egypt—conservative or relatively liberal regimes have sought to accommodate (or at least to appear to accommodate) Islamist views. In still other countries, such as Jordan, regimes have tried to balance Islamist concerns with secular politics, and to incorporate religious politics into a parliamentary system.

Over the long term, I think, rising literacy and education, together with the proliferation of new media, may well foster the growth of pluralism, tolerance, and civility. People learn from experience, at least sometimes. In the early 1980s, for example, I heard many people in the Gulf speak with admiration of the Islamic revolution in Iran. By the middle of that decade, the same people—committed Muslim activists who wanted to see Islamic values permeate political and social life—were decidedly cool toward the revolution. In Iran today, there is much frustration with the dominant conservative and extremist mullahs. The clash of views was evident at the Islamic summit meeting in Tehran in December 1997. Although Iran's supreme leader, Ayatollah Ali Khameini, excoriated the United States and the West, Iranian President Muhammad Khatemi, elected in an unexpected landslide in May 1997, spoke of Islam's "spirit of justice and tolerance" and urged learning from "the positive accomplishments of the Western civil society."

Meanwhile, both the Islamist extremism in Algeria and its state-sponsored counterpart has dampened the appeal to Moroccans of a more "Islamic" government, and Taliban rule in Afghanistan serves as a negative example to all its neighboring countries. In Jordan and Lebanon, where Islamists have been drawn into the electoral process, there has been a gradual shift away from radicalism, as Islamist parties seek to appeal to wider constituencies.

In Turkey, people's views have been evolving rapidly. In 1992, 1993, and 1994, rural and urban Turks were asked whether Turkey was "Muslim," "European," or "both." Some 20 percent consistently said "European." But the proportion who answered "Muslim" shrank from 37 percent in 1992 to 25 percent in 1994, while the segment that responded "both" correspondingly grew—from 25 percent to 36. Although figures for later years are not available, it is likely that this trend toward embracing both European and Muslim identities has continued. Islamic activists are seeking to encourage the spread of Islamic values, including respect for the rights of non-Muslims and education for both women and men, at all levels of Turkish society. Even the "fundamentalist" Refah Party was credited with drawing women into grass-roots politics, though it resisted giving them leadership roles.

The Muslim world has its share of militant fanatics, and they have been responsible for a great deal of death and destruction. In November 1997, for instance, Islamic militants who had been seeking to destabilize the Egyptian government massacred fifty-eight foreign tourists at a temple in Luxur. Just days before that, newspaper front pages told of the convictions of Muslim extremists in connection with the 1993 bombing of New York's World Trade Center, carried out to punish the United States for its support of Israel. But the Muslim world certainly has no monopoly on fanaticism or terrorism, as the 1995 bombing of the federal building in Oklahoma City attests.

It is dangerously misleading to view developments in the Muslim world in terms of a clash between Islamic "fundamentalists" and Western civilization. There is a "fundamentalist" crisis, Malaysia's Muhammad Mahathir said in 1997, but it is not the one perceived by religious and political authorities in many Muslim-majority countries and by some Western commentators. The real crisis, he said—correctly, in my view—lies in the need to encourage more Muslims to shun the extremism of the few and to get back to the true fundamentals of their faith—including a commitment to tolerance and civility. The Qur'an appears to give a final answer to the role of the Muslim community in a multi-community world: "To each among you, We have prescribed a law and a way for acting. If God had so willed, he might have made you a single community, but [he has not done so] that he may test you in what he has given you; so compete in goodness" (5:48).

Civility and tolerance will not prevail without struggle. The ideals of civil society, democracy, and open debate about basic values—ideals that are explicit in the works of Syria's Muhammad Shahrur, Turkey's Fethullah Gülen, and Iran's Abdokarim Soroush—are up against strong vested interests. These ideals threaten the sinecures of many preachers, specialists in religious law, educators, and clerics. Not surprisingly, some efforts at reform have been met with threats of violence.

But what I call the Islamic Reformation is nevertheless in progress. Many Muslims, of course, would resist the analogy with the Protestant Reformation. Shortly before writing this essay, I visited Fethullah Gülen. At the end of a spirited discussion on how the shift from face-to-face meetings to television had influenced his message. I told him of the title I had in mind for my essay: "Inside the Islamic Reformation." With polite amusement, he replied, "It's your title, not mine." Gülen explained that he saw his work—which includes the idea that there is no contradiction between an Islamic worldview and a scientific one—as an effort to persuade people to understand and live by the basic teachings of Islam. I pointed out that Martin Luther had said something very similar. Luther saw himself as returning to the fundamentals of belief, not creating anything new. Only later did others see his ideas and actions as instigating the "Reformation."

I must concede, however, that the analogy with the Protestant Reformation is imperfect. In the Muslim world today, there is no one central figure or hierarchy of authority against whom the people are rebelling. There are instead many authorities, and, despite numerous claims to the contrary, no movement or individual speaks for all Muslims. Many thinkers who write about Islam freely admit this. Muhammad Shahrur, for instance, acknowledges that his upbringing as an Arab nationalist has deeply influenced his thinking about Islam. Indonesia's moderate Nurcholish Madjid likewise recognizes that his writings on the future of Islamic civil society appeal mostly to Indonesians. Shiʿi thinkers such as the Iraqi Shaykh al-Rikabi, living in Damascus when I met him in 1997, admit that their primary audience is the Shiʿa.

The recognition by these and other leading reformers in the Muslim world today that different religious beliefs and practices exist, and that they should be tolerated and debated, is one reason to be hopeful about the eventual outcome of the Islamic Reformation. Perhaps even Muhammad Shahrur's notion that democracy is a fundamental tenet of Islam will take root and flower. In any case, whatever the outcome, the Islamic Reformation is under way.

23. The Sound of the Divine in Daily Life

Kristina Nelson

Muslims declare that the Qurʾan is proof of Muhammad's prophet-hood: only a divine source could explain the miraculous power and beauty of its language, for Muhammad was an illiterate merchant. Kristina Nelson writes here of the significance of the sound of the language of the recited Qurʾan and of the many levels of meaning it has for listening Muslims, and explains the pervasiveness of that sound in daily life. —Eds.

Muslims believe that the Qurʾan is the word of God revealed in Arabic to the Prophet Muhammad, and that it is the last of a series of revelations, including the Torah and the Gospels. The Qurʾan has been compared to these holy books, but Muslims consider it to be more than a book of scripture in which is set down God's law and promise for humanity, and the history of creation. For the Qurʾan must be heard, not merely read. As the word of God transmitted to the Prophet Muhammad, it is considered to be the actual sound of the Divine, the model of perfect beauty, and a testimony to the miracle of human and divine interaction. The revelation was not even written down, except in bits and pieces, until after the prophet's death, and then, the authoritative reference for the written text was the re-cited Qurʾan as it had been memorized by the followers of the Prophet.

An indication of the primary importance of the sound is the fact that the official text distributed to each community was accompanied by a re-citer. Since then, the primary source for learning the Qurʾan has been its recitation. Learning the Qurʾan is equated with reciting it from memory. Preschool children learn the verses of the Qurʾan and the correct phrases with which to begin and end a recitation. But they memorize more than words: They are encouraged to master the sound of the Qurʾan, even before they can comprehend its meaning. Throughout the Islamic world children are rewarded for memorizing the Qurʾan with cash prizes, media exposure and the respect of their communities. The child with a pleasing voice is encouraged to become a public reciter.

The actual learning process is rote memorization: the teacher recites and the student imitates. The teacher corrects until the student has it right. This tradition has great authority, for it is believed that the Prophet Muhammad was himself thus instructed by the Angel Gabriel over the twenty-year period during which the Qur°an was revealed, and that when the revelation was complete, the accuracy of the revelation was confirmed in a final review in which the Prophet was made to recite the Qur°an in full. Traditionally, the student may or may not refer to the written text, depending on the student's age and experience. But the basic premise of Quranic learning is that the written text is an aid to the oral tradition, and that to achieve full mastery, one must ultimately depend on what one hears.

To guard against the distortions and variants of oral tradition, Muslim scholars devised a code of rules which preserve the Qur°an in its oral manifestation. This code, called *tajwid*, regulates Quranic recitation in detail. Muslims believe that the sound thus preserved is that of the actual revelation; it is the language of God. Whereas the written text preserves the words, syntax, and order of materials, tajwid preserves the sound, from the pronunciation of each phoneme to the length and timbre or voice quality of each syllable. It is tajwid which differentiates Quranic Arabic from literary Arabic and gives the recitation its unique and characteristic sound. Even children have learned that, whether in the context of formal speech or informal conversation, the words of the Qur°an demand special rhythmic and pitch patterns which mark its divine origin.

The Qur°an is considered the miracle of Muhammad's prophethood. The proof of its divine source is in its inimitable euphony, eloquence, and wisdom, for Muhammad was neither poet nor sage, but an unlettered merchant. Most Westerners find the claim to the Qur°an's inimitable beauty baffling, for they have had access only to the written text, whether in translation or in the original Arabic. The ears hear more than the eyes see in the written text, and it is only in the sound that the full miracle is realized. Thus, while the meaning of each word may be translated from the Arabic, the Qur°an itself is untranslatable. In recognition of this, A. J. Arberry, an English scholar who tried to render something of the poetry, the imagery and rhythms, of the Qur°an into English, titled his work *The Koran Interpreted*. The point is made clear in comparing translations and the written Arabic text of a passage consisting of a simple list with the recitation of the same passage. What reads as a prosaic and boringly repetitive passage on who can marry whom (Qur°an 24/26) is, when recited, a lilting verse that draws one's attention to the subject with alternating rhymes, parallel syntax, and a catchy rhythm.

What does the Qur°an sound like? There are basically two sounds (and the following description should be considered a supplement to your listening), depending on whether the context is pedagogic and devotional or performative. *Murattal* is the style of recitation learned by all Muslims who want to recite correctly, that is, according to the rules of tajwid. Emphasis is on rendering the text correctly and clearly. The text is recited straight through, without repetition. Although differing from that of conversation, intonation is within the same range or even more restricted. The voice is pitched at conversation level or a bit higher. It is the characteristic rhythm of the text which dominates and most obviously marks this style. The sound of murattal has been variously described as "sing-song," soothing, restful, refreshing, and hypnotic. Except for radio broadcasting, murattal is usually heard only in the contexts of prayer, private devotions, and learning. Murattal is what most Muslims use when they recite.

What Muslims listen to, and what visitors to most Islamic communities are likely to hear, is the *mujawwad* style, which is used for public performance. In this style, clear and correct rendering of the text is taken for granted. The intent of the mujawwad reciter is to exploit the inherent beauty of the text with melody and artistry in order to "reach the hearts" of the listeners. This style is marked by repetition, elaborate melody, ornamentation, full voice, and, sometimes, an almost unbearable intensity. The audible release of tension on the part of listeners when the reciter comes to the end of a phrase is also characteristic of this style. Audience response may range from sighs and murmurs to weeping to ecstatic shouts.

Like all great art, recitation can be transforming, the participants touched and changed. But Quranic recitation is more than art. Indeed, Muslim scholars and reciters are careful to distinguish between recitation and "mere" music. The late Shaykh Mustafa Ismail, one of the more elaborately melodic reciters, told of a meeting with a prominent Egyptian musician who handed him a lute and asked him to sing. "I don't sing," said Shaykh Mustafa. Later the musician asked him, in effect, how he could make such sublime music when reciting and then say he does not sing. "I believe in God," said Shaykh Mustafa.

The public reciter is sensitive to what distinguishes him from the singer. He is not taught how to put text and melody together. He does not memorize melodies or set pieces. In performance, he has no back-up chorus or instrumental accompaniment. Although he may command as great a fee as the most popular singers, it is paid by a patron or group of sponsors, and his performance is free to the public. Whereas the singer may bend the text to his melodic inspiration, the reciter has no such license. He must not be carried away by melodic improvisation at the expense of the correctly rendered text. For it is not just any text, nor even just any religious text; it is the Qurʾan.

The meaning of the Qurʾan is not restricted to the words: the meaning transcends the words. In listening to the recited story of Joseph and his brothers, one hears not only a particular narrative but the sound of the Divine, the moment of revelation. No wonder listeners have been known to weep, swoon, and even expire on hearing the recited Qurʾan.

Indeed, the approved response to Quranic recitation is weeping; it is a sign that one is profoundly moved by the experience. An extensive tradition of stories attests to the affecting power of recitation, and anecdotes are continually being added to this tradition. I was told, for example, that every Christmas season the BBC used to broadcast the late Shaykh Muhammad Rifʿat's recitation of the story of the birth of Jesus. An American heard five minutes of such a broadcast and "dropped everything to come to Egypt and devote himself to the study of Islam." It is said of the same reciter that, when it was time for his regular broadcast, "all of Cairo fell silent, listening, even the foreigners in restaurants." A well-respected patron of Quranic recitation told me that he used to drink heavily, and while drinking, would often listen to recitation. "My friends told me this was blasphemous [it is forbidden to drink alcohol in Islam], but gradually, I began to listen more and to drink less. Now I don't drink at all." You do not have to be Muslim to appreciate the recited Qurʾan. Jews, Christians, and nonbelievers have all testified to the power of the sound. Comments of non-Muslims often acknowledge that the recitation is somehow more than music, and they include references to the character of the reciter, his piety, sincerity, or lack thereof.

Obviously not every recitation fulfills the ideal. There are reciters who misuse their skills to attract a following, whose inspiration is not the Qurʾan, but financial reward and personal popularity, just as there are listeners who seek out performances for the thrill of a particular reciter's music genius. ("He is like a tightrope walker: when he goes high, you are breathless.") In some Islamic countries Quranic recitation is severely restricted melodically to preclude such transgressions, and even in Egypt there is continuing discussion over the appropriateness of the use of artistry in recitation. But none of this affects the essential orality of the Qurʾan, nor its impact on the listener. Whatever the style of the recitation, the basic reality is that the Qurʾan is recited.

Quranic recitation is a common, daily event, not restricted to special occasions, nor even to strictly religious contexts. You may hear a beggar, sitting with palm outstretched on a corner in a residential neighborhood, reciting in full voice. You may take a taxi to the accompaniment of recitation played on cassette tape. You may deliver your laundry, buy meat, and find that most shopkeepers along your route have their radios turned to Quranic recitation. Halfway up the block, a group of men, sitting formally on small stools which spill out of the store onto the sidewalk, are listening to a recording of recitation. They are there to honor the memory of a deceased colleague. A business is opened, and the event is marked with lights, flowers, and the sound of a reciter broadcast into the surrounding streets. At a summit conference in Tunisia, reciters representing the participating countries perform in turn. Radio stations open and close their daily programming with recitation. Radio and television stations program recitation regularly during the course of the day. On the religious radio station in Egypt, you can listen to live performances of recitation in the context of commemorative and official events, or of religious liturgy. Or you may listen to a program that presents selections from a heritage of forty years of recordings of Quranic recitation.

Think of the characteristic sounds that define your day . . . the sound of the alarm clock, of dishes clattering, of disc jockeys and newscasters, the noise of traffic, of telephones and xerox machines and typewriters. Whereas you might be lucky enough to hear a piece of sublime beauty in a concert of religious music, or in the context of religious liturgy, or to hear even a Bach cantata in your local delicatessen, it would be a rare occasion, and it would not be the Qur'an. Imagine what it would be like to have, as an integral part of your day, a sound with all the implications and power and beauty and prestige of the recited Qur'an. There is no equivalent to that experience.

24. Abu Illya and Zakat

Donna Lee Bowen

The teachings of the Qur²an emphasize the responsibility of the individual to society and of society to the individual. The indigent, widows, orphans—those without a family to supply their needs are to be watched out for by the community as a whole. Sayyid Qutb, a twentieth-century Muslim ideologue and activist, stated in his book Social Justice in Islam *"Again every individual is charged with the care of society, as if he were the watchman over it, responsible for its safety. Life is like a ship at sea, whose crew are all concerned for her safety . . . No individual, then, can be exempt from this care for the general interest. Similarly the welfare of the community must be promoted by mutual help between individuals—always within the limits of honesty and uprightness. 'Help one another in innocence and piety, but do not help one another in crime and hostility' (5:3)."*

Each adult Muslim is expected to pay annually one-fortieth of his property for the care and welfare of the less fortunate in the Muslim community. In most parts of the Muslim world zakat (tithes) is no longer collected by the state as it was during the early years of Islam. Its donation has become voluntary and is given directly to the needy as well as being dispensed through a mosque. —Eds.

Abu Illya, the father of my friend Illya Muhammad, is the baker for the Moroccan town of Bou Jad. Each morning he rises at 3:30 A.M. and begins work at the bakery at 4:00 A.M. He and his second oldest son, Abdul Latif, mix, knead and bake hundreds of loaves of bread in large hot ovens set in the walls of the bakery. When the doors of the ovens are opened to retrieve the bread, the bakery resembles an inferno. Despite the strength needed to operate the bakery, Abu Illya is a slight, quiet, unassuming man. In family gatherings he sits quietly and contributes little to the conversation, preferring to puff on his pipe. The more time I spent with Abu Illya, the more I grew to respect him and the values that guided his life. My first meeting with him, however, was unusual.

At the family party preceding the wedding of Illya's second cousin Fatima's daughter, puffs of illicit *kif* (hashish) smoke drifted past Illya, me, and a few others. We sniffed, paused and looked at each other. I began to scan the room for a tell-tale huddle of young kif smokers, but I was stopped by a blushing Illya. "It's my father," he said. "I wish he would stop smoking." Abdul Latif joined in. "Don't you think it is bad for his health? No father should smoke in front of company. Talk with him, help him see he'd be better off without kif." Both sons were clearly embarrassed and worried about their father's pastime, but could do nothing more than gently tease him about it.

Later Fatima and I cornered Abu Illya and asked about the kif. "Don't you know that it's illegal in America?" I asked. Fatima countered with "What kind of example are you setting for your sons? Do you want them to turn into kif smokers too?"

He smiled. "I get up before dawn every day of the week and work hard to prepare bread for the town. The work is strenuous, routine, and with the heat of those giant ovens, I feel like I face the fires of hell each day. I return home at lunchtime exhausted and wanting only some quiet for a few hours. Furthermore, Bou Jad is the most boring town in Morocco. What else is there to do? Can I be blamed for smoking to relax? Haven't I earned the right to be left alone in peace with my pipe and my thoughts?"

From then on, Abu Illya and I sat together in the salon after lunch. He smoked and I read books and generally tried to make sense of all I saw in Bou Jad.

One afternoon a knock at the door shattered our quiet and the rest of the family's siesta. Illya's sister, Khadija, ran to the door and admitted a woman dressed in a shabby gray caftan. They held a whispered conference then Khadija came into the salon to consult her father. He reached for his wallet, pulled out several bills, and handed them to Khadija, who ran back to the entryway and pressed them into the woman's hand. The women called out thanks to Abu Illya and faded back into the alleyway.

That evening I asked Illya and Abdul Latif about the woman. They answered in an off-hand fashion that it must have been Lalla Fatiha needing something for her son's schooling since autumn classes had just begun. Who was Lalla Fatiha? No, she isn't a relative; she is our neighbor. Down the *derb* (alley), the doorway on the right. The one painted orange for her daughter's wedding. You've seen her younger children playing soldiers and soccer in the street. She is a widow. My father pays his *zakat* to her.

Zakat? No it isn't zakat as in the Prophet's time when it was paid as a tax to the community coffers. We don't have any collection of zakat in Morocco now. Instead we pay income tax to the government. And then we give alms to the poor. Most people don't pay zakat regularly, just give alms during Ramadan or perhaps support a particular beggar, although Bou Jad has far fewer beggars than Marrakesh or Casablanca Medina.

Abu Illya, it seemed, believed in the responsibility of Muslims to pay zakat whether or not it duplicated income tax. He also believed that one should pay zakat as it said in the Qurʾan, that Muslims should know their neighbor's situation and look after their welfare without being asked for help.

Abu Illya had known Lalla Fatiha and her husband, Si Mukhtar, since he was a boy. Si Mukhtar had been a clerk in the super caid's office making a low but sufficient wage. After he had fathered seven children, two of whom died before they reached one year of age, he developed unexplained pains in his stomach, was treated by a variety of doctors from Bou Jad to Khenifra, but died within the year. A horde of relatives descended upon Lalla Fatiha to mourn her husband's death, but within a week they had all left for their homes having eaten enough food to feed her children for three months.

Lalla Fatiha quietly went about her life. Gradually her children's clothes grew shabbier; the older boys stayed in school, but each year Lalla Fatiha looked more worn as she struggled to buy them shoes and books from the small savings her husband left. Finally, Um Illya, Illya's mother, in conversation with Lalla Fatiha about the upcoming feast discovered that she was not planning to sacrifice a sheep but to purchase a little meat for brochettes instead. In Morocco, failing to buy a sheep for sacrifice on 'Id al-Adha is a sure sign of financial insolvency. Um Illya rushed home, consulted with Abu Illya, and the next day Illya and Abdul Latif delivered a small sheep to Lalla Fatiha's door. That began the systematic zakat.

From then on, Lalla Fatiha and her children could hardly make a move without Abu Illya, his wife, or his children knowing. When money was short for the coming school term, an envelope was delivered to the orange door. When the oldest married daughter fell ill during the final months of her pregnancy and needed special food and medicine her husband couldn't afford, Abu Illya set up a credit line at the pharmacist. When the second youngest daughter discussed leaving school to apprentice herself as a maid, Um Illya was sent to speak to Lalla Fatiha about the need for her daughter's education in the fast-changing world that was modern Morocco. Each week, Abu Illya deposits sacks of flour at the orange door on his way home from the bakery. Illya's sister Khadija tutors the little girls in mathematics; Khalid, the youngest brother, tutors the children in English, his best subject.

After a few years of help, Lalla Fatiha reconciled herself to the omnipresence of Abu Illya's zakat after she tired of the lectures she received when he realized that she had not sent word to him when she lacked for anything. Again and again he told her: "This is only temporary. When your Abdul Rahman finishes the Bac then he can be responsible for you. If he or his brothers don't get an education, how can they support you or the little girls on an errand boy's or a dustman's wages? Little ventured, little gained. We must be willing to invest if we want a return. What would Si Mukhtar say if he knew you thought of sacrificing the children's education?" Weary Lalla Fatiha would nod her head, try to kiss Abu Illya's hand, and be brusquely told to get back to her work.

"But what about Lalla Fatiha," I asked. "Doesn't she resent all the charity? Always taking from others?" Illya was astonished at the question. "This isn't charity," he retorted. "This is zakat. Our honor is to proffer zakat, her honor is to use the zakat. All is provided by God, not by us. This time we have sufficient for our needs; later it may be Lalla Fatiha's turn to provide for us when her children are educated and work as doctors and engineers, and Abdul Latif and I are worn out from working in the bakery. God provides for us; he gives us our wherewithal, our brains, our health with which we work. If we have enough, then we share with our neighbor. If we lack, our neighbor is to share with us. Lalla Fatiha helps us be better Muslims, and in turn is a good Muslim herself. Isn't this the way Islam is to be lived?"

25. An American Woman on the Hajj

Michael E. Jansen

Each year, between the eighth and thirteenth days of the twelfth month (Dhu al-Hijjah)*, more than 800,000 Muslims from all parts of the world arrive in the Hijaz, the area where the holy cities of Mecca and Medina are located, for the pilgrimage* (hajj)*. A lesser pilgrimage* (umra) *can be made at any time of the year and marks the respect the Prophet Muhammad paid to the city of Mecca. —Eds.*

I was in Mecca at last.

Before me was the *Kaʿba*, a great black cube partly submerged in a torrent of white-robed pilgrims circling round and round. Around us, like a dam containing the torrent, stood the massive walls and the seven slim minarets of the Sacred Mosque. High above, the muezzin began the evening call to prayer: *"Allahu, Akbar!—*God Is Most Great!" Up on the hills the thin reedy voices of the muezzins in the smaller mosques joined in, each voice picking up the call in a fugue of prayer soaring into the golden crest of the afternoon.

In response, the crowds circling the Kaʿba slowed and stopped while new thousands flooded into the courtyard. In unison we bowed, fell to our knees and touched our foreheads to the earth, the familiar words of prayer filling the courtyard and cloisters with the hoarse whisper that spilled out into the streets of the hushed city.

Like most pilgrims, I could barely resist the desire to pay my formal respects at the Kaʿba immediately, but the crowds were so dense that I thought it wiser to wait. In the interim I stood in the arched cloisters and looked out at the marvelous spectacle taking place in the great courtyard before me.

The center of the spectacle, of course, was the Kaʿba, shrouded in black silk, with a wide band of golden calligraphy two-thirds of the way to the

Adapted from "An American Girl on the Hajj," *Aramco World Magazine* 25, no. 6 (November–December 1974).

top. Just that morning the Kaᶜba had received its ceremonial washing and, as is customary, the corners of the covering had been raised for the duration of the Pilgrimage, exposing the dark-gray blocks of Mecca stone, of which it is constructed, roughly cemented together.

Around the Kaᶜba, following their *mutawwifs* (guides for pilgrims) and repeating the customary prayers, swirled men and women of every race and nation, from every corner of the earth. There were brown men, black men, yellow men, and white men; some young, some old; some with the bearing of ancient patriarchs, others with the faces of medieval peasants and warriors, many with the clean-shaven look of modern businessmen. It was as if the sea had risen in a great tide around the world and swept us all to Mecca and into the whirlpool spinning about the massive black cube.

After a short time I realized that the crowds were not going to diminish, and decided to delay no longer. Leaving the cloisters, I walked along one of the nine broad stone walks that lead to the wide marble oval pavement which surrounds the Kaᶜba. I tucked my sandals (which I had removed before entering the mosque) into the gravel near a bench. Then I engaged a mutawwif and, left shoulder to the Kaᶜba, edged into the current.

Although this first ceremony is a moving experience for a pilgrim, the *Tawaf*, or "the Circling"—that is, making seven circuits around the Kaᶜba— is not, at that point, considered part of the Hajj. Along with the *Saᶜy*, or "the Running," it comprises the *Umra*, or "Lesser Pilgrimage," which is a gesture of respect to the Holy City made by the pilgrim on his first visit. It begins, traditionally, with the pilgrim's kissing or touching the Black Stone, but on that night there was no question of my getting near enough to touch it. The throng, gently but firmly, had carried me off.

Despite its size, the Hajj multitude is surprisingly gentle. Occasionally, as one group or another would attempt to cross the mighty stream, there would be an angry wave of pushing and jostling, but even that was understandable. To many pilgrims, who may never have gone further than the next village before making the Hajj, getting lost or separated was an experience too terrifying to contemplate.

On the seventh circuit the mutawwif steered me from the center of the stream to the outer bank and found a place for us to perform *Salat*—the recitation of a prayer while bowing, kneeling, and touching the forehead to the earth. This Salat, which completes the Circling, is performed near the Place of Abraham, a spot where Abraham prayed.

For the next rite I mounted the small rocky hillock called al-Safa, turned toward the Kaᶜba, raised my hands in salutation and declared my intention to perform the rite of Saᶜy. Then, descending from al-Safa, I entered the Masᶜa, a spacious promenade bisected lengthwise by two narrow, railed pathways for the wheelchairs of the infirm, and joined another throng of believers, walking briskly to al-Marwa, another hillock, in the first of seven Runnings between the hills.

This throng, I found, was more relaxed than the crowds outside. Although there were occasional groups of determined peasants from the Anatolian steppes or the plains of the Punjab who, arms firmly inter-locked, swept other pilgrims aside as they rushed at a headlong pace down the Masᶜa, most were exceptionally considerate. Children unconcernedly followed their parents; proud fathers bore infants in their arms and on their shoulders; the old, the blind and the crippled, who either could not afford or would not countenance wheelchairs, slowly but safely made their way.

After the Saᶜy, I visited the Well of Zamzam, where Hagar, the mother of Ishmael, found water. I descended the white marble steps to a large, divided chamber with a long pipe equipped with brass spigots running along its back and side walls. Crowding round the taps were ample Egyptian women, who wept as they splashed themselves and everyone else with the warm water, which I found had a slightly brackish smell but little or no taste. At the top of the steps I saw two men wringing out a long piece of white material: "A burial shroud," someone said, explaining that some simple folk bring their shrouds to Zamzam because they believe that a shroud bathed in its waters will help them gain entrance to Paradise.

In the dark corners of the mosque, pilgrims slept wrapped in blankets, shawls, and even prayer rugs. During the Pilgrimage, the Sacred Mosque becomes a part of the daily life of the pilgrims as well as a center of Pilgrimage. This may seem surprising to Westerners, but to a Muslim religion is a part of living; it is not folded up like a churchgoer's Sunday best until the next service. A prayer rug may serve as a bed, blanket, shawl, or turban, as well as for devotions. Only the Qurʾan is kept apart, wrapped carefully in a cloth and placed respectfully on top of one's goods.

As I walked on, the peace and serenity of the mosque crept into my heart. At the rail of the dim gallery above the cloisters, a man sat facing the Kaᶜba transfixed, a Qurʾan in his lap; and an Iranian woman stood alone quietly weeping. In the courtyard, where great throngs still circled the Kaᶜba, the sedan chairs of pilgrims unable to perform the Tawaf on foot bobbed above the heads of the multitude like boats plying through waters.

The next morning, with the thunderous refrain, "*Labbayk, Allahumma, Labbayk!*" the Pilgrimage began. Thundering through the streets of Mecca, the crowds swept out of the city in a great river that flowed along the broad road to Mina and past Jabal al-Nur, "the Mountain of Light."

For many, the Pilgrimage begins with this first glimpse of Jabal al-Nur, where Muhammad received his first revelation. To them, the mountain where the Prophet was summoned to God's service finally becomes a reality. Here Muhammad was commanded, "Read: In the name of thy Lord Who createth; createth man from a clot. Read: And thy Lord is the Most Bounteous, Who teacheth by the pen, teacheth man that which he knew not." Here, with these words spoken in this place, Islam began, and here we joyfully responded, "*Labbayk, Allahumma, Labbayk!*," knowing that God was indeed with us in this lonely, inhospitable valley. The sky was a hard ice blue and the air like crystal, sparkling with the rising dust. Yes, this was indeed a place fit for revelation, an intense solitary place, brown and blue and filled with white-robed believers as far as the eye could see.

With new understanding in our hearts, we streamed into the little desert town of Mina, where Muhammad and his Companions spent the night on their way to Arafat. Following in his footsteps we halted at Mina, set in a steep-sided wadi, barren and brown, only three quarters of a mile across on the Mecca side but widening into the plain of Muzdalifah. At the narrow end of the wadi stand the three stone pillars, the Jamarat, which represent the three attempts made by Satan to prevent Abraham from sacrificing his son. As the wadi broadens there are streets of pastel-painted buildings, three to four stories high, in which pilgrims are housed. At the edge of the built-up area are the Mina field hospital, the public bathhouse, blocks housing the Hajj Administration, and the vast tent city, sprawling as far as you can see, filling the wadi, creeping up its rugged sides and spilling forth upon Muzdalifah.

I immediately set out to explore Mina and found it fascinating. Stalls selling iced drinks, cloth, ready-made clothing, toys, and strings of beads lined the streets. There were goods from the world over: watches from Japan, bananas from Guatemala, apples from Lebanon, citrus fruits from Jordan, bolts of cloth from Hong Kong and India, dresses and shirts from Africa, chocolates from Switzerland, sandals from China—an accumulation of goods as heterogeneous in origin as the pilgrims themselves.

In the afternoon I also explored the tent city where most of the pilgrims live—and found that it was a city in every sense of the word, with broad avenues and narrow streets, sanitation facilities, and running water. Along the highway I saw free dispensaries, first-aid tents, a small Swiss plane spraying the area against fleas and flies, and some helicopters hovering overhead to help ambulance teams find pilgrims in need of medical attention. The tents were of all shapes and sizes, and for many purposes. There were striped tents and flowered tents and multicolored tents; soaring pavilions with beautiful patterns inside and long low halls with partitioned rooms; tents for sleeping and tents for eating; privy tents and bathing tents.

Before dawn the next day—the ninth of *Dhu al-Hijjah* and the second day of the Hajj—I rose to the call of prayer, made my ablutions and performed the Salat, and opened my Qur'an to the introduction to refresh my memory on the life of the Prophet, particularly on his Farewell Pilgrimage, which Muslims have ever since tried to emulate. Thus, it became my practice during the Pilgrimage to turn to the Qur'an, or to a book on the meaning of the Prophet's message, whenever I felt puzzled or when I had a problem.

At about eight o'clock I tossed my gear onto the roof of one of our mutawwif's little coaster buses, climbed up, and made myself comfortable among the bedrolls and bundles of the pilgrims inside the bus. The street was jammed with cars, buses and trucks brimming with hajjis and their goods waiting for the signal to begin the journey to Arafat. The din of the engines drowned out this signal—but there must have been one, for in one instant we all were moving, sailing smartly and smoothly above the traffic, waving gaily to other happy passengers, all part of the mighty river flowing from Mina to Arafat. "*Labbayk, Allahumma, Labbayk!*" cried a group of Africans from the back of a small truck, and the multitude joined in, each nationality responding in its own accent, to the divine call issued more than thirteen centuries before: "And proclaim unto mankind the Pilgrimage. They will come to thee on foot and on every lean camel; they will come from every deep ravine" (Qur᾽an 22:27).

At Arafat I set out at once for Jabal al-Rahmah, the Mount of Mercy, where, at the foot of a dark granite hill on the edge of the plain, the Prophet had stood to deliver the sermon during his Farewell Pilgrimage. At the base stood many pilgrims, eyes uplifted to the dazzling white pillar erected near the top of the two-hundred-foot slope. Some prayed, others sat on mats talking, family groups had their photographs taken and a knot of Africans, crowded beneath a striped beach umbrella, chanted "*Labbayk.*" One mutawwif, leading a long line of Turks, exhorted them through a loudspeaker. Television cameras scanned the goings-on from a scaffold, perched high above our heads. Keeping pace with me was an obviously sophisticated pilgrim, chatting animatedly to his wife, apparently oblivious of where he was and what was happening around him. But then he looked up and seeing the Mount just before him, stopped in his tracks and burst into a flood of tears.

As I began to ascend the Mount, a tall African generously shared the shade of his green silk umbrella with me and I recalled the Prophet's words: "Above all else, never forget that each Muslim is the brother of all others: for all Muslims in this world form one race of brothers."

Back in the tent, I found that the Pakistani ladies—now part of my group—had not visited the Mount of Mercy. Instead, they sat on their bedrolls, reading their Qur᾽ans. For me the meaning of those words was enhanced outside in the streets of Arafat, at the foot of the Mount, and on the barren plain enclosed by stark, azure mountains on three sides. I went out and walked alone until I found a place I could peacefully stand and gaze at the Mount, in my own private commemoration of the *Wuquf* or "the Standing," of the congregation for the Prophet's sermon. There were many of us who stood in the streets of Arafat that day, under the noon sun, recalling that God had given His last revelation to Muhammad at Arafat: "This day I have perfected your religion for you, completed My favor upon you, and have chosen for you Islam as your religion" (Qur᾽an 5:4). When they heard those words, the Prophet's Companions wept, for they knew that he would not remain with them long, and every pilgrim who has "stood" at Arafat since has felt the same sense of loss.

After the noon prayer, the multitude at Arafat seemed to heave a great sigh of relief, and the atmosphere changed from grave devotion to light-hearted serenity. There is a lovely story about the Prophet which explains the transformation at Arafat, a story few pilgrims know, but the essence of which they all feel in their hearts.

While he was at Mina during his Farewell Pilgrimage, Muhammad seemed glum, but his Companions, who felt his mood, hesitated to ask him why. At Arafat the next day, however, the Prophet's face glowed with happiness. One of the Companions asked him what had happened, why his spirits had changed from gloom to gaiety. The Prophet replied that the day before he had been depressed because he had asked God to forgive the pilgrims all their sins and God had replied that He could forgive only the sins against Himself. He could not forgive the sins they had committed against one another. But now He had said that He would forgive all the sins of the pilgrims at Arafat. And from that day onward pilgrims have left Arafat free men and women, reborn and without sin, for there is no concept of original sin in Islam.

Back in our compound, I found the magic of Arafat had made everyone serenely happy. A picnic atmosphere had swept across the plain. In our tent we were served enormous dishes of lamb and chicken cooked in spices with rice, and a sweet saffron-rice pudding.

After lunch the streets filled with people, long trains of pilgrims marching behind banners proclaiming their nationalities, families gathering in the shade of the little striped awnings attached to their cars, men and women sipping tea in refreshment tents.

At dawn cannon announced the morning prayer. In the chill mist that blanketed the plain, I began to walk from Muzdalifah to the pillars at Mina. In order to keep their little groups together, some hajjis had raised distinctive standards on long poles: teapots and paper bags, rags and plastic bottles, posters and flags were solemnly held aloft. The problem of losing hajjis was solved by the mutawwifs in various ways. Some gave their charges little cards with their addresses at Mina which a lost hajji could present to the nearest Boy Scout or policeman so that they could be sent to the correct tent. Desert tribesmen traveled in tight little rings, women and children on the inside, men forming an elastic outer circle. But it was the Iranians who had devised the most ingenious way of keeping track of their ladies: they simply stitched their addresses onto the back of the billowing white cloaks in which the women enveloped themselves from top to toe.

Because I was well ahead of the mass of pilgrims coming from Muzdalifah, I was able to approach the Jamrah quite easily. I took careful aim and cast the first seven pebbles home: one . . . two . . . three. They flew in shallow arcs . . . tic . . . tic . . . tic as they hit the pillar. I felt complete solidarity with the people all around, both great and humble; people who were at that moment striking out at their weaknesses, their misdeeds against God and one another . . . tac . . . tac . . . tac against the pillar. The earnestness with which the majority of the pilgrims—peasants and villagers of Africa and Asia—approached the Jamrah shamed the more worldly of us who, feeling foolish, initially hesitated on the edges of the crowd. But with each stone I felt more strongly the link between past and present, between the Patriarch Abraham and this vast assemblage: the millennia dissolved and the good intentions and resolutions of all the pilgrims who had cast their stones over the ages were fused into the collective Muslim will to follow "the Right Path."

As it was now time for the Sacrifice, I explained to my companion that I would perform it only if I could arrange to have the animal cooked, eat a part of the meat, and give the remainder to someone who was less fortunate than I. (Some hajjis follow this procedure, but most leave the carcass with the attendants at the Place of Sacrifice for distribution among the poor.) We proceeded, therefore, to the Place of Sacrifice, purchased a sheep from one of the bedouin shepherds who were selling their flocks, sacrificed it, and took it, cleaned and ready for cooking, to the proprietor of a shop where a charming rascal called Hajj Muhammad Atiq had agreed to cook it for me.

As we watched the meat cook, an old man, obviously without means, drifted by clutching a loaf of bread from the bakery next door, and asked Hajj Muhammad timidly the price of the meat. But it was too costly and he turned to go. My companion leapt up and offered him some of our meat as it lay simmering in the dish. Shakily the old man held out a nylon bag while Hajj Muhammad spooned in pieces from the pan. "Go in peace," the old man said as he ambled away.

After eating our fill, we left the shop of Hajj Muhammad in search of a recipient for the rest of the Sacrifice. As we thrust through the crowd in the street, a thin dark hand reached up from the pavement and plucked at my sleeve: "Some bread please, some bread." And we gave the lot to this crippled man, sitting on a mat with his crutches beside him.

After packing some clean clothing into a bag, I caught a bus to Mecca to perform the Tawaf and Saʿy of the Pilgrimage. The ride gave me a moment to reflect on what had happened to me since I had left Mecca two days earlier. Before I had embarked on the Pilgrimage, its rituals seemed to me just so many curious exercises. But as I participated in the events of the Pilgrimage, the meaning of these rites unfolded, my understanding of Islam was deepened, and I learned more fully what it meant to be a Muslim. Indeed, this is why God had commanded Muhammad to issue the call for the Pilgrimage: "That they (the pilgrims) may witness things that are of benefit to them" (Qurʾan 22:28).

Back at the Mecca Hotel, the time had come to doff the Ihram, shower, and put on fresh clothing for the Tawaf: "Let them make an end of their unkemptness and pay their vows and go around the Ancient House" (Qur'an 22:29).

The courtyard was not as crowded as it had been when we performed the Umra. After engaging a mutawwif I began the circuits, graceful gray and white pigeons fluttering overhead. From the minarets above us the call to prayer pierced the silence of the Sacred Mosque and my guide led us to the edge of the oval floor, where we prepared for the congregational devotions of the evening Salat. In the radiant evening the throng stood and knelt in unison round the House build by Abraham to proclaim the oneness of God and the unity of mankind. At that moment I understood why Muslims turn toward this great black cube in prayer.

Back in Mina I called on a man recommended to me by a friend, a man learned in the ways of religion, whose face simply radiates his inner peace and goodness. "When you come here," he said, "you are calling on God, you are entering His House. The *Talbiyah* is your application for admittance to His House, a request for an appointment with Him. And that you were able to make the Pilgrimage at all is a sign of God's willingness to accept you. It is a very great blessing for you, for all of us."

26. Abdul Qadar and the Sheep of ʿId al-Adha

Donna Lee Bowen

ʿId al-Adha, or Big Bairam, the Feast of Sacrifice, is the greatest feast day of the Muslim year. This feast, held on the tenth day of Dhu al-Hijja, commemorates the Prophet Abraham's sacrifice of the ram in the place of his son, Ishmael or Isaac (the Qurʾan is not clear about which, but Muslims largely believe it was Ishmael). The feast lasts for three days. Offices and shops close, and everyone celebrates the holiday. After a morning prayer, Muslims spend the feast days in visiting relatives and friends, hanging out with family, and cooking and eating good food. In some countries, such as Morocco, the sacrifice of a sheep is universal; in other countries, fewer households sacrifice. If a family sacrifices, they are expected to keep one third of the meat and give another third to a neighbor and the rest to someone in need. Since the price of meat is high today, the cost of such a sacrifice can run from $125 for a lamb to $400–500 for a full-grown sheep, which is a considerable financial burden for many. This high cost, along with the waste of meat in areas where refrigeration is scarce, has led many to call for a relaxation of the social "rule" that each family must sacrifice its own sheep. But, as is the case with Christmas in the West, social expectations for holidays often become more powerful than their religious purposes. —Eds.

As is the custom on ʿId al-Adha, Abdul Qadar's employers gave him presents of money. Sidney, the American, gave him a particularly generous sum in appreciation of Abdul Qadar's diligent help in running errands night and day. Abdul Qadar proudly took the money home and began to tell his wife how he planned to use it. This year, he said, we can buy meat for the ʿId, and still have enough to begin assembling the banquettes filled with wool for the salon. Perhaps we could buy a larger tray instead. Then he noticed his wife had tears in her eyes.

"No sheep for the ʿId?" she burst out. "Here we are, new in this neighborhood. How can we only buy a kilo of meat for the ʿId and still hold our heads up before our neighbors? What will they think of us? I don't care about the banquettes. I don't care about the tray. Everyone else in Marrakesh will have a sheep to sacrifice. How can we ever go out of our house proudly again? We Muslims know that sacrificing a sheep is the proper way to celebrate the ʿId." She paused for breath and the tears streamed down her face.

Abdul Qadar had never seen his wife weep before. He quietly left the house, mounted his motorcycle, and drove off to the sheep market, mentally counting his money. Sheep were expensive that year—most were going for well over 2,500 riyals—and although he had more money than before, he didn't have that much. After much searching and haggling with the canny sheep merchants, Abdul Qadar set off for home with a small sheep slung over the handlebars of his motorcycle.

He arrived home to a celebration. His wife dried her tears and the sun shone in her smile. His children danced around the sheep and sang songs of delight. That evening, as they planned the feast-day festivities, the children noticed that their sheep was not a sheep, strictly speaking, but a ewe. And strictly speaking, she was not just one ewe, but a pregnant ewe.

In the middle of the night, the ewe gave birth to a little lamb. Morning came and Abdul Qadar was again surrounded by tears. His children wailed, "If we eat the mother ewe, our lamb will die." His wife wept, "What will the neighbors say?"

Defeated, Abdul Qadar wheeled out his motorcycle. Back to Sidney to convince him of the necessity of borrowing next month's salary, and then back to the sheep market to find an animal to sacrifice before everyone left for the ʿId.

Home again, Abdul Qadar, who would have been satisfied with wool-stuffed banquettes and one holiday meal of brochettes, found himself surveying a small sheep herd—three where one day ago there had been none. His family's tears again transformed into shouts of joy. One unlucky sheep was sacrificed and the other two lived on to face another religious festival.

27. Muslim Women and Shrines in Shiraz

Anne H. Betteridge

Islam is often described as a male-dominated religion and most forms of public worship—prayers, Ramadan sacrifices—are predominantly attended by men. The woman's daily tasks and schedule preclude her attendance at the mosque to pray; she typically snatches a few moments when the large noon meal is finished and children are quiet to pray in a corner of her house. Group religious activities are favorite outings, and relatives or neighbors like to make short pilgrimages together to a local shrine as acts of general religious devotion; in times of stress, people prefer to make a solitary visit to pray for aid. Since the Islamic Revolution, the Iranian government has instituted changes which have altered the ways that women visit shrines. Betteridge visited Iran in 2000 and notes the differences between pre- and post-Revolution patterns. —Eds.

Muslim women in Shiraz, Iran, are more likely to make local pilgrimages (*ziarat*) than are men. In writing about pilgrimage in Shiraz, I at first regarded this fact as rather unimportant, meriting only brief mention and cursory explanation. However, in the course of piecing together the relationship between women and ziarat, I began to realize that the relationship is significant and fundamental to understanding local pilgrimage as I observed it in Iran.

The nature of women's association with pilgrimage is twofold. First, on a social or behavioral level, women make pilgrimages to local shrines more often than men. Doing so enriches their lives both spiritually and socially. Second, women's local pilgrimages have a cultural aspect which touches the realm of belief and assumptions about the way the world is constituted. Because local pilgrimage is regarded as basically female in character, it is

Adapted from *Mormons and Muslims,* ed. Spencer Palmer (Provo, Utah: Brigham Young University Religious Studies Center, 1983).

a ritual practice simultaneously suspect and beloved, not totally orthodox but one to which many Iranians have a deep-rooted emotional attachment.

Shiraz is located in southwestern Iran; at the time of my residence there the population numbered just over four hundred thousand. The character of religious observances in Shiraz, including local pilgrimage, is colored by the fact that most Iranians adhere to the Shiʿi sect of Islam and revere the Shiʿi imams, a series of men regarded as the rightful leaders of the Islamic community after the death of the Prophet Muhammad. The majority of Shiʿa, including the people of Shiraz, recognize a succession of twelve imams. Most of the shrines located in the city are the tombs of men and women supposed to be the descendants of the Shiʿi imams. These descendants of the imams, or *imamzadehs*, are respected for their nearness to God by virtue of their descent and their great piety. On account of their privileged position, these saints are often appealed to by Shirazis who are in need of assistance, both material and spiritual. Men and women visit the shrines seeking cures, help with personal and family problems, and forgiveness of sins.

Men tend to frequent larger, more important shrines that are considered formally legitimate by religious authorities. Women predominate at small, back-street shrines, often ramshackle sanctuaries of doubtful antecedents, mocked by men.

The extent of a woman's participation in and devotion to pilgrimage activity depends on a number of factors. The degree of her religious orthodoxy is important; those with strict backgrounds and orthodox education may regard the practice as a distortion of religion based on ignorance or misunderstanding. Others with a more strictly businesslike or scientific outlook may see it either as a diversion for women who don't know better or simply as a waste of time. A woman's age and stage of life also influence her ability to spend time visiting shrines. It is difficult for those with extensive responsibilities for young children or meal preparation to get away as often as they might like. Class membership alone appears to be less relevant; women tend to show fewer status-group differences in religious behavior than do men. At the shrines one sees well-to-do women as well as those with tattered veils. The expense of their vows and the status of the shrines they visit may vary, but the women are differentiated more by dress and wealth than by the degree of their attachment to pilgrimage.

One of the attractions of visiting local shrines is that it is not a formal, highly structured religious activity. Muslim women's participation in formal religious activities is to some extent circumscribed by rules pertaining to their sex. A woman may not pray, enter a mosque, or touch a line of the Qurʾan while menstruating. For young mothers the care of children and household duties make attendance at the mosque difficult. Should women, usually older or childless, go to the mosque, it is often very hard for them to become deeply involved in the services. There women are physically separated from the men, who sit in the central part of the mosque in front of the speaker. The women may, for example, be on a high balcony at the rear of the hall or seated in a side section of the mosque, often marked off by a curtain. In either case, it is none too easy to see the speaker or hear clearly, especially if the sound is piped to the women's section by a faulty loudspeaker. The occasional presence of children in the women's area and the social atmosphere which may prevail can also affect the seriousness of women's attendance.

Interested in hearing a sermon, I went to the mosque one evening and was directed to a balcony over the courtyard where the men were gathered at the feet of the speaker, who was already seated on the *minbar* (stepped pulpit). The women around me were chatting, cracking the shells of seeds, and arranging themselves comfortably to get a good view. I felt as though I were at a movie house rather than a serious religious gathering. Needless to say, I was not able to attend to the sermon in detail. This is not to suggest that I agree with the view men sometimes state, that women are constitutionally unable to involve themselves in the serious business of Islam. It is simply that the formal, public setting of the mosque, even when a woman is able to attend, works against her involvement.

Rather than attempt to integrate themselves into the male pattern of religious behavior, where they are often assigned the role of spectators and kept on the ceremonial sidelines, women have become very much involved in their own forms of religious activity, which give them greater scope for religious expression and allow them full ritual participation. Among these activities are the preparation and serving of ritual meals, sermons recited by and for women, classes conducted especially for women and girls, and pilgrimage to local shrines. On these occasions women are not relegated to peripheral positions and passive roles.

In contrast to the mosques, the structure of shrines and the way in which they are used encourage informal religious activity and allow women more freedom of movement. Particularly during those times of day when men are at work, local shrines become women's territory, popular places to gather and perform religious activities ranging from prayer to Qurʾan-reading classes.

Saturday evening is set aside as the time for visits to Qadamgah, a very popular shrine in Shiraz. At that time a great deal goes on within the shrine building and in its courtyard. Inside, women circumambulate the glass case which marks the footprint of ʿAbbas, half brother of the third Shiʿi imam, Husayn. Off to the side a group of women may be praying, while others are seated on the floor playing with children and exchanging news. A few women may prefer to sit alone and weep. Some listen to a sermon which they have paid a blind man to recite for them. Outside in the courtyard people are seated on the ground eating, drinking tea, and sharing a sweet, halva, which they have made in fulfillment of vows.

On one Saturday night when I was seated inside the shrine, two young men entered the building to pay their respects. As they went straight to the

glass case and circled it, they were the object of intense and decidedly unfriendly scrutiny from the assembled women. The young men soon became
uncomfortable, no doubt aware that they, apart from a blind man and the
shrine employee, were the only men present. They left abruptly. I was later
told by an old man who works at the shrine that men visit it on Fridays
when they are not at work.

Even at those times when men are also present at a shrine, women
are not cut off from participation in activities in the sanctuary. In larger
shrines, separate rooms, alcoves, or large areas to one side of the entrance
or tomb become women's areas as a result of popular usage. There they can
enjoy nearness to the tomb and the company of other women without compromising themselves by coming too close to the men who are also paying
their respects to the saint.

There is usually no formal, central activity at a shrine, such as a sermon, from which women can be excluded. Activities are more a matter of
personal choice than of group involvement. Women freely circumambulate
the tomb[1] and make requests of the saints; they may also pray, sit a while
with friends, or nap if they choose.

There are many reasons for women to be fond of visiting shrines. The
opportunity to get out of the house is not least among them. An older
woman, not able to get about as easily as she used to, envied me the time
I spent visiting shrines in the city. As she put it, "You see something. You
say something." In making local pilgrimages, women are able to escape
their household tasks and domestic responsibilities for a time and come
into contact with new people and situations. While men have varied experience of people in the course of their workday lives, women come into contact with such variety only on outings, such as shopping, visiting, and pilgrimage. Shopping is an end-oriented activity and one in which men often
assume an important role. Too much visiting would compromise a woman's reputation, suggesting that she was not seeing to her duties at home.
Visiting shrines, however, is a praiseworthy religious act and one which
the men of the house or other women would find hard to oppose.

Still, shrine visiting is not viewed uncritically by all men and women.
The relative freedom with which women may visit shrines has led to their
being viewed as places of assignation. Shrines may be the sites of innocent
flirtations or more questionable encounters. I was told, although I was unable to verify the report, that at major shrines such as the tomb of the
eighth imam, Reza, in Mashhad or that of his sister Maʿsumeh in Qum,
a woman may indicate that she is available by wearing her veil (*chador*)
inside out. Author Ibrahim Golestan has described illicit goings-on at a
shrine in his short story *Sefar-e ʿEsmat* (Esmat's Trip). In this story a destitute woman visits a shrine and is approached by a low-level clergyman,
who as it turns out is actually a thinly disguised pimp recruiting women.
It is sometimes said that the possibility of temporary marriage (*sigheh*) in
Shiʿi Islam has been exploited to facilitate this kind of relationship. How-

ever, these doubts about pilgrimage tend to surface in jokes and offhand remarks. I never encountered a woman who had been prevented from frequenting a shrine because of suspicions regarding her motives.

Apart from the obvious opportunity to get out of the house, women go to shrines for a number of different types of activities, religious, social, and personal. Women sometimes arrange events, such as Qur'an-reading classes and prayer sessions, at shrines. Special times appointed for visits are sometimes announced by the shrine or, more often, are a matter of tradition and so common knowledge. Women are frequently the majority of visitors at such times, especially at small neighborhood shrines. The women gathered there are likely to include groups of friends, all contributing to a convivial and supportive atmosphere. The women who visit the shrine share their faith and their sympathy. For example, on one visit to a small underground shrine I met an elderly woman who recounted to each woman at the shrine in turn the story of her son's automobile accident. Her son was at that moment in the hospital. In each instance, the other woman comforted her and assured her that her son would be fine, giving her the solace and encouragement she so much needed at the time.

Other pilgrimages occur as a woman chooses, not according to any specific schedule. A woman may prefer to avoid busy days and instead go to a shrine at a time when she knows it will be quiet, facilitating private prayer and communion with the saint. There are many immaterial benefits of pilgrimage. One woman told me that she enjoys ziarat because it is soothing, another described the experience as "heart-opening," and a third assured me that my heart would be enlightened by taking part in pilgrimage.

Anyone having a problem—emotional, spiritual, or material—may take it to a saint in the hope of finding some solution. The saints are felt to sympathize with men and women whose situations in some way parallel their own in life. Accordingly, women in Shiraz are able to find a sympathetic ear when appealing to female saints. Two shrines in Shiraz specialize in bringing about marriages, and at both the saint in residence was in life an unmarried woman. At another shrine it is said that the pregnant wife of its saint is also entombed there. Not surprisingly, the saint himself is inclined to assist women hoping for an easy childbirth and the birth of a son.

If a woman finds a particular imamzadeh to be helpful, she may continue to seek help at his or her tomb. The relationship established between the woman and the saint may last a lifetime and prove very comforting to her in times of need. She knows that there will always be someone to whom she can appeal.

The relationship individuals have with the imamzadehs is intensely personal, and one of its strengths lies in this quality. On one occasion I was surprised to find a woman shaking the grating around the tomb of Imamzadeh-ye Ibrahim, demanding his help. She threatened that if he failed, she would inform his father, the seventh imam. I subsequently learned that the pattern of alternately imploring and haranguing is very common and that people often have personal conversations with the saints and address letters to them.

Clearly one attractive element of the local pilgrimage is the fact that pilgrims can make requests of the imamzadehs. The way in which the process of asking for and potentially receiving favors proceeds is also important, which, as Fatima Mernissi has pointed out, is particularly appealing to women.[2] In making vows at the shrines, women are able to take charge over some aspect of their lives and attempt to bring control into their own hands. A doctor must be paid for his services regardless of success, but a saint is recompensed only in the event that he or she proves to be of help. This is especially important to women who, whether for social, economic, or political reasons, are unable to exert much control in their everyday lives. Even for those strong women who conduct their daily affairs as they wish, there are always discrete events which do not yield to conventional means of redress and on account of which women may seek divine aid. Difficult in-laws, barrenness, the desire for a son, or problems with a husband all may prompt visits to shrines.

The performance of local pilgrimage, then, has much to offer women. On a religious level, it allows them to play a central role in ritual; on a social level, it provides women with an opportunity to visit with one another in an approved setting; and on a personal level, it offers women a place in which to experience contact with divinity and attempt to control their lives in ways meaningful to them as individuals in their own right.

Discussions with men in Shiraz suggested a basic connection between beliefs about women and the character of local pilgrimage. In general, men tended to make disparaging remarks about women's participation in pilgrimage activity. They attributed the amount of time women were able to spend visiting shrines to women's leisure, unburdened as they supposedly are by men's important tasks. This opinion is related to the general understanding of the nature of women I encountered in Shiraz. On numerous occasions I was told that women are emotional creatures, easily swayed by sentiment and inclined to be irrational. Men were described as serious, likely to reason clearly, immune to emotional concerns. In support of this stereotypical view, I was referred to passages in the Qur²an concerning women (4:34) and reminded that a woman cannot act as a legal witness (2:282). Two women can serve as one witness, I was told, because two would correct the emotionally colored report provided by only one. I found that women generally accepted this view of their nature, some feeling that the weaknesses were inevitable, others regarding them as tendencies which could be surmounted.

These beliefs are related to views of women's religious behavior. Most men I consulted felt that women place too much emphasis on the social aspects of religious gatherings and are less well educated about Islam in general. Considering the pleasure women derive from the social atmosphere sometimes present at shrines and the fact that they find attendance at the mosque so problematic, these criticisms are not entirely without foundation. However, women's religious activities may be viewed in other, more flattering lights. Women who live opposite the shrine of Seyyed Fakhr al-Din in the south of Shiraz agreed that women make local pilgrimages more often than men (although men do so too) but felt that, since women have more time for these activities, they developed more faith by doing them.

A more penetrating explanation of women's involvement in pilgrimage was implied by a young man who worked at a local handicrafts shop. He had made a vow to a popular local saint but had not gone to the saint's tomb at a local shrine to do so. When I questioned further, he first voiced the same scorn as other men had: "Women everywhere devote more time to practices such as ziarat than men; women are more idle than men." Then he added a revealing statement: If he has a request for a saint, he may send his wife to the shrine to make it for him. She has the time to go, but also "women are without pride." Men have pride and do not like to display weakness or need in public.

It is in keeping with the view of women as more emotional and less rational than men that women perform ziarat to local shrines on behalf of their family members. In doing so they discharge part of their responsibility for the health and well-being of their relatives. This is not to suggest that men are not interested in local pilgrimage or in making vows, just that they express their religiosity in different ways.

The young man's remarks also suggest that much of the behavior that occurs at a shrine, such as expressing deep emotion and stating one's needs and perhaps shortcomings publicly, is not in keeping with notions of manliness. In effect, much of what takes place at a shrine involves a female mode of behavior, regardless of whether the pilgrim is a man or a woman. It is these "female" aspects of the pilgrimage which are often called into question. In the course of a discussion I had with men at a religious bookstore in Shiraz, the man behind the counter recommended a book to me: *Ziarat: Truth or Superstition?* The title indicates the crux of the problem. Men and some women formally educated in religion are ill at ease with the practice, while many other women are devoted to it. There is no definite proscription of the practice, and some traditions (*hadiths*) support and encourage it. Paying one's respects at a gravesite is laudable, but the way in which it is done during the performance of local pilgrimage is regarded by many as questionable.

In making pilgrimages to local shrines, men and women have the opportunity to argue with their "betters" and, within limits, to challenge the given order of things. They are also able to express their feelings in ways that are otherwise inappropriate. In so doing they are able to shape their ritual practice to their own requirements.

The pattern of challenge, harangue, expression of deep emotion, and voluntarism in ritual is foreign to the mosque. The opposition between the shrine and the mosque is described by Brian Spooner in connection with his descriptions of the religion of the shrine and the official religion, which "contains rules of ritual prayers, fasting, celebration, mourning and general conduct, which concern the will rather than the heart."[3] He identifies the first of these two strains of religion in Iran as unconscious, while the official religion is the conscious religion. I suggest that this opposition is at base a description of the difference between female and male modes elaborated in a religious context.

It is not surprising that funeral observances in which women are involved are more likely to take place within the home or in a shrine than in a mosque. It is not a time for dry observance of the passing of a fellow human being and loved one but a time to rage and lament, in so doing accentuating the sense of one's own life, and this is inappropriate in the formal setting of a mosque. The way in which shrine space is used at a funeral reflects differences in men's and women's styles of interaction, styles reflected in overall religious behavior. Men tend to be restrained and formal. They sit on folding chairs in the shrine courtyard, facing the officiating priest. They look down, their hands held over their eyes. At times they sob quietly or perhaps engage in muted conversation with the men seated in adjacent chairs. Tea is placed on small tables between the chairs. The atmosphere is highly formal and subdued; spaces are clearly defined, in keeping with the nature of official religion as Spooner describes it.

In contrast, women at a shrine funeral sit on the floor inside the wall and perhaps around the central tomb. At one end of the room, backs against the wall, sit the grieving women of the deceased's family. Women attending the funeral first approach them to pay their respects and extend condolences, perhaps sitting with the bereaved women for a time and weeping with them. Then the women move back as others come to take their place and commiserate with the "receiving line." As the guests move outward through the rows of seated women, the tone of the gathering becomes less somber until, in the outer circles, women are busily gossiping, catching up on the news of those more distant relatives and friends whom they see only on such formal occasions. All the while the seated women enjoy the tea and ice cream or sherbet that is served to the guests. The intimacy which prevails at women's gatherings is both physical, enforced by the pressure of bodies against one another as women plop down on the crowded floor, and social, as women exchange information and embraces and discuss their personal problems and their aches and pains. Just as the men's behavior suits the character of the "official religion," so do women behave in a way more consonant with the "religion of the shrine."

The fact that women are associated with local pilgrimage in Iran is neither accidental nor incidental. Men are associated with the mosque, religious texts, reasoned theological discussions, formal ritual assemblies—in short, with the intellectual aspects of religion. Women's association with local pilgrimage points out that it is bound up with things of the heart, the troubling aspect of life which questions, unsettles, and answers obliquely. Women in Muslim Iran are regarded as frivolous, emotional, irrational, and at times dangerous; the things with which they are associated are consequently dismissed as either inconsequential or at times downright suspect. Even women's dreams are described in Persian as *chap* (unreliable, off the mark), literally "left."

Women are ritually polluted with the messy business of menstruation and childbirth, but these polluting elements are paradoxically life-giving. Similarly, local pilgrimage is disorderly and informal, but what goes on at the local shrines energizes religion. Ziarat gives scope to the personal and difficult aspects of life and allows both men and, especially, women to express their emotional sides—to grieve and wail in an approved setting and to celebrate joyously with others.

AFTERWORD

Some shrine sites have altered in specific ways since I left Iran in January of 1979. I did not return to Iran until the spring of 2000, when I was able to spend almost six weeks there, primarily in Shiraz. During that short time, I visited many places, including shrines, where I had done research over twenty years before. I was not in Shiraz long enough to conduct a detailed survey of all the shrines and shrine-related activity that interested me, but I did come away with some sense of the changes that had occurred in the intervening years. This afterword provides an update that illuminates changes in the relationship between women and shrines in Shiraz under the Islamic Republic. The changes I observed and which I feel most confident discussing are physical; they reflect distinct alterations in the ways shrines are used and managed.

The first changes I noticed in Shiraz were evident immediately upon leaving the airport. Traffic was far heavier, and pollution consequently greater, than when I had lived in the city twenty years before. The crush of traffic was related to a phenomenon evident throughout the city: the enormous growth in population. The streets and some buildings appeared in poor repair, a fact that was later commented upon by some city residents. They felt that, while Isfahan had been much improved during recent years due to the efforts of the city's citizens and an active mayor, Shiraz had enjoyed no such positive attention. However, it did not take long for me to learn that buildings of historical and religious importance had undergone or were in the process of renovation.

Before the revolution of 1979, religious symbolism in Iran was most apparent on religious holidays, and especially during the Shi'i mourning months of Muharram and Sefar, when bazaars and some homes were decorated with black banners and pennants. Now colorful paintings of religious leaders and martyrs decorate the sides of buildings; religion is officially present and called to mind daily, rather than on a seasonal basis, in government and other institutions. The Islamic aspect of the Islamic Republic of Iran manifests itself in the design of shrines as well. Twenty years ago, the design of large shrines conformed to what might be called an official shrine style, which incorporated certain predictable elements. Domes decorated with tilework, interior walls bright with mirror mosaics, polished stone floors covered with high-quality carpets, and cage-like silver tomb enclosures (*zarihs*) made the largest shrines resemble one another, although their exact forms and degree of elaboration varied. Smaller shrines, where women were able to pay brief visits, or longer ones when they felt so inclined, were more individual. They were not fancily decorated with fine, bright stuff, but, like those who visited them, appeared less showy. Domes seldom capped small neighborhood shrines; interior walls of plaster were decorated with pictures, some framed; flooring was simple and, when covered, spread with locally made tribal carpets or simple cotton rugs (*zilus*). The green drapery occasionally spread over sarcophagi was described as the saint's garments, often donated by grateful petitioners. Modest wooden enclosures, sometimes but not always painted green, surrounded the saints' tombs. Frequently the tombs were topped with vases of artificial flowers. The degree of dustiness suggested the frequency of attention given to the small shrines. A fan, perhaps inscribed with a dedication, might hang from the ceiling near a simple light fixture. The entrance to the shrine might be marked only by the green paint around a door or window. And yet these simple shrines were often cozy and welcoming places where women could stop by, secure in the knowledge that they would encounter neighbors or other women. Men were very unlikely to be present at certain times, especially during the workday. The only men who might be around during the day were the shrine custodian, a cleric, and perhaps a blind man ready to recite a sermon for a modest fee.

It seemed right to begin my visits by paying my respects to the city's senior saint, Shah Cheragh. I had heard that metal posts had been put in place to divide women pilgrims from men who might jostle against them as they circumambulated the tomb. Rather than what I had supposed would be a line of posts ringing the tomb to direct and divide circumambulation, I was surprised to find the shrine divided in two by a fence: the right side as one faced the tomb was for women, while men were directed to the left. Fence is too common a word for the lovely divider that separated men's from women's space. The divider was perhaps just over six feet tall; visitors on both sides could see the top of the tomb enclosure and admire the grand ceiling and upper walls with their beautiful mirror mosaic. The divider was made of arched sections of silver, embossed with the same floral designs that elaborated the zarih. Frosted glass filled the spaces in what would otherwise have been open areas beneath the arches. The fence was opaque and effective and, most surprising to me, it prevented circumambulation by both men and women. I had thought of circumambulation as an essential element of a pilgrimage visit; clearly that was no longer the case. On their side, women walked along the section of the zarih available to them, clung to the bars, rubbed them, kissed the enclosure, and often wept, prayed aloud, or mumbled their requests to Shah Cheragh. Other women sat further away on the carpeted floor to read, pray, or tend children.

The shrine complex had been much renovated and expanded since last I was there. The large courtyard shared by Shah Cheragh and another, smaller shrine—that of his brother, Seyyed Mir Mohammad—was paved, included a large fountain, and was surrounded by new buildings. A book and souvenir shop had been added just outside the entrance gate to the courtyard. Just up the street the Bazaar of Shah Cheragh had been built, and included shops with goods likely to appeal to shrine visitors. Inside the courtyard official offices stretched along one wall; a large museum and extensive facilities, including restrooms, occupied buildings that formed a facing wall. When I visited the museum at No Ruz, the two-week New Year holiday in Iran, the museum featured an exhibit of personal effects of local young men killed in the recent war with Iraq. The exhibit and its location in the shrine museum underscored the connection of religion and government. Personal effects on view included soldiers' prayer beads, compasses, eyeglasses, shoes, headbands printed with religious inscriptions, letters, and personal photographs. I was struck by the conjunction of religious objects, military paraphernalia, and items of personal importance; the young men who died were powerfully present in their few displayed possessions. Religious paintings and other objects in the shrine's collection, which had been on view in a small museum in the main shrine building before, were now arranged in cabinets and on the walls round the room; exhibit cases filled the central space and contained temporary exhibits. Also on show was a model section of battleground territory, probably well known to most visitors. The government's presence and a reference to political circumstance were as evident in an addition to the Seyyed Mir Mohammad shrine across the courtyard. Added to the shrine since last I was there was a smaller zarih, wrought in the same form as larger zarihs around important saints' tombs. Inside was buried Ayatollah Seyyed Abd ol-Din Husain Dastgheib, former Friday imam of the important nearby congregation mosque. Ayatollah Dastgheib was assassinated in a politically motivated bombing during the early years of the Islamic Republic, and so is a martyr. The fact that the guardianship of the Seyyed Mir Mohammad shrine had long been in his family dictated Dastgheib's burial in the shrine. The form of his burial place, akin to saints' tombs, was more surprising to me, especially because visitors to the shrine circumambulated his zarih and addressed him just as they did the nearby saint. No dividers separated men's and women's space at the shrine.

The Shah Cheragh shrine complex was decorated for No Ruz, well appointed, and prepared to welcome large numbers of visitors, including foreign tourists. This fact was made evident to me on the first day that I visited the shrine. As I was seated in the ladies' area inside the shrine, a young employee came up and asked if I was foreign and, if so, could I speak English. When I answered yes to both questions, wondering why he inquired, he was very pleased. He asked me to correct the speech he had prepared in English to introduce foreign tourists to Shah Cheragh. It was a very welcoming talk, designed to acquaint visitors with the resident saint and his importance. On a subsequent visit I saw a cluster of European tourists gathering around their tour guide outside the entrance to the courtyard. Never once had I seen foreign tourists at Shah Cheragh during my previous stay in Shiraz.

A plan for the expansion of the Shah Cheragh complex, and the traffic circle and streets immediately outside it, was in place before the Islamic Republic was established. Although the renovation had not begun by the time I left Iran in 1979, I was not surprised by it. The extent of attention lavished on smaller shrines, however, did take me by surprise. Not only were popular small shrines enjoying renovation, the style of renovation mimicked the decoration of larger shrines, such as Shah Cheragh. A tiled dome, a much smaller version of that over Shah Cheragh, had been placed over the Seyyed Taj al-Din Gharib shrine building. Lovely older tiles, with floral designs and medallions depicting Imam Husain's half brother, Abbas, a descendant of whom is buried in the shrine, had been left in place around the doorway. But the courtyard had been paved, an office with an Iranian flag on the desk inside added at its far side, a silver zarih placed inside; mirrorwork was being affixed to walls as I visited. I knew that renovations had been planned years ago, but I never expected them to take the standard, official form I encountered. Most surprising was the aluminum fence that proceeded from just inside the door to the centrally located tomb; another segment of fencing continued on the other side to the far wall and divided the shrine space in two. Just inside the door a sign directed women to the left, men to the right. Women seated inside the shrine, but not far from the entrance, were able to carry on conversations with the men who sat near the doorway. Other women preferred to sit further inside, where they could not be seen from the door. The fence was exactly that, an aluminum fence made of upright pieces with spaces between them. To make the division opaque, pieces of green canvas were draped casually over it. The fence had a makeshift look about it; I suspected it was temporarily in place while a more appropriate formal divider, perhaps like that at Shah Cheragh, was being fabricated. I later saw a similar temporary divider in place at the larger and very popular Seyyed Ala ol-Din Husain (Astaneh) shrine. Since my last visit that too had been much expanded, with new minarets, an impressive paved entrance area, and a large hall and clinic under construction to the rear and side of the shrine building. At neither of these very popular shrines was circumambulation possible.

The separation of men's and women's public spaces in the Islamic Republic was at times convenient. Women's areas at the back of buses were invariably less crowded than the front sections where men stood, crushed together at busy hours; women usually found places to sit comfortably. And yet I lamented the separation of women's space in shrines, and the apparent creation of an officially mandated shrine style. Perhaps I simply suffered from nostalgia, and yet I wondered how women's experience of shrines, and what I had understood as their enjoyment of relative freedom of movement and proximity to the saints, would be affected by the changes. In part, because of the new dividers and official offices where men supervised activities, I felt that there was a more pronounced male control of religious space at the most popular shrines. The most extensive renovations and addition of what appeared to be bureaucratic offices occurred at shrines most likely to generate sizable incomes from visitors' contributions. Shrine enclosures were equipped with slots, like mail slots, into which contributions could be placed. The heap of bills inside the shrines suggested that there has been no diminution in the importance of requesting the saints' help. Perhaps the money could underwrite the costs of shrine renovation, some of which resulted in greater comfort for visitors. But the addition of shops and other formal buildings appeared calculated to increase the income shrines would generate, and to facilitate control of the space as well as its revenue. In some cases, the control of space might be necessary. Over twenty years ago the Seyyed Taj ol-Din Gharib shrine was presided over by a custodian whom I always saw there. It was he who explained the shrine's specialization as a site where oaths were sworn, and he who lamented that we now live in an age of deceit. Twenty years ago the custodian assured me that the resident saint's illustrious ancestor, Abbas, would punish those who took his name in vain when they swore oaths. Then the custodian added that it took longer for the punishment to take effect in the increasingly corrupt society in which we lived. I was saddened to learn that some years ago he became a victim of the deterioration he decried; he was murdered during a robbery of the shrine, and is now buried in the shrine's courtyard. The aspects of control I regret may be necessary to safeguard the shrine and its visitors. Increasing population density and economic pressure, particularly in certain areas, have affected shrines as well as the people who are their neighbors.

Some smaller shrines have also enjoyed renovation, but without the division of male and female space. I don't know how decisions are made to divide certain spaces and not others, but I did enjoy visits to two, admittedly less crowded, shrines popular with women. I wondered if they were slated for the installation of dividers in the future, or if the small, less popular shrines were regarded as not requiring them. In any case, the shrines I visited were frequented by women, some of whom spent large amounts of time in praying, simply sitting, or talking quietly with friends. At one shrine, watched over by an elderly couple, the wife welcomed women to the redecorated shrine. The painted zarih I remembered had been replaced by a silver-toned metal structure, a crude imitation of the zarihs at better-known shrines.

I was left with many questions and without the time to search for answers. Apart from the obvious absence of circumambulation, do women use divided shrine space differently from that in undivided shrines? Do women favor one type of shrine over another for particular kinds of activity? If women do feel that some shrines' spaces have been appropriated by male authorities, have other forms of religious activity exclusive to women developed to take their place? How will the new hall attached to Seyyed Ala ol-din Husain (Astaneh) be used? Will it be devoted to large gatherings primarily, if not exclusively, attended by men, such as those I saw broadcast on television during Muharram from a large hall in Tehran? Such new spaces for collective ritual activity are associated with gatherings on a scale that seldom occurred when I was in Iran in the 1970s. Do women have a place in these activities? How are decisions about shrine renovation and allotment of space reached, and to what extent are decisions made locally or nationally? Are renovations paid for by shrine revenue, or from the general coffers of the government Endowments Office? Does the official attention given to shrines imply that local pilgrimage has entered the realm of orthodox Shiʻi behavior? Official sanction has seldom influenced personal opinion in Iran, but I would like to know more about the relative approbation of various forms of religious activity, particularly those involving women, in present-day Iran. My questions await answers, and what I hope will be another trip to Iran in less than twenty years.

NOTE

1. I was advised that, to avoid pressing against men performing the same action, women should hold back and not circumambulate the tomb when a shrine is crowded. In this instance, as so many others, ideal prescriptions and actual behavior often differ markedly.

2. Fatima Mernissi, "Women, Saints, and Sanctuaries," *Signs: Journal of Women in Culture and Society* 3, no. 1 (autumn 1977): 104.

3. Brian Spooner, "The Function of Religion in Persian Society," *Iran* 1 (1963): 93.

28. Islamic Teaching among Sunni Women in Syria

Annabelle Böttcher

Within Islam, devout women may emerge as scholars and teachers on both local and university levels. Women may teach religious studies at schools, in homes, or in the mosques. In some countries, women are now emerging as teachers in Quranic schools as well as professors of religious studies at graduate schools. Well-educated women are writing books on Islamic feminism. Women combine their desire to master the basic texts of Islam with work and their care of their families; for instance, some stop by the mosque for a lesson on their way home from work. In socially conservative countries, discussions of religion and social issues may occur in private salons held in homes. These discussions may focus on both classical and reformist religious writings. They take place privately because in many countries governments interpret public displays of religious interest as political acts and forbid them. —Eds.

In contemporary Syria the transmission of religious knowledge among Muslim women has undergone a revival to an extent previously unknown in the Middle East. Over the past few years, most Muslim women and girls have participated in some form of Islamic teaching. Female Sunni Muslims play a major role in propagating Islamic practices and values in Syria. Many of them teach Sufism, a form of spiritual or mystical Islam. Women who are searching for alternative, flexible approaches to religion often feel attracted to Sufism because it offers more opportunities for female participation in worship.

Within Sunni Islam, Sufism constitutes an approach to religion which focuses on spiritual concerns—a Muslim's relation to God. Sober interpretations of conservative or *Wahhabi*-influenced Islam (the dominant interpretation in Saudi Arabia) often criticize Sufism. The division between these two currents in Islam is less clear-cut than it often appears in the polemic literature or in contexts where conflicts might arise for political reasons. In Syria, Sufi Islam has a long-established tradition of peaceful coexistence with other Islamic interpretations. While Sufi Muslims may belong to either of the two major sects of Islam (Sunni, Shi'a), in this paper I look at Sufi Sunni Muslims as well as Sunni Muslims who do not follow a Sufi path. Since many Muslims affiliate with a Sufi order as well as being observant, practicing Sunni Muslims, it can be hard to single out Sufis, and in the material I present below, the reader will notice that these lines blur. The Alawi tradition, which the Asad family and other members of the military and political elite follow, is distinct from both Sufism and Sunni Islam.

There are social, economic, political, and religious reasons for women's enthusiastic response to the new opportunities which Islamic revivalism opens up for them outside the private sphere of their houses. In a society as conservative as Syria, girls and women hardly ever leave the house unaccompanied and usually only for a legitimate reason, like visiting family, shopping, or going to the doctor. Pursuing an Islamic education and practicing religion are considered appropriate reasons for leaving one's domestic space. Sixty-year-old traditional women from conservative Damascene neighborhoods like al-Midan join their grandnieces alongside the Western-educated daughters of government ministers for prayers and weekly Quranic lessons. These lessons are a means of transmitting Islamic knowledge to all social levels in Syrian society.

Women pray and study together, but they also exchange news about family problems and help each other. They buy and sell a wide variety of items, such as clothes, prayer beads, fabrics, books, and even apartments. They arrange marriages among their sons and daughters, and they inform each other of job openings. In an economic situation which is particularly burdensome for the lower and middle classes, marriage has become an important way for girls and women to enlarge their family network by adding non-kinship units. A conservative Muslim girl does not have many opportunities to meet a suitable candidate for marriage. In the poor economy Syrian men have difficulty paying for the high cost of a wedding and the establishment of a household. Quite often they marry foreign women, thus adding foreign competition to the already tight domestic marriage market. And when Syrian men decide to marry Syrian girls, the general trend of Islamization has led many of them to choose a more traditional bride. For them, a wife who wears a veil represents a guarantee against "Western influences" in their family life. This places the responsibility of teaching both practical and theoretical aspects of Islam on the wives, who have become increasingly responsible for teaching Islamic knowledge and values to their children and safeguarding a proper Islamic lifestyle. This development is based on a consensus among women and men on the important role Muslim women play in preserving Islamic values.

The mounting interest of Sunni Muslim women in their religious and cultural heritage has become a sensitive political subject for a regime which is skeptical of any activity related to Sunni Islam. In Syria key military and political positions are mostly held by Alawis, a Shiʿi sect representing a minority of Syrians. Since 1963 they have taken an increasingly large role in political and economic decision making. In 1970 Hafiz al-Asad, himself an Alawi, took over the presidency, and Sunni influence declined further. The Sunni majority never accepted the power shift. Since a series of bloody confrontations between the regime and the Sunni majority in the 1980s, the regime has begun to show more subtlety in responding to the strong demand for religious participation. In this policy shift Sunni women have become key players. The regime knows that it cannot easily interfere in the female sphere, which is sacrosanct for both religious and cultural reasons. If the Syrian secret service started harassing female Sunnis by interrogating or imprisoning them, this would cause an outburst among Muslims in Syria and the Islamic world. In traditional Muslim societies female space, including that of devotional practice, is not easily accessible to men. Thus it has remained one of the few spaces which are difficult for the regime to control. The women have taken advantage of governmental hesitation by working toward their religious, and hence political, goal of Islamizing Syrian civil society.

TRANSMITTING AND STRENGTHENING SUFI KNOWLEDGE

One of the major tenets of Sufism is that students must be taught by Sufi guides, as opposed to studying on their own. Most Sufis are usually affiliated with a Sufi order, an organized group with a hierarchical structure and a *shaykh* as its leader. Men and women participate equally in the activities of a Sufi order, as members of sisterhoods and brotherhoods. In the past two decades Sufi women have begun to assume more prominent roles in teaching Sufi Islam. The teaching is usually done in one of two ways: a *dars* or a *dhikr*. A dars is a lesson about some aspect of Islamic belief or practice, taught from a Sufi perspective. A dhikr is a religious ceremony which includes prayers and the repetition of the *silsila*, the names of the leading shaykhs of the Sufi order from the Prophet Muhammad's day until the present. While a dars teaches principles of religion, participation in a dhikr is worship. Both methods of learning have the same goal: to advance on the path to God, to experience God.

In September 1994 I was invited to participate in two dhikr sessions held by members of the Naqshbandi sisterhood in Bait ʿAmr, in the traditional al-Midan quarter of Damascus. This area is one of the strongholds of traditional Sunni Islam in the capital, where many of the social and religious customs of previous centuries have been preserved. A large majority of the Muslim women living in al-Midan are veiled. A growing number even cover their faces partly or totally with the *mandil*, a black veil placed on top of the ordinary veil and folded to cover the lower half of the face, the chin, the mouth, and sometimes the nose. Usually they cover their eyes with dark sunglasses as well.

To reach Bait ʿAmr, where the sessions are held weekly, one has to pass the Sinan mosque in al-Midan. From Shahrur Square, a long street on the right leads one directly to the Naqshbandi mosque, through narrow lanes lined with entrances to small shops and traditional Arabic houses, often built of mud and wood. Occasionally modern concrete buildings break brutally into the pattern of the traditional quarters. The two-story Arabic house of Bait ʿAmr is adjacent to the Naqshbandi mosque. Everyone in the neighborhood knows that on Wednesday a dhikr for women is held there. After having passed through the front door one enters a vast courtyard with lemon trees and a stone fountain, around which the family rooms are grouped. Three families of the same clan share the house; one family lives on each side. The main part is occupied by the female head of the sisterhood, Umm Nabil, and the other parts by her two sons and their families. Large pictures of the tomb of Shaykh Khalid al-Naqshband are hung in the *liwan* (the reception room adjoining the courtyard). Shaykh Khalid is one of the most prominent shaykhs of the Naqshbandi Sufi order. His tomb is located at the foot of Mount Qasyun in Damascus. Umm Nabil's most famous ancestor, Shaykh ʿAbd al-Qadir al-Khani, was a close companion of Shaykh Khalid at the beginning of the nineteenth century. Umm Nabil is a direct descendant of Shaykh al-Khani and thus her lineage qualifies her to preserve the traditions of the Naqshbandiyya. Even though she is the head of a sisterhood, she modestly refuses the title of a shaykha and instead is called *al-Hajja*, a title bestowed on all who complete the pilgrimage to Mecca, or Umm Nabil. According to her daughters, she was taught by her mother, the Shaykha Khadija. After she had spent years studying and practicing Sufism, her mother issued her a written *ijazah*, a certificate of competence to teach the subject, and then appointed her to succeed her in the path. Umm Nabil's designation as her mother's successor had been preceded by a dream her mother had in which the prophet Muhammad confirmed her decision. In 1984 the shaykha died and Umm Nabil took over a flourishing Sufi order with about 250 female disciples. Since then, the number has diminished to around a hundred. Now that Umm Nabil herself has become an elderly lady with many grandchildren, she wonders if her daughter, Umm Fawaz, will succeed her in leading the sisterhood.

About half an hour before the start of the dhikr, groups of women in black or dark blue coats flock through the main entrance, chatting and laughing. Once they have reached the privacy of the inner courtyard, they take off their coats and mandil. All are dressed in white blouses, white veils, and black skirts. Uniform clothing is quite common among the various female Islamic groups in Damascus. A knowledgeable local can tell from the color, cut, and style of the clothes which movement or group a woman belongs to and even where she is situated within the group hierarchy. In a Sufi order the disciples often indicate their degrees of spiritual experience by the way they bind their scarf, but the al-Khani women do not do this. For the time of the dhikr, which lasts about one hour, no men are allowed inside the house. This prohibition is respected by the male members of the family as well as the neighborhood. The women gather in the liwan, where they greet each other and engage in conversation while sitting on couches, on the windowsills, and on the ground. News about families, weddings, births, children, and travels is exchanged, and then the dhikr starts. Umm Nabil usually sits opposite the entrance door, on a sofa below a picture of the tomb of Shaykh Khalid al-Naqshband.

On the two occasions I participated in the dhikr, the shaykha could not attend because of illness. The dhikr still had her blessings, since she stayed in the same house, in her bedroom on the second floor. One of her disciples led the dhikr while Umm Nabil's daughters went back and forth between their mother's bedroom and the session. Small booklets were distributed, each one containing a different section (*juz²*) of the Qur²an. Each of the participants quietly recited a different section, so that at the end of the first part of the dhikr the whole Qur²an had been read. This brings special blessing to the session and is done each time. After the reading the booklets were collected. The woman leading the dhikr started to recite the *khatm*, a collection of repetitive prayers, such as *astaghfiru allah:* I ask forgiveness of God. In this she was helped by an assistant. The repetitive recitation of the names of God and other phrases are the essential part of the dhikr. No music was allowed; however, the collective chant of the women had its own melodic rhythm.

At the end of the dhikr the women left the liwan to take some refreshments in the courtyard. They were served by one of the shaykha's daughters, who was dressed elegantly in a long red *galabiyya* and jewelry. Some of the guests were admitted to the bedroom upstairs to visit the sick shaykha. A long set of stone stairs led to the upper floor and into a cozy apartment. The bedroom of the shaykha was furnished with wooden furniture and a carpet. From her windows she could see into the courtyard. Smoking a cigarette, she sat in her bed and chatted with her family and guests, who sat on chairs around her bed. Other members of the family entered the room with trays and served the shaykha and her guests, who were telling anecdotes and laughing at jokes. Relatives came and left constantly; children played at the end of the bed. Older children returning from school poured in and were greeted by the attendants.

Many of those participating were born into the Sufi order. It is part of their religious heritage. Some join the Sufi order by choice. One woman in her twenties told me that while living in her parents' house, she had participated in a nearby Naqshbandi sisterhood. Then she married and moved to the al-Midan quarter at the other end of the town. She had neither the time nor the means to travel the distance from her house to the mosque where the dhikr was held, so she changed sisterhoods. She described herself as being on the verge of "taking the path," taking the oath of allegiance and becoming a disciple.

The demand for lessons in Islam—among Sufis as well as Sunni Muslims with no Sufi affiliation—has been so overwhelming among all levels of society that informal study groups in private houses and courses in mosques and schools can hardly cope with the demand. Classes are mushrooming all over Damascus. Many of them are improvised and given weekly or on occasions such as the celebration of the birth of a child, a family member's recovery from illness, or during *mawlid*, the celebration of the birth of the Prophet Muhammad. Engagement and wedding parties in conservative families often include a short lesson on the duties of husband and wife. At some occasions a female band and choir perform religious songs. These lessons or religious lectures can last from ten minutes to several hours, as the audience wishes. Some of them just teach the basics of Islam, like prayer or fasting; others explain complex issues and demand decades of study as background.

TEACHING ISLAM

The classic setting for teaching Islam is usually called a dars (lesson) or *majlis al-ᶜilm* (session of knowledge). There are variations depending on the Sunni school of law being taught. In Syria the majority of Sunni Muslims belong to either the Hanafi or the Shafii school of law. In Damascus to attend or give a dars, and thus to make *daᶜwa* (a mission or call to Islam), has become very fashionable for girls and women at all social levels. In a dars, the basics of Islam are taught, like prayers, almsgiving, fasting, and how to apply divine rules in daily life. The latter area concerns all aspects of life; for women, areas of interest include child education, marital life, and family management. Lessons are organized in two different settings, an informal one in private houses and an institutionalized one in mosques, schools, and universities.

Shaykha Waffa Kaftaru has the largest following of all officially tolerated female Muslim leaders in Syria. She has been allowed by the regime to teach in one of the biggest mosques in Damascus. Her father, Shaykh Ahmad Kaftaru, is the Syrian Grand Mufti and a close friend of the Asad family. The Kaftaru family network enjoyed more privileges in the Islamic arena than any other family network or group in Syria. Anisa Waffa, or al-Hajja, as she is called by her followers, has studied Islamic law with a number of Syrian shaykhs, including her father. She graduated from the

Faculty of Islamic Law of the University of Damascus and from her father's private Islamic university in the Abu al-Nur Islamic Center (ANIC). She began teaching in public as a teenager and has continued an unprecedented career as one of the most active and successful missionaries in Syria. She headed women's academic education at her father's Islamic center, the ANIC, until 1999. Her most popular dars was given there on Wednesdays in the main prayer room, with about two thousand female followers in attendance. Even though Shaykha Waffa is a Naqshbandi Sufi, her dars was a general lesson in Islam and did not include explicit reference to Sufi Islam. It was aimed at both Sufi and non-Sufi Muslims. The dars started in the late afternoon and lasted about two hours, during which four out of seven floors, including the main prayer room, were reserved for the female participants. They entered the mosque from the women's entrance, but at the end of the dars the crowd left through the main entrance of the ANIC, while the men discreetly turned their heads away until the main prayer room was reopened for them. Women had their preferred sitting places on the floor of the mosque, and when they belonged to a study group within the female Sufi order with a female teacher—herself a disciple of Shaykha Waffa—they usually sat with her. Seats in the first row close to the shaykha were reserved for special guests and members of the Kaftaru family. The shaykha sat in a little wooden chair which was put in front of the *mihrab* (prayer niche). It looked like a small box into which the shaykha climbed by means of a little ladder on the side.

Girls from the ANIC school and the four Islamic universities, as well as women from the neighborhood, attended the dars. Most of them came from simple educational backgrounds and wanted to learn the basics of Islam. The arrival of the shaykha was announced by a band playing drums and singing. The band members were trained in the ANIC in how to compose and sing songs about Allah and the Prophet Muhammad. Usually the musical introduction lasted twenty minutes to half an hour. After the arrival of the shaykha the dars began. I regularly attended the lessons for a period of four years during the 1990s. The basics of Islam, the Qurʾan, general features of Islamic history, the biography of the Prophet Muhammad, the background of the religious calendar, and so on were taught in a way that was understandable to girls and women with little previous background. Political and economic conditions in Syria were never criticized. In the end the shaykha always included the Syrian president Hafiz al-Asad in her prayers.

FEMALE ISLAMIZATION AND THE REGIME

This dars is a classic example of teaching a version of official Islam, the Islam of the state, which contributes to the religious and political legitimization of the ruling elite. The female members of this movement constitute a tightly knit network providing a wide variety of social and educational services. They organize charity bazaars, finance the education of girls and women, and help sustain needy families—not to speak of the moral support they give many female Muslims who would otherwise be left isolated in their family or clan. They often mediate for families with problems, especially conflicts between women and their husbands or fathers.

Since any activity among Sunni or Shi'i Muslims is closely watched by the authorities, only very few meetings, in private houses, can be considered "private." As soon as a group of men or women meet, they immediately attract their neighbors' attention, and subsequently that of the secret service. Up to the present many of their activities have been tolerated because the regime has realized that such a broad-based search for religious values within the Sunni society cannot be suppressed in the long run. Besides sincerely searching for spiritual values to counter a trend of globalization and Westernization, many people now find it fashionable to be a practicing Muslim.

Given the difficulty of preventing Islamic education, the political leadership has sought to coopt it by setting up institutes sponsored by the state. Families with an interest in Islamic values start teaching their children at early ages to memorize Quranic verses. The children usually learn parts of the Qur'an by heart and may later join one of the "Hafiz al-Asad Institutes for the Memorization of the Noble Qur'an." These institutes flourish in mosques all over the country, and there the older students usually assist the younger ones. Children join at the age of three and are rewarded for their work with small gifts or sweets. Later, when it is time for the child to enter school, the family can choose an Islamic or a secular school. A growing number of Islamic schools are opening all over the country, where religious subjects are taught in addition to the general curriculum. One of these schools is in the above-mentioned ANIC in Damascus, which is run by Shaykh Ahmad Kaftaru and his clan. The certificates awarded by the Islamic secondary schools are recognized by the state, which enables these students to continue their studies at a state university.

Institutions of higher education, such as the Faculty of Islamic Law of the University of Damascus, also offer training in Islamic law. A number of private universities, such as the ANIC, also teach Islamic law. Here licenses and master's and doctoral degrees are offered. Some introductory courses in Islamic law are also scheduled at the Faculty of Law (*kulliyat al-huquq*) at the University of Damascus and at the University of Aleppo. Even though the number of female students in these programs is quite limited, it is rising. And what is even more important, these young women transmit their knowledge outside the formal academic setting, in small circles in mosques and private houses. I have attended a number of these circles, where renowned Syrian shaykhs and shaykhas teach a group of hand-picked young girls and women such subjects as Arabic grammar, logic, and Islamic jurisprudence. Each week the circle would discuss a paragraph of a famous scholarly work which the students had read and prepared at home. Some particularly talented girls and women come for private lessons.

TOWARD A FEMINIST APPROACH IN ISLAMIC THEOLOGY

Parents can send young girls to private lessons in the neighborhood. Later they move on to more advanced groups covering all aspects of Islamic life, such as the rituals of fasting and praying. Lessons in more advanced topics, such as Quranic exegesis, Islamic law, Islamic history, and Arabic grammar are often given by established male scholars, who open their houses to a small number of female students. These groups concentrate on one book, which they discuss weekly. Each student brings her own copy of the book, in which she takes notes in the margin, continuing a long tradition of annotating the works of previous scholars. The passages are discussed in depth, and other questions not directly related to the subject may evolve. Study of a single book might take several years. Often female members of the shaykh's family participate in the lessons. This makes participation even more acceptable to other families, because they trust the shaykh and know that the girls and women are in an environment suitable to their convictions and reputation. Specially talented girls and women are usually encouraged to continue their studies in their field of interest.

Still, not enough women feel qualified enough to take over advanced Islamic teaching from the shaykhs. With the strong role women are taking in propagating Sunni Islam, one might expect a trend toward an Islamic feminist theology. But these Syrian women still accept the hierarchical order set for them by a patriarchal society. For example, the female Sufi order of the al-Khani family has made no attempt to establish a clear-cut genealogy of female shaykhas, even though any qualified man descending from a line of shaykhs would naturally draw up his ancestry. Their female spiritual leaders do not even assume the title of "shaykha," while less-educated male Sunni Muslims in Syria confidently call themselves shaykhs without meeting resistance. Publications of women Islamic scholars in Syria are still rare and confined to collections of *hadith*, traditional sayings. The few women's works which appear on the market have been encouraged and published by the ANIC, which means that state Islam actively sponsors women's Islamic studies. The number of female teachers of Islam is far higher than the number officially nominated and paid by the Ministry of Religious Endowments (*wizarat al-Awqaf*). About half of the teaching activities in the Syrian Sunni arena are performed by women. This silent and almost invisible contribution of women Muslims to the development of

Islamic culture and religion is at the same time a struggle for more civil rights and for more participation by women in the shaping of political, economic, and religious life. So far, Syrian women have been much more successful in wresting compromises from the regime than have their male counterparts.

REFERENCES

Ahmed, Leila. 1992. *Women and Gender in Islam: Historical Roots of a Modern Debate.* New Haven and London: Yale University Press.

Beck, Lois, and Nikki Keddie, eds. 1978. *Women in the Muslim World.* Cambridge: Harvard University Press.

Böttcher, Annabelle. 1998. "L'élite féminine kurde de la Kaftariyya, une confrérie Naqshbandi Damascène." In *L'Islam des Kurdes, Les annales de l'autre Islam,* no. 5, ed. Martin van Bruinessen, 125–39. Paris: INALCO-ERISM.

———. 2001. "Portraits of Kurdish Women in Contemporary Sufism." In *Women of a Non-state Nation: The Kurds,* ed. Shahrzad Mojab, 195–208. Costa Mesa, Calif.: Mazda Publishers.

Chodkiewicz, Michel. 1995. "La sainteté féminine en Islam." In *Saints orientaux,* ed. Denise Aigle, 99–115. Paris: De Boccard.

Orsi, Robert A. 1996. *Thank You, St. Jude.* New Haven and London: Yale University Press.

Schimmel, Annemarie. 1995. *Meine Seele ist eine Frau.* Munich: Kösel.

———. 1983. "Women in Mystical Islam." In *Women and Islam,* ed. Azizah al-Hibri, 145–51. Oxford: Pergamon Press.

Wadud, Amina. 1999. *Qur'an and Woman: Rereading the Sacred Text from a Woman's Perspective.* New York and Oxford: Oxford University Press.

29. Internet Islam: New Media of the Islamic Reformation

Jon W. Anderson

With the advent of the Internet, a Muslim can find numerous Web sites with information about ritual, discussions of the many dimensions of ritual practice, and even religious edicts (fatwa, pl. fatawa). Such sites may invite chat groups to discuss the pros and cons of interpretations of ritual and belief. Indeed, a modern-day Muslim can find and choose religious guidance electronically. This aspect of globalization, turning many religious discussions over to lay Muslims and making the pronouncements of national religious figures available to Muslims worldwide, may have repercussions on the future development of Islam. Programs on the UAE's al-Jazira television network have already countered other Middle Eastern nations' attempts to control religious discourse. —Eds.

The Internet has become a significant venue of Islamic expression and its contemporary reformation. Both traditional Muslim texts and contemporary Muslim conversation have found their way to the information superhighway's current leading edge. The venerable Al-Azhar University in Cairo, the establishment voice of Sunni Islam, and Shiʿi counterparts in Iran, make use of the Internet to disseminate texts for religious education; conservative preachers such as Egypt's Shaykh Qaradawi post sermons and fatawa on the Web. Internet surfers find not only traditional models of Muslim witness but also tech-savvy students' and activists' contemporary versions of Muslim piety and advice. Many Islamic schools (*madrasas*) and training institutes, from the Tablighi-Jamaʿat Islami in Pakistan to an International Islamic University established by the international Organization of the Islamic Conference and the government of Malaysia and a modern-form School of Islamic and Social Sciences in northern Virginia, have Web sites; traditionally international organizations such as the Naqshbandiyya Sufi order have also come on-line. Muslim student associations provide guides to these burgeoning on-line resources, as do Web sites maintained by Arab press groups and information services, to which the faithful are directed by advertisements and notices in print and broadcast media from Morocco to Indonesia.

Muslims worldwide have taken to the Internet, and taken their religion to the Internet, in the context of a media expansion which began with print in the nineteenth century and a rise in mass education over the past three decades. Today, the Muslim world is awash in religious media, from cassette tapes of sermons to Islamic novels to multimedia instructional material, from new journals for the discussion of legal codification to banners announcing new preachers and organizations, in megacities like Cairo and small towns throughout the Muslim world—indeed, wherever Muslims are in the world (Eickelman and Anderson 1999).

The Internet absorbs these trends in its own social dynamics. Whereas the mass media depend on expensive presses and studios, publishing organizations, and licenses to utilize public airwaves, it takes little more skill or investment to produce content for the Internet than to use it. Nearly all the initial uses come from ordinary Muslims bringing the texts of Islam and its propagation on-line.

Among the first to bring Islam to the Internet were students who went or were sent abroad in the early 1980s for study in technical fields where the Internet was developed out of interactive, multi-user, networked computing. In these high-tech precincts, students and researchers in non-Muslim societies of the West followed the example of their colleagues, who also used this medium, developed for scientific communication, to bring other interests on-line and to establish "virtual communities" of like-minded individuals everywhere the Internet reached. As pious acts of witness for Islam in cyberspace, they scanned and posted translations of the Holy Qur²an and collections of *hadith* that together are principal sources of the *shariᶜa*, the practical guides to correct belief and practice, and created a series of on-line discussion forums. They utilized each new format of the Internet, from file archives to discussion groups to electronic bulletin boards and now the World Wide Web, both to establish contact and to bear witness to their religious interests.

These activities were combined with pious acts and networking with others, particularly with other members of the contemporary diasporas of Middle Eastern and South Asian Muslims. Other academics and, around them, other professionals gained access to the Internet throughout the 1980s, and more Muslims became adept in the new medium. To the common texts, they often added personal "spin" in selection and emphasis on practices and views. Their outreach was typically, but not exclusively, to other Muslims with access to this on-line information space. A notable early example was "Selim, the Cybermuslim," the virtual alter ego of the diaspora, creator of a *"Masjid* [mosque] of the Ether," with brief accounts of Muslim beliefs and practices updated to the life, times, and vernacular of the World Wide Web.

Individual efforts to foster on-line communities and services were followed by the early 1990s by organizations, again largely among the contemporary Muslim diaspora, particularly in the West. Early examples, such as Muslim student associations on North American campuses, were followed by national Muslim associations in the United Kingdom, the U.S., Europe, and Australia that posted practical information relevant to leading a Muslim life, particularly in non-Muslim societies, from where to find mosques and *halal* butchers to prayer timers, matrimonials, and cheap flights home. Links to religious bookstores and providers of materials for children's religious instruction also attest to the diaspora character of organizations trying to meet the individual, familial, and community needs of Muslims living in modern societies of both Muslim-majority countries and in countries where Muslims find themselves minorities.

These Web pages expanded early on to include intense discussion of issues in home countries, particularly Islamic politics but also strictly religious matters, notably of interpretation (Anderson 1997). In the absence of the conventional guidance of ʿulama (scholars) and without madrasas or other forums where seekers could meet the learned, these diaspora pioneers developed a contemporary creolized discourse (Anderson 1995). Pioneers of on-line Islam drew on the intellectual techniques of their modern educations to address religious issues, problems, and, above all, interpretations. Such interpretations are often scorned or dismissed by those with more traditional religious training; or they are tolerated as intermediate steps. But the characteristic feature of these efforts is that they return to religious matters from perspectives of adulthood and alternative schooling (Eickelman 1992). An example might be the Web site created by a Muslim student to offer fatawa to others like himself in situations like his own.

From these efforts emerges a contemporary continuum of Islamic discourse and networking between communities otherwise separated by styles and channels of communication. This is not new in Muslim history: intermediate communities have frequently arisen between the spiritually minded and the scripturalist, between the often detached Islam of the madrasa and more engaged, more socially embedded, vernacular expressions of religiosity. Islam on-line is part of such a continuum, with the difference that cyberspace transcends distance and limitation to physical places, substituting for them a more purely social "space."

This Islamization of cyberspace has deepened with each new technology of the Internet, beginning with simple file archives and electronic mailing lists and culminating in the World Wide Web, which has become a major medium of publication (Anderson 1998). It is a medium, moreover, in which any number can participate as message creators nearly as easily as they participate as message receivers, and its techniques spread as fast as the Web itself. So diaspora pioneers have been followed on-line by more conventional Islamic organizations dedicated to witnessing, outreach, and proselytization, and finally by educational institutions, which all grasped the potentials of the new technology. The Internet can not only spread messages far and wide, in the way that since the Iranian revolution audiocassette tapes have carried the sermons of prominent and obscure preachers alike. It can also reach a modern vanguard, the technical intelligentsia in the engineering professions that created and first made use of the Internet—in other words, an up-market audience, transnational in habits, training, and other social resources.

Organizations that rose to the challenge that the medium poses to more orthodox voices included both activists and traditional *da ʿwa* organizations, which offer justifications of the faith for non-Muslims and instructional material for the faithful, particularly for the dispersed faithful who need it for their children's education as well as their own growth as Muslims. Access to technology intersects what Dale Eickelman has called the contemporary Islamic Reformation, which is marked by wider participation in public discussion of Islam's requirements in the modern world and how to lead a Muslim life where practices and beliefs cannot be taken for granted to the extent customary in traditional Muslim societies (see chapter 22, this volume). This is already a worldwide phenomenon, having begun before the Internet with newer and more accessible forms of print (Eickelman and Anderson 1997), and it has been well underway throughout the past century in mixed traditional and modern organizations (Gilsenan 1973; Hefner 1993; Bowen 1998). The Internet is a useful medium as new interpreters and new interpretations form a widening public sphere of debate and discussion, in which new views are measured against old and against new situations, above all those situations in which the growing professional middle classes find themselves.

This new meeting ground not only enforces its distinctive leveling on those who enter it. It also rebalances the expressive ecology of Islam that traditionally channeled impulses of spiritual renewal into Sufism, the organized expression of Islam's more spiritual side, sometimes contradicting and sometimes complementing the scripturalism of the ʿulama. Sufism has served as a conduit for new persons and practices, new accommodations of Islam, and new ways of integrating religion with contemporary experience. Contemporary professional middle-class people, who often already use the Internet for other purposes, already know its techniques, already accept its logic as a new public space with open access and participation, often find that it is peculiarly fitted to their expressions and participation in interpretation. Indeed, it is too much so in the view of some officials and scholars, who find their authority in this medium discounted and who have to master a new one. In this, the Internet joins existing trends toward wider participation and more diversity of techniques and views, trends already set in motion by the print media that also spread Islam's more in-stitutionalized forms. The Internet encourages the diversification both of Islam and of authority, religious and secular, and provides a space for grass-roots interpretations of religious beliefs and practice and their integration into organizational and everyday life.

Although ʿulama were initially suspicious of new *ijtihad* (reasoning about religion) and disdainful of the qualifications of its practitioners, they rarely express this disdain in their own on-line efforts. Instead, they create a sense of meeting Muslims as such, of invigorating traditional views of the equality of all believers, if not quite of all beliefs; this last is still widely adjudged part of Western "individualism" (Sardar 1993). Islamic expression extends from sermons and fatwas by Shaykh Qaradawi and others to movements and parties with Islamicizing political programs; on-line, it easily includes everything from political-religious movements like Hizbul-lah to new apologetics, particularly among the middle classes and the growing professional classes that increasingly dominate the contemporary Muslim as well as wider world.

The registers of this participation are the willingness to state and to take responsibility for interpretations accessible to everyone, the advantage earned by Internet skills, and a new internationalism that marks its scope and reach. These extend the range of interpretation and communication, which are, in practice, part of Islamic tradition and the right and responsibility of believers (Rahman 1982). In the long run, perhaps the more profound effect of the Internet and its predecessor technologies, from print to cassette recordings to satellite television, is the elevation of these principles from the background to the foreground of Islam.

REFERENCES

Anderson, Jon W. 1995. "Cybarites, Knowledge Workers, and New Creoles of the Information Superhighway." *Anthropology Today* 11, no. 4 (August): 13–15.
———. 1997. "Globalizing Politics and Religion in the Muslim World." *Journal of Electronic Publishing* 3, no. 1 (September). At http://www.press.umich.edu/jep/archive/Anderson.html, April 2001.
———. 1998. *Arabizing the Internet.* Occasional Paper no. 30. Abu Dhabi: Emirates Center for Strategic Studies and Research.
Bowen, John. 1998. "Qurʾan, Justice, Gender: Internal Debates in Indonesian Islamic Jurisprudence." *History of Religions* 38, no. 1 (August): 52–78.
Eickelman, Dale F. 1992. "Mass Higher Education and the Religious Imagination in Contemporary Arab Societies." *American Ethnologist* 19, no. 4 (November): 643–55.
Eickelman, Dale F., and Jon W. Anderson. 1997. "Print, Islam, and the Prospects for Civic Pluralism: New Religious Writings and Their Audiences." *Journal of Islamic Studies* 8, no. 1: 43–62.

———, eds. 1999. *New Media in the Muslim World: The Emerging Public Sphere.* Bloomington: Indiana University Press.

Gilsenan, Michael. 1973. *Saint and Sufi in Modern Egypt: An Essay in the Sociology of Religion.* Oxford: Clarendon Press.

Hefner, Robert. 1993. "Islam, State, and Civil Society: ICMI and the Struggle for the Indonesian Middle Class." *Indonesia* 56 (October): 1–35.

Rahman, Fazlur. 1982. *Islam and Modernity: Transformation of an Intellectual Tradition.* Chicago: University of Chicago Press.

Sardar, Ziauddin. 1993. "Paper, Printing, and Compact Disks: The Making and Unmaking of Islamic Culture." *Media, Culture, and Society* 15, no. 1 (January): 43–60.

Salah El-Ouadie at a Day of the "Disappeared" demonstration in Rabat, Morocco in 1999. Photo by Susan Slyomovics.

A youth group supporting President Asad marches in a parade in Hassiki in 1999 during the election. Photo by Evelyn A. Early.

Teachers cultivate the banks of the Blue Nile when school is out of session, Sudan. Photo by W. S. Howard.

Youth dancing at a village near Daraᶜa, Syria. Photo by Evelyn A. Early.

Selling nuts and seeds in Hama, Syria. Photo by Donna Lee Bowen.

An anti-smoking billboard in Aleppo, Syria. Photo by Donna Lee Bowen.

A new mosque in
Aleppo, Syria.
Photo by Donna Lee
Bowen.

Recipient of a microloan displaying handmade solar panels in Al Akraba, Syria.
Photo by Gilles François.

Potter at a Noor al-Hussein Foundation development project in Iraq Al Amir, Jordan. Photo by Gilles François.

Recipient of a microloan in his bakery in Al Mukhaibeh, Jordan. Photo by Gilles François.

Women mixing *qaiq,* a special cake dough, in Gaza. Photo by Brian Barber.

Men enjoying tea, Gaza. Photo by Brian Barber.

Ironing pants
for work in
Gaza.
Photo by
Brian Barber.

Preparing
stuffed
eggplant for
the main
meal in Gaza.
Photo by
Brian Barber.

Boys from the
refugee camp,
Khan Yunis,
in Gaza.
Photo by
Brian Barber.

Fishmonger, Meknes,
Morocco.
Photo by Donna Lee
Bowen.

Traffic in Casablanca,
Morocco.
Photo by Donna Lee
Bowen.

Cinema in a popular quarter of Fes al-Bali, Morocco. Photo by Donna Lee Bowen.

In a restaurant outside Amman, Jordan. Photo by Gilles François.

Chefchaouen, Morocco. Photo by Donna Lee Bowen.

Film poster for *Looking for My Wife's Husband* (1993). Courtesy of M. A. Tazi.

Film poster for *A Woman's Fate* (1999). Courtesy of Centrale Africaine Cinématographique.

National Information Center in Damascus, Syria. Employees transcribe and translate television newscasts from several Western languages into Arabic. Major Arab news items are translated into Western languages as well. Photo by Evelyn A. Early.

A Damascus corner during the 1999 Asad election. The little girl in the sign on the right is saying "yes" to President Asad. Photo by Evelyn A. Early.

PART FIVE

Performance and Entertainment

In the Middle East, as elsewhere, art expresses the spiritual and intellectual concerns of the culture, both through formal public performances in plazas and on theater, radio, and television and in the more personal reflections of poets and dreamers. Some cultural expressions, such as the jokes shared among two or more people, are embedded in specific social interactions. Others, such as movies or popular music, are independent of social context and may be consumed by a dozen or a thousand people, each experiencing a performance in a personal way.

In the last decade, a communications revolution has transformed the stage for performance and entertainment in the Middle East. The advent of the Internet, bringing the World Wide Web, the satellite dishes which blanket the rooftops of every city in the Middle East, and CNN, MSNBC, the Middle East Broadcasting Company, and other foreign media sources, has changed the way Middle Easterners view the world and view themselves. It has also altered the ability of Middle Eastern governments to restrict the content of entertainment available to citizens. The Web and satellite television have dealt a death blow to in-country censorship and have freed citizens—at least to some extent—to comment on their national situations. Evelyn Early describes the popularity of Syrian television dramas and their use in circumventing national censors. Another area benefiting from the technological revolution is human rights. The increased publicity, via satellite and Internet technology, of human rights violations has resulted in some loosening of government control over citizens. Former prisoners are writing accounts of their imprisonment and appearing on satellite television interview programs to discuss it. Susan Slyomovics translates and presents Salch El-Ouadie's account of imprisonment and torture in Morocco.

Despite the alternative programming offered by satellite television, radio and national television channels are freely used as conduits of political propaganda by most Middle Eastern governments. Most journalists—press and television—self-censor rather than risk disciplinary measures. Television news producers who neglect to lead off the evening news with that day's schedule for the head of state risk rebuke or even dismissal. It is small wonder that leaders of coups simultaneously storm radio and military headquarters; military dirges on the radio signal an overthrown government more often than a funeral.

VCRs and videocassettes have made mass culture accessible not only in cities but also in remote Syrian and Algerian villages without wired electricity, where generators provide power for crowds huddled around sets. Film theaters show grainy fifth- and sixth-run martial arts films alternating with Egyptian romances. CDs of local artists are sold in shops and kiosks alongside pirated CDs of such famous Arabic singers as Um Khulthum, Fairuz, and Abdel-Halim Hafez. Next to them customers find Dolly Parton, Celine Dion, U2, and Eminem.

Cultural expression may take a national and even international form. Kevin Dwyer writes that the film industry in North Africa is simultaneously artistically successful and financially troubled. While Middle Easterners happily attend Jackie Chan knock-off films from Asia, French romances, and Bruce Willis adventure epics, they also have formed large audiences for local films which comment on local situations. Walter Armbrust analyzes a television quiz show broadcast during Ramadan in Egypt. This "riddle" program is popular throughout the Muslim world and plays a part in transforming Ramadan from a family-centered religious observance into a full-blown cultural phenomenon.

Cultural expressive forms may also be offered in small gatherings, quite private and hidden. The women of Awlad Ali in the Egyptian desert, described by Lila Abu-Lughod in this section, express their feelings in the private venue of personal poetry: lyrics recited in conversations with intimate friends or sung while working alone. Poetry and other expressions may be popularized in public recitations or in the media. Art for the masses can be subject to ideological manipulations. In the public venue of tribal politics in Yemen, as Steven Caton shows, war is waged with words as well as with weapons. Here, the poets are *shaykhs*, the tribal political leaders, and their poetry is a vibrant element of political discourse. Less lively, but of equal political importance, is the Bedouin poetry broadcast on Syrian, Iraqi, and Gulf television by governments aiming to publicize pure Arab, Bedouin heritage.

Entertainment and performance in the Middle East probably best exemplify the contrast between the global and the local. In most Middle Eastern capitals and large cities, the discriminating diner can choose among McDonald's, KFC, and Dairy Queen as well as local restaurants. Like

Americans, Middle Easterners complain about the impact of globalization on their local culture. They grumble about the Latin American soap operas that infest television schedules, and about the rap music, hamburgers, and Arnold Schwarzenegger films undermining their cultural heritage. Globalization has offered many benefits, for the global force of technological changes gives students access to the Web and allows them to stay in contact with their families through e-mail. It offers the technology for cheap satellite dishes and broadcasts Middle Eastern news from London. At the same time, Middle Easterners value their local culture: music, folklore, cuisine, literature, and now films and drama. Every year, Morocco holds a folklore festival and invites groups from all over the country to perform at the ruined seventeenth-century Saadian palace in Marrakesh. It sells out rapidly, and the uncomfortable bleacher seats are filled with Moroccans and a few lucky tourists who managed to get tickets. At the conclusion of the festival, the audience jumps to its feet and loudly and lengthily cheers its cultural heritage.

Some selections in this section explore the inner soul of private songs and poetry, and others look at the mass soul of film and popular music. But all investigate the expressive experiences of Middle Easterners in a realm set apart from that of everyday life as it plunges ahead. All allow us to see the affective side of Middle Eastern life as those who live it laugh, cry, despair, and triumph.

30. Syrian Television Drama: Permitted Political Discourse

Evelyn A. Early

The introduction of satellite television to the Middle East has had a powerful influence not only on broadcast media but also on politics and culture. Even in countries such as Syria where dishes are theoretically controlled through government licensing, many citizens brazenly display unlicensed dishes on roofs and balconies with no real worry; public opinion holds that satellite dishes will soon follow in the path of fax machines, which were controlled via high license fees until in the mid-nineties there were so many illegal ones that the government stopped attempting to license them. Satellite television beams programs from all over the Arab world to Syrian, Iraqi, or Moroccan Arabs previously restricted to their own local Arabic programming. While Moroccans have long watched European television, eastern Arabs have not had as much access to subtitled European and American programs. In the late nineties satellite television talk shows in Arabic were becoming more and more adventurous on stations such as the quasi-independent al-Jazira TV of Doha, Qatar. Two of its programs, "The Opposite Direction" and "The Other Opinion," dealt with such delicate subjects as succession to the then-ailing President Asad of Syria and the political future of the Muslim Brotherhood in Jordan.

The following article discusses how historical dramas have flowered on Syrian television in the past decade, how satellite television has boosted the viewership of Syrian Ramadan serials—now seen across the Arab world—and how Syrian television dramas have challenged previous understandings of censorship in this authoritarian regime. Early suggests that such art forms provide an alternative discourse in a repressive political environment. —Eds.

One chilly winter night in Damascus in 1998, I threw a fancy dinner party in a restaurant in one of the renovated homes in central Damascus. The kerosene stoves purred and glowed with heat, and the candles reflected off intricately carved wooden walls and tiled geometric ceilings. I was seated with a philosopher on my left and a film star on my right. The philosopher was dressed casually in a shirt and sweater, drove a beat-up car, and lectured at international conferences; the film star wore the latest French-cut suit, drove a fancy sports car, and starred in shaving cologne ads on television screens across the Middle East. In the middle of dessert, they launched into an argument. Although they seemed to have little in common, they were both passionate about whether Syrian history had been distorted in the recent television serial *Khan al-Harir* (*The Silk Market*). The serial had just aired the month before in the prime slot just after *iftar*, the sunset meal which breaks the daily fast during the month of Ramadan. A writer and a businessman at our table soon joined in. They argued about the roles played by national pride, regional xenophobia, and government censors' ideas of politically correct scripts in the production of popular historical television serials each Ramadan. During many similar discussions in my three years in Syria in the late nineties, such discussions of Ramadan serials seemed to be a subtle discourse of politics in a country where explicit political discourse was tightly controlled. But first I wish to set the scene for this Ramadan activity.

RAMADAN

Ramadan, based on a lunar month, moves backward about a dozen days every year in the solar calendar. In 1998 it fell during the winter, when shorter days meant a relatively easy day of abstention from food, drink, and other sensual pleasure, including tobacco and sex. One abstains for ten to twelve hours, from break of dawn (the point at which white and black threads can be distinguished) until sunset. The Muslim fast during the month of Ramadan is performed to learn discipline, self-restraint, and generosity. Fasting, one of the five pillars of Islam, is compulsory for all who are mentally and physically fit, past puberty, and in a settled situation, and who will not be mentally or physically injured by the fast. Thus children, the elderly, the sick, travelers, and others are exempted from fasting.

In summer months, when heat makes forgoing water so much more excruciating in the blistering environments of Muslim countries like Sudan, Muslims who are fasting sip special thirst-quenching grain drinks at sundown. Every country has its classic Ramadan meal, but all include the traditional water and dates to break the fast. In Egypt, Muslims break their fast with dates, water, and lentil soup, followed by a table stacked with rice, meat, vegetable delicacies of fried eggplant and cauliflower, crème caramel, puddings, and fruits. The choicest pudding is Qamar ad-Din, a thick apricot confection with nutmeats and coconut. Mococcans break their fast with dates and a special Moroccan soup, *harira*, composed of pastas and of legumes such as chickpeas. Accustomed to Egyptian spreads, I was puzzled by my first Moroccan iftar, since it appeared relatively scant, with soup, dates, and special powdered sweets. Too polite to ask my prosperous host why the iftar was so simple, and ravenous because I had abstained from food and drink that day in a sign of spiritual solidarity, I worked my way through a heap of dates and sweets and two bowls of soup. To my horror, a full-scale dinner appeared a couple of hours later with several meats, vegetables, and salads followed by an esplanade of cakes, custards, and fruits. At that point my guest status was severely challenged as I half-heartedly chewed on the main course. I had been fooled by previous Egyptian experiences. In Syria, Ramadan iftars were marked by a familiar splash of soups, meats, vegetables, and rice.

Ramadan is a time to hone personal piety, but it is also a time to socialize and, in recent years, to watch special Ramadan television programs. In the Muslim Middle East, as the sunset call to prayer approaches, television carries Quranic readings with footage of the holy shrines in Mecca; a favorite shows the massive crowds circumambulating the Kaʿba, the symbolic ritual centerpiece of Muslim faith, in Mecca. At sunset the muezzin sounds the call to prayer and the screen freezes on a scene of a minaret at sunset as Muslims sit down to break the fast. Iftars can be at home, with friends, in a hotel, or in a restaurant, but wherever they are, there is a wide spectrum of observance. Devout Muslims drink some water, eat some dates, and immediately proceed to the space set aside for the sunset prayers, which are followed by special prayers called *taraweeh.* Some Muslims may go to a mosque and then return to finish iftar. Others pray at home and then go to the mosque after iftar, for evening prayers. Some Muslims plunge into iftar and then relax and socialize.

Whatever the pattern, most iftars in the Middle East are accompanied by flashing television screens. First there are the Quranic recitations, then the call to prayer, religious songs praising the Prophet Muhammad, then a stream of classical Arab music followed by a host of commercials which clear the way for the evening news and the first show of the evening. This first show is usually a quiz or other light show, followed by Ramadan dramatic serials. Viewers have had time to eat, pray at the mosque, and head for the coffee house or to a friend's home or their own to relax in front of the television by the time the evening fare of quiz shows and television serials begins.

RAMADAN HISTORICAL, SATIRICAL, AND COMIC TELEVISION SERIALS

Arabic Ramadan serials have an air of the drama of American soaps like *As the World Turns,* and of the glitz of American serials like *Dallas,* but their rambling plots are much more intertwined with epic history, much as *Roots* combines a strong story with history. They are a unique genre that reflects social and historical consciousness. Syrian historical television dramas have emerged at the forefront of Arab television serials in the last few years. The great Egyptian serials like *Layali Hilmiyya* (*Nights in the Hilmiyya District*), which dominated Ramadan post-iftar viewing in the eighties and early nineties, have been challenged by Syrian serial dramas. A Western journalist arriving from Gaza told us that Syrian serials were all the rage there and that viewers there thought Syrian dramas were head and shoulders above the Egyptian. "The Syrians really know how to act," they told the journalist.

Satellite television allows Syrians to choose what they want to see from the menu of Middle Eastern networks such as the Saudi-owned Orbit and Middle East Broadcasting stations or the Qatari al-Jazira station. This, coupled with the Syrian government's promotion of Syrian television, has led to an explosion of Syrian productions. The average cost of a Ramadan serial production is about a half million dollars. However, the Syrian government has reportedly subsidized some productions—those with "appropriate" messages—to the tune of one million dollars. Producers of more experimental, less politically compliant serials may receive considerably less than a half million from foreign backers.

In the past twenty years, historical serials have swept the Middle East, starting with Egyptian classics like *Layali Hilmiyya*, which spanned a half dozen Ramadans in Egypt. In Syria in the past ten years, the emergence of energetic private companies run by the sons of influential Syrians, coupled with a relative relaxation of censorship, has led to a flowering of Syrian historical television dramas. Every Arab young person is familiar with pre-Islamic figures like Queen Zenobia of Palmyra (a Roman fortress city in eastern Syria) and classical Islamic figures like the Umayyad and Abbasid caliphs or the famed geographer and world traveler Ibn Batatu, as well as twentieth-century Arab history. Every Syrian history class studies imperialist occupation by outsiders such as the Turks, French, and British; opposition to the occupiers; and independence movements. While opposition to Western powers and to Zionism is a leitmotif in all twentieth-century historical dramas, none of the programs reflect the unremitting anti-Zionist rhetoric of contemporary Syrian politics. Rather, the serials are Syria-centric, dwelling on the Syrian-Egyptian union in the late fifties and the Syrian nationalist groups of the fifties and sixties.

The Silk Market, written by Aleppan engineer Nihad Sires, spanned three Ramadans in Syria to present the life of merchant families, their political activism, and of course requited and unrequited love in nineteenth- and twentieth-century Aleppo. It showed the people of Aleppo under the heavy hand first of the Ottomans and then of the Egyptians, through the eyes of a silk factory magnate (whose factory was nationalized in the fifties) and family associates. These associates included merchants in the

Aleppo market and student friends of the magnate's son. Syrians and Arabs with access to Syrian satellite television across the Middle East gathered after iftar to watch the blockbuster couple Suzanne Nejem ad-Din and Jamal Suleiman court on screen. In a typical scene, Suzanne peers from a narrow slit in the wooden window shutter to convey a message to Jamal, moping about in the street below: "I will wait for you although my father is trying to force me to marry another man." Some Aleppans told me they were proud to see their city and its history presented for the world to see, but others complained about the fabrication of history.

THE ARGUMENT OVER POLITICAL HISTORY

During Ramadan iftars, one can start a lively discussion just by mentioning serials, history, and the screen. That crisp night in Damascus, we became embroiled in a long debate over the creation and interpretation of history. The first group, siding with the philosopher, felt that historical dramas like *The Silk Market* were superficial, manipulated, shallow renditions of history and that these renditions had been fashioned to serve contemporary political purposes. The group pointed to evidence of political manipulation; Syrian television had cut some parts critical of history as the ruling Baʿth party saw it in that Ramadan's home broadcast version of *The Silk Market*. The second group, siding with the actor, countered that such dramas presented history thorough the eyes of everyday historical figures such as a silk merchant's family, an opportunist merchant, and a blind religious man whose uncanny sense of what is going on about him gives him a timeless wisdom. They felt that dramas like *The Silk Market* stimulated national debate of both historical issues, such as the Syrian union with Egypt, and contemporary political and social problems, such as relations between generations.

Everyone knew what the actor meant when he spoke of "contemporary political problems," but even he, secure in his Syrian television contracts, chose not to elaborate on how historical opposition to autocratic personalities might also reflect contemporary political realities, or how popular disgust with the government might be felt but not expressed today. Indeed, Syrians are accustomed to holding debates about current politics using a historical idiom. Most history professors who have lectured in authoritarian states report the experience of students telling them in whispers how closely their lecture on a past revolution or change of government fits the "current situation." So, for example, after a lecture on the life of Abdul Rahman Kawakibi, a turn-of-the-century nationalist who opposed Ottoman rule in Damascus and was banished to Egypt, many Syrians said in soft asides how exciting it had been to hear about the need for opposition to the central government.

Almost everyone in Aleppo watched *The Silk Market* during Ramadan. Cynics suggested that another popular Ramadan series, *Hammam al-Qishaani* (*Qishaani's Baths*), was commissioned by Syrian TV to counter an Aleppan drama with a Damascene one. This four-year-long serial presented the social and political history of Damascus in the twentieth century. Echoing debates among *Silk Market* viewers, Syrians who followed *Qishaani's Baths* were divided into critics of the drama as a superficial art form and supporters of its presentation of history and provocation of social debate. Critics found it overly negative toward the nationalist leaders of the fifties. They cited such examples as a drastic overdramatization of the assassination of President Shashakli as an act of revenge for Shashakli's attack on the town of Sweda. Critics felt that the smearing of nationalist leaders was calculated by the Syrian government to make the ruling Ba'th party look better.

PUBLIC OPINION POLLS AND SYRIAN HISTORICAL SERIALS

Debates about Ramadan television serials, which rippled through the restaurants and parlors of Ramadan Syria in the late nineties, spurred the government-owned Arabic daily newspaper *Al-Thawra* to survey two thousand viewers in major Syrian cites. The paper announced on March 23, 1997, that the year's favorite was the historical drama *al-Thurayya*, which resembled *The Silk Market* and featured the same two stars. A political satire, *Maraya 97* (*Mirrors 97*), ranked second in popularity. Respondents said they preferred plays about national topics that employed good texts and intelligent actors.

Al-Thurayya presented the story of relations between tenant farmers and their Turkish pasha landlords in northern Syria in the early twentieth century. Viewers who favored it praised it for its "dramatic story line." This is puzzling, since the film resolves nothing historically; its story starts and finishes with the aristocracy in control. Al-Thurayya, the daughter of the local pasha (governor and large landholder), rebels against her family and marries a Robin Hood–like man named Akash, an outlaw and rebel against the feudal lords. Al-Thurayya's rebellion seems more of an intergenerational struggle than a challenge to Turkish feudal control of Syria. Indeed, al-Thurayya buys land for herself and Akash to recreate her aristocratic environment; her father promptly disowns her for "defecting" to the peasant class, but her mother sneaks off to assist her with the birth of her first child. Even Akash, clearly no Robin Hood at heart, declines to go fight the French when they occupy Aleppo because he "must look after his wife and his land."

It would seem that proponents of the position that "television historical drama is superficial" have a point. Readers surveyed felt this set piece about relations between oppressor and oppressed to be a dramatic story, but certainly the drama's message is lean. But, like a new hairdo or a political speech, success is not so much in the event as in its perception; to succeed is to be widely discussed. While some intellectuals might scoff at the thin gruel of television dramas and suggest that government censors control them, many of my interlocutors felt that such serials provoked spirited debates on history and politics. Intelligentsia reserved their true scorn for historical extravaganzas like Zenobia's story, called *al-Ababid* after the name of her tribe, which aired in 1997. The most elaborate serial of the season, *al-Ababid* was replete with elaborate battle scenes filled with charging horses and flashing swords, and plenty of crowded markets and long ceremonial processions. The serial disappointed viewers. They had expected a complex historical drama, but instead were treated to a progression of stereotypic complications in Zenobia's life. As one viewer described the plot of the extravaganza: "So what? Zenobia works thorough a series of lovers as she fights, is surrounded, escapes, is captured, and finally commits suicide. In the end everyone dies!" Most critics dismissed such extravaganzas as a government effort to distract viewers with politically convenient history. Indeed the rise and fall of Zenobia's kingdom was far simpler than her trail of lost lovers; the lover of the moment dictated the fortunes of her kingdom. The true cynics circulated the rumor that this entire serial was a government effort to counter a book published in Italy, which reportedly claimed that Zenobia was Jewish, not Arab.

The spirited public discussion of *al-Ababid* spurred the Syrian Ba'thist Youth Union to sponsor a seminar, upon which the government daily *Tishreen* reported. The scenarist, the producer, several actors, and other Syrian producers and writers attended. According to newspaper accounts of the seminar, the scenarist said that he had been influenced by the American film *Gone with the Wind.* He created Zenobia to be similar to Scarlett O'Hara, and situated the drama in a setting similar to the Atlanta plantation of *Gone with the Wind.* He said that history mentions three ends for Zenobia, and he chose the one, suicide, which he felt would satisfy the viewers. It was difficult for me to recognize the ambience of Tara in the palm-tree groves to which Zenobia's jubilant warriors returned, but Scarlett O'Hara's brashness did shine through in the character of Zenobia.

Other recent Syrian historic drama extravaganzas include the 1998 serial *Al-Qala* (*The Castle*), which was based on Shakespearean figures and presented a critique of autocratic Arab leaders, and the 1999 *Yaqout Al-Hamawi,* which related the travels of Yaquout, as a representative of Khalifa al-Ayyoubi of Iraq, to such Islamic countries as Azerbaijan and Samarqand to mobilize them against the Mongols. When his intended in Baghdad marries another man, Yaquout dedicates his life to traveling throughout the Muslim world to collect geographical information and to call for unity. The theme of Muslim unity is unmistakable; a bit more subtle is the symbolism some viewers suggest, with the Mongols representing the super-powers of America and Israel and Yaquout as an Arab leader like Hafez al-Asad, then president of Syria. Yet another Ramadan serial, *Taj al-Shawq* (*Crown of Thorns*), based on *King Lear, Hamlet,* and *Macbeth,* is about a king who lived during the pre-Islamic period and struggled to stay in power. When he discovered that his crown was made of thorns, he went to the desert to live in isolation. The king represents every Arab ruler who refuses to give up power.

POLITICAL SATIRE PUSHES THE ENVELOPE

While historical drama is implicitly political, contemporary satire is explicitly political. Two comedians dominate Syrian political satire: Dared Laham and his buffoon character Gawar, and Yasser al-Azmi and his serial *Maraya* (*Mirrors*). Laham's television dramas, such as *Dayya Tishrin* (*Tishrin Village*) and *Hadud* (*Borders*), were on the hit list of video shops across the Arab world in the seventies and eighties. Laham's Gawar character developed from a slapstick buffoon in the sixties to a political satirist by the late seventies. In an early film, *Gawar James Bond,* Gawar plays pranks such as holding up a bank with a hair-dryer-turned-pistol and is nothing more than a slapstick joke, a lovable, well-meaning fool. As Laham's character moves toward political satire in a middle-period film, *Samak Bila Hassik* (*A Boneless Fish*), Gawar is the confidant and protector of a widowed fishmonger and her daughter. When the unmarried daughter becomes pregnant, Gawar gallantly offers to save the daughter's reputation and marry her, saying, "I will be your husband in front of people and remain your brother before God."

Dared Laham attributes his turn from slapstick to political comedy to the situation in Syria. In a 1982 interview he said, "When we began, we did not want to talk about politics. But the loaf of bread was moldy.... Political events were affecting the price of bread.... Our generation has lived through six wars: 1948, 1956, 1967, 1973, 1982, and World War II. I was five years old when World War II occurred. It is impossible to live far from these events. Our plays must reflect them." By the 1970s Gawar had moved into political satire. *Tishrin Village* is a television play in which village rulers are thinly veiled versions of Arab—particularly Palestinian—politicians. In the 1979 *Kassak Ya Watan* (*Cheers, My Homeland*), Gawar is a common man fighting bureaucracy and corruption. When he cannot find a job, the government officials tell him that it is his fault. When his newborn baby boy dies, the physician at the government hospital says the same thing.

Dared Laham's plays are replete with jabs at inefficient government officials and generic Third World bureaucrats, as well as at tyrannical rule by stereotypic officials criticized by Gawar. These officials resemble those of the Syrian regime as well as other Third World rulers; they are the generic baddies of Third World government. One might question how a political satirist who implies critiques of the Syrian regime—a regime that until recently brooked no criticism—could have survived all these years. Indeed, some critics have suggested that Dared Laham was tolerated by the central government, perhaps as a kind of safety valve. When I asked Dared Laham about this in the eighties, he replied that there are only two forms of political theater, a government mouthpiece and a government critic, and that his form was clearly the second.

In the 1998 Ramadan season Dared Laham made a comeback with a fairly successful serial called, appropriately enough, *Awdat Gawar* (*The Return of Gawar*). During the thirty episodes, three plots unfold. In one, a simple man (Gawar) is accused of killing his wife and imprisoned; after twenty years he searches for his daughter. In another, a man who loves to live in jails because he gets better treatment there than on the outside is chosen by prisoners to be their boss. In the third, opportunists become rich by exploiting the system; soon they control the country's trade and politics. All three scenarios critique the repressive, inefficient, exploitative Arab governments. In one scene a donkey says to Gawar, "The kingdom of donkeys is better than the kingdom of man. In our kingdom we do not cheat or lie, we do not fear the secret police, and we have democracy."

The newest and most popular Syrian political comedian, who came to fame in the nineties, is Yasser al-Azmi, whose yearly rendition of *Mirrors* was eagerly awaited throughout the Arab world by the viewers of post-iftar television. The episodes were thinly veiled critiques of the Syrian establishment, and it is surprising that he had as few run-ins with government censors as he did. This is probably due in part to government awareness that no matter how much they censor at home, Syrians can always view the original product on satellite television. In "In Parentheses," a popular episode that aired in 1999, six parties pursue their political goals in six different ways. One follows a plan step by step to reach its goal. Another party struggles on without a plan. A third party, called "The Party of the Past," bases its program on culture and history, saying, "Those who do not have a past have nothing." The fourth party is the party of "A Look at the Future," which suits a country with "no past." The fifth party is against all religions and ideologies. The sixth party is "No Party" and its members are ready to join any party that becomes important. In addition to criticizing all parties as ineffective, the episode takes a swipe at the Baᶜthist obsession with continuing the Arab past into the future. Most Baᶜth party public events include poetry or speeches eulogizing the glories of the Arab past.

Another episode, "Election," presented an election in which candidates bribed voters with money and food, and in which candidates who received no votes were elected. One character mused, "How does it happen that in this unusual country a rascal becomes a *mufti* [religious leader], and a thief becomes a minister?" In the episode "Parents and Sons," the spoiled son of an important official tries to kill his teacher. When the teacher tries to complain to the boy's father, the teacher's friends and relatives work to dissuade him, warning that he will only land himself in trouble. This episode resonated with Syrians, who are accustomed to the outrageous behavior of the sons of high officials. Daily escapades of these spoiled brats include drag racing through residential districts, flirting with schoolgirls, and partying in flashy nightclubs. The episode "The Tribal Conference" was a transparent parody of Arab summits where leaders cannot agree; in this case a mock meeting ended in petty squabbles about soccer and in mock fights with paper and fists. In an episode lampooning the Syrian press's practice of publishing boilerplate praise of bilateral relations with any country whose ruler is visiting, a newspaper editor writes a long congratulatory article about the visit of a foreign delegation, which includes the delegation's praise of Syria's architecture. The article is published, although the delegation never arrives.

Some *Mirrors* episodes are slapstick scenarios, such as the 1997 one of the men who set off to sell a pickup truck full of watermelons. By the time that they arrive at the market they have given almost all the produce away in bribes to inspectors and officials along the way. The two men, defeated in their business venture, sit down to eat the remaining few watermelons. The episode "Ox or Tractor" criticized the bad quality of Syrian heavy machinery. The word for ox, *thawr*, is close to the word for revolution, *thawra*, and the ox stands for the Baʿthist social system. The message is that the Baʿthist social system is the cause of industrial and other problems, and that if Syrians could choose they would buy tractors, and possibly politics, from Germany.

A 1997 episode poked fun at the Syrian national pastime of the previous fall: watching a late-afternoon Mexican soap opera, *Cassandra*. So many Syrians attached themselves to the TV set during the daily feed of *Cassandra* that evening appointments were often glossed as "before Cassandra" or "after Cassandra." In the satire, Cassandra visits Damascus, where she is met with great pomp and circumstance. But when her promoters invite the Mexican ambassador in Damascus to dinner, he is not interested and says, "In my country Cassandra is a nobody." The episode ends with the question "If Cassandra is a nobody in Mexico, then why is she so important here?" prompting gales of laughter from Cassandra-addicts watching the program.

THE CENSOR OR THE SUITCASE?

Throughout the Middle East, satellite television and the Internet have knelled the death toll of censorship. That said, in Syria, the shadow of political power still falls on Syrian productions. First of all, families of the politically influential own most of the film companies in the private sector. Second, in theory Syrian television reviews all television productions made in Syria, even if they are made under contract to a foreign-owned satellite television station or company. Third, writers continue to self-censor to avoid hassles. There have been some joint ventures of Syrian and Gulf companies, a couple with France, and many productions whose Syrian scenarists and directors have solicited direct funding from Arab satellite television networks.

Nevertheless, Syrian producers feel that they are in a strong position to convey a message to the Arab world. In a March 5, 1999, interview with the London-based Arabic daily *Al-Hiyat*, Syrian director Basel Khatib noted, "Films can be strong messages to the world as they express any country's civilization and progress. . . . My aspiration is to tackle the tragedy of the Palestinian people. Most of the films that were produced on this cause have done a great deal of harm, rather than serving the cause." The blossoming of Syrian television drama has challenged the previous predominance of Egyptian drama on Arab satellite television. In an October 2, 1997, article by Scott Peterson in the *Christian Science Monitor,* director Hani al-Roumani notes, "Syrian drama is dealing with reality, and we have the freedom to say what we want." His drama deals with problems in the Syrian army during the 1940s and 1950s, a period of coups d'état and countercoups. Roumani says, "I don't think that in Egypt they can do it . . . all the thoughts and conflicts. In Egypt they have a model, and all their TV series are based on this model. There is nothing new." Actor Jihad Saad remarks in the same article, "There is a new vision, a new look, new ideas, a new generation of actors, and a real wish to do something serious on TV." Saad also feels that the Syrians have outstripped the Egyptians. "The new Syrian drama is soft, with elegant acting. . . . The Egyptians are very professional, but also very local and don't compare their experience with outside." Indeed, while Syrian television drama is privatizing, the Egyptian government still controls Egypt's eight television channels and most of their means of production; government television pays little for feature films, which it in turn sells for big profits to Arab satellite stations.

Syrian serial dramas are often financed by and produced for foreign stations, and so theoretically they are not subject to government censorship. Most producers choose to "donate" broadcast rights to their films—after the network buying first rights has broadcast them—to Syrian television. This can lead to bizarrely interesting juxtapositions of censored and uncensored versions. For example, *The Silk Market* was partially financed by the Orbit network, which showed it nightly to a wide Arab audience, including Syrians with dishes. The copy given Syrian television was also shown every night, but with some obvious cuts, such as of speeches by nationalist leaders and depictions of Syrian police as drunken fools.

Syrians may produce dramas in Syria for Gulf satellite channels; nevertheless, the government can still pressure them. Anything produced in Syria is supposed to pass through government censorship. While a producer can theoretically tuck all of the original reels of his production into a suitcase or the trunk of his car and smuggle them into Beirut or Amman (the government controls the earth station, so uplinking the film is not an option), most producers choose to submit to censorship. Syrian officials will see the film when it airs on a foreign satellite television station, after all, and if they are not pleased, they will thwart any further work by that producer in Syria. For example, the 1998 *Mirrors* was broadcast by the Saudi-owned, London-operated Middle East Broadcasting Company (MBC). This company's nickname, based on its incessant reruns of old Egyptian flicks, is "Ma Bonne est Contente" ("my maid is happy"); presumably the maid is happily watching MBC reruns rather than doing housework. One of the episodes, which landed al-Azmi in trouble with Syrian censors, was about a math teacher hired to tutor the children of the president. As the episode unfolds, the math teacher is never summoned to teach, but instead is by accident thrown into prison. No one notices until someone asks where he is. The search for the tutor, his dramatic exit from prison, and his elevation to "royal tutor" status drives home the message that anyone can fall in and out of favor at the drop of a hat. The Syrian censor saw the series and approved all of it but some lines from this episode. The producer than passed the series to MBC, which broadcast it over its satellite station during Ramadan, and neglected to make the minor dialogue changes. When MBC aired the episode without the changes, the director of Syrian Television summoned the producer and read him the riot act.

Sometimes the censor may interdict an entire series, but that does not stop its being seen by the several million viewers who illegally own satellite dishes, and their friends. A recent series, *Ayyam al-Ghadab* (*Days of Anger*), set in the coastal town of Latakia during the French invasion in the early twentieth century, was not passed by the Syrian censors. Either the censors did not like the show's presentation of the history of the predominantly Alawite region of western Syria (the Alawites, the country's current ruling sect, compose some 16 percent of the population), or they felt the Syrian government would not wish to offend the French with such an uncomplimentary portrayal of the French occupation. The serial features a folk figure who mobilizes the destitute peasants against the local leaders, who are collaborating with outside powers—first the Turks and then the French. Although the series did not play on Syrian TV, everyone with a dish could see it nightly during Ramadan. The fact that a film is banned locally makes it all the more attractive on satellite television and spices up any discussion of how accurate its history is.

There is no going back. Syrian television viewers, both during and outside of the month of Ramadan, are hooked on serials. They watch them on local channels and on regional satellite channels. They calculate when to watch so as to catch the best—that is, least censored—version. The fact that censorship tends to be minimal, and in fact almost symbolic in its cutting of clips that might make the Baʿthist party look degenerate, is due in large part to the censors' knowledge that what viewers don't find on Syrian television, they will find on satellite channels. Located somewhere between the glossiness of *Gone with the Wind* and the historicity of budget documentaries, these serials are, regretfully, not yet of the caliber of *Masterpiece Theater*, but are, mercifully, better than the truly slick and superficial serials like *Dallas* or *Cassandra*. They are a genre unto themselves, and the debate is not yet over on whether they are critiques of current politics or dispassionate historic accounts with no present-day agendas. What is clear is that the Syrian establishment monitors their contemporary message and censors it more lightly than it might were there not foreign satellite television competition. Clearly, satellite television has opened up an opportunity for political dialogue in Syria.

NOTE

This article is based on personal observations and on comments from Syrian colleagues during 1996–99, when I worked as director of the American Cultural Center in Damascus, Syria. I am particularly grateful to all my friends and colleagues who helped me to understand Syrian culture in general and Syrian television drama in particular. There are so many to thank that I will not try to name them here. I want to be clear, however, that the views expressed in the article are in the end mine and do not necessarily reflect the opinions of my friends and colleagues or the views of the U.S. government.

31. The Riddle of Ramadan: Media, Consumer Culture, and the "Christmasization" of a Muslim Holiday

Walter Armbrust

Religious ritual is often accompanied by much secular activity. For instance, the pilgrimage to Mecca occurs in the context of a traveling group, and prayers at the mosque may often be followed by a chat about the day's events. So also, fasting during Ramadan is framed by secular activities such as visiting and watching television. Walter Armbrust discusses the media quiz shows aired during Ramadan in Egypt and points to the consumerism which accompanies secular accoutrements of fasting. —Eds.

The basic outlines of the Ramadan fast are familiar to all practicing Muslims. During the month of Ramadan Muslims are to refrain during daylight hours from eating, drinking, and sex (indeed, all activities that involve introducing a substance into the body, including smoking, snuffing tobacco or other substances, and injection). Certain categories of people are legitimately excused from the fast, such as pregnant women, young children, and the physically infirm, whose health would be harmed by not eating; travelers; and combatants in a war. Of course the observance of Ramadan does not always adhere strictly to an unchanging and abstract ideal. Just as American celebrations of Christmas have changed enormously, so too have practices associated with the observance of Ramadan evolved in response to new cultural and material realities. For many people the quiet contemplation during Ramadan of values such as piety and humility constitute the meaning of the ritual. Virtually nobody opposes the contemplative character of Ramadan in the abstract. Nonetheless Ramadan has, in certain times and places, become associated with a wide range of values and practices. Among these local Ramadan practices are new habits of consumption and consumerism.

It is this new consumerism and forms of mass media which concern me here. The centerpiece of this essay is a description and analysis of a television program called *Fawazir Ramadan* (*fawazir* means "riddles"; the singular is *fazzura*). The program tells a riddle each night of the month of Ramadan. The riddle is not just stated, but is enacted in lavish song-and-dance routines broadcast roughly an hour after the *iftar*, the breaking of the fast just after sundown. Currently there are many other fawazir programs on the air; the original *Fawazir Ramadan* is Egyptian, and for at least the past two decades it has been a post-iftar dance extravaganza.

I hypothesize that the fawazir program promotes a "Christmas-like" association of materialist mass consumption with cultural value. *Fawazir Ramadan* has been increasingly tied to the promotion of the interests of multinational corporations, as well as those of the state. The most obvious manifestation of these interests is the lucrative prizes given to those who guess the correct answers to all the riddles. In 1990 the prize for *Fawazir Ramadan* was LE 30,000 (then approximately $10,000), offered by the program's main sponsors, Noritake China and the Fitihi Center (a shopping mall) in Jidda. A 1994 riddle program broadcast from the United Arab Emirates paid as much as 30,000 dirhams (also about $10,000) per question. In both cases commercial and political sponsorship have transformed what began as entertainment for children to something considerably more complex.

A NON-ISLAMIC RAMADAN PROGRAM

Fawazir Ramadan is not an "Islamic" program in terms of its content. It is not, and does not pretend to be, "Islam on television." It is, however, a program geared to the Islamic calendar, and therefore has relevance to the practice of religion in the contemporary Middle East. Although much media attention in Egypt and elsewhere is given to the "lighter side" of Ramadan (riddle shows, electronic greeting cards, etc.), many books and Web sites on Ramadan take the form of a quite sober discourse on the meaning of fasting. These sites consider not only the rules of fasting but also such values as piety, humility, uniformity of the Islamic community, sincerity, and struggle in the Way of God. Here is an example of one such explication of the meaning of fasting:

> The prescribed fast . . . make[s] people realize the hardships which others endure for lack of sustenance for their life. Only those who themselves undergo the hardship of hunger and thirst can understand the miseries of those who, in spite of labor, are not able even to meet their basic needs. This naturally induces people to help others in need and to abstain from hoarding wealth. (Ali 1995, 7)

A Pakistani scholar made this statement, but it conforms to widespread Islamic understandings of the significance of fasting. The fast is not meant to be an extreme form of asceticism, nor is it a mere reversal of normal activities. One is not supposed to simply sleep during the day (which of course would greatly ease the discomfort of fasting) and stay awake at night.

In practice, of course, peoples' daily routines are often interrupted. In the days leading up to the 1999–2000 Ramadan fast one person posted to an Internet newsgroup an announcement published in the Egyptian paper *al-Ahram:* "The working hours for all governmental agencies during the month of Ramadan will be from 9 A.M. to 2 P.M. five days a week, Thursday and Friday holiday. The Cabinet will confirm the decision tomorrow" (*al-Ahram,* December 12, 1999). The poster of this message followed it with a plan for what he described as a "realistic" work day: 9:00–9:30 arrival; 9:30–10:00 chat; 10:00–12:00 "work"; 1:30–2:00 leave. His intent in posting such a "schedule" was obviously ironic, but such jokes point to the gap between real-life behavior and the "meaning of Ramadan." Certainly, for many Muslims, anything that could be considered excess during the month of Ramadan, even during the non-fasting hours, is to some degree reprehensible. One can, with very little effort, find Internet sites about Ramadan that clearly disapprove of eating to excess during the night. Here is one example:

> Excessive intake of food is avoided (this regulates the stomach from being pot-bellied and distinguishes Muslims from kaafir whom Qurʾan describes as those who eat like cattle (47:12)); etc. All these good things which Ramadan fast teaches Muslims are the means to attain piety. This is why the verse on Ramadan fast says: "O ye who believe, fasting is prescribed for you . . . so that you will (learn how to attain) piety" (2:183). (As-Sunna Foundation 2001)

Despite such injunctions against overconsumption (which are readily available in print form, as well as on the Internet, throughout the Muslim world), the description of the *Fawazir Ramadan* television program that appears below suggests that it takes very little imagination to class such productions as excess. The social setting in which the television sequence described below occurs is a middle-class home just after the iftar. After the meal is over, the dishes are cleaned, and everyone usually sits in some common room, chatting. Typically everybody is stuffed from having consumed an abnormally large meal on an empty stomach. Most people have not yet left the home to visit friends and relatives, a practice widely observed in Egypt and elsewhere. In my videotaped sample, before the main riddle program is broadcast comes a "pre-*Fawazir Ramadan* fazzura," a kind of a warm-up before the main event. After that comes a commercial interlude, which I believe is an important and underanalyzed aspect of television. After the "little fazzura" and the commercials comes the introduction to the *Fawazir Ramadan* song-and-dance routine, followed ultimately by the main event: the evening's installment of *Fawazir Ramadan*.

The "little fazzura" described here is from 1990. It was sponsored by Sharikat Nasr lil-Kimawiyat al-Wasita (the Nasr Company for Middle Chemicals). This appears to be a public-sector company, possibly in the throes of being privatized, as many government-owned companies have been since the 1980s. Its market appears to be middle- to lower-middle-class consumers, judging from its product line, which includes insecticides, detergents, and cheap perfumes. A matronly woman not wearing a *hijab* (veil), who is identified as Fayza Hasan, hosts the program:

> Ladies and gentleman, happy holidays. The Nasr Company for Middle Chemicals gives you its best wishes for the blessed month of Ramadan. Each day of the month, after the Arabic serial, the company presents to you a cartoon riddle. The Nasr Company for Middle Chemicals offers valuable prizes:
> —*hajj* and *umra* tickets [for pilgrimages to Mecca]
> —a color television
> —an automatic washing machine
> —a four-burner stove
> —ten bicycles
> —five tape players
> —one hundred prizes from among the products of the Nasr Company for Middle Chemicals
>   Before we tell you the riddle we'll see it together in a cartoon. Pay close attention, because the solution to the riddle is contained in the drawing.

Then comes a series of cartoons, which the audience sees being drawn in fast motion, punctuated by shots of the cartoonist smiling at the camera. The cartoons represent a certain kind of food being eaten in humble circumstances. The riddle is absurdly easy. The first thing the cartoonist draws, in fact, is some letters being pulled out of a *ful* (bean) pot and formed into the words *ful sadiqi* ("beans are my friend"). Anyone who is minimally literate thus learns the answer immediately. One might surmise that the goal of the program is entertainment for young children. On the other hand, one wonders just what a toddler would do with the prizes. A four-year-old winning *hajj* tickets? A four-burner stove?

After the cartoonist is through, Fayza Hasan comes back on and restates the riddle in a poem:

> Shall we say the riddle?
>   ᵓAmm Zaghlul al-Zanati
>   When the cannon sounds

Says, "Woman, bring me some protein from the restaurant."
She smiles, and says to Zaghlul al-Zanati,
"We have some vegetarian protein
Its scientific name is *vichya faba*
Food of the poor
Add a bit of lemon and oil, and let's go
Everyone eat, and whoever gets full should thank God
For a loaf of bread and the vichya faba.

After restating the riddle she tells the audience the terms of the contest: "We hope the riddle is easy, and we wait for you to send the answers to Egyptian television. Don't forget to attach to the answers two proof-of-purchase coupons for products from the Nasr Company for Middle Chemicals. The company wishes you good luck."

One thing that can be easily inferred from this program is that fawazir put a premium on localized imagery. They are often tied, with varying degrees of explicitness, to efforts to construct imagined communities. I think this is true even of the far more elaborate fazzura that I will describe below.

INTERLUDE

Before *Fazzura Ramadan,* which is the main event of the immediate post-iftar period, comes an advertising interlude. In Egyptian television, as in most of the world other than the U.S., advertising occurs between shows, not during them. In the early and middle 1990s, when I was watching Egyptian television most often, advertising intervals could last up to half an hour.

Egyptian advertising production is far different from American. In the mid-1990s I witnessed the production of the sound track for a television advertisement for chocolate-covered croissants. The creative process began with a musician in his recording studio playing various tunes on his synthesizer for an advertising agent until the agent heard one that he liked. The winner proved to be Chubby Checker's "The Twist." Next a singer was brought in and words were made up on the spot about a sad man dragging himself through his morning until eating a delicious chocolate-covered croissant, at which point the "Twist" music kicked in. It took about an hour and a half for the studio owner, in consultation with the advertising agent, to fine-tune the lyrics, and for the singer to perform it to everyone's satisfaction. The tape was made and sent on to the television studio, where someone else would have the responsibility of creating visuals to go with the music.

My studio-owner informant insisted that the process of making advertisements such as this was every bit as haphazard as it appeared. According to him, one of the main reasons for such quick-and-dirty (and presumably very cheap) productions is that the state does not permit marketing research. He told me disdainfully that the advertising executives had absolutely no idea whether their commercials really worked. He believed that for many of the companies who advertised on television the advertisements were entirely a product of vanity. If true, this suggests that the advertising industry in Egypt is organized very differently from that of the U.S. Television advertising time in the U.S. is an expensive high-stakes game. Why invest in advertising if its effectiveness is dubious? This makes one wonder how much can be assumed about the value of advertising during "prime-time" viewing hours in Egypt. Indeed, my impression is that the advertising on Egyptian television is always roughly the same throughout the day. But confirming or rejecting such an impression must await both a more systematic survey of advertising and interviews with those who do the programming.

Audience reaction to advertising would also be a natural concern of a future field research project. In the mid-1980s, when I first began spending time in Egypt, I often heard that many people considered the advertising segments more interesting than official programming. At the time it was said that advertising on local television was still to some degree a novelty —a product of the economic *infitah* ("open door" policy) initiated in the 1970s. If it was ever true that advertising segments were something of an event in and of themselves, I doubt it is true now, in the much more advertising-saturated media environment of the present.

* * *

About twenty minutes of advertising come between the rather low-budget fawazir program described above and the much more elaborate and expensive *Fawazir Ramadan* described below. The ads begin just after the ʿishaʾ—the evening call to prayer. Although most of the advertisements were not tailored specifically to Ramadan, their placement relative to the prayer times appears to be deliberate (at any rate, this is my working hypothesis until I can conduct more field research). During the non-Ramadan year calls to prayer come in the middle of films, dramatic serials, news broadcasts, and advertising intervals. Whatever happens to be on will be interrupted. But post-iftar television is scheduled around certain fixed points:

1) the *maghrib* call to prayer, which marks the end of the daily fast;
2) the ʿishaʾ call to prayer, which occurs a certain time later (roughly an hour and a half, depending on the length of time between twilight and evening at a given latitude);
3) the *Fawazir Ramadan* program, which airs after the ʿishaʾ.

Fawazir Ramadan marks the end of the segment because for many people it is only after it that visits to friends and neighbors commence.

In Cairo the end of the daily fast was customarily signaled by a cannon blast (now broadcast on television and radio), which announced the time of the maghrib prayer, after which the iftar food is served. Many people implicitly synchronize their television watching to ritual time. In effect, the overall structure of the post-iftar television segment facilitates a transition from fasting time to "normal" time. *Fawazir Ramadan*—the program that, as we will see, features imagery that is not just non-religious, but aggressively secular—occurs after the day's last call to prayer. From the 'isha' until the next day's *fajr* prayer people have the greatest possible license to indulge in activities forbidden during the fast.

* * *

The television segment I am describing here begins just before the 'isha' prayer and continues to *Fawazir Ramadan*. The child-oriented (but highly commercialized) cartoon fazzura described above comes first. Between that program and the *adhan* call to prayer there is a brief interval. This interval is filled not by advertising but by a religious song. Although I am fairly sure I have heard it sung outside of Ramadan, I can only describe it as a "Sufi Christmas carol." Its lyrics are perfectly ordinary:

> God is greatest of all
> Praise be to God
> Thanks to God the provider
> By your light, O Lord, guide me
> Make fast my faith and strengthen me
> Give me victory over my enemies
>
> . . .
>
> From your blessings the light of belief
> Making humanity what it is
> You also give man a soul
> Revealing the truth is not a dream
> I contemplate your earth and your heaven

This is sung by a woman who wears a scarf over part of her light brown hair—not a hijab, or at least not one worn as most women wear them. As she sings the image of her face fades to scenes of a Sufi order circling a tomb (the tomb in Cairo of the Prophet Muhammad's grandson Husayn, which is particularly revered by Egyptian Sufis). It is an unusual Arabic song in that its arrangement includes a harmony, which makes it sound like a Christmas carol. The song ends with the *shahada* (witness to the unity of God) sung in harmonized rounds, suggesting pealing bells far more than it suggests either Quranic recitation or any conventionally Arabic style of music.

This Christmasized, harmonized, and lavishly orchestrated Sufi song performed by a woman wearing a hijab incorrectly is clearly intended as a transition to the call to prayer. In many ways the Sufi song is an expression of the state's vision of a domesticated, "modernized," and non-oppositional Islam. The buffering function of the song is clear from the fact that the adhan cuts the song off. Although during normal television programming the adhan can occur anywhere, during Ramadan there is greater sensitivity to juxtaposing religious discourse with the highly commoditized post-iftar discourse.

The actual call to prayer in this case is quite long (during normal programs it can be as minimal as a window inserted into one corner of the screen showing first a clock, then whichever adhan it is time for. It includes filmed scenes of pilgrims circumambulating the Kaʿba and recitation of a *hadith* (teaching) appropriate to the ritual occasion. After the call to prayer comes more buffering material, at least in the sense that the viewer still sees a state-sanctioned message. It is, however, a message that not only buffers sacred language (the call to prayer and the recitation of a hadith) from the profane world of commercialism but also, perhaps, benefits from the proximity of both. It is a family planning advertisement, a compilation of scenes from a number of other such ads: a kind of "best of" selection orchestrated by an authoritative white-jacketed female doctor figure. Then follow other gradual steps toward the outright profane, beginning with an ad for Bank Faysal al-Islami. This is one of the few ads specifically tailored to Ramadan. It extols the bank's charity work and gives holiday greetings to the audience. After it comes a slightly anomalous ad for wedding dresses by Abudi—anomalous because the religious portion of the advertising segment is not quite over. There is, however, still a connection between the product (wedding dresses) and the season (Ramadan). People do not generally marry during Ramadan, because it would be improper for the newlyweds to engage in intercourse during the fasting hours. But a spate of weddings typically occur just after the completion of the fast, hence the sale of wedding dresses can be seen as connected to Ramadan. This is followed by a quick spot for volumes of religious commentary by a thirteenth-century Islamic scholar, Tafsir al-Qurtubi. On twentieth-century Egyptian Ramadan television, al-Qurtubi finds himself sandwiched between Abudi wedding dresses and an ad for crystal chandeliers.

From al-Qurtubi on to the end of the advertising segment all the ads are completely secular and very materialistic. Chicken bullion, al-Ahram locks, Toshiba VCRs, Riri baby formula, the Filfila restaurant; then a delightful Meatland advertisement in which chickens and cows cluck and moo to the tune of the *1812 Overture* as their carcasses are efficiently hacked up in a clean industrial packing plant; juice concentrate; corn oil; smoker's toothpaste; more wedding dresses; more crystal chandeliers. An intriguing Juhayna Yogurt ad in which a cow metamorphoses into a beautiful spinning woman. A perfume ad showing a woman going out on a date (or perhaps the man shown picking her up in a spiffy red sports car is her brother?). Sa'd cars. And finally the advertising segment ends.

THE MAIN EVENT

Now comes the main program, *Fawazir Ramadan*. It is announced by an attractive, un-veiled woman: "Ladies and gentlemen: *Fawazir Ramadan,* by the title 'World of Paper, Paper, Paper.' The program consists of thirty pieces of paper that have a special significance in our lives. The star of the show is the *fannana isti'radiyya Nelli* [Nelli, the revue-show artiste] . . . " Various other important contributors to the project are named. Then comes the familiar, grandiose sign-on for the Egyptian Radio and Television Union, Economic Section. The sign-on is accompanied by a spinning wheel of colored pie-slices that fades into an illustration of an oversized radio and television building, instantly recognizable by its rounded façade and tall antenna. This sign-on is either culled from Egyptian television archives or deliberately retro in design. But before the program can actually begin, an ad is inserted into the flow. This is a fairly recent practice. The insertion of ads into program introductions caused some comment in the early 1990s, though it is now quite common. The ad is for this year's sponsor of *Fawazir Ramadan:*

> [deep, ponderous voice] Name of the manufacturer—Noritake; type of product—fine quality china; name of the manufacturer—Noritake; place of sale —Fitihi Center, Jidda; name of the manufacturer—Noritake; type of product—finest tableware and tea sets for the best taste; name of the manufacturer—Noritake; mark of the manufacturer—concern for detail. The Fitihi Center in Jidda presents LE 30,000 in cash prize money for *Fawazir Ramadan.* Good luck.

Before I continue, let me set the scene of fawazir programs. *Fawazir Ramadan* attracted a large audience during several of the Ramadans I spent in Egypt. Particularly in 1986, the *Fawazir* seemed to attract a large crowd. That year I was in Cairo studying Arabic at the American University. Most nights during Ramadan I attended iftar with a lower-middle-class family whom I had met through mutual friends. The family consisted of a divorced woman and her two daughters, one a teenager and the other around ten years old. Although the *Fawazir* are an aggressively secular counterpoint to a religious holiday, I can only say that this family watched them religiously, missing few, if any, episodes. They were also trying to guess the answers to the riddles in order to have a chance to win the prize.

My impression at that time—in 1986—was that watching the *Fawazir* was a mass ritual. I generally joined the iftar, then stayed through the *Fawazir,* which began about an hour and a half after iftar (just after the ʿishaʾ) and lasted for roughly an hour. When the *Fawazir* ended I went home or to other social engagements. My habits were fairly typical. When the ending music of the *Fawazir* program played I said my good-byes and headed for the street. When I left their apartment the streets were filling rapidly. Everyone seemed to be leaving at the same time. On the occasions when I left early the streets were empty, and the sounds of the program could be heard wafting from many a window.

In 1994, when I last spent significant time in Cairo, the *Fawazir* program seemed to be either losing its hold over audiences or simply getting lost in an increasingly large number of programs. However, this may have been a function of the company I was keeping. Most of my friends and acquaintances by this time were male college students. Possibly such people have never been very interested in this program. Maybe the 1986 *Fawazir* were just more successful than the ones broadcast in 1994. And maybe the *Fawazir Ramadan* targeted a particular segment of the television audience—i.e., women and children, and possibly the lower middle class more than the more affluent.

Fawazir Ramadan is nominally for children. Some informal queries to Egyptian friends and acquaintances, as well as a query to an Internet discussion group devoted to Egypt and things Egyptian, yielded a basic profile of the custom of watching it:

- The *Fawazir Ramadan* is clearly an invented tradition. Most of the people I queried agreed that the mass media's posing of riddles on each night of the holiday dates from the 1950s. Some suggested that its origins are further in the past—in the 1930s. Others believe that the custom of telling riddles during Ramadan is ancient. The radio version of the program was originally the brainchild of the vernacular poet Salah Jahin and a radio hostess named Amal Fahmi. Amal Fahmi became known by the phrase *"wi niʾul kamaan"* ("and we'll say it again"), after which the riddle was repeated. Ten years after the program's mid-1950s radio debut *Fawazir Ramadan* migrated to television.
- After a five-year hiatus due to the 1967 war the program was revived.
- In 1975 the program metamorphosed into *Sura wa Fazzura* (A Picture and a Riddle). A vivacious dancer known on the stage as Nelli acted out the riddle.
- Also in 1975 the manager of Casio, the electronics company, began

to offer prizes for guessing the riddles. The first prizes were digital wristwatches. Next, the owner of the local BMW dealership offered luxury cars.

- In the mid-1980s Islamic investment companies used their sponsorship of the program to promote their businesses. By the late 1980s these companies had been accused of massive fraud and dissolved by the government.

Nelli, the main performer in the episode I analyze here, was described by the announcer as "the revue-show artiste." She is essentially a dancer, though not in the "oriental" or "belly-dancing" style. Nelli, though vivacious and often presented in form-fitting outfits, is considered by Egyptians I met to be more "cute" than "sexy." She has an obvious flair for comedy and a special appeal to children. She is also getting too old to be the main fannana istiꜥradiyya of *Fawazir Ramadan*. Others have tried their hand, but few have had as much success as Nelli.

Each year *Fawazir Ramadan* has a theme. It is always secular—for example, folk proverbs or tales from *A Thousand and One Nights*. In the program I discuss the theme is "paper"—birth certificates, graduation diplomas, marriage licenses, etc. It is a playful swipe at the bureaucratization of everything in the life of an individual. A surreal introductory dance segment—the longest part of the show—shows Nelli dressed in a luxuriant variety of outfits. She dances with such glitzy companions as a male ensemble clad in sparkly-blue overalls (they look like the Village People), a Turkish pasha, and a fleet of baby carriages pushed by chic women. All the while she sings about "ꜥalam waraʾa waraʾa waraʾa" ("world of paper, paper, paper"). She ends the introductory segment dressed as a gypsy. Speaking in a heavy pseudo-gypsy accent, she then tells the riddle to a different character each night. In this episode, the riddle is told to a sea captain—the captain of the Love Boat, apparently. Nelli asks the riddle ("What paper does one need?"), then enacts it as a stowaway on the Love Boat, ending the spectacle dancing in a ballroom with the captain. Then Nelli returns to her gypsy persona and restates the riddle:

The gypsy to the captain:
There's a piece of paper in your life, captain—not a passport or a map or a card. Your trip doesn't start until you've gotten one from everyone who has one. Get it, captain?

The fazzura (at the end of the dance routine):
The train travels and pulls into the station,
The Love Boat arrives at a foreign port.
Even a plane landing on the ground, sweetie.
There's no difference between first class and some trashy passenger.

What's more important? The chairs, or getting there?
Hintish bintish garrab wintish. Get it?

That is a sample fazzura. (The answer is "a boat ticket.") The playful anarchy of the program is noteworthy. "World of Paper, Paper, Paper" is a joke about the iron cage of bureaucracy. The moral value attached to the over-the-top commercialism of this vehicle for Noritake china sold in a Saudi shopping center is related to that of the humble cartoonist in the "Beans are my friend" riddle program mentioned earlier. Both are about local identity. Nelli's surreal anarchy is part of a series: by 1990 the audience has seen her do this something like ten times before. Every time her performance was associated with breaking the fast during Ramadan: a well-deserved pleasure after a day of doing God's will. The repetitiveness of the ritual makes it part of Egyptian Ramadan. Holiday traditions include *fawanis* (Ramadan lanterns that children play with); *kunafa* (a very sweet pastry) and various other foods associated with the holiday; certain songs and poems; the *misahharati* going around the neighborhood waking everyone for their final predawn meal; the cannon going off to signal the end of the fast; and now *Fawazir Ramadan*. The program is analogous to such American holiday programming as *Frosty the Snowman, How the Grinch Stole Christmas,* and *Miracle on 34th Street.*

Fawazir Ramadan is also eminently emulatable. Versions of it have spread all over the Middle East. The United Arab Emirates, for example, has its own fawazir program. The 1994 version of the Emirati program emphasized nation-building far more than did the Egyptian show. It was set around a simulacrum of a Bedouin campfire set on a stage and surrounded with folkloric objects. The "camp" was at one end of an open-air arena. Emirati men in national dress sat on one side of the arena, women on the other. At the opposite end of the arena a large black Mercedes was parked, within which sat a son of Shaykh Zayed, the ruler of the U.A.E. Prize money was sometimes passed out through the window of the car. A master of ceremonies, in national dress, stood on the stage by the campfire and asked the riddles. In this invented tradition the riddles were all about vanishing traditions: Emirati place names, folk games, riflery, and falconry. These were all practices that the younger generation was, according to the program, in grave danger of losing. The program was a spectacular illustration of a community imagined, particularly given that the state is identified with a family, a representative of which looks on from a black Mercedes, giving official sanction to the event and dispensing largess.

One challenge that phenomena such as the *Fawazir Ramadan* present to us is to resist dismissing such programs as "inauthentic." In his history of Christmas in the United States Stephen Nissenbaum notes that the idea of "invented tradition" is inescapable in the context of such practices as celebrating Christmas (and, increasingly, celebrating Ramadan). But, he continues,

> The easiest and most tempting way to abuse the idea of invented traditions may be to believe that if a tradition is "invented," it is somehow tainted, not really authentic. . . . There are several reasons why such a belief is false. But the most important of them is that it is based on a profoundly questionable assumption—that before there were "invented" traditions there were "real" ones that were *not* invented. (Nissenbaum 1996, 315)

The *Fawazir Ramadan* television program is as invented a tradition as there ever was, and precisely for this reason it makes an intriguing comparison to Anglo-American Christmas. I believe that the comparison could ultimately even be extended to include an investigation of the influence of globalized Christmas observances on commoditized celebrations of Ramadan. To my surprise, when I first spent Christmas in a Muslim country (in Tunisia in 1983) my Muslim hosts insisted that I celebrate the holiday with them. Two years ago a friend in Cairo sent me a Ramadan Christmas card: Santa by the pyramids under an Islamic crescent moon. A visit to a department store in the United Arab Emirates during Christmas of 1994 brought me face to face with a chubby, red-cheeked Santa (from Kerala, India).

A crucial part of this phenomenon is that the materialism of the newly invented rituals enables a discourse of disapproval. I remember a friend who adamantly refused to watch the fawazir programs. *"Al-Fawazir al-Burgwaziyya,"* he called them: "the bourgeois riddles." A discussion of "the spirit of Ramadan" requires a profane twin. This is akin to the demand of one of my own relatives, a Christian fundamentalist, for a traditionalism that will counter the accretions of pagan and Victorian celebrations that became Anglo-American Christmas: he makes the historically nonsensical call to "put the Christ back in Christmas" (to which a more historically astute traditionalist might plausibly reply, "put the carnival back in Christmas"). There are undoubtedly many in the Muslim world who want to refocus the prescribed fast of Ramadan into a quest for purity, Islamic community, and religious merit, and they are, of course, as justified in this as my relative is in demanding a more Christ-centered Christmas. All the same, it seems likely that the ingenious coupling of materialism with moral value is intensifying. A religious holiday blurs into a ritual of mass consumption. In public culture disseminated by the mass media, the religious obligation of fasting during the month of Ramadan has become the twin of the holiday Ramadan. Ramadan the holiday is associated with Ramadan the period of ritual fasting. The two aren't exactly the same, but it is becoming increasingly difficult to pull them apart.

REFERENCES

Ali, Syed Anwer. 1995. "Setting the Goal of the Prescribed Fast." In *Ramadan: Motivating Believers to Action: An Interfaith Perspective,* ed. Laleh Bakhtiar, 4–10. Chicago: The Institute for Traditional Psychoethics and Guidance.

Nissenbaum, Stephen. 1996. *The Battle for Christmas: A Cultural History of America's Most Cherished Holiday.* New York: Vintage Books.

As-Sunna Foundation of America. 2001. "Why Do Muslims Fast?" http://sunnah.org/ibadaat/fasting/fast.html. February 9.

32. Moroccan Filmmaking: A Long Voyage through the Straits of Paradox

Kevin Dwyer

In the past two decades, national film industries in the Middle East have told stories important to their local cultures which have challenged the dominance of Egyptian, Indian, Asian, American, and French cinema. The flourishing Iranian film industry has received the most honors and the greatest distribution in the U.S. and Europe and has relied on subtlety to exist within the strictures of the Islamic state. Other national cinemas, like the North African ones described below, are struggling to emerge with independent voices. Perhaps surprisingly, their greatest problems do not stem from political or social resistance to their socially sensitive messages. Middle Eastern audiences welcome local representations of local situations in local languages. However, the filmmakers face the same financial production problems which struggling artists face worldwide. —Eds.

INTRODUCTION: THE PARADOX OF PERILOUS ECONOMICS AND PROMISING ATTENDANCE

Most filmmakers today are in difficult straits and face nerve-racking economic pressures, for their work requires mobilizing vast amounts of money and human resources. Moroccan filmmakers and most of their Third World counterparts, struggling in peripheral locations in an increasingly global marketplace, are in an even more perilous predicament. In Morocco, movie attendance is down, many movie theaters have closed, and theaters that still exist mostly show foreign imports. The sector suffers from lagging technical capabilities and training opportunities, severely limited investment capital, and a small local market; the use of local languages in films hampers international distribution. Also, foreign films being shot in Morocco often push aside local filmmakers, increasing the demand for actors and technicians and pricing local producers out of the market. Indeed, in 1998, foreign films made in Morocco invested sixteen times as much as Moroccan films and employed almost eight times as many actors and extras. These factors complicate a film's voyage from creative inspiration to effective realization and diffusion, and make a mirage of the goal of profit.

The Moroccan film scene is particularly poignant because Moroccan audiences, after decades of showing no interest in Moroccan films, have begun to flock to them. However, the Moroccan film world's dire straits present a bewildering dilemma to the Moroccan filmmaker. Like Odysseus, he (or, in rare cases, she) is lured by sirens singing of high attendance figures, yet should he honor his vocation and follow their call he risks economic destruction. Indeed, many filmmakers do not survive. Half of the forty-four directors (only two of them women) who produced the eighty-six Moroccan feature films made through 1997 never made a second film.

What, then, are the prospects for Moroccan filmmaking? First I will trace the history of changes in Moroccan film practice, then look at audience trends, and finally examine four films of the 1990s. Although significant gains have been made in this decade, structural problems remain unresolved.

Moroccan film production took off more slowly than that in Algeria or Tunisia. After gaining independence from French colonial rule in 1956, Morocco produced fewer than twenty feature films through 1979, while Tunisia, with one-third the population of Morocco, produced about twenty-five, and Algeria produced over forty from its independence in 1962 through 1979. When public financing first became available in Morocco in 1980, the rate and variety of film production increased. Between 1980 and 1997 Morocco produced sixty-seven features, more than either Algeria (fifty-eight) or Tunisia (thirty-nine) (Armes 1996, n.d.a, n.b.d). Moroccan state aid rarely covers all the cost of production, and many filmmakers seek European, Canadian, and U.S. support. But financing is not the only issue, for Moroccan filmmakers face problems in production, distribution, and screening. As a result, many Moroccan films are never shown and even the most successful ones fall short of recouping expenses. Two of the four films I discuss below, both very successful, recouped only 60 percent and 15 percent of their budgets. Indeed, Moroccan filmmakers are an embattled species, although a healthy number of Moroccan films—about fifteen in 1998, for example—have appeared in the last few years, and the public has responded positively at the box office. One of Morocco's premier filmmakers, Muhammad Abderrahman Tazi, describes this paradox: "Making a film in Morocco is like the flight of the bumblebee—all scientific laws say that it is impossible for that insect to fly, yet it does fly."

TRENDS OF THE 1990S: CHANGING AUDIENCES,
CHANGING FEATURES

What accounts for the turn toward Moroccan films? Up until the 1990s, Moroccan films were poorly distributed. In 1992, a Moroccan distributor released Abdelkader Lagtaa's film *A Love Affair in Casablanca,* which was seen by two hundred thousand people, an exceptional number. The following year, almost a million saw Muhammad Abderrahman Tazi's *Looking for My Wife's Husband.* Since Tazi's film, it is not rare for a Moroccan film to be seen by more than a hundred thousand people. Home-grown films are increasingly popular in Morocco, reflecting the changing tastes of film audiences and their growing desire to see themselves and their own society represented on the large screen, rather than yet another representation of life in the West. No doubt, their popularity is also related to demographic developments, such as the preponderance of youth, unmarried women, and students among the viewing audience. A survey (Jaidi 1992) of filmgoers in the early nineties showed a slightly higher proportion (12 versus 8.5 percent) of women than men exhibiting a strong preference for Moroccan films, and students most apt to view Moroccan films.

Supporters of Moroccan films will likely increase. A preference for Moroccan film correlates with higher educational levels, and the Moroccan population grew considerably more educated in the 1990s. Women prefer Moroccan films more than men do, and the proportion of women filmgoers should increase as women become better educated and as more of them postpone both marriage and their first child. Another trend that may increase women's attendance is the construction and expansion of better-appointed theaters, because women hesitate to attend films in crowded, seedy theaters with predominantly male audiences.

CHANGING FILMS

What are the aspects of these films that have led to increased audience interest in Moroccan films? To answer this, I will examine four films of the past decade, two that launched the popular success of Moroccan films in the early 1990s (Abdelkader Lagtaa's *A Love Affair in Casablanca,* 1992; Muhammad Abderrahman Tazi's *Looking for My Wife's Husband,* 1993) and two that have prolonged it into the present (Nabyl Ayouch's *Mektoub* (*It Is Written*), 1998; Hakim Noury's *A Woman's Fate,* 1999). Taken together, the four films exemplify the work of three generations of filmmakers. Tazi, near sixty years old, belongs to the first generation, which was trained in the early years of Moroccan independence. Noury and Lagtaa, from Casablanca, belong to the second generation, those in their forties and early fifties. Ayouch belongs to the new generation, many of whom have spent most of their youth in Europe. I will consider these films in chronological order, and will single out one feature that has contributed to each film's success at the same time that it suggests a new trend in Moroccan filmmaking.

A Love Affair in Casablanca *(1992): "Nerve" and Transgression*

Salwa, a young woman in her final year of secondary school, is having an affair with Jalil, a much older man. At a party one evening she meets Najib, a melancholy, vulnerable young photographer. They begin seeing one another, first casually, then more seriously, making love on at least one occasion at Najib's home, where he lives with his divorced father. The father, it turns out, is Jalil; one day he happens on his son's photographs of Salwa and realizes that he and his son are involved with the same woman.

Jalil, jealous and possessive of Salwa as well as uncaring toward his son, humiliates Najib by getting him drunk and coaxing from him his love story. Then Jalil attempts to break up the young couple's relationship by impugning Salwa's morality in anonymous letters he sends to her father, who responds by banishing her from home. Finally Salwa chooses to continue with Najib and breaks off her relationship with his father.

However, Najib, discovering Salwa's affair with his father, despairs and loses his grip on life. The film ends with Najib's tragic suicide and, as the credits roll, Salwa and Jalil accuse each other of having caused it.

Although Moroccan films have often been strongly critical of various social mores (among them the situation of women, the treatment of children, and problems related to emigration to Europe), most Moroccan filmmakers share the modesty and reticence (*heshma*) that characterize their broader cultural environment. Consequently, their films rarely display open sexuality, bare bodies, or bloody violence, nor do they depict violations of certain norms of social behavior, such as the respect and distance that mark father-son relations.

Abdelkader Lagtaa has had the nerve to challenge and transgress such cultural norms, and he publicly states that he aims to do so. *A Love Affair in Casablanca* was his first feature, and in it the camera passes slowly over Salwa's body as she lies on the beach, clad only in a bathing suit; later, we see Jalil drinking with his son and egging him on to drunkenness. Both of these sequences were offensive to many Moroccans, but are mild compared to the very premise of the film, that the father and son (for the most part unknowingly) share the bed of the same young woman. The film's final scene, the suicide of the young hero, also shocks by being very bloody. Lagtaa's more recent films, *Casablancans* (1999) and *The Closed Door* (2000), treat other taboos: the police and local officials are butts of sharp ridicule, a father and a religious teacher are discredited, a young man has an erotically charged relationship with his stepmother, male homosexuality is suggested.

Looking for My Wife's Husband *(1993): Humor and the Comic Mood*

Hajj Ben Moussa, a stocky, relatively youthful sixty-year-old, is a well-off jewelry merchant in Fez, Morocco's most traditional city. He has three wives, the youngest of whom, Houda, has a flirtatious manner and excites him sexually. One day, while a delivery man and Houda are bantering harmlessly with one another, the Hajj returns home unexpectedly and bursts into anger at Houda's behavior. Tempers flare on both sides, the two other wives are unable to cool things down, and the Hajj repudiates Houda for what turns out to be the third time. In Islamic law the third verbal repudiation definitively ruptures a marriage, and Houda must leave the Hajj and return, divorced, to her parents.

While Houda is experiencing the freedoms and constraints of the single life, the Hajj grows increasingly morose and irascible. Sexually deprived, he spends one evening drinking and then, growing maudlin, he seeks the sexual favors of his two remaining wives, neither of whom has had such attention from him for some time. They do not relish it, and both send him back to his own bed. The Hajj, clearly, is still in love with Houda, and his wives and young children also miss her lively personality. Repenting his rashness, the Hajj wants to take her back but realizes that according to Islamic law he may only do so if Houda first marries another man and consummates that marriage.

So, to regain her, the Hajj begins looking for a new husband for Houda and weathers ever more humiliation as he follows several false, farcical trails. He finally settles on a man home on vacation from Belgium. As the Hajj sullenly endures the wedding ceremony he himself has paid for, he is laughed at from all sides and finally, in another fit of anger pierced with jealousy, rudely dismisses the celebrants and, like a spoiled child in a tantrum, waits petulantly at home until the next morning, when he hopes to fetch Houda.

However, immediately after consummating the marriage, the new husband has to flee Morocco because the police are after him. There is no time or thought for divorce. The film ends as the Hajj, hoping to retrieve the husband and then regain Houda, and willing to risk his life in the effort, sets off in a makeshift boat to cross the Mediterranean, in the company of other men desperate to emigrate to Europe.

Tazi's 1993 *Looking for My Wife's Husband* was the first Moroccan film that sparked audiences' laughter from start to finish. Many films since then have used humor, but none as fully or successfully. Up to now this humor has been either gestured, burlesque, or ridicule. Burlesque largely speaks for itself, but a few words should be said about ridicule, which requires establishing distance between the audience and the object of ridicule. A comparison between Tazi's *Looking* and its sequel, *Lalla Hobby* (1997), may help us understand the delicate nature of ridicule and the reasons for its success or failure.

In *Looking,* Hajj Ben Moussa is the chief source of laughter, a laughter that grows out of his ridiculous situation, his risqué problem, and the actor's mastery of a broad repertoire of pouts, sneers, frowns, and grimaces. All of these elements work well together, in part because the action is somewhat theatrical—at a distance from the audience, playing out in the relatively timeless venue of Fez.

In the sequel, the Hajj scours Belgium for Houda's husband but, in contrast to the previous film, rarely evokes laughter. Hajj Ben Moussa is played by a different actor and has been brought up to date: he is a Moroccan illegally in Europe, ignored, sneered at, belittled, even beaten up. He has acquired an identity different from the timeless one of Fez; his experiences, no laughing matter, are those shared by Moroccans in Europe both legally and illegally. Hajj Ben Moussa has become an identificatory and pathetic figure, no longer an appropriate target for ridicule. The halfhearted reception Moroccan audiences gave the sequel certainly had something to do with the clash between the public's desire for another installment of ridicule-based humor and a main character too close to the audience for comfort. We see here how finely tuned ridicule must be to succeed, the discomfort it engenders when distance from the audience is not maintained, and how difficult it may be for some audiences to laugh at themselves.

Mektoub *(1998): Action, Suspense, and Narrative Style*

Mektoub's point of departure is a notorious early 1990s scandal in which a police commissioner and his accomplices systematically lured young women into apartments, raped them, and videotaped the abuse. Two women had the courage to bring a complaint against the commissioner, leading to a 1993 trial in which 118 videotapes were introduced as evidence, showing him and his associates sexually abusing more than five hundred identifiable women. He was sentenced to death and later executed by a firing squad, and a number of his co-conspirators were imprisoned for life.

Tawfiq is a young ophthalmologist. While he and his wife are attending a conference in Tangiers, she is abducted, raped, and abandoned on the street. Still in shock, she manages to return to the hotel to tell her husband of her ordeal. Tawfiq seeks out his brother, a police detective, but impulsively runs off with his brother's gun and then forces a hotel executive involved in the abduction to take him to the scene. There he finds a videotape of his wife's rape. As he pockets it he is attacked from behind and in the struggle shoots his assailant dead. Returning to his wife, he overhears that the murdered man was a police commissioner and a widely respected hero of the independence struggle. Fearing he will be arrested for the murder, Tawfiq and his wife, aided by his brother, flee into the Rif mountains. A sinister inspector is put on the case and is charged by the police commissioner's accomplices with recovering the tape. The inspector begins to track the couple, and first finding the brother at home and shooting him dead.

Tawfiq and his wife, although under threat, have nonetheless begun to enjoy the pleasures of community life in the Rif mountains. They witness hashish cultivation (for which the region is well known), the wife participates in Sufi ritual trances, and the tempo of the film slows down, even as the couple has to flee several more times to evade capture.

Tawfiq manages to give the tape to an intermediary who will use it to bargain for the couple's freedom. Soon after, Tawfiq and his wife hear over the radio that the tape has been returned to those who recorded it, that the conspirators will most likely go unpunished, and that those who shot the police commissioner will not be pursued. The film ends as Tawfiq and his wife head toward a village where they hope to meet Tawfiq's brother. As they near the village, they come upon a funeral procession and the hero realizes that the cortege is marking his brother's death.

Over the years, Moroccan films were often criticized for "not knowing how to tell a story," for a weakness of plot, intrigue, suspense. *Mektoub's* innovative narrative style placed these elements at the center of the film's construction. In the film's first half hour, the husband is drugged, the wife raped and abandoned, the husband is reconciled with his estranged brother, the husband murders a police chief, and the couple flees into the mountains. The rapid action and heightened suspense attracted the Moroccan public, which may also have appreciated the cynicism of a dénouement in which police corruption and abuse are not prosecuted.

A Woman's Fate (1999): Televisual Style at the Movies

A Woman's Fate is one of several films contributing to ongoing public discussion of the rights of women and Morocco's personal status code. This code governs marriage and divorce; known as the *Mudawwana*, it follows the teachings of the Maliki school of Islamic law as it is practiced in Morocco. Whereas *Looking* targets a man's right to have up to four wives and especially his prerogative to gain a divorce at will, *A Woman's Fate* focuses on the fact that, according to the Mudawwana, if a woman wants a divorce she must gain her husband's consent. In such situations, once a marriage turns sour the wife becomes extremely vulnerable: she may be able to get her husband to agree to divorce only after enduring humiliation, coercion, extortion, or other forms of mistreatment at his hands. This is true even where, as in this film, the woman is an accomplished professional. (Although these films have called attention to controversial aspects of the Mudawwana, and it has been the subject of heated debate in recent years, none of the above provisions has been significantly modified as of this writing.)

> Saida, a young, unmarried executive in a Casablanca firm, meets Hamid, a computer technician. They begin a full-fledged love affair, with smiling close-ups, walks in the park, romantic music, and muted colors. The film then jumps far forward, past their marriage and to the birth of their first child, a daughter. From this moment on, the marriage rapidly disintegrates, as Hamid cannot tolerate having a daughter instead of the son he desired so much. He begins to behave like the mirror image of the loving suitor he had formerly been: he insults Saida, beats her, attempts to extort money from her to finance his own business, and finally brings his mother and sister to live in the couple's home, exerting further pressure on his wife to give him money in return for a divorce.
>
> The film ends as Saida, no longer able to resist and with no other way out of a wretched situation, agrees to meet Hamid's conditions. She signs a check providing her husband with all the money he has asked for; only now will he divorce her and enable her to regain her freedom.

Whereas *Looking* developed its critique of aspects of the Mudawwana through humor and ridicule, Hakim Noury's *A Woman's Fate* does so through the earnest, melodramatic, and televisual style that is his hallmark. Many features distinguish televisual from cinematic style, among them the privileging of voice over image, close-ups, the signaling function of music, stripped-down images with less detail and density, and a simple story-line (Ellis 1992). Film critics and directors often devalue televisual style, and *A*

Woman's Fate was an easy and frequent target for such criticism. Yet this style did not discourage the public, for *A Woman's Fate* and several other similar films were box-office successes. This may not mean that the public prefers these films to those with cinematic style, but it does mean that the televisual style is widely accepted among Moroccan filmgoers.

A Feature in Common

Having highlighted a key feature of each of these four films, I wish to note another feature that all four films share with each other and with many other films of the 1990s, setting them off from earlier films.

While Moroccan films produced into the 1980s were typically set in rural or lower-class urban male settings, many of the films of the nineties take place in urban, young, white-collar, or bourgeois settings. The characters are just beginning their careers or marriages; women frequently play main parts. In fact, women characters have recently become so central that filmmakers and critics have begun to speak of female "saturation." Filmmakers and critics are overwhelmingly male, however, and filmgoers do not appear to share this view. Of the five most popular Moroccan films shown in 1998 and 1999, three privilege women's points of view rather than men's; also the word "women" appears in these films' titles four times out of a total of nine nouns.

Taken together, these shifts may reflect not only general demographic changes but perhaps also the growing importance of filmmakers from Casablanca, Morocco's largest city and its economic capital. As well, by showing formerly hidden details of upper-bourgeois life, they hint at the filmmakers' growing recourse to the voyeuristic appeal of film.

The features that appear to have contributed to the popularity of Moroccan films include a wider variety of social settings, a broader repertoire of expression in both televisual and cinematic styles, heightened use of intrigue and suspense, acceptance of a critical and occasionally even provocative attitude toward social and cultural conventions, and a growing use of humor. These features suggest increased social openness, tolerance, and mutual understanding and increased audience acceptance of differences in perspective and forms of expression. They suggest, too, the improved capacity of filmmakers to meet public taste while not necessarily understanding it.

Another positive element is a very fertile political and cultural environment, in which discussion is open and almost any issue can be raised. Important indicators of this climate are the installation in March 1998 of a *"gouvernement de l'alternance"* led by opposition parties, the crowning of King Muhammad VI in July 1999 (following the death of his father, King Hassan II, who had ruled the country for almost four decades), and the removal just four months later of a minister of the interior closely associated with the previous regime. When we see the police ridiculed in Lagtaa's recent *Casablancans*, we need only recall a period not very long ago when it was impossible for Moroccan filmmakers to show a policeman's uniform, still less mock those wearing it. Although limits have occasionally been imposed, this new freedom is seen by filmmakers and almost everyone else in civil society as extremely liberating and supportive of many forms of cinematic expression, including new settings, experiments in visual and narrative style, growing audacity, and a diversity of humor.

Despite these encouraging developments, such cautionary tales as that of Morocco's neighbor Tunisia inspire wariness. Two breakthrough Tunisian films of the early 1990s, Férid Boughedir's *Children of the Terraces* (1990) and Moufida Tlatli's *Silences of the Palaces* (1994), established an international reputation for the Tunisian cinema, enhanced funding and international distribution, and produced waves of optimism. Yet their effects were short-lived. Not only has the number of Tunisian theaters fallen drastically (even more drastically than in Morocco), but Tunisian films since 1994 have faltered on the international market, and 1996–1997 was the last good year nationally. The Tunisian Ministry of Culture, at its July 1999 meeting on aid to production, responded by rejecting every request for funding of a feature film for the first time in history. At the same time, over the past few years the Tunisian government has curbed freedom of speech, a development which filmmakers, among others, find very discouraging.

Yet Morocco's more favorable conditions—political, cultural, and in terms of film-going and the films themselves—have not yet led to a film that could be considered an international breakthrough, although Nabyl Ayouch's second film, *Ali Zaoua* (2000), honored with many international prizes, may become one, and *A Love Affair in Casablanca* and *Looking for My Wife's Husband* were certainly national ones. Even more worrying, many of the fundamental problems in the film sector remain: inadequate infrastructure, finance, market size, and training. There is also the unstated view in official circles (in both Morocco and Tunisia) that national films should, somehow, promote the country's image. Such implicit censorship no doubt dampens filmmakers' creativity.

It would therefore be a great mistake to be complacent regarding the future of Moroccan filmmaking. The delicate balance of the filmmaking environment was emphasized when an official of the Moroccan Film Center, which aims to encourage Moroccan filmmaking, remarked that the Tunisian Ministry of Culture's rejection of film proposals was perhaps the best course of action since it made little sense to invest in a sector unable to pay its way. Attitudes like this help explain the unease of one Moroccan distributor who, while enthusiastic about the future of Moroccan films, described to me threats to Moroccan film production (perhaps with visions of an American western in his mind) as assassins lurking in the dark, preparing an ambush. He might have referred instead to a well-known Mediterranean epic and compared the filmmaker to Odysseus, who, returning in rags from a long voyage, is finally reconciled with his wife Penelope, his privileged audience, after he has vanquished the other suitors for her attention. Or perhaps, unlike in the Odyssey, the suitors—in the guise of satellite television, video clubs, and big-budget films from the West—will be the victors. Or then again, after reuniting with his audience for a time, the Moroccan filmmaker may set off on a new long voyage . . .

NOTE

An early version of this essay was presented at the annual meeting of the Middle East Studies Association, December 1999, Washington, D.C. The research was funded by the National Endowment for the Humanities.

REFERENCES

Armes, Roy. 1996. *Dictionnaire des Cinéastes du Maghreb*. Paris: Editions ATM.
———. n.d.a. "The Role and Status of Women: Silences of the Palaces." Unpublished paper.
———. n.d.b. "Chronology and Dictionary of 124 Filmmakers from the Maghrib." Unpublished paper.
Ellis, John. 1992. "Broadcast TV as Sound and Image." In *Film Theory and Criticism,* ed. Gerald Mast, Marshall Cohen, and Leo Braudy, 4th ed., 341–50. Oxford: Oxford University Press.
Jaidi, Moulay Driss. 1992. *Public(s) et Cinéma*. Rabat: Al-Majal.

33. *Al-Aris* (The Bridegroom): Prison Literature and Human Rights

Salah El-Ouadie

Translated and introduced by Susan Slyomovics

No family in the Middle East has not been threatened by the spec-
ter of arrest and violation of human rights at some point in the
past fifty years. Too many of today's adults lived in fear of the
secret police knocking at the door or—as was and is common in
Iran and Iraq—were forced to inform on family and friends for
the intelligence forces. Torture and imprisonment without habeas
corpus were common political tools under every regime in the
Middle East, including the Israeli rule of Palestine. In 1994, King
Hassan II of Morocco stated in a speech that "we have decided to
definitively turn the page on those whom we call political prison-
ers." One effect of these words has been the circulation of prison-
ers' stories throughout the Middle East. These stories, disseminated
in print and as interviews on satellite television, find ready audi-
ences, who are shocked and dismayed by what they learn. —Eds.

Al-Aris ("The Bridegroom") is the misnomer nickname assigned to the Moroccan poet Salah El-Ouadie by his torturers after the secret police kidnapped him as he was leaving a wedding party. Dressed in tuxedo and bow
tie, El-Ouadie was forcibly abducted into Casablanca's infamous torture
center, Derb Moulay Cherif. He was condemned during the celebrated 1977
Casablanca trial of leftists to twenty years' imprisonment for undermining
the security of the Moroccan state, and amnestied and released from Keni-
tra Prison in 1984. El-Ouadie's novel *Al-Aris* is written as a sequence of
clandestine letters from the author to his mother, from Derb Moulay Cherif
to the outside world, from memory—because El-Ouadie had no pen or paper—to autobiographical text, and from the memory of torture in 1976 to
publication to great acclaim in 1998. The letters describe his torture and

confinement in Casablanca's notorious prison, but are written as if by a Candide innocently and high-mindedly facing the whip. At the novel's end, the reader learns that the letters were discovered by a fellow political prisoner, who mailed them only after their author's death. The truth is that, although at the end of the book the reader is told that the author has perished, Salah El-Ouadie is still very much alive. He continues to publish poems and articles. Currently, he is vice president of Morocco's *al-Muntada min ajli al-haqiqa wa al-insaf* (Forum for Truth and Justice), a non-governmental association established in 1999 by victims of torture and repression seeking to establish a Moroccan commission for truth and reconciliation.

LETTER 1

Dear Mother,

I am writing you a letter you will never receive. I will write it in my memory because I lack pen and paper—how wretched a privation. I have many reasons to convince you that writing you now would be a grave imprudence even had I the means. I do not want—were I discovered, God forbid—to spend the night under a rain of abuse, of curses and gross insults, of beatings and random blows to my neck as if planned among them. I have already received today my share of offerings from the faithful who watch over our repose in this unique refuge. We eat, sleep, drink, keep silent, scream, hide our time, we cradle our hopes, praise God that we are still alive breathing the air of our country, and that our swollen bodies occupy space therein. When a well-trained prison guard arrives to call one of us ceremoniously for a high-level encounter with the agents that watch over our repose and that of our peers, he jumps for joy from his bed, leaves smartly in order not to miss the opportunity. Between you and me, how much time does it take an ordinary citizen to meet an official? Generally one year or two but here—long life to them—never is anyone left to wait. Personally, barely had I entered between their walls than I was given cast-off khaki, manacles; even more, they bestowed on me some black fabric whose use I did not immediately grasp, but finally, later, it protected my eyes from a light bulb illuminated day and night so they could follow all our movements. This I understood later. When they finished dressing me, somewhat energetically, they pronounced a number and said, "This is how we call you. When you hear it, say 'present.'" I said, "So be it." One of them smashed his fist into me: "Do not speak, dog, except when we order you to talk." I almost said, "Amen," but for a merciful God who restrained me. I will be silent now, Mother, they are coming shouting and I don't want to be surprised in the act. . . .

LETTER 2

Having conferred on me my own personal number, they put me in a humid place, and barely settled in, I heard one of them bellowing. Only then did I become aware that silence covered the place. I asked myself why silence on the one hand and yelling on the other. I had no leisure to answer the question. I felt a fist on my neck and a hand of iron grabbing me by my khaki shirt collar and lifting me into emptiness. The voice screamed at me: "Why didn't you answer the roll call?" I slid on my shoes like slippers to gain time, grasping instinctively that to take time to lace them up could bring upon me severe reprisals. I marched hurriedly after the voice, sincerely trying to make him understand that I was not yet accustomed to my number, but he was not the least convinced by my words; rather, he considered them nonsense. I was offended by this. I do not permit anyone to doubt what I say, especially if the skeptic is a citizen with this degree of energetic force.

This citizen grabbed and pulled me by my handcuffs, causing me pain. I was aware of entering a room, I believe by the door, because the citizen with the voice only lifted me when I was inside, where he was joined by other voices, other hands and feet that insulted, cursed, hit, smashed, and kicked. Finally they attached me to a pole, with my face and stomach down; their chief said to me, "Your nose to the ground." I thought to myself, "Good heavens, he is right," despite this small observation which is that my nose was in cold cement, when they lifted the pole into the emptiness, as it happened, it, me, and all my weight carried by my handcuffs and my feet tied with a rope, and it was there, dear Mother, to speak truthfully, I understood I was being tortured. I said to myself, "Be a man," and I started to howl. You know how silent I am, how I hate noise, but the torture was intense. They interrogated me between one slap and another and strokes of the whip about names, concepts, and big words, So-and-so, Such-and-such, democracy, socialism, classes, citizens, countries, revolution. Then they brought an engine that hummed and maneuvered it near my skull and I in the situation could see nothing. I believed at first that this affair concerned an enormous fly. But the story of a fly took wing when they placed the apparatus on my skull, my neck, my limbs, and I felt a shock and jolt travel through my entire body. I suddenly remembered that I knew this jolt from childhood, the day I was electrically shocked while playing; I remembered how you took me in your arms when I came in tears looking for you. Here was electricity being installed in my body long before reaching the countryside and the villages, even though I made no request to anyone. How can the government plead a lack of means—here they distribute electricity so generously without payment? I was brought out of my meditations by insults. Because they began to insult my father, you also, my descendants and my origins, saying my father was a big thief and you a big p——, not surprising I should be like you, I and my brothers, and that we would be extirpated (What is "extirpate"?), that I should be a man and speak the truth, neither more nor less. (Here they are returning to spit, threaten, yell, trailing behind them noise and the smell of tobacco. There is one who screams and has no fear of anyone: "Speak, who led you astray? Speak or I'll —— motherf——.")

LETTER 3

Mother,
They asked me, while I was in the air, to tell the truth and I replied as soon as they stopped hitting me: "It is not required to beat me for me to tell the truth. Lower me and I'll tell you." So they became quiet and I understood they believed me because they lowered me. The strangest thing, Mother, is that when they released me I could no longer feel my body. For the first time in my life I felt that I was a mere thought, that is all, without a body, and all this was as a result of an excess of pain. Two of them started pushing me while yelling, "Jump, jump, to make the blood circulate." And little by little, I was no longer a thought. Afterward, they sat me down so I could speak the truth. I began to speak with some pride because these citizens were hanging on my lips in quest of knowledge. I said, "The people are poor, most children do not go to school, liberties are oppressed, and our country, after years of independence, is still—" I could not complete the sentence, they threw themselves on me all at once. Very curious. They find someone who tells them the truth, freely, and they repay him in this way. Curse them! Thus they continued to repay me each time they called my number until I began to think that my lying would avoid torture. I said to myself, "Next time I will lie to them, perhaps this decision will solve my problem." For this reason, I prepared in my head what I would say: "The people are rolling in comfort, all children are learning and even learning the love of Morocco, with liberty for all, and our country, after years of independence. . . . " But this time, too, they suddenly threw themselves on me and began to hit me, whip me, and say gross words about you and my father. This time even my paternal uncles, my paternal and maternal aunts did not escape their insults. I said to myself, stretching out to rest after torture, "This is payment for liars." I had repeated these sentences in my mind to the point of almost believing them.
(I will sleep now; my body is completely desiccated after this round and only a kind of moaning emerges from my mouth. Here is what remains of me: a hoarse grunting from my mouth and heavy breathing from my nose.)

LETTER 4

After they finished whipping me, Mother, they threw me, as I told you before, into a smelly and very humid corner. The reason for this, as I understood subsequently, is because the sun never enters here. I lay down to rest; one would say I was carrying heavy stones on my shoulders. I remembered the slaves who long ago built the pyramids and I compared my fatigue to theirs. I wanted to reflect on the differences between these two fatigues but for the first time my skull hurt when thinking. For the time, I set all this aside and began to feel my head. I found my hair shaggy and solidified in many places. I said to myself, "What is this?" I began scratching something hard; it was blood that flowed from head wounds. Here I understood what one of them said during my torture session: "Hit him in the head so as not to injure the skin." I thought they were speaking about sheep. I understood instantly that the sheep in question was me and I understood suddenly why they suspended me. Consider the confusion in their brains between a sheep and a human being. Perhaps they do not see why we should enjoy human rights because they take us for sheep. Ah, I get it. We must convince them that we are human beings, surely then they will stop beating and whipping us and cursing our fathers and mothers. . . .

LETTER 5

I took it upon myself to enlighten their thoughts and I called one of them. He took me by the handcuffs and pulled me. I let him do it because he still took me for a sheep. I came to their chief, who sneered and said, "You have become reasonable? You have something to say?" His words surprised me. I thought, "Perhaps he understood what I am about to say," which encouraged me and I began to speak. Hardly had I begun to explain the manifest difference between sheep and human beings, in particular, the horns, the tail, and the walking on all fours, than the same blows, the same curses about my parents and entire family fell on me. So I said to myself while tasting the truncheon, "Are you more intelligent than the state? If the state tells you something there can only be sufficient reason." The beating continued as they yelled at me, "You make fun of us, you ass." You see the level of their knowledge about animals. Surely you want to know how the ordeal ended. Naturally with the baton, very quickly, and I was brought to my place where they threw me once again. I neither ate nor slept that night. I swore by the Lord of the Kaʿba not to take any new initiatives without thinking about it a thousand times. The silence served me well because I passed the night hearing groans from all sides around me. I understood I was not alone in this ordeal and other Moroccans were undergoing the same ignominy. This discovery encouraged me to patience and I found consolation in the age-old adage: Collective punishment is less painful. My imagination roved; I said to myself, "If this situation were extended to all Moroccan citizens, the ordeal would be minimized because there would be more people whipped than whippers; then the whip would become impossible, and citizens could speak freely about politics and wages. The problem for me would be if the formerly whipped decided to become the whippers, whence their multiplication. As for me, I am, as you know, against the whip whatever its source."

NOTE

The translator thanks Latifa El-Morabitine, Ahmed Jebari, Ahmed Goughrabou, and Mustapha Kamal for their advice.

34. "To Mount at-Tiyal He Declared": Some Poetry from the Yemeni Civil War

Steven C. Caton

The civil war in the Yemen Arab Republic (North Yemen) lasted from 1962, when a military coup put an end to a thousand-year-old imamate, until 1967. Gamal Abdul Nasser of Egypt supported the Republicans while King Faisal of Saudi Arabia supported the Royalists.

In 1967 South Yemen wrested power from the British colonists and established the Marxist-oriented People's Democratic Republic of Yemen. Skirmishes along the borders continued past the ceasefire and attested to political differences separating the two states although hopes for reunification were continually voiced. In 1990, the two Yemens, divided since the 1700s, reunified into one Yemeni state. —Eds.

At John F. Kennedy's inauguration in 1961, Robert Frost read a poem especially composed for the occasion, the opening lines of which are:

> Summoning artists to participate
> In the august occasions of the state
> Seems something artists ought to celebrate

When suddenly a gust of wind blew the piece of paper out of the poet's hands, the ceremony had to proceed without his being able to finish th prepared text. The event presaged what was to befall Kennedy's symbolic gesture of wedding poetry to power. Enthusiasm for this idea waned after the first few months of his presidency and he never referred to it again.

During the Kennedy era and long thereafter, a revolution and ensuing civil war broke out in North Yemen (southwestern Arabian Peninsula) where the association between poetry and power was not the exception but the norm of political rhetoric. Of course, poetry is only one of many verbal registers in which Yemenis tried to exhort or otherwise persuade their compatriots, but it was nevertheless one of the most important. In the dawn hours of September 26, 1962, Sanaa's radio listeners heard a tribal poet reciting his ode announcing the advent of the Revolution and a steady stream of verse was to issue thereafter on the civil war which lasted until approximately 1972. The following verses are only a small portion of that output but are nevertheless representative of a use of poetic discourse in marked contrast with our own sociolinguistic traditions.

To this day the most numerous and powerful element in Yemeni society is the sedentary, agricultural tribes. All the poetry in this section was composed by shaykhs from the area of Khawlan, whose territory stretches eastward from the capital Sanaa to the outskirts of Marib, site of the dam which was considered by the ancients as one of the "seven wonders" of the world.

The tribal shaykh is an important figure in Yemeni politics, though he is not an absolute ruler, having to shape consensus by persuasion rather than coercion. In times of crisis, however, such as intertribal war or the threat of foreign invasion, the tribe, probably an entire confederacy, might rally around an outstanding military leader and grant him considerable power. For example, Khawlan is composed of several tribes which are unwilling today to forfeit their independence to the authority of a "Shaykh of Shaykhs." This was not always the case. In the Yemeni civil war the Khawlanis elected one of their tribal shaykhs to head their joint armies—Naji bin Ali al-Ghadir—so renowned was he for his valor, wisdom, military prowess, and, as we shall see, poetic talent.

The one-thousand-year-old imamate was overthrown by army officers under the leadership of Salal, who was to become the first president of the Republic. Imam al-Badr, however, managed to escape to the northern part of the country, where he rallied the tribes in support of his cause. For the next ten years a costly and very bloody civil war inflicted deep wounds on Yemen which have still not healed.

Like other tribal areas, Khawlan was very fickle in its political allegiances during the conflict. A common joke of the era relates that they were Republicans by day and Royalists by night (the former maneuvering mainly in daylight whereas the latter's guerrilla forces carried out their operations under the cover of darkness). At the beginning of the Revolution many tribesmen of the region were sympathetic to the new government because it promised to institute badly needed social, political, and economic reforms. But when Salal in the early days of his regime asked President Nasser to send troops and matériel (by mid-November of 1962 there were reportedly about ten thousand Egyptian troops on Yemeni soil), Republican Khawlanis such as Shaykh al-Ghadir balked at what seemed to them to be a foreign invasion of Yemen and they threw in their weight with the Royalists.

One of the greatest poems to come out of this early period of the civil war was composed by Shaykh al-Ghadir. In it he proclaimed his political position:

> To Mount at-Tiyal he declared and shouted to every peak
>   in Yemen//We will never join the Republic, though we be
>   snuffed out of the world forever,
> though yesterday were to return today and the sun rise from
>   the south//though earth were to consume fire and clouds
>   rain bullets.

The poem is of the type called *zamil*. Meter and rhyme are among its chief aesthetic features, a satisfactory discussion of which would be too technical here. Alliteration and sound-symbolism are also quite intricate and demonstrate the skill of the poet. His artistic ability in this regard reflects positively on his reputation for honor. As for the content, it has to be compressed into the space of only two lines, which readers can see approaches the compactness of aphorism. The most important aesthetic appeal of the lines above lies in the clever use of paradoxes. For example, the poet cites a series of impossible events ("though yesterday were to return today" or "though the earth were to consume fire") and declares that even if these should occur, his side would still not join the Republic. Hyperbole is to be found in poetry around the world as a device by which to express emotional emphasis.

Zamil poems may be linked as parts of exchanges between poets who challenge each other. Indeed, the poem above was a poetic challenge hurled at the Republicans, one of whose shaykhs, Salih bin ar-Royshan, took up the gauntlet. The respondent in such exchanges is required to compose at least an aesthetically equivalent poem or, better yet, top his opponent by surpassing his metaphorical, alliterative, and humorous flourishes. If the poet is not up to scratch, he loses face, and the honor of his group is in turn diminished. Let us now turn to ar-Royshan's composition to see whether it manages to meet al-Ghadir's challenge.

> Beg pardon of one who's wended a crooked course.//
>   The MiG, the Yushin, the helicopter and phantom jet—
> Fighter pilots are not stopped by M-1 rifles and cartridges//
>   Tell Hasan and Badr, O Naji, silver has turned to
>   brass.

To appreciate how good ar-Royshan's response is we must delve into its sound texture in more detail than most nonspecialists have patience for.

Readers will have to take my word that its alliterations and sound symbolisms surpass the original. I cannot resist, however, pointing out one detail of this poet's superb craftmanship, a stunning use of allusion which comes at the end of the poem. Al-Ghadir is commanded to tell the deposed imam and his right-hand man Prince Hasan that "silver has turned to brass" (silver having been a symbol of the imamate). Many times I asked listeners what this line meant and received various, but not necessarily contradictory, answers. One person told me it referred to the collapse of the monarchy's army, another said it simply meant that the value of the imamate had been debased, and still another had a different interpretation. If we saw in the previous poem how hyperbole was used to get the listener's attention, here the technique is subtlety. This way of talking "between the lines" is in fact greatly admired even in everyday language.

This stunning poem was not only a reply to a challenge, it provoked the following retort from Shaykh al-Ghadir:

> The Yushin won't do you a bit of good—we have the means to
>   combat it. You're crazy!//
> The land mine is certain to leave the tank in pieces.
> Salal, the lunatic, won't help you, nor al-Amri Hasan.//
> O Satan, you're cursed! The curse is in a narrow grave.

While the meter, rhyme, and alliteration of the original are preserved, it does not match the sound symbolism of ar-Royshan's poem. It frankly deteriorates into name-calling against the president and his prime minister, al-Amri Hasan, and only partially succeeds in matching allusion with allusion at the end of the poem by a not-so-subtle reference to the death of the Republican soldiers. It nevertheless is judged by Yemenis to be a good, if not outstanding, zamil.

I was never able to elicit ar-Royshan's reply to this poem, if in fact one exists. Perhaps he thought it did not require one on the grounds that he had already won the zamil exchange with the second poem. However, he did produce another one on a different meter and rhyme scheme which was addressed to the Royalists:

> I ask you: where did the Imam go, the day the bullets
>   riddled his house?//
> O you who say the people will never join the Republic:
>   listen to the clamors and convulsions of its army.

The last line in Arabic is again sound-symbolic, the alliterations being eerily effective in mimicking the reports of guns on the battlefield.

One could add hundreds more examples of zamil poems, but the above are among the most famous ones remembered by Yemenis from this period of the civil war. Note that the poets are shaykhs, the political leaders of the tribes. Though any adult male may compose verse for various public occasions, the shaykh must cultivate the art for himself or prevail on one of his talented followers to perform the important routine of challenge-and-response. The exercise of power is commensurate with the practice of poetry. War is waged with words as well as weapons.

35. Sad Songs of the Western Desert

Lila Abu-Lughod

Performances can be public events with vast crowds or private ones with a few observers as in the case of the Awlad ʿAli bedouin women of Egypt. In their personal discourse, the women sing short poems to articulate intimate feelings which they could not convey in normal conversation. The Egyptian bedouin women's poems express their problems in a cultural form specific to, and understood by, those sharing the same life situation. —Eds.

Living in camps and towns scattered throughout the coastal region of the Egyptian Western Desert, the Bedouins known collectively as Awlad ʿAli are seminomadic pastoralists in the process of sedentarization. Their traditional economy was based on sheep and camel herding, supplemented by rain-fed barley cultivation and trade (recently replaced by smuggling and legal commercial ventures). Arabic speakers and Muslims who migrated from Cyrenaica (Eastern Libya) at least two hundred years ago, they proudly assert their separate identity within Egypt, where they are a minority living on the fringes of settled life. They differentiate themselves from the peasants and urbanites of the Nile Valley by the tribal ideology which shapes their social and political organization, not to mention interpersonal relations, and by their stricter adherence to a moral code of honor and modesty. Their cultural traditions are also distinct. They share with other bedouins a great love of poetry, which they use to express some of their most poignant sentiments.

During the nearly two years I lived in a small community of Awlad ʿAli Bedouins, I rarely tape-recorded anything but wedding festivities. Laughingly accusing my machine of being a tattler, people were loath to let me record their ordinary conversations and the songs or poems that frequently punctuated these. I was usually out of batteries anyway since people loved to listen to the tapes I had made. They enjoyed the wedding tapes even though the singing was barely audible over the din of multiple conversations, crying babies, and excited children. But one special tape was always requested. It had been recorded one afternoon when I happened to catch the spontaneous songs and conversation of two women sewing a tent. They were comfortable with me and with each other, and we were alone in the household. As they shredded fabric for the patchwork for the tent walls and sewed the pieces together, they talked and then began to sing short poems called "little songs" (*ghanaawy*, singular *ghinnaawa*) that I was beginning to discover were very important to the Awlad ʿAli. They took turns responding to each other's songs. ʿAziza initiated the singing with the following:

> Patience brought no fulfilled wishes
> I wearied and hope's door closed . . .

Her friend answered with a song implying that it was better for one to replace love with patience. ʿAziza rejoined with a song about the persistence of memories; her friend countered with an exhortation to forget those who cause pain.

Whenever I played this tape for women in the community, they sat quietly and listened intently. They always looked solemn and pained. Some shook their heads sadly and commented, "Her bad luck!" or "This is news that makes you cry." Some even wept. It took me a while to understand why.

The poems were sung mournfully and were not without the poetic graces of alliteration and internal rhymes. Yet the images in the poems were not remarkable, nor were the themes of patience and memories uncommon. What moved people who heard the songs was that they knew the difficult conditions under which ʿAziza lived, and they cared about her, having known her all their lives. She had been born in the community and had spent all but a few of her 33 years there. She had recurring problems with the moody and poverty-stricken brother with whom she lived. Barely able to support himself and unable to keep a wife, he resented having to support his divorced sister. Her marital history was sad. Her husband had taken a dislike to her shortly after their marriage and had become abusive. She escaped home only to be met with her father's death. After the funeral she was persuaded to return to her husband's household, where her sister-in-law (also her half-sister) mistreated her, and then got into trouble with her husband, who had been away in Libya. He divorced her and she never remarried. To make matters worse, she had a hideous and painful skin disease that had first manifested itself during the difficult period before the divorce and that broke out periodically. She conceded that her condition worsened whenever she dwelt too much on her misfortunes.

ʿAziza's revelation of painful personal sentiments in poetry moved people. Knowing the circumstances of her life, they realized that the despair of her poems was due to her unhappy marriage, her illness, her poverty and loneliness. When she sang about memories and her inability to forget, they understood that despite the passage of time, she was still concerned with her ex-husband and wounded by his unfair treatment of her. By singing about patience, ʿAziza betrayed her hopes and her faith that some reward would come from her suffering. Her discouragement troubled the listeners, as well as her friend who gave her poetic comfort, because they knew how few signs of hope really existed.

ʿAziza was not the only bedouin individual to use poetry in this way. Both men and women recite this type of oral lyric poetry in conversations with intimates or sing as they work alone. They admit that they sing about what is on their minds and it was my impression that they sing more often when they are facing some personal crisis. Those who hear the poems appreciate them for what they reveal about the experiences of those reciting. Despite the intrinsic ambiguity of such condensed and formulaic poetic statements, they are easily interpretable because friends and relatives usually have such intimate knowledge of the particular circumstances of one another's lives.

Since I spent more of my time with women, I came to understand the relationship between their poems and their lives more clearly and will confine this description to them. Women are moved by the poems of other women because the contours of bedouin women's experiences are so similar. Their lives follow much the same pattern: they grow up with kin, marry (sometimes moving to another community, sometimes not), have many children, and grow old. With luck, they will be given to a good husband who will not mistreat them, their husband's kinswomen will be kind, their kin will support them, and their children will be healthy. Most likely, they will face a number of difficult experiences and will suffer. Women agree that their lives are hard. They work hard, often handicapped by poor health due to inadequate nutrition and constant childbearing. More trying are the hardships in the interpersonal sphere.

Separations from loved ones are a fact of life, especially in a society until recently nomadic. For women, the most difficult separations, after their own from their natal families at marriage, are those from their children. Daughters marry and leave to live with their husbands' families. Their daughters' departure is hard on their mothers, who lose companionship and household help. But it is expected. With best wishes and prayers, daughters are sent off with songs like the following:

> The household and neighbors suffered
> when she left, the one with gazelle eyes . . .

When sons leave, mothers are heartbroken. One poor woman I knew had a son in Libya. He had gone there as a migrant laborer and then had been unable to return after the border closed in 1977. She had not seen him for five years. As she told me about him she began to weep and sang the following:

> If only you who're far away
> Despair could bring you close . . .

Her friend who was sitting with us responded with another song to comfort her:

> Nothing is odious but death
> In time hope brings the absent . . .

This sentiment was certainly felt by another woman I met. Her son had been killed recently in an altercation between some bedouin men and a group of Egyptian soldiers riding on a train through a bedouin area. She sang:

> A fog of despair shrouds the eye
> just when it starts to clear . . .

The intimacy of growing up in the same household and the central ideology of the primacy of blood ties combine to make bonds between brothers and sisters very close. These are intensified when a woman marries because she begins to depend on her brother for protection against mistreatment by her husband or his family. The loss of a brother leaves a woman feeling vulnerable. One young woman whose brother had died a few months earlier sang of her grief as she sat alone washing clothes:

> They shoved you between despair and fire
> you turned to ash, my little heart . . .

Women are also troubled by their relations to husbands. Most marriages are arranged by the families of the bride and groom. Although romantic love is glorified in stories, people think love marriages don't work out well, and they are not common. Nearly all brides are shy and won't admit to being happy about marrying, even if they are pleased. But some brides are genuinely unhappy with the mates chosen for them. One such bride, whose kinsmen were adamant that she accept the marriage they had arranged for her, could not express her objections without alienating her kinsmen or insulting the women in her new community, kinswomen of her husband. She rarely said much, but recited numerous poems and often sang to herself while she worked. One of the poems she recited was the following:

> On my breast I placed a tombstone
> though I was not dead, oh loved one . . .

More often, women have developed attachments to husbands to whom they have been married for years and are hurt if the men leave them or seem no longer to care. Women I knew who, in keeping with notions of modesty and social propriety, vehemently denied attachment to their spouses, professed a lack of concern with their marriages, and admitted no interest in sexual matters nonetheless recited poems expressing sentiments of attachment and emotional vulnerability to men.

A young widow whose husband had been killed in a fight did not speak of him. She was cheerful and her sense of humor endeared her to the community. She seemed content to forego remarriage, preferring to remain with her children and the women among whom she had grown up. One night she recited a number of poems, including the following, that saddened and moved the women who heard them.

> Drowning in despair
> the eye says, Oh my fate in love . . .

A married woman whose husband of fifteen years wished to take a second wife admitted no concern, expressing only anger at his failure to buy her the proper gifts and his unconventional decision to hold the wedding in his brother's house rather than her own. Yet she expressed the sense of hurt by myriad poems, including:

> Long shriveled from despair
> are the roots that fed my soul . . .
>
> Patience is my mourning for the loved one
> and your job, oh eyes, is to cry . . .

Other women in the community tried to console her by comparing her fate to that of other women ("Do you think you are the first woman whose husband ever took a second wife?"), cynically commenting that men are all like that (as soon as they can afford it, they seek another wife and more children), or telling her to be grateful for her six children. They indicated empathetic concern by reciting in her presence poems, such as the following, which voiced what they assumed she was feeling:

> Despair of them, dear one, made you
> a stray who wanders between watering places . . .

This poem evoked a despair so powerful it could drive someone to abandon human society and to roam outdoors like an animal. By expressing sentiments from her point of view, rather than offering advice, the women's friend emphasized the sense of community and commonality of experience.

Bound by conventions and traditions, this oral folk poetry would seem to be a highly impersonal form of expression. Yet individuals use the poems to express the supremely personal, in the double sense of that which touches on their own experiences and that which is confidential, to be shared only with intimates. What is most interesting is that people express feelings they could not ordinarily express without compromising their social reputations and images as proud and independent. More often than not, the poems voice sentiments of sadness, unfulfilled longing, or suffering caused by a sense of abandonment. Bedouin women, like the men, have great pleasures in their lives, and their conversations are generally marked by humor and laughter. But as one old woman explained when I commented that most poems seemed so sad, "When a woman gets what she wants, she gets happy and shuts up."

GLOSSARY

All are Arabic unless designated Persian (P).
al- before a word is the Arabic definite article.

adhan: call to prayer.

ahli: family.

Alawi: a Shiʿi sect representing a minority of Syrians.

ʿalim: a Muslim religious scholar (plural: ʿulama).

ʿaqd: a marriage contract.

ʿaroubiyya: a rural, unsophisticated woman.

awliya: saints or holy men who were the first teachers in Sudan.

awqaf: religious endowment lands (plural of **waqf**).

baladi: local or authentic, as opposed to foreign or inauthentic.

baraka: divine grace, a kind of charisma or blessing from God which individuals or objects can possess (Persian **barakat**).

Bedouin: Anglicized plural of **bedu** (**badawiyin**), nomad. Although it was originally a plural, in English it is singular.

chador: a full-length cloth which covers the body and hair but not necessarily the face, worn in Iran.

dars: a lesson about some aspect of Islamic belief or practice taught from a Sufi perspective.

daʿwa: a religious call; a term used by Islamists for a commitment or rededication to religion.

dawla: state.

dhikr: a religious ceremony which includes prayers and the repetition of names, usually the ninety-nine names of God.

Dhu al-Hijjah: the month in which the pilgrimage (**hajj**) is performed. Muslims use a lunar calendar.

din: religion.

dirham: a monetary unit used in Morocco, roughly equivalent to the French franc.

du'a: a personal prayer.

dura: sorghum, the staple grain of Sudan.

al-fajr: the dawn. **Al-Fajr** is the name of the major Arabic-language newspaper in Jerusalem (which also has an English edition).

Fatah: the largest constituent group of the Palestine Liberation Organization headed by Yasser Arafat.

fatwa: Islamic legal opinions pronounced by a religious authority (plural: **fatawa**).

fazzura: a riddle (plural: **fawazir**).

fellah: peasant (plural: **fellahin**).

fiqh: Islamic jurisprudence.

fitna: temptation, charm, fascination.

ful: fava beans, a staple food in Egypt.

galabiyya: a long outer robe worn by men (see **jalabiyya**); (Syrian usage).

gam'iyya: an informal savings association (plural: **gam'iyyat**).

al-giraya al-jama'iyya: group oral reading (Sudani Arabic).

gsella: a bath attendant (Moroccan Arabic).

hadith: a written account of the Prophet Muhammad or the early Muslim community, a primary source of Islamic law.

hajj: the pilgrimage to Mecca. A person who has made the pilgrimage to Mecca will take the title **Hajj** (m.) or **Hajja** (fem.).

hajji: a person who is performing the pilgrimage.

halal: religiously permissible. Halal butchers sell meat that has been prepared in accordance with Islamic law.

halqa: a circle; used for a circle of students or spectators.

hammam: a bathhouse, a steam bath.

haqq: right, correct, proper.

hara: a quarter, an urban neighborhood.

harem: female members of the family.

harim: a sacred place.

harram: forbidden, prohibited.

henna: a plant which when powdered yields a red dye used on hair, hands, and feet. Henna can be drawn into intricate designs, and is used for festive occasions such as weddings.

heshma: modesty and reticence.

hijab: this term can mean anything from modest Islamic dress to a full veil. It is often a headdress which covers a woman's hair in combination with long, loose clothing. It can also mean a veil which covers a woman's lower face.

hshim: to be modest, polite, know your proper place (Moroccan usage).

hshuma: shame, modesty, politeness (Moroccan usage).

Ibadi: a sect of Islam whose members are found mostly in Oman and Yemen.

ibn: son (of); also **ben.**

ᶜid al-seghir: the feast of cakes which immediately follows the end of Ramadan.

iftar: the breaking of the Ramadan fast just after sundown.

ijab: an offer of marriage made by the woman or her guardian.

ijhad: abortion.

ijtihad: religious reasoning about important questions.

imam: in Shiᵓi Islam, the head of the Muslim community; in Sunni Islam, a prayer leader.

imamzadeh (P): a descendant of the imams.

Intifada: the Palestinian uprising against Israel, 1987–1993.

ᶜishaᵓ: the evening call to prayer.

Islam: the religion which stems from the revelations Muhammad received from the angel Gabriel, now contained in the Qurᵓan. Islam literally means submission, with the sense of submission to a higher power: here, God.

ᶜisma: a mixture of authority, dominion, and protection.

jalabiyya: a long robe which covers the body, worn by both men and women. In some areas, it is hooded, in others not. Also **jellaba, galabiyya.**

jihad: struggle, holy war.

jinn: a spirit or demon, either harmful or helpful, often mischievous (plural: **jnoun**).

juzᵓ: a section of the Qurᵓan.

Kaᶜba: a sacred shrine at Mecca, whose site has been revered since pre-Islamic times.

khadima: a slave or servant girl.

khalifa: caliph, an administrative title, indicating the head or leader; literally "deputy," as of God (plural: **khulafa**).

khatm: prayers consisting of repetitive phrases.

khulᶜ: divorce by mutual consent; a type of divorce which can be initiated by the wife, who renounces her claim to the brideprice.

kubba: a domed shrine or tomb (plural: **kubab**).

liwan: a reception room.

madrasa: a religious school.

mahr: bride price; a sum of money or any valuable that the husband pays or pledges to pay to the bride upon marriage.

majlis: a session, gathering, or meeting.

majlis al-ᶜilm: a study session where knowledge is imparted.

makhazni: a person who works for the government, a soldier or guard.

makhzen: the central government (North African usage).

makruh: disapproved, detested, or reprehensible; one of the five categories of actions in Islamic law.

maktub: written, fated (Moroccan **mektoub**).

mandil: a black veil, placed on top of the ordinary veil and folded to cover the chin, the mouth, and sometimes the nose. Usually dark sunglasses are worn to cover the eyes as well.

mankalla: a game found all over Africa that uses seeds or stones as counters.

marabit: a saint or holy person, or the tomb of one (plural: **marabitiin**). Also **marabout.**

al-Masʿa: "the Place of Running"—a corridor appended to the Sacred Mosque in Mecca where the **saʿy** is performed.

masjid: a mosque.

mawlid: the anniversary of the birth of a saint or of the Prophet Muhammad.

mihrab: a prayer niche.

minbar: the pulpit in the mosque from which the sermon is delivered.

mosque: a meeting place for Muslims, designed for community prayer.

mousem: a festival (usually held annually) honoring a saint.

Mudawwana: Morocco's code of personal status, which governs marriage and divorce.

muezzin: the person who calls Muslims to prayer five times a day from the minaret.

mujawwad: a style of reading or chanting the Qurʾan.

mullah (P): a religious authority, generally in a town or village.

murabiyya: the postpartum visiting period.

murafiq: a companion, bodyguard, follower, or servant (plural: **murafiqin**).

Muslim: One who submits to the will of God; the proper term for an adherent to the faith of Islam.

mutʿa: temporary marriage (Persian **sigheh**).

mutasawwuf: a Sufi, a mystic.

mutawwif: a guide for pilgrims in Mecca.

nafaqa: maintenance, defined as shelter, food, and clothing. The wife's right and the husband's duty.

nasib: fate.

nushuz: disobedience; a husband's or wife's failure to perform legally required duties.

piastre (Egyptian Arabic, borrowed from Italian): a monetary unit.

qabul: acceptance of a man's offer of marriage.

qadar: fate.

qadi shariᶜa: a court judge.

qaeran: a coin (Afghanistan).

qahwa: a coffee shop.

qasbah: a fortified stronghold.

qasida: a poetic ode.

ᶜqel: mind, reason, maturity.

Qurʾan: the Muslim sacred scripture which records God's 114 revelations to Muhammad through the angel Gabriel.

Ramadan: the Muslim month of fasting.

rizq: sustenance supplied by God.

Salaf: the Companions of the Prophet Mohammed.

salat: prayer; the formal ritual prayer performed five times a day.

samovar (P): a large brass container which heats water for tea.

saᶜy: "The Running"; a ritual part of the pilgrimage which reenacts Hagar's search for water for the infant Ishmael.

shahada: the creed or statement of belief: There is no god but God and Muhammad is the messenger of God.

shariᶜa: Islamic law.

shaykh: a respected man, often older; the head of the tribe (fem. **shaykha**). Also **sheikh.**

Shiᶜa (collective n.), **Shiᶜi** (adj.): sectarian; the second largest sect of Islam, which follows Ali and his sons as leaders of the Muslim community.

sigheh (P): temporary marriage contracted by participants, dissolved after a set term.

Sufi: a Muslim mystic. Sufism is a form of spiritual or mystical Islam.

sulha: conciliation, arbitration, peace meeting.

sunna: the practice of the Prophet Muhammad or his community. Also, verbal accounts of the Prophet Muhammad and his community, a primary source of Islamic law.

Sunni: the largest sect of Islam.

suq: a market.

tahar: circumcision.

tajwid: a code of rules defining how to read the Qurʾan aloud.

talaq: repudiation, divorce.

tamkin: submission, defined as the husband's right to unhampered sexual access. The husband's right and the wife's duty.

tarbiyya: education and cultivation to encourage proper Islamic practices.

tariqa: a Sufi order, literally, "the way, the path."

tasawwuf: mysticism, Sufism.

tawaf: making the seven circumambulations around the Kaaba.

Tawjihi: examinations given at the conclusion of primary and secondary school.

taᶜziyeh (P): a Shiᶜi passion play commemorating the martyrdom of Hussein at Karbala, performed annually during Muharram.

thawra: revolution.

toman (P): an Iranian monetary unit.

umma: the Muslim community.

umra: the shorter form of the pilgrimage; the lesser pilgrimage undertaken in months other than Dhu al-Hijjah.

wadi: valley (literally a dry river valley); in North Africa, river. Also **wad.**

Wahhabi: the highly conservative official school of Islam followed in Saudi Arabia.

wali: a saint or guardian.

waqf: endowment properties or funds (plural: **awqaf**).

wasta: connections, "pull."

watan: a nation.

wilaya: guardianship; legal power.

wuquf: "The Standing," a ritual part of the pilgrimage which involves standing on the plain of Arafat, facing Mecca.

zajal: folk tales.

zakat: tithes.

zamil: a poetic form.

zar: a ceremony to release demons (**jnoun**) from a possessed person.

zawiya: an Islamic school.

ziarat (P): a visit paid to a shrine (Iran).

This section is designed to guide readers new to the area to basic works on aspects of everyday life in the Middle East. We concentrate here on works that address the themes and subjects that are the focus of this book. The list is, of necessity, selective. We emphasize books that have been published since the first edition of this book came out in 1993, but please refer to the first edition for excellent works which we do not have space to list here.

BACKGROUND ON THE MIDDLE EAST AND ISLAM

Any in-depth understanding of the Middle East requires a sense of the area's history and Islamic principles. Albert Hourani, *A History of the Arab Peoples* (Cambridge: Harvard University Press, 1990), remains a favorite history of the area. Numerous specialized histories shed light on Middle Eastern history, such as Beshara Doumani, *Rediscovering Palestine: Merchants and Peasants in Jabal Nablus, 1700–1900* (Berkeley: University of California Press, 1995). Marshall G. S. Hodgson's three-volume *The Venture of Islam* (Chicago: University of Chicago Press, 1974) is an important survey of the history and culture of the Islamic world from Muhammad to the modern period. A good source for the geography of the region is Colbert C. Held, *Middle East Patterns: Places, Peoples, and Politics* (Boulder: Westview Press, 1989).

This volume makes references to the politics of the Middle East. James A. Bill and Robert Springborg, *Politics in the Middle East,* 5th ed. (New York: Longman, 2000), is an introduction to the political dynamics and institutions of the area. Its references to other resources are highly useful. *The Middle East,* 9th ed. (Washington, D.C.: Congressional Quarterly Press, 2000), is a detailed sourcebook, with chapters on such topics as Middle East arms sales and Islam, country profiles, and a chronology. An introductory volume for students with no previous knowledge of the Middle East is Deborah J. Gerner, ed., *Understanding the Contemporary Middle East* (Boulder: Lynne Rienner Publishers, 2000). The Israeli/Palestinian conflict has generated libraries of documents and publications. Two books give a particularly good sense of the area and the people involved: Mark Tessler, *A History of the Israeli-Palestinian Conflict* (Bloomington: Indiana University Press, 1994); and Thomas Friedman's updated *From Beirut to Jerusalem* (New York: Anchor Books, 1995). Rashid Khalidi, *Palestinian Identity: The Construction of Modern National Consciousness* (New York: Columbia University Press, 1997), details the construction of Palestinian nationality.

The primary source on Islam is, of course, the Qurʾan itself. The Muslim scriptures are available in a variety of translations, although, as Muslims state, the language of the original can never be adequately replicated in any translation. N. J. Dawood, *The Quran* (Harmondsworth, Middlesex: Penguin Books, 1956), is readable and widely available. Oddly, it presents the *surah*s (chapters) in a non-traditional order. Muhammed Marmaduke Pickthall and Arafat Kamil Ashshi, *The Meaning of the Glorious Quʾran* (New York and Toronto: Mentor Books, Penguin Books, 1993), is a methodical translation which owes more to accuracy than lilt of language. A. J. Arberry, in *The Koran Interpreted* (New York: Macmillan, 1969), gives a sense of the flow and tone of the original Arabic.

The religion of Islam has been widely written about, and works on most of its aspects are available. Two general presentations of Islam in practice are John L. Esposito, *Islam: The Straight Path* (New York: Oxford University Press, 1988; revised editions in 1991 and 1998); and Frederick M. Denny, *An Introduction to Islam*, 2nd ed. (New York: Macmillan, 1996). Esposito's work is a concise, synthetic overview of the major tenets, organization, and movements of Islam. Denny considers both Islamic principles and contemporary religious practices. A newer work is Emory C. Bogle, *Islam: Origin and Belief* (Austin: University of Texas Press, 1998). John L. Esposito has edited a massive work, *The Oxford History of Islam* (New York: Oxford University Press, 2000), which will tell readers everything they could want to know about all aspects of Islam.

Fazlur Rahman's *Islam*, 2nd ed. (Chicago: University of Chicago Press, 1979) gives the point of view of a committed Muslim modernist whose work is influential throughout the Middle East as well as the West. Rahman also wrote *Major Themes of the Quran* (Minneapolis: Bibliotheca Islamica, 1989).

Questions raised by the intersection of Islam and politics have engendered a good-sized literature that takes strong positions both for and against Islamic activism. Different but representative and well-reasoned approaches include John Esposito, *The Islamic Threat* (New York: Oxford University Press, 1995); Nazih Ayubi, *Political Islam* (New York: Routledge, 1991); Bassam Tibi, *The Challenge of Fundamentalism: Political Islam and the New World Disorder* (Berkeley: University of California Press, 1998); Fawaz A. Gerges, *America and Political Islam: Clash of Cultures or Clash of Interests?* (New York: Cambridge University Press, 1999); and Bruce B. Lawrence,

Shattering the Myth: Islam beyond Violence (Princeton: Princeton University Press, 1998). The historian Carl Brown has written a synthetic study of Islam and politics, *Religion and State: The Muslim Approach to Politics* (New York: Columbia University Press, 2000).

An anthropological survey which gives a good sense of the pluralistic Middle Eastern society and culture is Dale Eickelman, *The Middle East and Central Asia: An Anthropological Approach*, 4th ed. (Upper Saddle River, N.J.: Prentice Hall, 2001). Another is Daniel Bates and Amal Rassam, *Peoples and Cultures of the Middle East* (Upper Saddle River, N.J: Prentice Hall, 1983). A useful reader is Nicholas S. Hopkins and Saad Eddin Ibrahim, eds., *Arab Society: Class, Gender, Power, and Development* (Cairo: American University in Cairo Press, 1997).

Researchers are attacking problems of human rights in the Middle East. Amnesty International, Human Rights Watch: Middle East, and the U.S. Department of State publish reports annually. Books on aspects of the subject include Ann Elizabeth Mayer, *Islam and Human Rights: Tradition and Politics*, 3rd ed. (Boulder: Westview Press, 1999); Abdullahi Ahmen An-Na'im, *Toward an Islamic Reformation: Civil Liberties, Human Rights, and International Law* (Syracuse: Syracuse University Press, 1990); Susan Waltz, *Human Rights and Reform: Changing the Face of North African Politics* (Berkeley: University of California Press, 1995); Kanan Makiya, *Cruelty and Silence: War, Tyranny, Uprising, and the Arab World* (New York: W. W. Norton, 1993); and Mahnaz Afkhami, ed., *Faith and Freedom: Women's Human Rights in the Muslim World* (Syracuse: Syracuse University Press, 1995).

MIDDLE EASTERN LITERATURE

Perhaps the best sources of material on Middle Eastern life are novels, essays, biographical accounts, stories, and poetry written by Middle Easterners. A brief selection of works available in English translation is listed here. The Middle East's most celebrated author is Nobel Prize–winner Naguib Mahfouz. A number of Mahfouz's novels have appeared in English. Among his best-known are *Children of Gebelawi*, trans. Philip Stewart (Boulder: Lynne Rienner Publishers, 1990); *Midaq Alley*, trans. Trevor Le Gassick (London: Heinemann, 1975); and *Miramar*, trans. John Fowles (London: Heinemann, 1978). Anchor Books (Doubleday) has made the following works by Mahfouz available: *Autumn Quail*, trans. Roger Allen (1985); *The Beggar*, trans. Kristin Walker Henry and Nariman Khales Naili al-Warraki (1986); *The Beginning and the End*, trans. Ramses Awad (1985); *Midaq Alley*, trans. Trevor Le Gassick (1975); *Respected Sir*, trans. Rasheed El-Enany (1987); *The Search*, trans. Mohamed Islam (1987); *The Thief and the Dogs*, trans. Trevor Le Gassick (1984); *Wedding Song*, trans. Olive E. Kenny (1984); *Akhenaten: Dweller in Truth*, trans. Tagreid Abu-Habbaro (2000); and *Arabian Nights and*

Days, trans. Denys Johnson-Davies (1995). Mahfouz's most famous work in Arabic is his trilogy, translated into English by William Hutchins. The three volumes are *Palace Walk* (New York: Anchor Books, Doubleday, 1990), *Palace of Desire* (New York: Anchor Books, Doubleday, 1992), and *Sugar Street* (New York: Doubleday, 1992). Two Middle Eastern authors who have also gained renown in France and in English translation are Amin Maalouf, with *Leo Africanus,* trans. Peter Sluglett (New York: New Amsterdam Books, 1990); *The Gardens of Light,* trans. Dorothy Blair (New York: Interlink, 1998); *Ports of Call,* trans. Alberto Manguel (London: Harvill, 1999); *The First Century after Beatrice,* trans. Dorothy Blair (New York: George Braziller, 1995); *The Rocks of Tanios,* trans. Dorothy Blair (New York: George Braziller, 1994); and *Samarkand: A Novel,* trans. Russell Harris (New York: Interlink, 1998); and Tahar Ben Jelloun, with *Corruption,* trans. Carol Volk (New York: New Press, 1996); *The Sacred Night,* trans. Allen Sheridan (Baltimore: Johns Hopkins University Press, 2000); and *The Sand Child,* trans. Allen Sheridan (Baltimore: Johns Hopkins University Press, 2000). Also worth noting is Shaw J. Dallal's *Scattered like Seeds: A Novel* (Syracuse: Syracuse University Press, 1998).

Two writers represented in this volume have written other works as well. The Moroccan writer Driss Chraibi has numerous works, including *Heirs to the Past,* trans. Robin Roosevelt (London: Heinemann, 1972); and *Flutes of Death,* trans. Robin Roosevelt (1985); *The Butts,* trans. Hugh A. Harter (1983); *The Simple Past,* trans. Hugh A. Harter (1990); and *Inspector Ali,* trans. Lara McGlashan (1994), all published by Three Continents Press in Washington, D.C. Emily Nasrallah, the well-known Lebanese writer, is the author of two books which have been translated into English and are currently in print: *Flight against Time,* trans. Issa Boullata (Austin: University of Texas Press, 1998); and *A House Not Her Own: Stories from Beirut,* trans. Thuraya Khalil-Khouri (Charlottetown, P.E.I.: Gynergy Books, 1992).

More Arab authors are being translated into English and are finding an audience. Among them are Simin Behbahani, *A Cup of Sin: Selected Poems,* trans. Farzaneh Milani and Kaveh Safa (Syracuse: Syracuse University Press, 1999); Yusuf Idris, *City of Love and Ashes,* trans. R. Neil Hewison (Cairo: American University in Cairo Press, 1999); Adalet Agaoglu, *Curfew: A Novel,* trans. John Goulden (Austin: University of Texas Press, 1997); Mohamed El-Bisatie, *Houses behind the Trees,* trans. Denys Johnson-Davies (Austin: University of Texas Press, 1998); Out El Kouloub, *Zanouba,* trans. Nayra Atiya (Syracuse: Syracuse University Press, 1996), and *Three Tales of Love and Death,* trans. Nayra Atiya (Syracuse: Syracuse University Press, 2000); Mohamed Berrada, *The Game of Forgetting,* trans. Issa Boullata (Austin: University of Texas, Center for Middle Eastern Studies, 1996); Elias Khoury, *The Kingdom of Strangers,* trans. Paula Haydar (Fayetteville: University of Arkansas Press, 1996); Hatif Janabi, *Questions and Their Retinue,* trans. Khaled Mattawa (Fayetteville: University of Arkansas Press, 1996); Jabra

Ibrahim Jabra, *The First Well*, trans. Issa J. Boullata (Fayetteville: University of Arkansas Press, 1996), and *In Search of Walid Masmoud* (Syracuse: Syracuse University Press, 2000); Ghada Samman, *Beirut '75*, trans. Nancy N. Roberts (Fayetteville: University of Arkansas Press, 1996); Sahar Tawfiq, *Points of the Compass: Stories*, trans. Marilyn Booth (Fayetteville: University of Arkansas Press, 1996); Khalid Kishtainy, *Tales from Old Baghdad: Grandma and I* (New York: Kegan Paul International, 1997); and Samia Serageldin, *The Cairo House* (Syracuse: Syracuse University Press, 2000). Hanan Shaykh is a popular novelist; her books include *Women of Sand and Myrrh*, trans. Catherine Cobham (New York: Anchor, 1992), and *I Sweep the Sand off Rooftops*, trans. Catherine Cobham (New York: Doubleday, 1998). André Aciman has written two autobiographical books, *Out of Egypt* (New York: Riverhead Books, 1996) and *False Papers* (New York: Farrar, Strauss, Giroux, 2000), about his youth in Alexandria and his later life.

Inea Bushnaq, editor of *Arab Folktales* (New York: Pantheon Books, 1986), and Hasan M. El-Shamy, editor of *Tales Arab Women Tell* (Bloomington: Indiana University Press, 1999), have collected tales told and retold in Middle Eastern families. Margaret Mills has written a study of folklore, *Rhetorics and Politics in Traditional Afghan Storytelling* (Philadelphia: University of Pennsylvania Press, 1991).

Poetry has traditionally been the primary literature of the Middle East. Pre-Islamic epic poetry about the thoughts, environment, and battles of Arab heroes is the source of all other literary works. Although various translations of the *muallaqat* (odes) exist, a good starting point is the translations of selected odes in Jacques Berque, *Cultural Expression in Arab Society Today*, trans. Robert W. Stookey, with poetry translated by Basima Bezirgan and Elizabeth Fernea (Austin: University of Texas Press, 1978). Michael A. Sells has translated and introduced *Desert Tracings: Six Classic Arabian Odes* (Detroit: Wesleyan University Press, 1989).

More contemporary collections include Salma Khadra Jayyusi, ed. and trans., *Modern Arabic Poetry: An Anthology* (New York: Columbia University Press, 1987); and Miriam Cooke, *War's Other Voices: Women Writers on the Lebanese Civil War* (New York: Cambridge University Press, 1987). Salma Khadra Jayyusi and Roger Allen have edited an anthology of modern writing for the theater: *Modern Arabic Drama: An Anthology* (Bloomington: Indiana University Press, 1995).

Two anthropologists with essays in this volume look at literary expression within a tribal context. Steven C. Caton's work on Yemen, *"Peaks of Yemen I Summon": Poetry as Cultural Practice in a North Yemeni Tribe* (Berkeley: University of California Press, 1990), looks at poetry from a practical and political as well as an aesthetic viewpoint. Lila Abu-Lughod, *Veiled Sentiments: Honor and Poetry in a Bedouin Society* (Berkeley: University of California Press, 1986), in looking at women's songs, sees poetry as expressive of interpersonal concerns and relations.

FAMILY AND COMMUNITY

Books which look at the family include Elizabeth W. Fernea, ed., *Women and Family in the Middle East: New Voices of Change* (Austin: University of Texas Press, 1985); and Andrea Rugh, *Family in Contemporary Egypt* (Syracuse: Syracuse University Press, 1984). Two books focus on children: Elizabeth Warnock Fernea, ed., *Children in the Muslim Middle East* (Austin: University of Texas Press, 1995); and Erika Friedl, *Children of Deh Koh: Young Life in an Iranian Village* (Syracuse: Syracuse University Press, 1997).

An increasing number of books have been written on aspects of family life in the disciplines of history, anthropology, political science, and law: Margaret Lee Meriwether and Judith Tucker, *A Social History of Women and the Family in the Middle East* (Boulder: Westview Press, 1999); Unni Wikan, *Tomorrow, God Willing: Self-Made Destinies in Cairo* (Chicago: University of Chicago Press, 1996); Saud Joseph, ed., *Intimate Selving in Arab Families: Gender, Self, and Identity* (Syracuse: Syracuse University Press, 1999); Ziba Mir-Hosseini, *Marriage on Trial: A Study of Islamic Family Law: Iran and Morocco Compared* (New York: St. Martin's Press, 1993); Homa Hoodfar, *Between Marriage and the Market: Intimate Politics and Survival in Cairo* (Berkeley: University of California Press, 1997); Diane Singerman, *Avenues of Participation: Family, Politics, and Networks in Urban Quarters of Cairo* (Princeton: Princeton University Press, 1995); Margaret L. Meriwether, *The Kin Who Count: Family and Society in Ottoman Aleppo, 1770–1840* (Austin: University of Texas Press, 1999); Barbara C. Aswad and Barbara Bilge, eds., *Family and Gender among American Muslims: Issues Facing Middle Eastern Immigrants and Their Descendants* (Philadelphia: Temple University Press, 1996); Samer El-Karanshawy, *Class, Family, and Power in an Egyptian Village* (New York: Columbia University Press, 1999); and Andrea B. Rugh, *Within the Circle: Parents and Children in an Arab Village* (New York: Columbia University Press, 1997).

As the Middle East becomes more urbanized, fewer ethnographies of Middle Eastern tribal life are being written. An older work, but one which is generally popular and conveys the traditional Western romanticism of the Middle East, is Wilfred Thesiger's *Arabian Sands* (New York: E. P. Dutton, 1959). Some more recent ones, focusing on change and adaptation, are Lois Beck, *The Qashqaʾi of Iran* (New Haven: Yale University Press, 1986) and *Nomad: A Year in the Life of a Qashqaʾi Tribesman in Iran* (Berkeley: University of California Press, 1991); William Lancaster, *The Rwala Bedouin Today*, 2nd ed. (Prospect Heights, Ill.: Waveland Press, 1997); Jibrail S. Jabbur, *The Bedouins and the Desert: Aspects of Nomadic Life in the Arab East*, trans. Lawrence I. Conrad (Albany: State University of New York Press, 1995); Donald Cole and Soraya Altorki, *Bedouin, Settlers, and Holiday-Makers: Egypt's Changing Northwest Coast* (Cairo: American University in Cairo Press, 1998); Dawn

Chatty, *Mobile Pastoralists: Development Planning and Social Change in Oman* (New York: Columbia University Press, 1996); and Richard Tapper, *Frontier Nomads of Iran: A Political and Social History of the Shahsevan* (New York: Cambridge University Press, 1997). Andrew Shryock's *Nationalism and the Genealogical Imagination* (Berkeley: University of California Press, 1997) takes up questions of historical tribal lineage and its application to personal identity.

Studies of community and social issues take up various aspects of Middle Eastern life. Edmund Burke III, ed., *Struggle and Survival in the Modern Middle East* (Berkeley: University of California Press, 1993), looks at issues considered in this book from a historical perspective. Susan Schaefer Davis and Douglas A. Davis, *Adolescence in a Moroccan Town* (New Brunswick: Rutgers University Press, 1989), considers how social change distances teenagers from the world of their parents and grandparents. Patrick Gaffney, *A Preacher's Pulpit: Islamic Preaching in Contemporary Egypt* (Berkeley: University of California Press, 1994), looks at religion in its social relationship with the community. Also noteworthy are Asef Bayat, *Street Politics: Poor People's Movements in Iran* (New York: Columbia University Press, 1997), and Michael E. Bonine, ed., *Population, Poverty, and Politics in Middle East Cities* (Gainesville: University Press of Florida, 1997).

Food and cooking are important aspects of family and society. Three books are worth mentioning both for recipes and for the context they set the food in: Claudia Roden, *The New Book of Middle Eastern Food* (New York: Knopf, 2000); Sonia Uvezian, *Recipes and Remembrances from an Eastern Mediterranean Kitchen: A Culinary Journey through Syria, Lebanon, and Jordan* (Austin: University of Texas Press, 1999); and Linda Dalal Sawaya, *Alice's Kitchen: My Grandmother Dalal and Mother Alice's Traditional Lebanese Cooking*, 3rd ed. (self-published by Linda Dalal Sawaya, P.O. Box 288, Vallego, CA).

ARTS, ARCHITECTURE, MUSIC

Researchers have begun studying performance in the Middle East in the areas of classical and popular art, drama, films, television, music, photography, and architecture from the vantage points of anthropology, literature, architecture, and ethnomusicology. New works include Karin van Nieuwkerk, *"A Trade like Any Other": Female Singers and Dancers in Egypt* (Austin: University of Texas Press, 1995); Sherifa Zuhur, ed., *Images of Enchantment: Visual and Performing Arts of the Middle East* (New York: Columbia University Press, 1999) and *Asmahan's Secrets: Woman, War, and Song* (Austin: University of Texas Press, 2000); Virginia Danielson, *The Voice of Egypt: Umm Kulthum, Arabic Song, and Egyptian Society in the Twentieth Century* (Chicago: University of Chicago Press, 1997); Wijdan Ali, *Modern Islamic Art: Development and Continuity* (Gainesville: University Press of

Florida, 1997); Theodore Levin, *The Hundred Fools of God: Musical Travels in Central Asia (and Queens, New York)* (Bloomington: Indiana University Press, 1999); Kathleen Stewart Howe and Patricia Ruth, eds., *Revealing the Holy Land: The Photographic Exploration of Palestine* (Santa Barbara: Santa Barbara Museum of Art/University of California Press, 1997); Walter Armbrust, *Mass Culture and Modernism in Egypt* (New York: Cambridge University Press, 1996); Walter Armbrust, ed., *Mass Mediations: New Approaches to Popular Culture in the Middle East and Beyond* (Berkeley: University of California Press, 2000); and Zeynep Celik, *Urban Forms and Colonial Confrontations: Algiers under French Rule* (Berkeley: University of California Press, 1997). Nancy Lindisfarne-Tapper and Bruce Ingham discuss questions of costume in *Languages of Dress in the Middle East* (Richmond, Surrey: Curzon Press, 1997). Dale Eickelman and Jon Anderson look at the interface of society, media, religion, and technology in their edited volume *New Media in the Muslim World: The Emerging Public Sphere* (Bloomington: Indiana University Press, 1999).

WOMEN AND GENDER

The study of women in the Middle East has boomed over the past two decades. Where once scholars were hard pressed to find material on women's lives and experiences, now studies branch out beyond basic ethnography to studies of specific locales, classes, and interests. Gender studies have now begun to include studies of men and their relationships with each other and with women.

The first important books on women in the Middle East are still highly useful. These include Elizabeth Warnock Fernea, *Guests of the Sheik* (New York: Doubleday, 1965) and *A Street in Marrakech* (Garden City, New York: Anchor Press, 1976); Elizabeth Warnock Fernea and Bassima Qattan Bezirgan, eds., *Middle Eastern Muslim Women Speak* (Austin: University of Texas Press, 1977); and Lois Beck and Nikki Keddie, eds., *Women in the Muslim World* (Cambridge: Harvard University Press, 1978). Fernea's accounts of family life in the Middle East are highly accessible and generally popular studies which focus on women's relationships, but are studies by an outsider attempting to enter Middle Eastern society. Fernea and Bezirgan and Beck and Keddie presented some of the first collections of material about women. In the former, women recount their own lives; in the latter, scholars present studies of women in the Middle East.

Middle Eastern women's accounts of their own lives are increasingly being written and translated. Fatima Mernissi has written a vivid and accessible autobiography with appeal for general readers, *Dreams of Trespass: Tales of a Harem Girlhood* (Reading, Mass.: Addison-Wesley, 1994). Others include Leila Abouzeid, *The Year of the Elephant: A Moroccan Woman's Journey toward Independence, and Other Stories,* trans. Barbara Parmenter (Austin: Center for Middle Eastern Studies, University of Texas at Austin, 1989), and *Return to Childhood: The Memoir of a Modern Moroccan Woman* (Austin: University of Texas Press, 1999), in which she writes of her own experiences. Nayra Atiya, *Khul-Khaal: Five Egyptian Women Tell Their Stories* (Syracuse: Syracuse University Press, 1982), presents accounts of women's lives in Egypt. Bouthaina Shaaban wrote *Both Right and Left Handed: Arab Women Talk about Their Lives* (Bloomington: Indiana University Press, 1991). Stories written by Iranian women are translated for Western readers in Soraya Paknazar Sullivan, *Stories by Iranian Women since the Revolution* (Austin: University of Texas Press, 1990). Michael Gorkin and Rafiqa Othman wrote *Three Mothers, Three Daughters: Palestinian Women's Stories* (Berkeley: University of California Press, 1996).

Nawal El Saadawi has long been considered one of the most important contemporary Middle Eastern feminists. Her works have been collected in *The Nawal El Saadawi Reader* (New York: St. Martin's Press, 1997). In *Women of Deh Koh: Lives in an Iranian Village* (New York: Penguin, 1989), Erica Friedl relates stories about the townspeople in an Iranian village gathered over decades of acquaintance. Lila Abu-Lughod has written *Writing Women's Worlds* (Berkeley: University of California Press, 1993), and edited a third, *Remaking Women: Feminism and Modernity in the Middle East* (Princeton: Princeton University Press, 1998).

Books about aspects of gender in the Middle East include Guity Nashat and Judith E. Tucker, *Women in the Middle East and North Africa* (Bloomington: Indiana University Press, 2000); Elizabeth Warnock Fernea, *In Search of Islamic Feminism: One Woman's Global Journey* (New York: Doubleday, 1998); Afaf Lutfi al-Sayyid Marsot, *Women and Men in Late Eighteenth-Century Egypt* (Austin: University of Texas Press, 1995); Evelyn A. Early, *Baladi Women of Cairo: Playing with an Egg and a Stone* (Boulder: Lynne Rienner, 1993); Alison Baker, *Voices of Resistance: Oral Histories of Moroccan Women* (Albany: State University of New York Press, 1998); Diane Singerman and Homa Hoodfar, eds. *Development, Change, and Gender in Cairo: A View from the Household* (Bloomington: Indiana University Press, 1996); Zahra Kamalkhani, *Women's Islam: Religious Practice among Women in Today's Iran* (New York: Kegan Paul International, 1998); Carol Delaney, *The Seed and the Soil* (Berkeley: University of California Press, 1991); Annelies Moors, *Women, Property, and Islam: Palestinian Experiences, 1920–1990* (New York: Cambridge University Press, 1995); Parvin Paidar, *Women and the Political Process in Twentieth-Century Iran* (New York: Cambridge University Press, 1995); Ashgar Ali Engineer, *The Rights of Women in Islam* (New York: St. Martin's Press, 1992); Ziba Mir-Hosseini, *Islam and Gender: The Religious Debate in Contemporary Iran* (Princeton: Princeton University Press, 1999); Judith E. Tucker, *In the House of the Law: Gender and Islamic Law in Ottoman Syria and Palestine* (Berkeley: University of California Press, 2000); Mohja Kahf, *Western Rep-*

resentations of the Muslim Woman: From Termagant to Odalisque (Austin: University of Texas Press, 1999); Marc Schade-Poulsen, *Men and Popular Music in Algeria: The Social Significance of Rai* (Austin: University of Texas Press, 1999); Laurie A. Brand, *Women, the State, and Political Liberalization: Middle Eastern and North African Experiences* (New York: Columbia University Press, 1998); Richard A. Lobban, Jr., ed., *Middle Eastern Women and the Invisible Economy* (Gainesville: University Press of Florida, 1998); Deborah Kapchan, *Gender on the Market: Moroccan Women and the Revoicing of Tradition* (Philadelphia: University of Pennsylvania Press, 1996); Eleanor Abdella Doumato, *Getting God's Ear: Women, Islam, and Healing in Saudi Arabia and the Gulf* (New York: Columbia University Press, 2000); Suha Sabbagh, ed., *Palestinian Women of Gaza and the West Bank* (Bloomington: Indiana University Press, 1998); Suha Sabbagh, ed., *Arab Women: Between Defiance and Restraint* (New York: Interlink Books, 1996); Mahnaz Afkhami and Erika Friedl, eds., *Muslim Women and the Politics of Participation: Implementing the Beijing Platform* (Syracuse: Syracuse University Press, 1997); Julie M. Peteet, *Gender in Crisis: Women and the Palestinian Resistance Movement* (New York: Columbia University Press, 1991); Valentine M. Moghadam, *Modernizing Women: Gender and Social Change in the Middle East* (Boulder: Lynne Rienner, 1993); and Judith Tucker, ed., *Arab Women: Old Boundaries, New Frontiers* (Bloomington: Indiana University Press, 1993).

LILA ABU-LUGHOD is Professor of Anthropology at Columbia University. Her studies of the Awlad Ali of the Western Desert of Egypt were published as *Veiled Sentiments: Honor and Poetry in a Bedouin Society* (1986) and *Writing Women's Worlds: Bedouin Stories* (1993). She is the editor of *Remaking Women: Feminism and Modernity in the Middle East* (1998) and co-editor, with Catherine Lutz, of *Language and the Politics of Emotion* (1990). Her book on Egyptian television serials, *Melodramas of Nationhood*, is forthcoming.

JON W. ANDERSON is Professor of Anthropology at the Catholic University of America and co-director of the Arab Information Project at the Center for Contemporary Arab Studies at Georgetown University. He is co-editor, with Dale Eickelman, of *New Media in the Muslim World: The Emerging Public Sphere* (Indiana University Press, 1999).

WALTER ARMBRUST is the Albert Hourani Fellow of St. Antony's College, Oxford University. He is the author of *Mass Culture and Modernism in Egypt* (1996) and editor of *Mass Mediations: New Approaches to Popular Culture in the Middle East and Beyond* (2000). Dr. Armbrust's research interests focus on popular culture and mass media in the modern Middle East.

BISHARA BAHBAH is the author of many articles on Middle Eastern politics and, with Linda Butler, the book *Israel and Latin America: The Military Connection* (1986). He is Chairman of the Board of the Palestine Children's Relief Fund and former editor-in-chief of the Palestinian newspaper *Al-Fajr* and magazine *The Return*. He taught at Harvard University's Kennedy School of Government and has been a member of the Palestinian delegation to the Multilateral Peace Talks. He may be contacted at imfra@home.com.

BRIAN K. BARBER is Associate Professor in the Department of Child and Family Studies, University of Tennessee, Knoxville. He is a social-developmental psychologist who specializes in researching adolescent development across cultures. He has been an Advanced Research Fellow for the Social Science Research Council, during which time he gathered much of the data included in the essay published here. He is currently writing a book on adolescent development in Gaza.

ANNE H. BETTERIDGE is Executive Director of the Middle East Studies Association (1990–2002) and Director of the Center for Middle Eastern Studies, University of Arizona. She has conducted extensive research in Iran and has authored articles on the anthropology of religion and symbolism, as well as on women in the Middle East. She has served on the board of the Association for Persianate Studies, on the executive council of the Society for Iranian Studies, and as chair of the National Council of Area Studies Associations.

ANNABELLE BÖTTCHER is currently a research scholar at the Center for the Study of the Arabic World, Saint Joseph University, in Beirut, Lebanon. Her main research topics are Sufi networks in the Middle East and the U.S., Islamic local, regional, and global networking, Islam in contemporary Syria, the training of Sunni and Shiʿi clerics, and Sufi women. She is the author of *Syrische Religionspolitik unter Asad* (1998). An English edition is in preparation.

DONNA LEE BOWEN is Professor of Political Science and Near Eastern Studies at Brigham Young University. She has published numerous articles on the interface of Islam and social policy in the Middle East and North Africa, notably aspects of family planning. She serves as treasurer for the American Institute of Maghribi Studies.

STEVEN C. CATON is an anthropologist who lived and worked in North Yemen from 1978 to 1981. He is Professor of Anthropology at Harvard University and the author of *"Peaks of Yemen I Summon": Poetry as Cultural Practice in a North Yemeni Tribe* (1990) and *Lawrence of Arabia: A Film's Anthropology* (1999).

DAWN CHATTY is a social anthropologist with over twenty years of field experience in the Middle East as a researcher, development practitioner, and university professor. She is currently Deputy Director of the Refugee Studies Centre, Queen Elizabeth House, University of Oxford. Her most recent book, edited with Annika Rabo, *Organizing Women: Formal and Informal Women's Groups in the Middle East* (1997) has been translated into Arabic by Al Mada Press in Damascus.

DRISS CHRAIBI is a popular Moroccan novelist who lives in Paris and writes in French about the contradictory emotions of longing and alienation which many North African immigrants there feel for their countries. His novels include *The Simple Past; Flutes of Death; Mother Courage;* and *Night in Tangiers*, for which he received the coveted French literary prize, the Golden Palm.

SUSAN SCHAEFER DAVIS, an anthropologist, is a former professor who is now an independent scholar and consultant on socioeconomic development in North Africa. She is the author of many articles and the books *Patience and Power: Women's Lives in a Moroccan Village* (1983) and *Adolescence in a Moroccan Town* (1989), the latter with her husband, Douglas A. Davis. She can be contacted at sdavis@uslink.net or through her Web site, http://www.marrakeshexpress.org.

KEVIN DWYER is Professor of Anthropology at the American University in Cairo, Egypt, and the author of *Moroccan Dialogues: Anthropology in Question* (1982) and *Arab Voices: The Human Rights Debate in the Middle East* (1991). His next book, on Moroccan filmmaking, is planned for 2002.

EVELYN A. EARLY, a symbolic anthropologist, has written on everyday life and narratives, popular etiology, informal business, and the cultural role of the information technology revolution. She has done research in Egypt, Lebanon, and Syria. Currently Director of the American Center, Prague, Czech Republic, she is the author of numerous articles and *Baladi Women of Cairo: Playing with an Egg and a Stone* (1993).

CHRISTINE EICKELMAN did fieldwork in the Sultanate of Oman with her husband and two-year-old daughter in 1979–80 and is the author of *Women and Community in Oman* (1984). She is indebted to her two adopted daughters, who were with her on a 1988 return visit to the Sultanate and whose presence led to conversations with Omani women on fertility, giving birth, birth control, and the value of children.

DALE F. EICKELMAN, Ralph and Richard Lazarus Professor of Anthropology and Human Relations at Dartmouth College, has conducted extensive field research in Morocco and the Arabian Peninsula since the late 1960s. He is co-author with James Piscatori of *Muslim Politics* (1996), co-editor with Jon W. Anderson of *New Media in the Muslim World: The Emerging Public Sphere* (Indiana University Press, 1999), and author of *The Middle East and Central Asia: An Anthropological Approach*, 4th ed. (2001).

ELIZABETH W. FERNEA is Professor Emeritus of English and Middle Eastern Studies at the University of Texas at Austin. Her most recent book is *In Search of Islamic Feminism: One Woman's Global Journey* (1998). Her other work includes *Guests of the Sheikh* (1965) and *A Street in Marrakech* (1976). She is editor of *Middle Eastern Women Speak* (1977, with Bassima Bezirgan), *Women and the Family in the Middle East: New Voices of Change* (1985), *The Struggle for Peace: Israelis and Palestinians* (1992, with Mary Evelyn Hocking), and *Children in the Muslim Middle East* (1995). Her films include *Some Women of Marrakesh; Price of Change; The Veiled Revolution* and *Women under Siege*.

ANGEL FOSTER is completing her D.Phil. in Modern Middle Eastern Studies at Oxford University and her M.D. at Harvard Medical School. A 1996 Rhodes Scholar, Ms. Foster spent over a year conducting fieldwork in Tunisia for her doctoral dissertation on women's comprehensive health care. Her post-doctoral research develops policy recommendations to address young women's health needs in rural and urban areas of Tunisia.

ERIKA FRIEDL is the E. E. Meader Professor emerita of Anthropology at Western Michigan University. She and her family have lived in Iran for nearly seven years of the past thirty-five, most recently in the fall of 2000. Dr. Friedl's latest book is *Children of Deh Koh: Young Life in an Iranian Village* (1997). She is also the author of *Women of Deh Koh: Lives in an Iranian Village* (1989), and with Mahnaz Afkhami has edited two books, *Muslim Women and the Politics of Participation: Implementing the Beijing Platform* (1997) and *In the Eye of the Storm: Women in Post-revolutionary Iran* (1994).

W. STEPHEN HOWARD is Associate Professor and Director of African Studies at Ohio University and founder and director of the Institute for the African Child. A sociologist by training, he has spent about five years teaching and doing research in Sudan and has worked in a number of other African and Middle Eastern countries as well (Swaziland, South Africa, Egypt, Yemen, Ghana, Chad, Tanzania). His publications are in the area of Islamic social movements in Sudan and education and democratic change in Africa.

MICHAEL E. JANSEN, an American convert to Islam after years of study of the religion, was possibly the first American woman to perform and then write about the *hajj*.

MARGARET A. MILLS is Professor in and Chair of the Department of Near Eastern Languages and Cultures at Ohio State University. She has conducted extensive fieldwork in Afghanistan and Pakistan, and has recently begun research in Tajikistan. She is the author of *Rhetoric and Politics in Traditional Afghan Storytelling* (1991).

ZIBA MIR-HOSSEINI is an independent consultant, researcher, and writer on Middle Eastern issues, specializing in gender, family relations, Islam, law, and development. She is currently Research Associate at the Department of Social Anthropology, University of Cambridge, and at the Centre for Near and Middle Eastern Studies, School of Oriental and African Studies, University of London. She is the author of *Marriage on Trial: Islamic Family Law in Iran and Morocco* (1993) and *Islam and Gender: The Religious Debate in Contemporary Iran* (1999), and co-director of the award-winning documentary *Divorce Iranian Style* (1998).

EMILY NASRALLAH is a well-known Lebanese novelist, journalist, teacher, and women's rights activist who resides in Beirut. She began her career in journalism and creative writing while still a student and is the author of six novels, six collections of short stories, and four children's books. Her collection of short stories *A House Not Her Own: Stories from Beirut* (1992) and her novel *Flight against Time* (1998) have been published in English. She is currently in the process of publishing six volumes of a non-fiction work in Arabic, *Nisaaᵓ Raidat* (Pioneer women).

KRISTINA NELSON is the author of *The Art of Reciting the Qurᵓan* (1986).

SUSAN OSSMAN is Associate Professor at the American University of Paris and visiting Professor at the Center for Contemporary Arab Studies at Georgetown University. She is the author of *Picturing Casablanca: Portraits of Power in a Modern City* (1994) and editor of *Miroirs Maghrébins: Itinéraires de Soi et Paysages de Rencontre* (1998). Her latest book, *Three Faces of Beauty: Casablanca, Paris, Cairo*, will be published in 2001.

TAYEB SALIH is the Sudan's most famous novelist and story writer. He was educated in Britain as well as in the Sudan. His most celebrated works include *Wedding of Zein* and *Season of Migration to the North*.

DIANE SINGERMAN is Associate Professor in the Department of Government, School of Public Affairs at American University, and Co-chair of the Council of Comparative Studies. She is the author of *Avenues of Participation: Family, Politics, and Networks in Urban Quarters of Cairo* (1995) and co-editor of *Development, Change, and Gender in Cairo: A View from the Household* (Indiana University Press, 1996).

SUSAN SLYOMOVICS, Geneviève McMillan–Reba Stewart Professor of the Study of Women in the Developing World and Professor of Anthropology at the Massachusetts Institute of Technology, is the author of *The Merchant of Art: An Egyptian Hilali Oral Epic Poet in Performance* (1987) and *The Object of Memory: Arab and Jew Narrate the Palestinian Village* (1998), and co-editor of *Women and Power in the Middle East* (2001).

JENNY B. WHITE is Associate Professor of Anthropology at Boston University. She has spent many years living and doing research in Turkey. She is the author of *Money Makes Us Relatives: Women's Labor in Urban Turkey* (1994) and *Vernacular Politics: Islamic Mobilization in Turkey* (forthcoming).

QUINTAN WIKTOROWICZ is Assistant Professor of International Studies at Rhodes College. He is the author of *The Management of Islamic Activism: Salafis, the Muslim Brotherhood, and State Power in Jordan* (2001) and a number of articles about Islamic activism, civil society, and democratization in the Middle East. Currently, he is conducting a comparative study of Islamist political violence in Algeria, Egypt, and Jordan.

INDEX